Positive H

Positive Psychology

A Critical Introduction

Giovanni B. Moneta

First published 2014 by
PALGRAVE MACMILLAN

Palgrave Macmillan in the UK is an imprint of Macmillan Publishers Limited, registered in England, company number 785998, of Houndmills, Basingstoke, Hampshire RG21 6XS.

Palgrave Macmillan in the US is a division of St Martin's Press LLC, 175 Fifth Avenue, New York, NY 10010.

Palgrave Macmillan is the global academic imprint of the above companies and has companies and representatives throughout the world.

Palgrave® and Macmillan® are registered trademarks in the United States, the United Kingdom, Europe and other countries.

ISBN 978–0–230–24293–7

This book is printed on paper suitable for recycling and made from fully managed and sustained forest sources. Logging, pulping and manufacturing processes are expected to conform to the environmental regulations of the country of origin.

A catalogue record for this book is available from the British Library.

A catalog record for this book is available from the Library of Congress.

Typeset by MPS Limited, Chennai, India.

Contents

List of Figures

List of Tables

Preface

There is nothing more important to people than how well they and their close ones feel. Positive psychology is the scientific field that tries to understand what 'feeling well' and 'functioning well' mean, and to identify the personal and social factors that influence the way people feel and function in any given moment of their everyday life and, in general, when they stop running after work or leisure engagements and reflect on their endeavours, achievements, relationships, and life experiences as a whole. Happiness and optimal functioning had been researched and debated by classic philosophers, such as Aristotle and Confucius, for thousands of years. Positive psychology aims to study these paramount topics using the theoretical and empirical approach of psychological science.

Since Martin Seligman and Mihaly Csikszentmihalyi published their 2000 manifesto outlining the theoretical foundation and research agenda of positive psychology, the field of positive psychology has expanded at an impressing pace and has influenced research and applications in other areas of psychology, social sciences, and even politics. The many scholars that have been joining the positive psychology movement share one common goal: to seek the 'better' for human beings. However, they have put forth a wide range of views of what constitutes the better, and they have developed research programmes and applications that differ markedly from one another. What, then, is positive psychology? Is it a coherent field of psychology or just a mishmash of views?

This book was written to help the reader find the answer, and uses three strategies to accomplish its goal. First, it proposes a unifying picture of the field of positive psychology organized by major topics, where each topic is dealt with in a separate and nearly self-contained chapter. Second, each topic-chapter presents approaches that differ in theoretical perspective, language, and research methods: reading diverse arguments in close proximity is designed to help the reader detect, process, and possibly resolve controversies. Finally, the review of the literature presents a balance of classic and recent sources: this is designed to help readers decide for themselves whether recent contributions to the field of positive psychology have an incremental value or repeat in different words what was said or found before in other fields of psychology. In all, this book invites the reader to take a critical approach to the field to gain a deeper understanding of the nature and implications of the controversies within the field of positive psychology.

This book is designed both as a support for teaching and for independent reading. For both uses, it is important to point out that this book takes an evaluative stance and hence differs, in the depth of the research covered and the effort required on the reader, from many other books that have a more didactic approach to the field. As a support for teaching, this book may be used as supplemental reading for an introductory undergraduate course and as main text for a second, more advanced undergraduate course. It can also be used as main text in a Master's level course, provided that students read in conjunction well-chosen research articles; in this connection, every chapter of this book ends with recommended further readings. Finally, because this book tries to use as little specialist jargon as possible, it can be read independently by readers from all backgrounds who have a strong motivation to tackle intellectually the problems of happiness and optimal functioning in their lives.

Acknowledgements

The author and publisher would like to thank the following for permission to adapt copyright material:

Figure 2.1 Plutchik's circumplex model of primary emotions and secondary emotions generated by pairing adjacent primary emotions, adapted with permission from Conte, H. R., & Plutchik, R. (1981). A circumplex model for interpersonal personality traits. *Journal of Personality and Social Psychology, 40*, 701–711, American Psychological Association.

Figure 2.2 Circumplex model of positive and negative emotions showing that emotions can be classified according to pleasantness (horizontal axis) and activation (vertical axis) as well as according to positive affect and negative affect, which are obtained by rotating the original axes clockwise of 45 degrees, adapted with permission from Russell, J. A., & Carroll, J. M. (1999). On the bipolarity of positive and negative affect. *Psychological Bulletin, 125*, 3–30, American Psychological Association.

Figure 3.3 The various types of motivation, with their self-regulatory style, organized according to the level of self-determination they allow, adapted with permission from Ryan, R. M., & Deci, E. L. (2000). Self-determination theory and the facilitation of intrinsic motivation, social development, and well-being. *American Psychologist, 55*, 68–78, American Psychological Association.

Figure 3.4 The pancultural model of life satisfaction, adapted with permission from Kwan, V. S. Y., Bond, M. H., & Singelis, T. M. (1997). Pancultural explanations for life satisfaction: Adding relationship harmony to self-esteem. *Journal of Personality and Social Psychology, 73*, 1038–1051, American Psychological Association.

Figure 4.1 The circumplex model of interpersonal behaviour, adapted with permission from Wiggins, J. S., & Broughton, R. (1991). A geometric taxonomy of personality scales. *European Journal of Personality, 5*, 343–365, John Wiley.

Figure 6.4 The octant model of the flow state, adapted with permission from Delle Fave, A., & Massimini, F. (2005). The investigation of optimal experience and apathy: Developmental and psychosocial implications. *European Psychologist, 10*, 264–274, Hogrefe & Huber Publishers (now Hogrefe Publishing).

Table 2.1 The Positive and Negative Affect Schedule (PANAS), adapted with permission from Watson, D., & Tellegen, A. (1985). Toward a consensual structure of mood. *Psychological Bulletin, 98*, 219–235, American Psychological Association.

Table 3.3 The 2×2 classification of achievement goals, adapted with permission from Elliot, A. J., & McGregor, H. A. (2001). A 2×2 achievement goal framework. *Journal of Personality and Social Psychology, 3*, 501–519, American Psychological Association.

Table 7.1 Child-rearing practices self-report items and teaching strategies rating items that were consensually judged as most typical of Rogers' creativity-fostering environment, adapted with permission from Harrington, D. M., Block, J. H., & Block, J. (1987). Testing aspects of Carl Rogers's theory of creative environments: Child-rearing antecedents of creative potential in young adolescents. *Journal of Personality and Social Psychology, 52*, 851–856, American Psychological Association.

Table 7.2 The types and domains of experiences in extracurricular activities measured by the Youth Experiences Survey (YES 2.0), adapted with permission from Larson, R., Hansen, D. M., & Moneta, G. B. (2006). Differing profiles of developmental experiences across types of organized youth activities. *Developmental Psychology, 42*, 849–863, American Psychological Association.

1 | What Is Positive Psychology?

THE BIRTH OF POSITIVE PSYCHOLOGY

Martin Seligman introduced the term *positive psychology* in his presidential address at the 1998 annual meeting of the American Psychological Association. He then fortuitously met Mihaly Csikszentmihalyi during a vacation in Hawaii, and together they set to provide the foundation of positive psychology as a long-term endeavour aimed at enhancing the way psychology chooses its research objectives, frames research problems, and contributes to the betterment of the human condition. In January 2000, the journal *American Psychologists* published an entire issue – often referred to as the 'millennium issue' – devoted to the theoretical foundation and research agenda of positive psychology. In the leading article, Seligman and Csikszentmihalyi (2000) identified the key limitations of psychology as it emerged from the end of World War II, and outlined the directions for a renewed, 'positive' psychology.

Seligman and Csikszentmihalyi (2000) pointed out that, before World War II, psychology had three missions: (a) understanding and curing mental disorders, (b) enhancing people productivity and sense of fulfilment, and (c) identifying talented individuals and helping them realize their potential. After the war, arguably because of the selective strategy used by research grant foundations, psychology increased its focus on the first mission and extended it to the understanding and prevention of all forms of human suffering. The key outcome variables became stress and its negative consequences to psychological and physical health. The key explanatory variables became negative environmental factors, such as disrupted families and inhumane work environments. Empirical research focused on how hostile and thwarted environments can cause stress and, in turn, psychological and physical disorder. In the study of the relationships among negative environmental factors, stress, and illness the individual tended to be considered as an essentially passive being, that is, as a mere respondent to incoming harmful stimuli.

Seligman and Csikszentmihalyi (2000) contended that absence of mental disorder, albeit a positive condition, is not the best human beings could aspire to and accomplish. There is a wide range of positive psychological processes and outcomes that go beyond mere absence of illness. These positive aspects of human psychology are more easily noticed at times of catastrophe, chaos, and despair, when only some individuals manifest resilience, maintain a state of serenity, and guide others with their example. These people are definitely not passive beings: they adapt and proactively strive in the midst of challenge. These people have remarkable strengths, virtues, and resilience. If we could learn how to foster those strengths in everyone, then we would have achieved more than mere absence of mental illness. As such:

> Psychology is not just the study of pathology, weakness, and damage; it is also the study of strength and virtue. Treatment is not just fixing what is broken; it is nurturing what is best. Psychology is not just a branch of medicine concerned with illness or health; it is much larger. It is about work, education, insight, love, growth, and play.
>
> (Seligman & Csikszentmihalyi, 2000, p. 7)

Finally, Seligman and Csikszentmihalyi argued that the expansion of the first mission of psychology to the study of strength would also redirect psychology to its two neglected missions: enhancing people engagement and productivity and fostering talent development.

THE ORIGINS OF POSITIVE PSYCHOLOGY

Positive psychology seeks the 'better' for human beings. What is the better? Positive psychology presents a wide range of views of the 'better'. Nevertheless, the origin of the different views can be traced back to the classic philosophical definitions of *hedonic well-being* and *eudaimonic well-being*. The former essentially states that the 'better' is a human condition characterized by happiness and pleasant emotions in the here and now, and a positive outlook on one's own life in respect to the past, present, and future. The latter essentially states that the 'better' is a human condition characterized by optimal functioning, including absorption in meaningful and challenging endeavours, environmental mastery, resilience in facing challenges and setbacks, and lifelong organismic growth. Both hedonic and eudaimonic well-being can be called 'happiness' in everyday jargon, but they do represent relatively independent constructs. As such, hedonic and eudaimonic happiness do not necessarily co-occur in the same individual. Moreover, activities that foster one form of happiness do not necessarily foster the other form of happiness. Therefore, the definitional choice of what constitutes the 'better' for human beings heavily influences the strategies and techniques that different positive psychologists prescribe for the purpose of bettering the human condition.

Emotions are important for both the hedonic and the eudaimonic approach to well-being. Both definitions of the 'better' imply that happiness comes with abundance of positive, pleasant emotions and paucity of negative, unpleasant emotions.

The difference is that, while for the hedonic approach emotions define well-being (e.g., feeling strong joy, interest, and love equates to being hedonically happy), for the eudaimonic approach emotions are a sign of well-being (e.g., feeling strong joy, interest, and love is a consequence of being eudaimonically happy). Either way emotions play a ubiquitous role in positive psychology. As such, positive psychology is grounded in a long tradition of emotion research, which classified emotions, examined their relationships, and identified their evolutionary functions.

Strengths, virtues, and resilience are all terms that refer to relatively stable characteristics of individuals, and implicitly assume that individuals differ in the extent to which they possess them. Therefore, positive psychology utilizes all the research methodologies that were developed in the field of personality psychology for the purpose of measuring state and trait variables. Moreover, all the strength constructs developed in positive psychology have some conceptual link to – and in some instances overlap considerably with – constructs that were previously studied in personality psychology. In particular, Rogers (1963) and Maslow's (1968) phenomenological and humanistic theories of personality provided the conceptual foundation for the contemporary eudaimonic approach to well-being. As such, positive psychology is constantly interpreting its findings in relation, and sometimes in alliance with personality psychology.

The ambition of positive psychology is to change all people for the 'better'. This raises the issue of whether there is a single 'better' for people from all cultures. Cross-cultural psychology began questioning the cultural invariance of personality processes and structures already in the early nineties (Markus & Kitayama, 1991, 1994). Given that positive psychology and personality psychology are deeply intertwined, cross-cultural psychologists have begun questioning and testing the universality of indicators of well-being and of explanatory factors for well-being that were primarily identified on participant samples from Western cultures. Moreover, some of the key cross-cultural constructs have driven, rather then followed, numerous investigations in the field of positive psychology. As such, positive psychology is grounded in cross-cultural conceptions of how cultural values and ways to perceive the self and the others influence cognitive and emotional functioning.

THE CHILDHOOD OF POSITIVE PSYCHOLOGY

Twelve years after the millennium issue, positive psychology has grown into a strong child. There are two peer-reviewed journals – *The Journal of Positive Psychology* and *The Journal of Happiness Studies* – entirely devoted to publishing theoretical and empirical research in the field of positive psychology. This is only the tip of the iceberg though: perusing the articles published in a wide range of peer-reviewed journals spanning across different fields of psychology – including personality and social psychology, organizational psychology, and educational psychology – one can see that theories, constructs, and measurement instruments that were originally developed in the field of positive psychology are being utilized in research that is not formally labelled 'positive psychology'. Positive psychology has thus been able to attract the attention of psychologists from all orientations, and has influenced their thinking and actions.

The fact that most of the research with a positive psychology connotation or nuance is published in 'peripheral' journals, and not in the two 'core' journals, constitutes both a threat and an opportunity. As the philosopher and historian of science Thomas Kuhn (1969) pointed out, core journals have the function to unite a 'paradigmatic' field of science, by providing a unified and coherent picture of what belongs to the field and what is external to it, including the topics to be dealt with in research, the methodologies that should be used, and the values that should guide the research endeavour and the interpretation of its results. As such, a key threat to positive psychology is that researchers who publish mostly in peripheral journals – and hence are not fully fledged positive psychologists – may with their work drive the field of positive psychology away from the ground that is agreed upon by the body of fully fledged positive psychologists. In turn, this external threat also constitutes a unique opportunity for positive psychology to grow in the direction of non-obvious research findings and applications.

Positive psychology is also facing threats and opportunities from within. The most obvious divide is the difference in the hedonic and eudaimonic approaches to what constitutes the 'better' for the human condition. Yet, this only is the tip of the iceberg: there are different emphases and areas within positive psychology, and these differences are so big that one wonders whether positive psychology is a coherent field of psychology or just a mishmash of views. As such, a key threat to positive psychology is that its internal divisions will prevent it from becoming what Kuhn (1969) called a fully fledged 'paradigm', that is a conceptually clear and coherent domain of knowledge that is managed effectively by a body of recognized experts and their institutions. In turn, this internal threat also constitutes a unique opportunity for positive psychology to become more far reaching and complex before 'crystallizing' into a stable paradigm.

Finally, positive psychology is facing both opportunities and threats from politics. Various national governments have developed a keen interest in positive psychology and launched exploratory research programmes aimed at promoting national well-being. For example, the British Government led by Prime Minister David Cameron has commissioned the Office of National Statistics to develop and administer a survey to measure national happiness (e.g., Cohen, 2011), and former French President Nicolas Sarkozy had commissioned a team of researchers to develop an index of citizens' happiness that could be combined with Gross Domestic Product to create a more comprehensive and satisfactory index of the well-being of nations (e.g., Easterly, 2011). These developments are a key opportunity for positive psychology to become more visible to the general public and to receive more research funding. In turn, this opportunity comes with a risk of seeing the concepts and theories of positive psychology translated into a wide range of administrative languages that might distort their original meaning and eventually lead to policies and practices that run against the agenda of positive psychology as we know it today.

THE GOAL OF THIS BOOK: FINDING AN ANSWER TO THE QUESTION

What, then, is positive psychology? As Alex Linley and co-workers (2006) put it, if you were to ask ten positive psychologists you would probably receive ten different answers. Taking this as a matter of fact, the only wise answer is to ask the reader of this book – you – to find the answer by yourself. This book was written to help you find the answer.

This book tries to accomplish its goal using three strategies. First, it proposes a unifying picture of the field of positive psychology organized by major topics, where each topic is dealt with in a separate and nearly self-contained chapter. Second, each topic-chapter presents approaches that differ in theoretical perspective, language, and research methods over and above the mere difference between the hedonic and eudaimonic approaches to well-being: seeing diverse arguments in close proximity is designed to help the reader detect, process, and possibly resolve controversies. Third, the review of the literature presents a balance of classic, root sources and recent sources: this is designed to help readers decide for themselves whether recent contributions to the field of positive psychology have an incremental value or are just a camouflaged repeat of what was said or found before in other fields of psychology.

A final note on criticism. Finding an answer to the question 'what is positive psychology?' requires critical thinking. Critical thinking is valued universally because it is the propeller of engagement in the subject matter, learning, and eventually scientific progress, but it comes at a price: negative emotions. Nobody likes to be criticized, and those who criticize typically do so because they are somewhat dissatisfied with what they read. As such, the reader of a critical introduction like the present one is bound to experience some level – hopefully moderate – of negative emotions. The reason for accepting such a reading mission is 'no pain, no gain', where the gain is engagement in the subject matter and learning. I hope that in reading this book your gain will largely exceed your pain.

THE NARRATED ROADMAP OF THIS BOOK

Overview

Every book that is designed both for independent reading and as support for teaching, such as this one, is reviewed by a number of anonymous referees who are experts in the subject matter and are actively involved in teaching it at undergraduate and/or graduate levels. A referee commented that, although each chapter could be read independently of the others, it would be better to read the whole book sequentially, from start to end, particularly if the reader is new to the field of positive psychology. Another referee added that, because some of the chapters are extensive and intellectually challenging, it would be good to provide some advance guidance to the reader.

This book is made of this introductory chapter (Chapter 1), a concluding chapter (Chapter 9), and seven intermediate, substantive chapters (Chapters 2–8). The first five substantive chapters tackle the core theoretical concepts of the field of positive psychology: the definitions and measures of well-being (Chapter 2), the workings of the self in seeking well-being (Chapter 3), the personality traits that foster or hinder well-being (Chapter 4), the set of dynamic variables – such as optimism and metacognition – that influence well-being and are potentially amenable to change (Chapter 5), and the key optimal state – flow – that fosters both achievement and well-being (Chapter 6). As a set, these theoretical chapters focus on the theoretical debates, empirical tests, and theoretical developments that have made positive psychology a distinct field of psychological research.

The remaining substantive chapters focus on applications of positive psychology to the real world: relations with partners, relations with work, and relations with children (Chapter 7), and psychotherapy (Chapter 8). These applied chapters are included in the present book for three reasons. First, no matter how much they love a purely scientific discourse, positive psychologists ultimately aim at improving people's lives. Second, applications help to gain a better understanding of positive psychology theories. Finally, the analysis of applications provides invaluable cues as to how positive psychology theories should be improved in the future. As a set, these applied chapters focus on preliminary attempts to make positive psychology work for people, and they portray succinctly the area of positive psychology that is most likely to grow in the years to come.

Whether you decide to read the whole book or only the chapters that interest you, the following sections provide you with a narrated roadmap of the flow of contents and arguments that are presented in each chapter. After reading a chapter, you may find useful to return to the narrated roadmap in order to recap the main points of that chapter and to orient yourself for reading another chapter.

Chapter 2: Positive Emotions and Well-Being

This chapter has three sections. The first section reviews conceptions of emotions. Several classification systems for primary emotions were proposed. Four principles are common to all of them: (a) primary emotions can be broadly classified into positive and negative, with positive emotions being relatively independent of negative emotions, (b) positive and negative primary emotions evolved over millions of years because they support both individual and group survival, (c) secondary emotions can be thought of as combinations of two or more primary emotions, and (d) not all emotions pass the threshold of consciousness to become feelings, meant as perceived emotions that individuals can report and assess. Researchers have developed valid and reliable scales to measure aggregates of feelings called positive affect and negative affect. The two types of affect are trait-like variables and are strongly influenced by genetic makeup. Nevertheless, momentary variations of affect occur as a function of whether persons judge their progress toward goals to be slow or right. Most important, momentary increases of positive affect and decreases of negative affect result in a broadening of attention, enhanced access to problem-relevant information, and more creativity in problem solving. In all, although one's overall levels of positive and negative affect are quite constant over time, momentary variations of affect provide useful diagnostic information on progress or lack thereof toward achieving one's goals in life, and they influence cognitive and behavioural approaches to problems.

The second section of Chapter 2 reviews empirical work aimed at measuring and understanding happiness and life satisfaction as global judgments people make about the quality of their lives. Research in this area has been descriptive more than theory-driven, and mini theories were proposed in order to explain some surprising but robust empirical findings. In particular, researchers found that happiness is not a linear function of income, and proposed two main explanations for the reasons why wealth does not necessarily result in more happiness: adaptation and social comparisons. Both processes make any attempt to enhance the happiness of all people via economical development short-lived, and hence somewhat useless: as on a treadmill, as people become richer, they will experience a peak of happiness that will rapidly deflate until there is another increment of wealth. Moreover, comparisons of happy and unhappy people revealed that the former tend to have a positive bias in evaluating their own lives, suggesting that happiness comes at the price of reduced objectivity. In all, there is no doubt that being unhappy is bad, but it is not clear the extent to which happiness can be enhanced and whether such an enhancement may have negative side effects.

The third and final section of the chapter reviews the opposing models of subjective well-being and psychological well-being, and analyses the empirical relationships between the indicators of the two types of well-being. On one hand, the model of subjective well-being is derived from empirical research on emotions and happiness, and defines 'the better' as a human condition wherein a person has highest happiness, life satisfaction, and positive affect, and lowest negative affect; any variation from this ideal pattern constitutes a departure from 'the better' and hence a lower level of subjective well-being. On the other hand, the model of psychological well-being is derived from humanistic and phenomenological theories of personality, and defines 'the better' as a human condition wherein a person has highest self-acceptance, positive relations with others, autonomy, environmental mastery, purpose in life, and personal growth; any variation from this ideal pattern constitutes a departure from 'the better' and hence a lower level of psychological well-being. Although the indicators of the two opposing models of well-being differ in meaning and were derived using different research strategies, they converge empirically to such an extent that the two types of well-being are virtually undistinguishable. In all, decades of research and debates between opposing camps have generated substantial agreement on what constitutes well-being, leaving unsolved only some apparently minor differences in views.

Chapter 3: Positive Self

This is the longest and most complex chapter of the book. It has three sections. The first section reviews conceptions of the self as a concept. Two main constructs are considered: self-esteem and self-efficacy. Self-esteem is a self-belief of capability, significance, success, and worthiness. As is true of every belief, it changes across social roles and contexts, so that one may have high self-esteem in a given role (e.g., as a student) and low self-esteem in another role (e.g., as a tennis player). General self-esteem represents a kind of average belief of self-worth across situations and times, and hence is a trait-like variable. For decades, advocates of the construct of general self-esteem have investigated the associations involving general self-esteem and another variable (e.g., aggressive behaviour), and every time they found one they claimed that general self-esteem was the cause and the other variable was the consequence. However, other researchers had a more critical approach, looked for evidence supporting reverse causality, and found plenty. In particular, they found that self-esteem is the consequence of academic achievement, and not vice versa as previously believed. Moreover, they found that self-esteem correlates strongly with self-rated physical attractiveness and is virtually uncorrelated with other-rated physical attractiveness, which suggests that general self-esteem is mostly thinking highly about oneself. Finally, some sub-types of high general self-esteem – such as narcissism and egotism – are more conducive to aggressive behaviour – particularly of the retaliatory type when one's own sense of grandiosity is threatened by others – than low self-esteem is. On the positive side, general self-esteem was consistently found to correlate fairly with happiness and life satisfaction while retaining the status of distinct variable. This finding makes general self-esteem one of the variables that can be included in models of well-being, with the caveat that it may flag problems on the high end of the scale.

Self-efficacy is a belief about one's own capability to handle difficult situations. Unlike the construct of self-esteem, the construct of self-efficacy is grounded in a comprehensive theoretical framework, which explains how self-efficacy interacts with other variables, such as expectations, goals and standards, to influence behaviour and how it changes over time in interaction with the environment. General self-efficacy correlates strongly with general self-esteem and other core self-evaluations, and it is thus a potential target for the heavy criticism that was directed against the construct of general self-esteem. Moreover, above a certain threshold, self-efficacy cannot explain why one keeps being interested in an activity. In all, the main conceptions of self as a concept are useful global constructs that can explain well the low end of the behavioural range (i.e., emotional and behavioural failure stemming from an ugly self-concept) but cannot explain the high end of the behavioural range (i.e., emotional and behavioural success). The bottom line is that success requires far more than a positive self-concept.

The chapter's second section reviews theoretical and empirical work aimed at understanding the self as a regulatory process. Ego psychologists introduced the concepts of effectance motivation, locus of causation, and sense of identity as central to the healthy functioning of the self. Self-Determination Theory further developed these concepts and integrated them into a broader framework that contains intrinsic motivation and self-determination as the core self-regulatory process for behaviours, motivations, and emotions. Cross-cultural psychologists contested the centrality of self-determination in Eastern, collectivistic cultures and developed a dual-process conception of self-construal that includes independent self-construal and interdependent self-construal as distinct and parallel processes, and allows for an individual to express more of one construal depending on the context of the activity. Reversal Theory pointed out that the self operates in two radically different modes, depending on whether a situation is perceived as work or play, and can shift abruptly between the two modes. Research on stress identified the various adaptive and maladaptive strategies the self adopts to cope with demanding situations, and highlighted that high levels of adaptation and resilience require coping flexibility, which consists of monitoring and responding proactively mostly to controllable stressors. Research on needs and motives pointed out that some of the most powerful forces that drive the self are somewhat below the awareness level, and take the form of imaginative and dramatic life stories that can have as recurrent themes achievement, power, and intimacy. Research on personal strivings and goals, instead, pointed out the powerful self-regulatory function exerted by conscious and volitional mental representations and anticipations of future desirable states, and found that avoidance goals and conflicts between strivings are important indicators of maladaptive self-regulation. Finally, decades of research on creativity highlighted that, in order to be fully functional, a self must work over and above convergent and goal directed behaviour, and must engage, in addition, in exploration of ideas and generation of new ideas. No less important is the need for the creative self to be armed with personal resources that are required to win acceptance of a novel idea by the gatekeepers of the field in which that idea would be most consequential. In all, this review of many theories of self-regulation clearly shows that self-regulation involves many simultaneous processes and is therefore complex.

The third and final section of the chapter reviews theoretical and empirical work aimed at understanding how the I – the self-regulatory processes as a whole – construes the Me – the self-concept – in a never ending writing and re-writing of one's own life narrative. This is primarily achieved by construing a sense of identity that makes one unique and yet consistent across situations and times as well as understandable to others. Although identity construction was originally regarded as an adolescent's task, further research pointed out that it is rather a lifetime endeavour. The I achieves this by writing personal stories that make sense of one's own life themes and life changes. This implies that there are risks inherent in construing a non-authentic sense of identity in that it may hinder rather than foster psychological well-being. In all, this line of research points out that what we tend to consider fixed objects under the umbrella of self-concept and traits are to some extent subjective constructions, and hence can change by re-writing parts of one's own life narratives.

Chapter 4: Positive Traits

This chapter has four sections. The first section reviews the empirically driven research on traits that led to the identification of the Big Five personality traits, and empirical findings on the relationships between traits and well-being. Extraversion or its sub-components emerged as the most positive trait in that it is associated with more subjective well-being and more psychological well-being. In a mirror image, neuroticism emerged as the most negative trait in that it is associated with less subjective well-being and less psychological well-being. The other traits – openness to experience, conscientiousness, and agreeableness – showed mixed associations with the different indicators of well-being, and hence could not be classified as consistently positive traits. Moreover, no single pattern of traits emerged as consistently positive. In particular, a pattern that would be optimal for subjective well-being would not be optimal for creative achievement – an indicator of psychological well-being – and vice versa. In all, it appears that, even if we were able to shape our Big Five traits at will, we could not have it all.

The second section reviews the conceptually driven research on traits that led to the identification of gender role attributes, general causality orientations, and intrinsic and extrinsic motivational orientations, and analyses what is known about the relationships between these traits and psychological well-being. Gender role traits emerged as consistently positive traits. Of the three causality orientations, autonomy emerged as a consistently positive trait, impersonal orientation emerged as a consistently negative trait, and control emerged as a mixed trait whose positivity-negativity depends on context. Finally, trait intrinsic motivation has reasonably consistent positive effects on performance, and trait extrinsic motivation has reasonably consistent negative effects, with some contextual variability. In all, it appears that, as predicted by Bakan's theory and its operationalization via the circumplex model of personality, the two broad traits of agency and communion are consistently positive.

The third section reviews the conceptually driven research on character strengths, meant as socially desirable and moral traits, that led Peterson and Seligman to the identification of 24 universal character strengths organized in six core virtues. All character strengths were found to correlate with life satisfaction, and the correlations were particularly strong for the strengths of hope, zest, gratitude, curiosity, and love. However, factor analytic studies questioned the proposed dimensionality of virtues and the organization of character strengths. Moreover, empirically driven research using the psycholexical method generated quite a different classification and interpretation of virtues. In all, it appears that character strengths and virtues are important contributors to well-being, but there is uncertainty about their number, nature and function.

The chapter's fourth and final section reviews criticism of Peterson and Seligman's conceptual model of virtues and of their recommended interventions aimed at enhancing character strengths. The criticism was first derived from the writings of two ancient philosophers, Confucius and Aristotle. The section then reviews the arguments raised by contemporary psychologists. The analysis reveals a generalized concern about the risks of treating character strengths as if they were independent of one another, cultivating only a limited a number of strengths, and ignoring the potentially negative effects of possessing and deploying too much of any one strength. In all, these concerns point to the risk of fostering a deformed, unbalanced, and excessive character that could hardly constitute a moral model.

Chapter 5: Optimism and Self-Regulation of Emotions

This chapter has two sections. The first section reviews psychological constructs that are theorized to foster persistence in goal pursuit, resilience, and ability to understand and utilize emotions toward goal achievement. The first reviewed construct is optimism. Seligman and collaborators defined optimism as an explanatory style, and proposed that optimists explain downturns with reference to external, unstable, and specific causes, whereas pessimists invoke internal, stable, and general causes. Preliminary empirical research suggests that an optimistic explanatory style fosters academic performance. Carver and Sheier defined optimism as the disposition generally to expect more good than bad events in life. Empirical research consistently showed that dispositional optimism fosters better health and adaptation, more approach coping under stress, and more well-being. The second reviewed construct is hope. Snyder and collaborators defined hope as a disposition characterized by the ability and willingness to set clear goals, viable strategies to achieve the goals, and the motivation to deploy the required strategies until the goals are achieved. Empirical research showed that hope is not redundant of dispositional optimism, and that it fosters well-being. The third and last reviewed construct is emotional intelligence. Salovey and Mayer defined emotional intelligence as the ability to understand and regulate emotions in the self and in other people, and to utilize emotions to guide one's own thoughts and actions. Empirical research found that the various instruments developed to date to measure emotional intelligence either as an ability or as a personality trait are not psychometrically sound, and that the positive effects of emotional intelligence on well-being are small once the effects of personality and general intelligence are accounted for. All three constructs reviewed in this section occupy a central position in the field of positive psychology.

The second and final section reviews psychological constructs that foster the self-regulation of emotions, particularly when one is engaged in challenging endeavours, encounters difficulties, and experiences negative emotions. The first reviewed construct is attentional control, which Derryberry and Reed defined as the executive function that allows to deliberately focus on the task at hand and to swiftly shift attention away from the task when it is no longer required. Empirical research indicates that attentional control reduces anxiety, depression, and aggression. The second reviewed construct is mindfulness, which is present-moment awareness, avoiding 'automatic pilot', and observing experience without judgment and reactivity. Empirical studies have consistently indicated that mindfulness fosters well-being. The third reviewed construct is meta-emotions, which are secondary emotions that have primary emotions as their object. Preliminary findings gathered by Mitmansgruber and co-workers suggest that positive meta-emotions, such as curiosity about one's own negative primary emotions, are powerful predictors of well-being. The fourth and last reviewed construct is metacognition, which is knowledge and beliefs about one's own cognitive and emotional processes. Empirical studies indicate that maladaptive metacognitions foster negative emotions and maladaptive coping strategies, whereas adaptive metacognitions foster positive emotions and adaptive coping strategies. All four constructs reviewed in this section occupy, to varying degrees, marginal positions in the field of positive psychology, and hence represent opportunities for theoretical and empirical developments of the field.

Chapter 6: Flow

This chapter is devoted to flow, defined as a state of profound task-absorption, enhanced cognitive efficiency, and deep intrinsic enjoyment that makes persons feel one with the activities they engage in, be they leisure, work or a combination of the two. This chapter has three sections. The first section reviews the different ways flow has been conceptualized into models and measured in empirical studies. Five models were proposed: the original model of the flow state, the quadrant model, the octant model, the dedicated regression models, and the componential model. Each model somewhat simplified Flow Theory and put it in a form that allowed for its empirical testing. The original model of the flow state drove the development of the Flow Questionnaire, which emerges as the best method for measuring prevalence of flow – whether a person has ever experienced the flow state as defined by the simultaneous presence of con-centration, merging of action and awareness, and loss of self-consciousness. The quadrant model, the octant model, and the dedicated regression mod-els were developed in conjunction with the Experience Sampling Method, which is the best method for measuring the level of various facets of subjective experience – and hence the level of flow – as they occur in everyday life activi-ties. The componential model drove the development of the standardized flow scales, which provide the most psychometrically sound method for measuring intensity of flow both as a state and as a trait. In all, this section points out that the various models are not perfectly consistent with one another, and that no measurement method emerges as the overall winner.

The second section reviews theoretical and empirical work aimed at under-standing the origins of flow. The analysis points out that flow can be viewed as a specific process and state within the framework of Self-Determination Theory. From that perspective, flow is caused by the need for competence, and it fosters intrinsic motivation to the extent that it satisfies the need for competence when the person engages in self-determined activities. Flow can also be viewed as originating from the teleonomy of the self, which drives all individuals – and particularly those with an autotelic personality – toward ever-growing levels of perceived challenges and skills. Finally, a small number of studies indicate that, although flow can be observed in many different cultures, culture shapes the type of activities wherein people tend to experience flow, and influences the optimal challenge/skill ratio wherein flow is more likely to occur. In all, this section highlights that more research is needed on the definition and measure-ment of the construct of autotelic personality, as well on cross-cultural differ-ences in the nature of flow, and its antecedents and consequences.

The third and final section of the chapter reviews evidence supporting the hypothesis that flow fosters creativity directly and indirectly, via the media-tion of talent development, and performance in sports, work, and studying. The evidence is strong overall, as it comes in some instances from well-controlled longitudinal studies. The section also reviews evidence in support of the broad hypothesis that flow fosters positive affect and happiness and hence subjective well-being. This evidence is weak and preliminary, as it was for most part gathered using correlational study designs that do not allow disentangling antecedents and consequences of flow. In all, this section highlights the need to investigate the antecedents and consequences of flow using longitudinal and experimental study designs, and controlling for alternative explanatory factors.

Chapter 7: Positive Relationships

This first of the two applied chapters has three sections. The first section reviews research on dyadic, romantic relations. Researchers proposed several componential definitions of love, the simplest being the two-component view of passionate love and companionate love. Studies using measures of passionate and companionate love or measures of more specific components of love consistently showed that love is positively associated with subjective well-being and psychological well-being, with a caveat: passionate love is more strongly associated with affect, whereas companionate love is more strongly associated with happiness and life satisfaction.

The second section reviews research on relationships in the work environment. Studies on what constitutes well-being at work pointed out that work engagement is the best predictor of work performance. Studies on managerial behaviour revealed that the task of leading project teams in organizations is multifaceted and complex. In order to foster individual and team performance, the team leader needs to perform a wide range of task-oriented and relationship-oriented behaviours that fall into the broad and interrelated categories of initiating structure and consideration. Recent research on the inner work lives of team members indicate that the key task of the team leader is to ensure that individual team members have a continuing, day-to-day perception that they are making meaningful progress in their work. Yet, contrary to popular belief, the negative emotions experienced at work seem to foster rather than hinder creative work achievement, provided that in the course of an endeavour the worker shifts from a state of heightened negative affect to one of heightened positive affect and low negative affect.

The third and final section reviews three studies on parent–child, teacher–child, and child–other relationships in the contexts of everyday parenting, classroom teaching, and extracurricular activities. The first two studies are inspired by Rogers' theory of democratic parenting. The first study found strong evidence in support of Rogers' idea that democratic parenting fosters children's creative potential. The second study found strong evidence in support of Rogers' idea that democratic teaching fosters children's proactive engagement in learning. The findings from both studies highlight the pervasive and enduring influence that parent–child and teacher–child interactions have on the current and future psychological well-being of children. The third study is exploratory, and assessed the extent to which structured, community-based extracurricular activities – typically conducted after school and under the supervision of adults other than parents or school teachers – foster developmental (i.e., positive) and negative experiences. The found ranking of activities is somewhat surprising and thought provoking for the many parents who wonder what could be best for their children. In particular, among all activities, sports and youth-based religious groups provide the highest opportunity for developmental experiences, but sports also provide the highest opportunity for negative experiences. This raises the issue of whether negative experiences are altogether 'negative' or are a necessary component of experience for developing hardiness in adult life.

Chapter 8: Positive Therapy

This chapter has four sections. The first section reviews the subtle and important distinction between mental illness and mental health. On one hand, the construct of mental illness originates in the fields of clinical psychology and psychiatry. For every known illness, it takes the form of a binary (present/absent) statement, which is based on whether the total number of illness-specific symptoms that are experienced by a person exceed a certain threshold. On the other hand, the construct of mental health originates in the field of positive psychology. For every person, it takes the form of a graded judgment weighing into a total score the extent to which a person feels well, copes well with everyday life problems, is functional at work, and is socially engaged. A review of studies indicate that mental illness and mental health are relatively independent variables; it is thus possible to have one or more mental illnesses and to score high on mental health ('flourishing'), as well as to be free of mental illness and score low on mental health ('languishing'). Moreover, longitudinal studies indicate that mental health predicts the occurrence of mental illness, so that a person who is flourishing now is less likely to develop a mental illness in the future. In all, this section points out the important contribution that positive psychology has made to the understanding of the aetiology of mental illness.

The second section reviews studies that tried to enhance happiness through character strengths interventions. Seemingly simple techniques were developed in order to enhance each character strength and virtue, and the effectiveness of some of these techniques was tested in randomized clinical trials. The review indicates that character strengths interventions can be effective in enhancing happiness, but in order to have durable effects they need constant rehearsal.

The third section reviews studies that tried to enhance positive emotions in experimental conditions. Some interventions were found effective within the limited follow-up time of an experiment. However, there is still limited evidence indicating long-term, durable effects stemming from a single intervention.

The chapter's fourth and final section reviews the theoretical framework of two novel and effective types of psychotherapy: Mindfulness-Based Cognitive Therapy and Metacognitive Therapy. These were originally developed in the field of clinical psychology, but depart substantially from the traditional clinical approaches to the treatment of psychological disorders. In particular, they emphasize acceptance of internal states such as worry and anxiety, no matter how negative these might be, rather than their modification. Likewise, these new psychotherapies clash with character strengths therapies, which essentially target the self-concept in order to induce a lasting modification of internal

states. The review suggests that, because they challenge the intervention paradigms that are dominant in both clinical psychology and positive psychology
and because they appear to be very effective, these new types of psychotherapy
should be carefully considered by positive psychologists.

Chapter 9: Future Directions in Positive Psychology

This is the final chapter. It provides an impressionistic picture of future directions for positive psychology and tries to convey a sense of the field as a movement in time. The history of science has shown over and over again that new
and good scientific ideas may take up to thirty years to be recognized as innovative. As such, any judgment of 'likelihood of impact' for a scientific idea rests
on shaky ground. The only certainty I have is that in selecting and presenting
the materials of this book I must have missed some excellent and creative ideas,
most probably proposed by young and less well-known researchers, and I anticipate the guilt and shame I will feel when proven blatantly wrong in due time.
As such, the final chapter humbly outlines three scientific themes that emerge
all along the seven substantive chapters of this book, and that I find personally
interesting, challenging and worth pursuing in future research and application.
These are proposed to you in a 'try it on for size' spirit.

Measurement Issues

A note on the measurement of positive psychology constructs is in order. There
is an important relationship between theory and measurement. A theory, such
as Self-Determination Theory, is a set of interrelated constructs and proposi-
tions that describe systematically the relationships among the constructs
with the purpose of explaining and predicting a set of measurable outcomes.
A measurement method, such as the General Causality Orientations Scale, is an
apparatus and a technique for using it that is designed to measure one or more
theoretical constructs in order to test some predictions made by the theory.
Therefore, when reviewing a theoretical construct, it is important to interpret it
considering the measurement method(s) that is(are) used to tap it. This means,
for example, that when considering a theory of happiness, one should ask the
question: how does that theory measure happiness?

Most positive psychology constructs are measured using self-report questionnaires. Although a detailed analysis of the properties of these questionnaires
is beyond the scope of the present book, sample items are provided whenever
possible in order to give a sense of how the constructs are operationalized and
measured. In terms of rights ruling their use, questionnaires can be broadly
classified in three groups. The first group includes all the copyrighted questionnaires: these can be used only by purchasing them, and not even sample
items can be published in a journal article or book. The second group includes
questionnaires that can be obtained from the authors by sending them a formal

request of authorization: after receiving a scale from its authors, one can use it for the authorized use, but often not even sample items can be published in a journal article or book. The third and final group includes questionnaires that are published in a journal article or book, typically as appendixes: these are sometimes available on websites and can be freely used for one's own research and teaching. This book will provide sample items and hyperlinks, if available, to the full text of the reviewed questionnaires in the third group. You are encouraged to follow the links and make your own judgment as to what those questionnaires actually measure.

◊ RECOMMENDED WEB RESOURCES AND FURTHER READING ◊

Before delving into the next chapters you are invited to engage in some self-orienteering. This section suggests websites and readings that are interesting and easily accessible, and that give a sense of the wide-ranging implications of positive psychology research and practice.

Websites

Associations for positive psychology, with information on their programmes and upcoming conferences:

- International Positive Psychology Association (IPPA) at: http://www.ippanet work.org/
- Global Chinese Positive Psychology Association (GCPPA) at: The Global Chinese Positive Psychology Association (GCPPA)
- The European Association of Positive Psychology (EAPP) at: http://www.enpp.eu/
- Positive Psychology UK, which presents clear definitions of theoretical concepts and reviews of empirical research, at: http://positivepsychology.org.uk/home.html
- Canadian Positive Psychology Association (CPPA) at: http://www.positive psychologycanada.com/

Virtually every nation has a positive psychology association; in order to find the one you are interested in, just type the name of the nation followed by 'positive psychology association' in a search engine.

The websites of the founders of positive psychology and their research centres:

- Martin Seligman's Positive Psychology Center, University of Pennsylvania, at: http://www.ppc.sas.upenn.edu/index.html
- Mihaly Csikszentmihalyi's Quality of Life Research Center, Claremont Graduate University, at: http://qlrc.cgu.edu/about.htm

Information on many of the other researchers that are referenced in this book can be found through the Social Psychology Network at: http://www.socialpsychology.org/.

The main positive psychology journals:

- The Journal of Positive Psychology at: http://www.tandfonline.com/action/aboutThisJournal?journalCode=rpos20
- The Journal of Happiness Studies at: http://link.springer.com/journal/10902

If your library does not have access to full-text articles, you can still browse titles and abstracts of papers.

- The Good Project at Harvard Graduate School of Education, whose main objective is to identify examples of good work carried out by individuals and institutions, at: http://www.thegoodproject.org/

Finally, two interesting column articles that highlight the political and economical implications of positive psychology:

- Cohen's (2011) *The happynomics of life* at: http://www.nytimes.com/2011/03/13/opinion/13cohen.html
- Easterly's (2011) *The happiness wars* at: http://www.thelancet.com/journals/lancet/article/PIIS0140-6736%2811%2960587-4/fulltext

Reading

- Seligman and Csikszentmihalyi's (2000) manifesto, which provides the founding principles of positive psychology
- Linley and co-workers' (2006) stimulating update on the state of the subject

This book assumes a certain level of understanding of the nature of the research process in psychology, and some familiarity with reading research papers. If terms such as 'longitudinal study' or 'correlation coefficient' sound mysterious to you, you will benefit from consulting an undergraduate textbook on statistics and research methods. There are many good ones; Stangor (2011) is the one I like the most.

2 Positive Emotions and Well-Being

When people who know each other meet in the street, in the bus or at work for the first time in an ordinary day, they greet each other using such expressions as 'how are you today?', 'how do you feel?', or 'are you OK?'. This social ritual emphasizes the importance that human beings across all cultures attribute to positive emotions in the here and now. The key indicator of such stable positivity is *happiness*, which is the key concern of the hedonic approach to subjective well-being. When people support a friend who is about to face a challenge, such as an upcoming exam or a job interview, they use expressions such as 'good luck', 'break a leg', or '*veni, vidi, vici*' (which in Latin means 'I came, I saw, I conquered'). This ritual emphasizes the importance that all cultures attribute to preparedness, adaptiveness, and resilience when facing challenges. The key indicator of such dynamic positivity is *optimal functioning*, which is the key concern of the eudaimonic approach to psychological well-being.

Emotions play a crucial role in both the hedonic and the eudaimonic approaches to well-being, although the two approaches treat emotions differently. The hedonic and eudaimonic approaches have generated definitional models of well-being, which normatively state what is the 'better' for human beings. As such, emotions, the model of hedonic well-being, and the model of eudaimonic well-being constitute the core constructs of positive psychology. This chapter tackles these constructs, and hence is the foundation of the whole book. Each of the following chapters will refer to the concepts presented here in two different ways. First, each chapter will review studies that identified antecedents of hedonic and eudaimonic well-being as defined in this chapter. Second, each chapter will review studies that identified antecedents of facets of well-being that are not yet included – and perhaps will never be – in the hedonic and eudaimonic models of well-being. In either case, understanding the hedonic and eudaimonic definitional models of well-being is paramount for understanding any research endeavour and application in the field of positive psychology.

The first section of this chapter reviews what psychologists have learned so far about positive and negative emotions, their functions, origins, and consequences. The second section reviews research conducted on happiness across cultures. The third section analyses the specific way emotions and happiness are combined in the hedonic approach to subjective well-being, the specific way emotions are viewed in combination with other psychological constructs in the eudaimonic approach to psychological well-being, and the relationships between measures of subjective well-being and measures of psychological well-being. The final section outlines issues open to discussion, ongoing controversies, and directions for future research.

NEGATIVE AND POSITIVE EMOTIONS

Emotions, Feelings, and Moods

Emotions are momentary reactions to environmental (e.g., the sudden appearance of a predator) and internal stimuli (e.g., a sudden feeling of fatigue). How many are there? The English dictionary contains about 600 words describing somewhat different emotions (Averill, 1997). Not surprisingly, numerous psychologists strived to reduce the number of emotions to a small set of distinct *primary* emotions from which a wide range of *secondary* emotions can be formed by combining two or more primary emotions (e.g., Ekman, 1992; Izard, 1977; Matsumoto, 1991; Plutchik, 1980; Russell, 1997; Shaver, Schwartz, Kirson, & O'Connor, 1987). Each researcher came up with a slightly different categorization of primary emotions, but the convergence of views is reasonably strong. We can focus, therefore, on one categorization as illustrative of the core concepts.

Plutchik (1980) postulated the existence of eight primary, bipolar emotions: joy versus sadness, acceptance versus disgust, fear versus anger, and surprise versus anticipation. Gaines (1998) provided a precise definition of each of these emotions:

> Joy is a positive, transitory emotion characterized by the establishment or gain of attachment, whereas sadness is a negative, transitory emotion characterized by the decline or loss of attachment. Acceptance is a positive, transitory emotion characterized by incorporation of concern with another person's psychological well-being into oneself, whereas disgust is a negative, transitory emotion characterized by rejection of concern with another person's psychological well-being from oneself. Fear is a negative, transitory emotion characterized by avoidance of a potentially pain-inducing stimulus, whereas anger is a negative, transitory emotion characterized by approach toward a potentially pain-inducing stimulus. Finally, surprise is a positive or negative, transitory emotion characterized by approach toward a novel stimulus, whereas anticipation is a positive, transitory emotion characterized by approach toward a familiar stimulus.
>
> (Gaines, 1998, p. 509)

Plutchik (1980; Conte & Plutchik, 1981) organized the eight primary emotions into a *circumplex model*, which represents discrete emotions as if they were hours in a rotary traditional watch. Plutchik's model is shown in simplified form in Figure 2.1. Similar emotions are adjacent, so that, for example, joy is closer to anticipation than it is to anger. Secondary emotions are formed by combining two or more primary emotions; for example, the pairing of joy and anticipation generates the secondary emotion of optimism, and the pairing of anticipation and anger generates the secondary emotion of aggressiveness. It is also possible to have secondary emotions that combine the opposite poles of a dyadic emotion, as for example when an athlete wins a competition (which generates joy) and at the same time decides to retire (which generates sadness). Finally, each emotion can vary in intensity, which can be represented in the circumplex model as a third, vertical dimension.

All theories of emotions embrace the evolutionary approach (e.g., Andersen & Guerrero, 1998; Berscheid, 1983; Buss, 2000; Plutchik, 1997) and posit that different emotions serve different biological and social functions. For example, joy predisposes the individual to play with ideas and functions as a signal for welcoming friendly interaction; sadness prepares the individual to gain a more realistic perspective and functions as a signal for attracting help from others; anger mobilizes resources to achieve one's own goals through aggression and functions as a signal to others that an aggression is imminent, in hope that they will back off without a fight. Therefore, each primary emotion can promote survival of individuals and their groups.

Are negative emotions always 'negative' and positive emotions always 'positive'? From an evolutionary perspective any emotion is 'positive' if experienced

Figure 2.1 *Plutchik's circumplex model of primary emotions and secondary emotions generated by pairing adjacent primary emotions (adapted from Conte & Plutchik, 1981)*

in an appropriate context and at an appropriate intensity, and is 'negative' if experienced in an inappropriate context or at an inappropriate intensity. For example, if you encounter a hungry tiger in the wild and experience intense joy – which conveys to the tiger that you are open to a friendly interaction – your life expectancy will be strongly reduced. For the sake of survival, it is way better if you experience a paralyzing fear: chances are that the tiger will play with you for a little while and then go away because it found you deadly boring. Therefore, from an evolutionary perspective emotions are positive or negative with reference only to their consequences to survival.

Are people aware that positive emotions are not always positive and negative emotions are not always negative? Berscheid (1983) found that people label an emotion as 'positive' when they think it facilitates their goal achievement, and as 'negative' when they think it hinders their goal achievement. Therefore, there is substantial convergence between the evolutionary approach to emotions and people's representation of goodness and badness of their own emotions.

However, the positivity or negativity of emotions should also be evaluated over and above the interest of the individual, by looking at the interest of the group in which the individual operates and, ultimately, at the common good. Building on Wright's (2000) work on the global economics of human endeavours, Seligman (2002) proposed an economical interpretation of emotions that considers the overall utility of social interaction as *games* based on the emotions of the interacting agents and the conceptual framework of *game theory*. He argued that, on one hand, negative emotions prepare individuals for *zero-sum games*, in which there will always be a winner and a loser. The overall utility of this type of game is equal to the gain of the winner minus the loss of the loser, which cancel each other to produce *zero utility* for the game as whole. On the other hand, positive emotions prepare individuals for *win-win games*, wherein both sides can be winners. The overall utility of this type of game is equal to the sum of the gains of both winners, which produces positive utility for the game as whole. For example, two companies competing for a limited market of customers can either compete with the aim of conquering new shares of that market at the expense of their competitor, or collaborate with the aim of expanding and differentiating the existing market of customers in such a way that both companies would end up with a larger share of the market. The first scenario represents a zero-sum gain that is energized by negative emotions, whereas the second scenario represents a win-win game that is energized by positive emotions.

Emotions can be detected and measured by looking at physiological indices, such heart rate, blood pressure, and cortisol level. Yet, no matter how physiologically real they are, not all emotions pass the threshold of consciousness. For example, a person may feel relaxed even if several physiological indices indicate otherwise; in this connection, *biofeedback* – a technique which consists of showing clients a live monitoring of their physiological indices and asking them to slow down using the monitoring as a guide – is used to realign perceptions and physiological indices hoping that the clients will learn how to slow down physiologically at will. The implication is that when researchers ask study participants to report the intensity of their emotions of joy, sadness, anxiety, or anger on a numerical scale, they are studying *feelings, feeling states,* or *emotion experience* (Frijda, 2009), not emotions. Feelings are perceptions of those emotions that passed the threshold of consciousness.

Sometimes, researchers use questionnaires to study *moods,* that is, feelings that are more general and more enduring than distinct and temporary feelings. Batson (1990) contended that mood is a complex affective state that entails simultaneously current emotions and *expectations* about the future development of those emotions. Based on this definition, a change of mood would represent 'the fine-tuning of one's own perception of the general affective tone of what lies ahead' (Batson, 1990, p. 103).

Positive and Negative Affect

Wyer, Clore, and Isbell (1999) defined affect as a general term representing 'positively or negatively valenced subjective reactions that a person experiences at a given point in time' (p. 3). Based on this definition, affect can be regarded as an umbrella for both feelings and moods, and according to Batson (1990) it is the most general and primitive of the constructs used in emotional research, whose major function for the individual is to provide information on one's own emotional 'state of affairs'. Because positive affect encompasses perceptions of positive emotions such as joy, love, and contentment, and negative affect encompasses perceptions of negative emotions such as fear, anger, and sadness (Baumeister & Bushman, 2013), the construct of affect is grounded in theories of emotions.

Positive affect and negative affect were initially regarded as relatively independent constructs, and represented graphically as two *orthogonal dimensions* like the two axes of a Cartesian space (Watson & Tellegen, 1985). Other researchers proposed to represent affect on other two orthogonal dimensions: *pleasantness* or *valence* (ranging from displeased to pleased) and *activation* or *arousal* (ranging from unaroused to aroused) (e.g., Diener, Smith, & Fujita, 1995; Larsen & Diener, 1992). Russell and Carroll (1999) proposed the circumplex model shown in Figure 2.2, which reconciles the two views on the dimensions of affect. The model locates eight emotions in a bidimensional space with pleasantness as the horizontal axis and activation as the vertical axis. The more similar two emotions are, the closer they are in space. The model shows that feeling happy is equally as pleasant as feeling satisfied, and that both feelings are much more pleasant than feeling dissatisfied or sad. The model also shows that feeling upset is equally as arousing as feeling elated, and that both feelings are much more arousing than feeling depressed or calm. Finally the model shows that if the pleasantness and activation axes are rotated clockwise (keeping them orthogonal to each other) of 45 degrees, they can be re-interpreted and labelled as 'positive affect' and

Figure 2.2 *Circumplex model of positive and negative emotions showing that emotions can be classified according to pleasantness (horizontal axis) and activation (vertical axis) as well as according to positive affect and negative affect, which are obtained by rotating the original axes clockwise of 45 degrees (adapted from Russell & Carroll, 1999)*

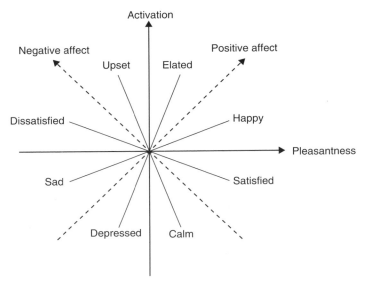

'negative affect' based on the relationships the rotated axes have with the eight emotions. After rotation, elated and happy are indicators of a high level of positive affect, whereas sad and depressed are indicators of a low level of positive affect; likewise, dissatisfied and upset are indicators of a high level of negative affect, whereas calm and satisfied are indicators of a low level of negative affect. Although the unrotated and the rotated representations of emotions are equivalent, researchers typically classify and interpret emotions in their research using as reference the dimensions of positive affect and negative affect.

The circumplex model represents positive affect and negative affect as reciprocally independent, uncorrelated variables. This in turn implies that by knowing your current level of positive affect one would not be able to predict your current level of negative affect beyond chance, and vice versa. In other words, at any point in time the four possible combinations of positive affect and negative affect (low–low, high–high, low–high, and high–low) are equally probable. This is counterintuitive: if one feels happy or elated, is it possible that one also feels sad or depressed, and, if so, how likely is it? Russell and Carrol (1999) showed that, although it is possible in some instances to be in a high–high or a low–low condition, when measurement artefacts are controlled for, the general tendency is to be in high–low or low–high conditions: 'Is a human being a pendulum betwixt a smile and a tear? Apparently so' (p. 25).

However, researchers typically investigate affect by asking study participants to provide measures of momentary positive and negative affect repeatedly over a period of time, and then calculate personal scores of positive and negative affect as averages over the whole set of repeated observations. Mean scores of positive affect and mean scores of negative affect – which are often called *trait positive affect* and *trait negative affect* – tend to be uncorrelated when the means are calculated over many repeated occasions (e.g., Diener & Emmons, 1984). In this specific sense, it is reasonable to state that trait positive affect and trait negative affect are relatively independent of each other.

Positive affect and negative affect can be measured validly and reliably using the Positive and Negative Affect Schedule (PANAS; Watson, Clark, & Tellegen, 1988; available at: http://www.authentichappiness.sas.upenn.edu/questionnaires. aspx), which is shown in Table 2.1, or the International Positive and Negative Affect Schedule – Short Form (I-PANAS-SF; Thompson, 2007), which was developed from the original scale by excluding somewhat redundant items and selecting items that have more stable psychometric characteristics across cultures (i.e.,

Table 2.1 *The Positive and Negative Affect Schedule (PANAS; adapted from Watson et al., 1988)*

This scale consists of a number of words that describe different feelings and emotions. Read each item and then mark the appropriate answer in the space next to that word. Indicate to what extent —————— [*see note*].

1 Very slightly or not at all	2 A little	3 Moderately	4 Quite a bit	5 Extremely
1. —————— interested		11. —————— irritable		
2. —————— distressed		12. —————— alert*		
3. —————— excited		13. —————— ashamed*		
4. —————— upset*		14. —————— inspired*		
5. —————— strong		15. —————— nervous*		
6. —————— guilty		16. —————— determined*		
7. —————— scared		17. —————— attentive*		
8. —————— hostile*		18. —————— jittery		
9. —————— enthusiastic		19. —————— active*		
10. —————— proud		20. —————— afraid*		

Note: Insert the appropriate time instructions in the filler, such as 'you feel this way right now, that is, at the present moment' or 'you have felt this way during the past week'. To calculate the positive affect score sum up all the odd-numbered items, and to calculate the negative affect score sum up all the even-numbered items.

*Items selected in the I-PANAS-SF (Thompson, 2007).

these items are more likely to have the same meaning for people from different cultures). The PANAS can be used flexibly in a variety of research contexts simply by writing the appropriate time instructions, such as 'you feel this way right now, that is, at the present moment', 'you have felt this way during the past week', 'you generally feel this way, that is, how you feel on the average', in the filler of Table 2.1. The asterisks in Table 2.1 indicate the subset of ten items that are included in the I-PANAS-SF. The I-PANAS-SF uses a different instruction: 'Thinking about yourself and how you normally feel, to what extent do you generally feel'. Moreover, the I-PANAS-SF asks respondents to rate each item on a five-point scale ranging from 1 (*never*) to 5 (*always*). Despite the differences in number of items, instructions and response scale, the I-PANAS-SF scale scores correlate strongly with the scale scores of the original PANAS, and hence the two scales provide nearly equivalent assessments of positive affect and negative affect.

Origins and Consequences of Affect

What are the origins of positive and negative affect? Naturally, good and bad events occurring in everyday life can cause momentary variations of affect. Yet, trait affect (i.e., the average affect over many occasions) correlates strongly with personality traits. In particular, controlling for measurement error, trait positive affect has a strong correlation of .8 with the trait of *extraversion*, whereas trait negative affect is virtually undistinguishable from the trait of *neuroticism*, so that trait negative affect and neuroticism can be regarded as nearly the same variable (Diener & Lucas, 1999). Moreover, studies on twins and siblings revealed that the heritability of trait affect is high: 40 per cent for trait positive affect and 55 per cent for trait negative affect, whereas shared family environment accounts for only 22 per cent and 2 per cent, respectively (Lykken & Tellegen, 1996). Therefore, trait positive affect and trait negative affect, in particular, appear to be rather stable and hence changeable only to a limited extent through active control of thoughts and interaction with the environment.

Are we therefore condemned to fixed overall levels of positive and negative emotions by virtue of genetic influence, through the mediation of personality traits? Some studies suggest that we are not. For example, David and co-workers (1997) investigated simultaneously the effects that extraversion, neuroticism, and daily events have on daily levels of positive affect and negative affect on 96 35- to 55-year-old US male participants, who provided daily self-reports on affect and daily events for eight consecutive days. The daily values of positive affect and negative affect were used as the criterion variables in two distinct regression models. In the model of positive affect, extraversion accounted for 2 per cent of the total variance, neuroticism accounted for 2 per cent, daily events accounted for 7 per cent, and the remaining 89 per cent of the total variance remained unexplained. In the model of negative affect, extraversion accounted for nearly 0 per cent of total variance, neuroticism accounted for 11 per cent, daily events accounted for 11 per cent, and the remaining 78 per cent of the total variance was unaccounted for. On the whole, daily affect appears to be affected more by events than by personality. Perhaps the most interesting finding is that about 40 per cent of the variance in daily positive affect and negative affect was explained by 'dummy' variables indicating only the identity of each participant: this 'participant vector' represents unknown individual difference components that are not captured by extraversion and neuroticism. Therefore, the findings from this study suggest that individual variables – other than extraversion and neuroticism – and situational variables – other than daily events – may play a relevant role in shaping daily affect.

Carver and Scheier's (1981, 1990, 2000) *cruise control model* assumes that people keep trying to achieve a goal only if their expectancies of eventual success are sufficiently positive. In that case, if people perceive that their progress towards the goal is sufficiently rapid, they will experience positive affect; otherwise, if people perceive that the progress towards the goal is too slow, they will experience negative affect. In turn, affect functions as a signal to regulate effort and goal setting. In particular, if people experience positive affect, they will reduce effort ('coasting') and may start looking for and pursuing other goals. Instead, if people experience negative affect, they will increase effort towards the original goal and, if effort does not pay off, will eventually abandon the goal altogether. For example, if a student believes to have made good progress in preparing for a specific exam, he will experience positive affect, reduce effort in studying for that exam, and (ideally) start preparing for another exam. On the other hand, if a student believes has made no or insufficient progress in preparing for a specific exam, he will experience negative affect, increase effort in studying for that exam, and may (regrettably) surrender if the additional effort does not pay off. In all, the cruise control model considers affect as a signal that the organism uses to assess and modify goal-directed behaviour.

The Broaden-and-Build Theory of Positive Emotions

Are positive emotions good only at reducing effort and switching attention to new goals? The *broaden-and-build theory* of positive emotions (Fredrickson, 1998, 2001) posits that positive emotions have surprisingly far more reaching effects on cognition, adaptation, and health. The theory integrates and extends prior conceptions of emotions. On one hand, the theory acknowledges the evolutionary benefits of negative emotions, in that they narrow our thought-action repertoires to those that were selected in the evolutionary process because they best promoted our ancestors' survival in life-threatening situations. On the other hand, the theory highlights that positive emotions carry evolutionary benefits for individuals and groups that had been previously downplayed. In particular, even if people seemingly act only to feel good, the underlying motivation to do so has deep evolutionary roots: by pursuing activities that elicit positive emotions, we accrue resources that enhance our odds for survival and reproduction. The theory is articulated in three main hypotheses.

The first hypothesis – the *broaden hypothesis* – concerns the way positive and negative emotions influence attention processes: whereas negative emotions narrow cognition and behaviour, positive emotions expand thought and action repertoires, and encourage play and exploration, and hence creativity. Positive affect and negative affect are viewed as having very different effects on specific emotions and behaviours. On one hand, the theory regards negative affect as a promoter of specific negative emotions, which in turn promote narrow and target-focused action tendencies. For example, negative affect may foster the emotion of fear, which in turn fosters an escape action sequence, or the emotion of disgust, which in turn fosters an expel action sequence. On the other hand, the theory regards positive affect as a promoter of specific positive emotions, which in turn promote broad and exploratory action tendencies. For example, positive affect may foster the emotion of joy, which in turn urges one to play with a problem, push the limits, and be creative, or the emotion of interest, which in turn drives one to seek new information and learn.

The second hypothesis – the *build hypothesis* – states that, although positive emotions are short-lived, they can have enduring effects by enhancing cognitive, physical, psychological, and social resources. Cognitive resources include learning new information and developing problem-solving skills. Psychological resources include developing a strong sense of identity, goal orientation, and resilience in facing life challenges. Physical resources include developing strength, coordination, and cardiovascular health. Social resources include strengthening existing bonds and developing new ones.

The third hypothesis – the *undoing hypothesis* – states that positive emotions correct or offset the deleterious influence that negative emotions have on physiological and psychological well-being. As such, the hypothesis is actually constituted of two joint hypotheses. The first hypothesis is that there is an association between negative affect and a given negative outcome; for example, the more anxious students feel about an upcoming exam, the faster their heartbeat will be during the exam. The second hypothesis is that positive affect moderates (buffers) the effect that negative affect has on that outcome. For example, if students, in addition to feeling anxious about the upcoming exam, perceive the exam as a positive and interesting challenge, their heartbeat during the exam will not be as high as it would be in absence of positive affect.

All three hypotheses were tested. The broaden hypothesis was first tested in experimental settings. For example, an experiment measured participants' baseline affect and then asked them to classify geometric figures, and found that people with more positive affect were more likely to use global attributes of the figures in carrying out the task (Experiment 2 in Gasper & Clore, 2002). The difference between global and local attributes can be best defined in relation to human faces. For example, the picture of a face can be processed globally, by looking at broad features such as symmetry and height/width ratio, or locally, by looking at narrow features such as colour of lips and shape of nose in a piece-meal fashion. No matter what the figure being shown is, when people experi-ence positive emotions they pay more attention to its broad features. As such, positive emotions seem to foster a focus on the forest, whereas negative emo-tions seem to foster a focus on the trees.

The hypothesis was also tested using longitudinal study designs in real-life contexts. For example, a study measured affect and *cognitive analysis* – which is a coping strategy that requires broadened cognition (e.g., 'think of different ways to deal with the problem' or 'try to step back from the situation and be more objective') – on 138 US undergraduate students on two separate occasions five weeks apart (Fredrickson & Joiner, 2002). Regression analyses revealed that time 1 positive affect (but not time 1 negative affect) predicted more time 2 cognitive analysis, and time 1 cognitive analysis predicted more time 2 positive affect (but it did not predict time 2 negative affect). Therefore, positive affect and broad-ened cognition in everyday life seem to have a reciprocal causal relationship. In another study, the affect and creativity at work of 222 employees from seven companies were measured daily using an end-of-day diary (Amabile et al., 2005). Time-lagged analyses revealed that positive affect on any given day predicted creativity on the same day as well as on the following two days. Moreover, quali-tative analysis of the open-ended descriptions of the day at work suggested that creative achievement on any given day predicted positive affect on the following days. Therefore, positive affect and creativity at work seem to have a recipro-cal causal relationship. We will examine more closely the relationship between affect and creativity at work in Chapter 7 (section *The Inner Work Life, the Progress Principle, and Positive Team Leadership*), also considering the functions exerted by negative emotions (section *The Missing Bolt in the Affect-Creativity Yoke: Negative Emotions*). In all the support for the broaden hypothesis is strong.

Because the build hypothesis claims long-term effects of positive emotions, it could only be tested in longitudinal studies. For example, a study on 86 col-lege students measured daily affect for 30 consecutive days, and *life satisfaction* (e.g., 'So far I have gotten the important things I want in life') and *ego resil-ience* (e.g., 'I quickly get over and recover from being startled') at the beginning and the end of the month of the study (Cohn et al., 2009). Regression analyses revealed that mean positive affect predicted increases of life satisfaction and ego resilience that took place from the start to the end of the month of the study, whereas mean negative affect was not a predictor. This and other studies (e.g., Fredrickson et al., 2008) provide preliminary support to the hypothesis limit-edly to relatively short durations of the build effect.

The undoing hypothesis was first tested with regard to the physiological impact of negative emotions in experiments (Fredrickson & Levenson, 1998; Fredrickson et al., 2000; Tugade & Fredrickson, 2004). With some differences, these experiments used a time-pressured speech preparation task in order to induce negative emotions and increase cardiovascular reactivity, and then randomly allocated participants to four groups in order to watch one of the films that were designed to elicit contentment, amusement, sadness, or neutrality. Consistent with the undoing hypothesis, the participants who watched films inducing contentment or amusement had a faster cardiovascular recovery than the participants who watched films inducing sadness or neutrality.

The undoing hypothesis was also tested using longitudinal study designs in real-life contexts. For example, an experience sampling study conducted on 60 workers measured positive affect and negative affect at work four times per day, on each working day, for two consecutive weeks, and job satisfaction at the end of the follow-up. Consistent with the undoing hypothesis, the study found that (a) mean negative affect over the two weeks of the study was negatively associated with job satisfaction at the end of the study, and (b) mean positive affect mitigated the association (Dimotakis, Scott, & Koopman, 2011). These findings are consistent with the claim that positive affect buffers the deleterious influence of negative affect on behaviour.

In all, the broaden-and-build theory of positive emotions received substantial empirical support. In particular, the broaden hypothesis was consistently supported by numerous studies, and hence stands solid. The build hypothesis received initial support but needs more testing with longer follow-up times. Finally, the undoing hypothesis was fairly well supported, but at present lacks a compelling rationale – put simply, the undoing process works but it is not clear why. For example, a plausible explanation for the undoing effect is that when positive affect is experienced in conjunction with negative affect, it will enhance the appraisal of negative affect, so that a person would be more inclined to consider negative emotions as a signal of the existence of a problem that can be solved if attended to properly. This and other plausible explanations should be tested in future research on the undoing hypothesis. In this connection, Chapter 7 will review constructs – such as mindfulness and positive meta-emotions – that represent adaptive ways to attend to negative emotions, thus reducing their deleterious consequences.

The Dual Nature of Affect: Signal and Cause of Progress

Although both Carver and Scheier's (1981, 1990, 2000) cruise control model and Fredrickson's (1998, 2001) broaden-and-build theory highlight the importance of affect in the self-regulation of cognition and behaviour, the two theories differ in the directionality of the hypothesized causal link. On one hand, the cruise control model views affect simply as an indicator of progress towards a goal; as such, progress would be the cause and affect one of its consequences. On the other hand, the broaden-and-build theory views affect as a causal factor of progress towards a goal, so that affect would be the cause and progress one of its consequences. Which theory best fits the available empirical evidence? Arguably, it is too early to tell, and it might be that both theories hold simultaneously: affect might work as both a cause and a consequence of progress.

A recent study highlights the practical importance of determining whether affect is just an indicator of progress or also a causal factor for it. Rogaten, Moneta, and Spada (in press), hypothesized that university students' positive affect in studying would be positively associated with academic performance, whereas students' negative affect in studying would be negatively associated with academic performance. A sample of 406 undergraduate students from a London university completed the PANAS-SF (Thompson, 2007), and their end-of-semester and past-semester academic performance was recorded across all the courses in which they were enrolled. Regression analyses showed that positive affect predicted better examination grades, better coursework grades, and better Grade Point Average, whereas negative affect predicted worse examination grades and worse Grade Point Average. These associations held after controlling statistically for students' evaluation anxiety, approaches to studying, and past-semester academic performance. Because the regression analyses controlled for past academic performance, the findings rule out the alternative hypothesis that high-performing students enjoy studying and low-performing students do not. Therefore, the more students enjoy their study activities, the better their grades will be.

Yet, does students' enjoyment simply signal the extent to which learning progress occurred, or does it, in addition, cause performance? What are the implications of these differing interpretations for intervention? On one hand, based uniquely on Carver and Scheier's (1981, 1990, 2000) cruise control model, one should use affect as a warning signal and concentrate the intervention on facilitating learning through traditional educational practices, such as delivering well-organized lectures and providing real-life examples. On the other hand, based on Fredrickson's (1998, 2001) broaden-and-build theory, one should use affect both as a warning signal and as a target for intervention, through less traditional educational practices, such as infusing students with enthusiasm and challenging them intellectually. In all, affect appears to be important to students' academic performance, but more sophisticated studies are needed to understand whether and to what extent affect in studying can be manipulated in order to improve students' academic performance.

The Ratio of Positive to Negative Emotions

Fredrickson and Losada (2005) extended broaden-and-build theory in an attempt to explain human *flourishing* and *languishing*. Keyes (2002) had previously introduced the view in which mental health lies along the flourishing–languishing continuum. Flourishing is more than just absence of mental disorder, and includes generativity, growth, and resilience. Languishing represents lack of generativity, growth, and resilience, but does not necessarily imply the presence of mental disorder. The key difference between flourishing people and languishing people is that the former describe their life as 'full' whereas the latter describe it as 'empty'. Compared to flourishers, languishers tend to experience more distress and impairment in their daily lives (Keyes, 2002). Chapter 8 (section *Mental Illness and Mental Health*) will look more closely at the operationalization of the construct of mental health continuum and its relationship with psychopathology.

Fredrickson and Losada (2005) adopted a nonlinear dynamic model of positive and negative affect to explain the separate processes leading to flourishing and languishing. Nonlinear dynamic systems have a chaotic behaviour that tends to be fast reacting and adaptive in rapidly changing environments. Fredrickson and Losada argued that, because positive affect broadens thought-action repertoires whereas negative affect narrows them, positive affect makes individuals more chaotic and hence less predictable. In turn, unpredictability supports flexible adaptation to turbulence and crises, and hence leads to more resilience. Based on these assumptions, they used a nonlinear dynamic model to estimate the mean ratio of positive to negative affect (*critical positivity ratio*) in everyday life that separates the trajectories towards flourishing and languishing as stable states. They concluded that the critical positivity ratio of 2.9 separates flourishing from languishing. This implies that for a higher ratio people's trajectories point towards flourishing as an attractor state, whereas for a lower ratio people's trajectories point towards languishing as an attractor state. Finally, they tested the model on two samples totalling 188 undergraduate students at a Midwestern university in the United States. Participants first were classified into flourishing and non-flourishing, using Keyes (2002) criteria, and then completed end-of-day measures of positive and negative affect for 28 consecutive days. The positivity ratio for the flourishing individuals in the two samples was 3.2 and 3.4, respectively, whereas the positivity ratio for the non-flourishing individuals was 2.3 and 2.1, respectively. In all, flourishing mental health seems to require at least a 3:1 ratio of positive over negative emotions in everyday life.

Cross-Cultural Differences in Emotions

Are emotions universal? More precisely, is the structure and function of emotions the same across cultures? On one hand, the structure of feelings (i.e., experienced and reported emotions) as represented in the circumplex model (shown in Figure 2.1) appears to be the same across numerous samples from a wide variety of cultures (e.g., Russell, Lewicka, & Niit, 1989). On the other hand, the associations of feelings seem to vary across cultures. In particular, positive feelings appear to be less 'positive' for Asians than they are for Westerners (e.g., Leu, Wang, & Koo, 2011). As such, the function of positive emotions may differ across cultures, and this difference has implications for the theoretical development and application of positive psychology.

An even more basic source of cultural differences concerns the co-occurrence of positive and negative emotions in momentary experience. Bagozzi, Wong, and Yi (1999) pointed out that Western cultures view positive and negative emotions as antithetic, and this explains to a large extent why momentary measures of positive emotions and negative emotions are negatively intercorrelated in Western samples. More precisely, because Western people believe 'if I am happy, I cannot be sad' and 'if I am sad, I cannot be happy', they tend to rate 'happy' and 'sad' items consistent with their beliefs. Instead, Eastern cultures uphold a dialectical view, such that positive and negative emotions are complementary rather than contradictory. As such, Bagozzi and co-workers hypothesized that the (negative) correlation between positive emotions and negative emotions at any point in time will be less strong for Asians than it is for Westerners. Numerous empirical studies supported the hypothesis. In particular, Schimmack, Oishi, and Diener (2002) assessed affect in a composite sample of 5,886 undergraduate students from 38 nations, and found that the correlation between positive affect and negative affect ranged from −.49 (Egypt) to .09 (Hong Kong). In general, the correlation in Western countries was more negative (e.g., Australia −.37, USA −.36, and Germany −.31) than it was in Eastern countries (e.g., Hong Kong .09, Japan .07, and Thailand .03). Moreover, the West–East dimension did not fully account for the ranking of correlations, which indicates that other, more specific cultural factors influence the co-occurrence and reporting of positive and negative emotions.

The cross-cultural differences found in the consequences of emotions to well-being, and on the compatibility of positive and negative emotions in momentary experience, basically mean that emotions work somewhat differently on members of different cultures. The key implication is that virtually each of the research findings concerning the antecedents and consequences of positive and negative emotions that are reviewed in this book should be read holding a doubt: might this finding be specific to a group of cultures, or even to just a single culture?

Affect and Emotional Complexity

Although positive affect and negative affect account for a large portion of variance in feelings at the aggregate level of samples of participants, it is reasonable to ask if these two dimensions are sufficient to account for the emotional complexity of all individuals in those samples. In other words, are there marked individual differences in emotional complexity? Is it possible that the affect of more complex and discriminating persons has a dimensionality greater than two?

Larsen and Cutler (1996) addressed these questions on a sample of 43 US undergraduate students. Participants provided ratings of 21 mood adjectives three times a day for eight consecutive weeks. The researchers performed a separate *exploratory factor analysis* (a family of multivariate statistical techniques that allow determining the number of independent item groups in a multi-item questionnaire, and identifying the item groups so that they have maximal intra-group correlations and minimal inter-group correlations) for the data provided by each participant in the sample, and obtained two somewhat conflicting findings. On one hand, if the number of extracted factors was limited to two, the explained variance ranged from 31 per cent to 60 per cent across participants, and the grouping of mood adjectives in the two factors supported the interpretation of the factors as positive affect and negative affect for the whole sample. On the other hand, if for each participant the factors were extracted up to explaining 50 per cent of the variance, the number of extracted factors ranged from two to five across participants. Therefore, there are marked individual differences in emotional complexity: whereas the broad classification of feelings into positive affect and negative affect works fine for the average individual, it is too tight a classification for emotionally complex individuals.

Finally, even if positive affect and negative affect are sufficient summaries of feelings for the average individual, we will see in the next chapters that distinct feelings are sometimes linked more directly and strongly to relevant psychological phenomena than are the broad dimensions of positive and negative affect. In particular, we will see in Chapter 3 (section *Intrinsic Motivation, Extrinsic Motivation, and Self-Determination*) that *enjoyment* of the activity and *interest* in the activity are emotions specifically linked to *intrinsic motivation*, the motivation to pursue an activity for its own sake, and arguably are the best among all the positive emotions in predicting creative output from the activity.

The Role of Emotions in Positive Psychology

Finally, it is important to recognize that the study of emotions is one of the fastest growing fields of psychology, and one that yields wide differences of views between researchers. Izard (2011) conducted a survey with 34 scientists in the field of emotion research asking open-ended questions about the structure of emotions and their functions. The qualitative analysis of the responses identified the following common themes:

> Emotion consists of neural circuits (that are at least partially dedicated), response systems, and a feeling state/process that motivates and organizes cognition and action. Emotion also provides information to the person experiencing it, and may include antecedent cognitive appraisals and ongoing cognition including an interpretation of its feeling state, expressions or social-communicative signals, and may motivate approach or avoidant behavior, exercise control/regulation of responses, and be social or relational in nature.
>
> (Izard, 2011, p. 367)

It follows from these statements that emotions underlie and contribute to virtually every psychological phenomenon that is covered in this book. Consistent with this, emotions will have a relevant role in each chapter of this book.

HAPPINESS AND LIFE SATISFACTION

Feelings of Happiness and Happiness

Are you happy? Is your neighbour happy? The simplest way to answer these questions is to administer a single bipolar item:

Sad	1	2	3	4	5	6	7	Happy

There is an ambiguity though: it is not clear if the item refers to feelings in the here and now, or to feelings about one's own life as whole. In the first meaning the item would measure a feeling, whereas in the second meaning the item would measure a mixture of feelings and evaluations of one's own past, present, and possibly future prospects. This second meaning is what people and psychologists normally attribute to the word 'happiness'. Research comparing 'narrow' (e.g., how happy are you now? How happy are you with your new car?) and 'broad' (e.g., how happy is your life?) questions about happiness suggest that people frame answers to narrow questions by retrieving and evaluating actual experience, whereas they frame answers to broad questions by retrieving experience that is both salient to them and congruent with their sense of identity. Research on happiness has mainly used broad questions to measure happiness.

The Measurement of Happiness

Several questionnaires were developed to measure happiness. We will consider the four most frequently used in research and practice. The first questionnaire in history was the Delighted-Terrible Scale (D-T Scale; Andrews & Withey, 1976), which consists of the following single item:

How do you feel about your life as a whole?

Terrible	1	2	3	4	5	6	7	Delighted

The strength of this scale is simplicity. Its weakness is that one cannot estimate its *internal consistency* (i.e., the extent to which the different items of a scale measure the same construct) simply because it is made of a single item. However, it correlates fairly well with the longer scales that were proposed afterwards, and hence has good convergent validity.

A close variant of happiness – life satisfaction – can be measured validly and reliably by means of the Satisfaction with Life Scale (SWLS; Diener et al., 1985; available at: http://internal.psychology.illinois.edu/~ediener/SWLS.html). The scale includes five statements that respondents are asked to rate on a seven-point scale ranging from 1 (*strongly disagree*) to 7 (*strongly agree*), with neutral midpoint 4 (*neither agree nor disagree*). The first three statements are similar to the single item of the D-T Scale in that they are broad, global statements about one's own life (e.g., 'I am satisfied with my life'). The last two statements are different in that they ask to evaluate life in respect to the past (e.g., 'So far I have gotten the important things I want in life').

Happiness can be measured validly and reliably using the Subjective Happiness Scale (SHS; Lyubomirsky & Lepper, 1999; available at: http://www.ppc.sas. upenn.edu/ppquestionnaires.htm). The scale includes four statements, which respondents are asked to rate on a seven-point scale, with anchors of 1 and 7 that vary in meaning depending on the statement. The first item is a broad, global statement about one's own life ('In general, I consider myself: 1 not a very happy person – 7 a very happy person'), and hence it is similar to the D-T Scale and items 1–3 of the SWLS. The remaining three items are different in that they require comparing oneself with others (e.g., 'Compared to most of my peers, I consider myself: 1 less happy – 7 more happy'). As such, this scale can be regarded as a social-comparison measure of happiness.

Finally, the longest happiness questionnaire, and a popular one in the United Kingdom, is the Oxford Happiness Questionnaire (OHS; Hills & Argyle, 2002; available at: http://happiness-survey.com/survey/). The scale includes 29 statements that respondents are asked to rate on a six-point scale ranging from 1 (*strongly disagree*) to 6 (*strongly agree*), with no neutral midpoint. Kashdan (2004) criticized the content validity of the scale heavily, pointing out that it contains items measuring constructs – such as *self-esteem* (item 1, 'I don't feel particularly pleased with the way I am'), *autonomy/locus of control* (items 19 and 26, 'I feel that I am not especially in control of my life' and 'I usually have a good influence on events'), *agreeableness* (item 4, 'I have very warm feelings towards almost everyone'), and *extraversion* (item 2, 'I am intensely interested in other people') – that mix up indicators of subjective well-being with its antecedents and consequences, without proposing a theoretical model that justifies such aggregation (these constructs will be covered later in this book). In all, Kashdan's criticism compels researchers to ponder carefully the pros and cons of this scale and to consider the alternatives before choosing a happiness scale for their studies.

Finally, researchers have often combined single-item measures of happiness with either single-item or multi-item measures of life satisfaction to create an aggregate happiness-satisfaction score. This is justified empirically as measures of happiness and measure of satisfaction have fair correlations in the range of .40–.60, which indicates that happiness and satisfaction are related but distinct constructs.

Background Variables and Happiness

In the early stages of happiness research, psychologists investigated the effects of background variables on measures of happiness. This was done by selecting specific groups of people and comparing their mean levels of happiness or life satisfaction. The research was exploratory in nature and descriptive. Myers and Diener (1995) investigated differences between religious and non-religious people and found that the former are happier than the latter. Moreover, Myers (2000) found that for religious people there is a positive correlation between frequency of attendance at religious services and happiness. Diener and co-workers (1999) investigated differences between married and unmarried people, and found that the former are markedly happier than the latter. Moreover, there are virtually no differences in happiness among the three sub-groups of unmarried people: never married, separated, and divorced. Finally, these and other studies indicated that there are small differences in happiness between genders, and that happiness is not linked to level of educational achievement.

Special consideration was given to age, as most cultures attribute a high value to youth, health, and physical beauty. Surprisingly, studies conducted in different cultures show that life satisfaction does not decline with age (Butt & Beiser, 1987; Diener & Suh, 1998; Horley & Lavery, 1995; Inglehart, 1990). Moreover, life satisfaction correlates more with perceived health than with objective health (e.g., Brief et al., 1993). These findings have been interpreted as evidence that people adjust their goals and standards of reference as they age (Campbell, Converse, & Rodgers, 1976; Rapkin & Fischer, 1992), shifting progressively from assimilative coping, in which life conditions are modified to fit personal preferences, to accommodative coping, in which personal preferences are modified to fit constraints such as poor health and reduced income that are typically associated with age (Brandtstadter & Renner, 1990). As pointed out by Diener and co-workers (1999), these and other findings converge in showing that people's expectations mediate the effects that potentially negative age-related processes and events, such as the deterioration of health and financial conditions, have on their life satisfaction. In all, demographic variables are not good predictors of happiness.

Income and Happiness across Nations: Basic Needs and Human Rights

Diener, Diener, and Diener (1995) investigated national differences in mean life satisfaction using data from the World Values Survey (World Values Study Association, 1981–2013), which was conducted on representative samples totalling more than 100,000 participants in the period 1989–1993. Life satisfaction was measured using a single item asking how satisfied they were with their life 'as a whole these days' to be scored on a 1–10 scale with anchors 1 (*dissatisfied*) and 10 (*satisfied*). They tried to explain national differences in life satisfaction using an indicator of wealth, *purchasing power parity*, as the predictor. The purchasing power parity of a nation is the average standard basket of goods that persons in that nation can buy with their yearly income pro capita, divided by the purchasing power of the United States, which is the country with greatest purchasing power. Is there a relationship between purchasing power parity and happiness? Before proceeding with your reading, think of yourself: would

Figure 2.3 *Mean life satisfaction as a function of national purchasing power (based on a subset of data tabled in Diener, 2000)*

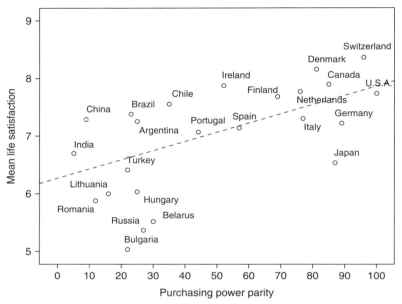

you be happier if you could afford purchasing more 'gadgets' – say the double amount – in your daily life?

Figure 2.3 shows the scattergram, with superimposed regression line, of the data tabled in Diener (2000) and using a sub-sample of nations. The graph shows that only two nations – Russia and Bulgaria – fall below the 5.5 midpoint value of the life satisfaction scale; most of the nations are on the satisfied side. Most important, satisfaction appears to grow linearly as a function of purchasing power: the more purchasing power, the more satisfied. In the full sample of nations, purchasing power and life satisfaction have a strong correlation of .69, which means that purchasing power explains nearly 48 per cent of the variance in mean life satisfaction, and hence is a good predictor (Diener, 2000). Why does purchasing power explain differences in national levels of life satisfaction? What are the specific reasons that make people from wealthier nations more satisfied with their lives?

Wealthier nations differ from poorer nations in many factors that may promote happiness and life satisfaction, including more support for basic needs (e.g., food, shelter, and health care), more or better human rights, lower crime rates, more or better education, longer life expectancy, and better health. Of course, wealthier nations also provide more potentially negative factors, such as more competitiveness in work and career development, more materialism and less spiritualism, and less time available to socialize and engage in leisure activities. Which one of these factors could best explain the relationship between purchasing power and life satisfaction?

In an attempt to find the answer, Diener and co-workers (1995) and Myers (2000) analysed the World Values Survey Association's (1981–2012) data in different ways. They found that the relationship between various indicators of wealth (such as purchasing power parity and Gross National Product pro capita), on one hand, and life satisfaction, happiness, or the average of the two, on the other hand, conforms to an *inverted U curve* such that the correlation is stronger for poorer countries and weaker for wealthier countries. Moreover, wealth indicators and human rights records are better predictors of life satisfaction and happiness for the poorer countries than they are for the wealthier countries. Therefore, both Diener and co-workers (Diener et al., 1995; Diener, 2000) and Myers (2000) proposed that life satisfaction and happiness are higher in wealthier nations because those nations are more capable of fulfilling basic human needs and provide more or better human rights.

An interesting implication of the findings from these studies is that the economic growth of a nation and the enhancement of its human rights record will have a different impact on its residents' happiness and life satisfaction depending on the nation's baseline level of wealth and human rights record: an improvement of wealth and human rights is likely to have a big impact in a poor country and a small impact in a wealthy country. Eventually, all the fast growing economies of the world will reach and some will overtake those economies that are considered wealthy now. What will happen then? Will income still have an impact on happiness and life satisfaction? We can wait and see or snoop into the future by looking at what happens in wealthy countries.

Income and Happiness within Wealthy Nations: The Hedonic Treadmill

Myers (2000) investigated how inflation-adjusted income and percentage of 'very happy' people in the population changed in the United States from 1956 to 1998, and found that, while income grew throughout the studied period and nearly tripled, happiness remained substantially stable. This puzzling pattern of findings, which was labelled the *Easterlin paradox* after the name of the scholar who first identified it (Easterlin, 1974), suggests that in wealthy nations income does not foster happiness. The Easterlin paradox was replicated on similar data in various wealthy countries, including Japan for the period 1958–1990 (Frey & Stutzer, 2002), the United States for the period 1973–2003 (Clark, Frijters, & Shield, 2008), and five European countries (France, Germany, Italy, Netherlands, and United Kingdom) for the period 1973–2004 (Clark, Frijters, & Shield, 2008). Therefore, the Easterlin paradox is the norm in wealthy nations.

What about the emerging economies such as those labelled *BRIC* (Brazil, Russia, India, and China)? Kahneman and Krueger (2006) analysed data from

China – which is the largest of the growing economies and currently the second in the world behind the United States – for the period 1994–2005: the percentage of people who are satisfied with their lives decreased consistently over the period, whereas the percentage of people who are dissatisfied increased consistently, despite a continuous and fast economical growth for the nation as a whole. Moreover, Brockmann and co-workers (2008) found that happiness in China declined continuously throughout the decade 1990–2000. Therefore, the Easterlin paradox is even stronger in China than it is in wealthy nations. In all, it seems that both in wealthy countries and in countries that are bound to become wealthy in the near future, money does not bring happiness. Why?

Two main explanations for the Easterlin paradox have been proposed. The first explanation is *habituation* or *hedonic adaptation*, which is a re-make of the principle 'good things satiate and bad things escalate' (Coombs & Avrunin, 1977, p. 224). In times of economic growth, the principle translates into the following: as income increases, income expectations rise too and, in turn, higher expectations offset or even neutralize the positive impact from the higher income on life satisfaction (e.g., Stutzer, 2004; Di Tella, Haisken-De New, & MacCulloch, 2010). Habituation implies that, although it is possible to raise the level of life satisfaction by acquiring more resources, the growth in satisfaction will last only until the process of habituation is completed.

The second explanation is *relative income effects* or *social comparisons*. The principle is that people attribute value to money and what they can buy with it both in absolute terms and relative to what their acquaintances earn and can buy. The power of relative income effects was captured in a study of married women who had a married sister (Neumark & Postlewaite, 1998): an unemployed woman married to someone who earned less than her sister's husband was about 20 per cent more likely to find a job than an unemployed woman married to someone who earned more than her sister's husband. To put it simply, it appears that these women's motivation to find a job and earn a salary was fostered by a comparison of their family income with their sisters' family income.

Are the relative income effects confined to close acquaintances? A study of about 10,000 people leaving in nearly 1,000 different neighbourhoods (Luttmer, 2005) found that people's happiness is not influenced by their neighbours' income if that income is stable. Yet, they feel happier if their neighbours' income decreases, and they feel less happy if their neighbours' income increases. Therefore, relative income effects are pervasive, and have the potential to offset the positive impact that income has on happiness, even in times of economic growth.

Relative income effects can be even more important than the average economical trend. For example, Brockmann and co-workers (2008) explained the decreasing happiness in China in the 1990–2000 decade as the result of 'frustrated achievement'. Although the average person in China became richer, the distribution of earnings in the Chinese society became increasingly skewed towards the high-income end, with a minority of people becoming extremely rich and the majority of people falling below the average yearly income. Thus, Brockmann and co-workers (2008) pointed out that most Chinese did not fare well when comparing their income with the average income, and this unfavourable social comparison in turn determined the overall decrease in happiness of the Chinese population.

Habituation and relative income effects can lead to a three-stage loop often referred to as the *hedonic treadmill*: (1) higher past consumption and unsatisfactory comparisons with wealthier acquaintances foster higher income expectations, (2) higher income expectations foster higher income, higher consumption, and more satisfactory comparisons with poorer acquaintances, and hence higher life satisfaction, (3) the higher level of consumption becomes the new standard and hence life satisfaction returns to the level of stage one. The main implication of the hedonic treadmill is that the majority of people living in a wealthy country (i.e., those who are not markedly rich) are 'condemned' to look beyond money in order to become happier persons.

Differences between Happy and Unhappy People

Diener and co-workers (2002) analysed data from two large surveys conducted on undergraduate students from more than 30 nations using a measure of happiness to classify participants into 'happy' and 'unhappy', a measure of global life satisfaction, and measures of domain-specific satisfaction in eight domains of life (health, finances, family, friends, recreation, religion, self, and education). They investigated how happy and unhappy individuals differently produce global life satisfaction scores as a function of domain-specific life satisfaction scores. They found that happy individuals tend to weight more their best domains when rating their global life satisfaction, whereas unhappy individuals tend to weight more their worst domains when rating their global life satisfaction. On one hand, happy people seem to wear rosy lenses when they rate their global life satisfaction: they pay more attention to those domains of life wherein things are going well, and less attention to those domains wherein things are going poorly. On the other hand, unhappy people seem to wear dark lenses when they rate their global life satisfaction: they pay more attention to those domains of life wherein things are going poorly, and less attention to those domains wherein things are going well. Therefore, both happy and unhappy people produce biased ratings of their global life satisfaction, and the bias is 'positive' for the former and 'negative' for the latter. It follows, that the only unbiased raters of their global life satisfaction are those in the middle of the happiness scale, that is, the majority of people who see the glass either half empty or half full.

Diener and co-workers' (2002) study has two methodological implications. First, in order to obtain a valid assessment of life satisfaction researchers should collect both a global rating and domain-specific ratings. Second, measures of happiness and measures of global life satisfaction capture somewhat distinct psychological processes; hence should both be used on the same study participants.

Lyubomirsky (2001) argued decisively in favour of the use of global measures of happiness, and used the SHS (Lyubomirsky & Lepper, 1999) as a global measure of happiness in numerous studies trying to understand the specific motivational and cognitive processes that distinguish happy from unhappy individuals. She identified four main discriminating factors.

The most important factor discriminating happy and unhappy individuals is that the former tend to engage less in social comparisons. This seems to hold both when they evaluate their own life condition and when they evaluate the condition of a team to which they belong. For example, in an experiment undergraduate students received either positive or negative performance feedback on a teaching task, and witnessed peers to receive either more negative or more positive feedback on the same task (Lyubomirsky & Ross, 1997, Study 2). This experimental design creates two conditions of inferiority in respect to a peer: (a) a poor performance that is even worse than that of a peer, and (b) a good performance that is however less good than that of a peer. In both conditions, compared to unhappy individuals, happy individuals were less influenced by the superior performance of their peer. Another study investigated what happens when individuals are members of a team that competes with other teams and found that, compared to unhappy individuals, happy individuals are less influenced by the relative performance of their team (Lyubomirsky, Tucker, & Kasri, 2001). In all, these findings concur with the economic interpretation of the Easterlin paradox (e.g., Luttmer, 2005) in that they point out that to engage in social comparisons by monitoring other people's achievements and trying to bolster one's own achievement is a key to unhappiness.

The second factor discriminating happy and unhappy individuals is that the former tend to have more positive *postdecisional rationalizations*, namely less regret for how things eventually went. For example, in an experiment, undergraduate students rated the attractiveness of desserts in a menu before and after being told which one would be served to them (Lyubomirsky & Ross, 1999, Study 2). The study found that, compared to unhappy individuals, happy individuals modified less their ratings of desserts after knowing which one they would receive. Moreover, in cases when participants learned that they would receive a less desirable dessert, the unhappy individuals rated the options they did not receive even lower than the option they would receive; to put it simply, they lowered the value of all other options in order to see the received option as the least negative. In all, these findings indicate that the tendency to reduce dissonance between the desirability of a good when it is an option and the desirability of the same good when it becomes reality is a key to unhappiness.

The third factor discriminating happy and unhappy individuals is that the former construe life events – whether big or small and whether real or imaginary – more favourably. For example, in a longitudinal study undergraduate students were asked to report on their current life events, and were then asked to remember those same events weeks later. There was no difference between happy and unhappy individuals in the number of positive and negative life events they initially reported. However, compared to unhappy individuals, happy individuals remembered on average more positively both types of events at a later time. For example, they were more likely to remember negative events using sense of humour and to emphasize the lessons learned. In all, these findings indicate that the tendency to construe positively and adaptively life events is a key to happiness.

The last but not the least factor discriminating happy and unhappy individuals is that the former tend to engage less in monitoring of, and self-reflection on their negative life outcomes and associated moods. This in turn implies that happy individuals retain comparatively more cognitive processing capacity following a downturn. For example, in an experiment, undergraduate students were given to solve impossible anagrams without being told that they were impossible (Lyubomirsky et al., 2011a). After the forced-failure experience, participants were given a reading understanding task. Happy students outperformed unhappy students on the reading task. These findings indicate that excessive monitoring of negative outcomes and rumination about those outcomes and one's own associated negative feelings is a key to unhappiness. In this connection, we will see in Chapter 5 (sections *Mindfulness* and *Adaptive and Maladaptive Metacognitions*) that lack of mindfulness and presence of maladaptive metacognitions are theorized to be the key individual factors fostering perseverative thinking on negative outcomes, and we will see in Chapter 8 (section *Mindfulness-Based Cognitive Therapy and Metacognitive Therapy*) that novel psychotherapies that target clients' mindfulness and maladaptive metacognitions appear to be remarkably effective.

In all, comparisons between happy and unhappy people revealed that happy people have a more self-enhancing attributional style. Self-enhancement comes with costs and benefits. The main cost of self-enhancement is loss of objectivity, whereas its main benefit is maintenance of happiness when facing downturns.

MODELS OF WELL-BEING

The Hedonic Definitional Model of Subjective Well-Being

By the end of the nineties hedonic research had identified the three main components of subjective well-being: global life satisfaction, trait positive affect, and trait negative affect (e.g., Diener et al., 1999). The estimated correlation of life satisfaction with trait positive affect is .46, and with negative affect is −.25, whereas positive affect and negative affect are virtually uncorrelated

Figure 2.4 *The hedonic model of subjective well-being*

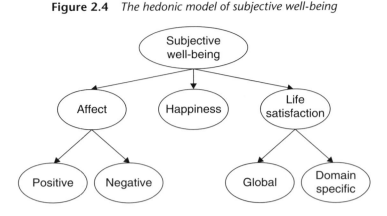

(Emmons & Diener, 1985). Moreover, all three components show fair temporal stability over periods ranging from four to seven years (Headey & Wearing, 1992; Magnus, Diener, Fujita, & Pavot, 1993). As such, the three components are related but distinct constructs, and represent relatively stable dispositions. As a whole, these three main components define subjective well-being as a trait-like variable.

The study showing how the relationships between global and domain-specific life satisfaction differ between happy and unhappy people (Diener et al., 2002) reveals that happiness and domain-specific life satisfaction should also be included in the definition of subjective well-being. Figure 2.4 shows the hedonic definitional model of subjective well-being that includes all five key components. The model states that the highest hedonic condition is one in which individuals are very satisfied with their lives in general and in each relevant life domain, are very happy, and experience consistently high levels of pleasant affect and consistently low levels of unpleasant affect in their everyday lives. This represents the hedonic view of 'the better', such that every hedonic attempt to change human beings for the better consists of maximizing one, two, or all of these key components of subjective well-being. We will see in each of the following chapters of this book that a large share of empirical research in the field of positive psychology is dedicated to the identification of psychological factors and processes that either foster or hinder one or more components of subjective well-being.

What is the theoretical foundation of the model? By admission (e.g., Diener et al., 1998) hedonic psychology has consistently used an empirical, bottom-up approach. Hedonic psychology has imported theories, measurement methods, and findings from the field of research on emotions and has integrated those inputs with methods and results developed somewhat independently in the field of research on happiness. Indeed, hedonic psychology has never made explicit its theoretical foundation. Yet, Ryan and Deci (2001) argued that hedonic psychology has an implicit theoretical foundation that fits well within the expectancy-value approach (e.g., Oishi et al., 1999), mixed with behavioural theories of reward and punishment. This fundamentally means that subjective well-being can be maximized by maximizing expectancies on the 'goods' one values the most and by minimizing speed and effort in getting those goods. This in turn leads to maximal pleasure and minimal pain, whereas pleasure and pain can be derived in everyday life experiences as well as through appraisals of past events and anticipation of future events. In this respect, affect represents the pain/gain account balance of everyday life experience, whereas global happiness and life satisfaction represent the pain/gain account balance of appraisals and expectations.

The Eudaimonic Definitional Model of Psychological Well-Being

The contemporary eudaimonic approach to psychological well-being is rooted in Maslow's (1968) and Rogers' (1963) phenomenological and humanistic theories of personality. Both theories posit that *self-actualization* is the main force driving human experience. Self-actualization is a natural and inborn tendency towards organismic growth, meant as expansion of the inner world and increase in cognitive and emotional complexity. An individual who reaches self-actualization is labelled *actualizing person* (Maslow) or *fully functioning person* (Rogers).

In their relationships with others, actualizing persons are acceptant of self, others, and nature; they identify fully with the human species, and have good and deep interpersonal relations, but they are detached from the more mundane aspects of the social world, seek privacy, and do not believe that they always need approval from others. In their private experience, they are spontaneous, rich in emotional reactions, and creative, and they often have *peak experiences*, that is, contemplative states in which they have a sense of deep connectedness with the world.

Self-actualization is a motivation that does not conform to the so-called *tension-reduction model*. Tension-reduction motivations, such as the sex and hunger drives, produce three-stage behavioural loops: (1) tension builds up to direct the organism towards a desired object, (2) the organism 'consumes' the desired object, and (3) consumption satisfaction reduces tension. Self-actualization does not drive the organism towards consumption of a desirable object as an end in itself, and consumption does not necessarily reduce tension. As such, self-actualization may lead to tension-seeking behaviours, such as exploring new environments, choosing to engage in difficult activities, and making choices that expose oneself to criticism from others.

Whereas a tension-reduction motivation drives the organism to approach desirable objects and to avoid undesirable objects, self-actualization drives the organism to approach and maintain experiences that help or are in accord with the organismic-actualizing tendency, and to avoid or minimize experiences that hinder or are in contrast with the organismic-actualizing tendency. Therefore, self-actualization is not a hedonic tendency: even if self-actualization may foster pleasure and prevent pain, this happens not as an end in itself but as a consequence of organismic growth. In all, whereas the hedonic person seeks pleasure and avoids pain, the actualizing person seeks meaningful experience and avoids meaningless experience.

Is the actualizing person just a camouflaged hedonist who substitutes 'meaning' for 'pleasure'? The answer is no, for two reasons. First, because meaning is not given by the situation or society: the actualizing person construes it. Second, because the construal of meaning is a never-ending process, as actualizing persons keep exploring and probing experience in order to find more meaning to their own existence. In all, Maslow's and Rogers' phenomenological approach to personality is inherently eudaimonic, and emphasizes the role of meaning over that of pleasure and happiness: meaning in life is paramount, whereas pleasant affect and happiness are by-products.

Meaning in life can be measured validly and reliably using the Meaning in Life Questionnaire (MLQ; Steger et al., 2006; available at: http://www.ppc.sas.upenn.edu/ppquestionnaires.htm). The questionnaire contains ten items that respondents rate on a seven-point scale ranging from 1 (*absolutely untrue*) to 7 (*absolutely true*), with neutral midpoint 4 (*can't say true or false*). The questionnaire measures meaning in life as two sub-scales: *presence of meaning* (e.g., 'I understand my life's meaning'), representing the attained fullness of meaning in life, and *search for meaning* (e.g., 'I am searching for meaning in my life'), representing the engagement in searching for more or deeper meaning in life. The two sub-scales capture well the core features of self-actualization.

Ryff and Keyes (1995) proposed a model of psychological well-being that is rooted in Maslow's (1968) and Rogers' (1963) phenomenological and humanistic theories of personality. After reviewing the progress made by the hedonic approach to subjective well-being, Ryff and Keyes argued that a basic and fundamental question – 'What does it mean to be well psychologically?' (p. 719) – still awaited an answer. They further emphasized that all the definitional components of subjective well-being – affect, happiness, and life satisfaction – had been identified using a data-driven research strategy, often using data sets that were originally collected for a purpose other than the study of well-being. They finally claimed that the definition of well-being should instead be based on psychological theory.

Drawing from Maslow's (1968) and Rogers' (1963) personality theories, as well as from Erikson's (1959) conception of how the self develops – which is reviewed in Chapter 3, section *Ego* – Ryff and Keyes (1995) took the theoretical stand that well-being is grounded in the satisfaction of a limited number of fundamental needs. There are many needs, and what all needs have in common is that their satisfaction results in pleasure. Therefore, pleasure is not the key issue. The key issue is that only a limited number of needs are such that their satisfaction or realization leads to organismic growth and hence produces well-being. For example, a physiological need such as the sexual drive does not foster

Figure 2.5 *The eudaimonic model of psychological well-being*

organismic growth unless it is integrated with a higher-order need such as the need to love someone. From this theoretical stand, the first question a psychology of well-being should ask is, which needs are fundamental?

Ryff and Keyes' (1995) answer to the question is the eudaimonic model of psychological well-being shown in Figure 2.5. The model states that the highest eudaimonic condition for human beings is one in which individuals have developed fully all six distinct components of actualization shown in the figure. *Self-acceptance* means holding positive attitudes towards the self and one's own past life. *Positive relations with others* means having developed warm, empathic, intimate, and trusting relationships with others in the form of romantic love, other types of love, and deep friendship. *Autonomy* means self-determination (a construct that is covered in depth in Chapter 3, section *Intrinsic Motivation, Extrinsic Motivation, and Self-Determination*), independence of the approval of others, and harmonious self-regulation of emotions and behaviour. *Environmental mastery* means being able to catch opportunities and use them to select and change the environment. *Purpose in life* means to have discovered one's own mission in life, and to have a sense of identity and direction, and hence strong intentionality in one's own life choices. Finally, *personal growth* means being willing always to face new challenges, being open to new experiences, and developing talents and potential. The six components can be measured validly and reliably using Ryff's (1989) six Scales of Psychological Well-Being, each of which consists of three items. This represents the eudaimonic view of 'the better', such that every eudaimonic attempt to change human beings for the better consists of maximizing one, two, or all of these key components of psychological well-being. We will see in each of the following chapters that a large share of empirical research in the field positive psychology is dedicated to the identification of psychological factors and processes that either foster or hinder one or more components of psychological well-being.

Empirical Comparison of Subjective and Psychological Well-Being

Given that the hedonic and eudaimonic models of well-being identified completely different sets of components of well-being, it is not surprising that there has been a strong controversy between the developers of the two opposing models. On one hand, Ryff and Singer (1998) criticized the hedonic model on the ground that it is not theory driven, and that it was developed according to a purely exploratory research strategy. On the other hand, Diener and co-workers (1998) admitted the descriptive nature of the hedonic model, and rebutted that this is a strength, not a weakness, in that the model is an authentic representation of peoples' view of subjective well-being. Moreover, they criticized the eudaimonic model in that, precisely because it is theory driven, it represents experts' (and not people's) views of well-being. Regardless of the different ways the hedonic and eudaimonic models of well-being were derived, how do they empirically relate to each other?

Keyes, Shmotkin, and Ruff (2002) measured the three key components – life satisfaction, positive affect, and negative affect – of the hedonic model of subjective well-being and all six components of the eudaimonic model of psychological well-being on a sample of 3,032 adults residing in the continental United States. The correlations between the two sets of constructs are shown in Table 2.2. All the correlations were statistically significant at least at the $p < .001$ level. All six components of psychological well-being correlated positively with happiness and positive affect, and negatively with negative affect. Looking at the size of the correlation coefficients, one can notice that self-acceptance and environmental mastery are the two psychological well-being constructs that are most strongly correlated with the subjective well-being constructs. Autonomy is the psychological well-being construct that correlates the least with the subjective well-being constructs. In all, the two models of well-being seem to overlap to some extent. Does this mean that they tap the same underlying construct?

In order to answer the question, Keyes and co-workers (2002) used *confirmatory factor analysis*, which is a form of factor analysis that controls for measurement

Table 2.2 *Correlations between components of subjective well-being and components of psychological well-being (selected correlation coefficients from Keyes et al., 2002)*

Psychological well-being	Subjective well-being		
	Life satisfaction	Positive affect	Negative affect
Self-acceptance	.48	.50	−.50
Positive relations	.32	.38	−.39
Autonomy	.16	.19	−.21
Environmental mastery	.45	.50	−.49
Purpose in life	.21	.19	−.27
Personal growth	.25	.28	−.28

error and hence allows estimating a more valid ('disattenuated') single correlation coefficient representing the strength of the relationship between the factor of psychological well-being and the factor of subjective well-being. The estimated correlation between the two factors was .83. Does this mean that the two factors are indistinguishable? The psychometric 'rule of thumb' is that if two variables correlate .85 or higher they are indistinguishable. Therefore, technically, psychological well-being and subjective well-being are nearly undistinguishable, with the caveat that autonomy does not seem to be fully captured by subjective well-being.

Tay and Diener (2011) investigated the relationships between components of subjective well-being and satisfaction of six needs (basic, safety, social, respect, mastery, and autonomy) using survey data collected by The Gallup Organization (1999–2013) on community samples totalling more than 60,000 participants from 123 countries. Two of the studied needs – mastery and autonomy – correspond closely to the environmental mastery and autonomy components of psychological well-being, and a third one – social – converges to some extent with the component of positive relations. Two sets of findings are relevant here. First, the correlations between the extent to which the three needs are satisfied and subjective well-being were weak for life satisfaction (range: .12–.18) and negative affect (range: –.14–.18), and moderate for positive affect (range: .26–.29). Second, regression analyses controlling for income revealed that life satisfaction is best predicted by the satisfaction of basic needs, positive affect is best predicted by the satisfaction of respect and social needs, and negative affect is best predicted by the satisfaction of respect, basic, and autonomy needs. Therefore, the relationships between the three studied components of psychological well-being – environmental mastery, positive relations, and autonomy – and the three main components of subjective well-being are from weak to moderate, and the three studied components of psychological well-being related differently to the components of subjective well-being.

In all, the findings from studies that compared measures of psychological well-being with measures of subjective well-being indicate that the two underlying constructs have a lot in common. Therefore, the most interesting findings in future research will be those showing that distinct indicators of well-being have differing patterns of relationships with a set of relevant variables. In this connection, we will see in Chapter 4 (sections *The Big Five and Subjective Well-Being*, *The Big Five and Psychological Well-Being*, and *The Big Five and Consonant–Dissonant Well-Being*) preliminary evidence suggesting that subjective and psychological well-being have somewhat different patterns of relationships with personality traits. Nevertheless, until more evidence is gathered, the issue of whether psychological well-being and subjective well-being are one and the same will reside as a ghost in the castle of positive psychology.

DIRECTIONS FOR FUTURE RESEARCH

The integration of the several points made in this chapter suggests seven broad issues that call for debate and empirical research.

1. *Which indicators of subjective well-being?*

   It is somewhat disturbing that there is no definitional overlap between the indicators of subjective well-being and the indicators of psychological well-being, as this implies that the two models of well-being cannot 'speak to each other'. Yet, this is only the tip of the iceberg, as we will see in the next chapters that there is a wide range of views in positive psychology as to what variables are true indicators of well-being and what variables are antecedents of well-being. In particular, we will see in Chapter 3 (section *Intrinsic Motivation, Extrinsic Motivation, and Self-Determination*) that Self-Determination Theory considers autonomy as the key antecedent of well-being, and not as one of its definitional components. Moreover, both the model of psychological well-being and the model of subjective well-being may have missed components of well-being that have been valued and researched for decades. In particular, we will see that creativity is regarded by many researchers as a key component of eudaimonic well-being (Chapter 3, section *The Creative Self*), particularly in the work context (Chapter 7, section *The Missing Bolt in the Affect-Creativity Yoke: Negative Emotions*), that creativity requires a particular pattern of personality traits (Chapter 4, section *The Big Five and Creative Achievement*), and that creativity can be traced back to the parenting one had in childhood (Chapter 7, section *Positive Parenting*). Surprisingly, despite its centrality, creativity is included in neither model of well-being. Therefore, the empirical convergence between the two models of well-being masks a substantial fragmentation of views about well-being that needs to be resolved in future research.

2. *Componential models as 'body builder' models.*

   Both models of well-being are componential models, meaning that their definitional components can be regarded as correlated dimensions of the well-being construct that can trade-off in determining the overall level of well-being. If the level of all components is highest, a person will be in the highest possible well-being status. If some components reach highest level whereas others reach only medium or low levels, the contributions to well-being of the different components will sum up in producing a well-being condition that is overall less positive than the highest possible well-being status. This implies that the more complete the development of well-being indicators is, the greater the overall well-being of the person will be. For this reason both models of well-being can be called 'body builder' models, in that they state that the perfect human body (an analogy for well-being) is one in which each of the thousand muscles of a human body is fully developed. As is well known, body builders run more slowly than runners do, punch more slowly than boxers do, and jump both less high and less far than jumpers do, and because of this, they generally do not compete in the Olympic Games. The reasons why a complete muscle development is inefficient in virtually every sport is because, for any given sport: (a) some muscles are more important than others, and (b) the development of less important muscles interferes with the functioning of the more important muscles. For example, a gymnast specialized in the rings apparatus will benefit from an overdevelopment of the muscles of the arms and torso, and will be hindered by an overdevelopment of leg muscles. By analogy, why should a 'body builder' model that does not work for sports instead work for well-being? Future research should investigate whether completeness of well-being components is possible and, if so, whether it is indeed desirable. This issue will return and be further analysed in the subsequent chapters. In particular, Chapter 3 (point 2 of section *Directions for Future Research*) will consider whether it is feasible and advisable to attain a complete development of all indicators of psychological well-being, and Chapter 4 (section *From Confucius and Aristotle to Schwartz, Sharpe, and Grant*) will weigh the pros and cons of complete versus specific development of character strengths and virtues.

3. *Beyond positive affect and negative affect.*
   The constructs of positive affect and negative affect are undoubtedly useful for classifying and simplifying the otherwise complex spectrum of emotions and feelings. However, as usual, simplification comes at a price. We have seen that some individuals are more discerning of their emotions than others are, that is, they have more emotional complexity. Moreover, we will see in the following chapters that there are theories of eudaimonic well-being, such as Self Determination Theory (Chapter 3, section *Intrinsic Motivation, Extrinsic Motivation, and Self-Determination*) stating that specific emotions – such as interest and enjoyment – play a fundamental role in the self-regulation of cognition and behaviour. Therefore, in

order to understand self-regulatory processes one needs to go beyond pleasantness and activation of emotions.

4. *Is negative emotionality always and necessarily bad?*

An implicit assumption of the hedonic approach to well-being is that negative emotionality is always negative, except for when fighting or fleeing are the only options. However, this in turn implies that negative emotions are substantially uncontrollable. We will see in Chapter 5 (section *Self-Regulation of Emotions*) a number of theories stating instead that negative emotions can be self-regulated and can even provide invaluable information for problem solving. For example, the executive function of attentional control allows shifting attention away from threatening stimuli when it is no longer needed, and rapidly returning to a positive emotional state (section *Attentional Control*). Moreover, metacognitions – beliefs about one's own cognitive and emotional processes – play an important role in determining whether negative emotions will escalate or simply vanish as a result of task focus: if a person regards negative emotions as cues that there might be a threat – and not as reality – negative emotions help, rather than hinder, task focus and problem solving (section *Adaptive and Maladaptive Metacognitions*). Consistent with this tenet, we will see in Chapter 7 (section *The Missing Bolt in the Affect-Creativity Yoke: Negative Emotions*) that negative emotions have a positive and necessary effect on creativity at work. In all, the assumption made by the hedonic approach to well-being ignores a wealth of theories and empirical findings highlighting the positive and, in some contexts, necessary function that negative emotions have in the pursuit of eudaimonic well-being.

5. *The more positive affect the better?*

An implicit assumption of the hedonic approach to well-being is that positive emotionality is always positive. In contrast with this view, we will see in Chapter 5 (section *Mindfulness*) that mindfulness – a contemplative and non-judgmental state characterized by tempered emotionality – is theorized to play a fundamental self-regulatory role. Moreover, we will see in Chapter 6 (whole chapter) that flow – a state of profound task-absorption accompanied by feeble emotionality – is regarded as a peek instance of eudaimonic well-being. As such, a constantly high level of positive affect may be viewed as inability to 'unplug', rather than as indication of subjective well-being. Future research should investigate whether healthy fluctuations of positive affect are more indicative of well-being than is a constantly high level of positive affect.

6. *Is ruminating about happiness any good?*

   All the components of subjective well-being are quite constant over time. In particular, trait affect has a strong genetic determination, whereas the hedonic treadmill puts a cap on how long an increase in happiness will last. Is it, therefore, wise to encourage people to think about their happiness and to take action to improve it? The risk is that if people fail in their strivings to feel happier, they may start ruminating about happiness (or lack thereof), and eventually feel even less happy. Future research should investigate the effects on well-being that stem from casting happiness as the main target of self-development.

7. *Unconstrained and decontextualized well-being.*

   Both models of well-being implicitly assume that growth in one component of well-being will not interfere with growth in the other components of well-being, and that the growth in any single component of well-being will have an overall positive effect; this implies that growth is unconstrained. Moreover, neither model considers special circumstances, such as individual differences in natural abilities and characteristics of the environments wherein individuals live; both thus implicitly assume that a single well-being recipe will work for all, no matter whom they are and where they are. These assumptions may be unrealistic. For example, a growth in environmental mastery most often requires intense and prolonged personal strivings (e.g., earning a graduate degree), which in turn reduce the time and energy one can devote to, for example, a growth in positive relations with others. If indeed, the growth of a specific component of well-being is incompatible or even harmful to other components of well-being, the best advice one could give is to choose well among competing endeavours, rather than pursuing them all at the same time. We will see in each of the following chapters that numerous theories and empirical findings suggest that one cannot 'have it all', and hence it is wiser to search for 'the better in context' than for 'the absolute better'.

SELF-DEVELOPMENT AND UNDERSTANDING EXERCISE

This exercise requires carrying out a simple *event history analysis* on your daily changes of positive and negative affect, trying to determine the effects that significant everyday life events have on your affect. Event history analysis is a broad family of techniques that monitor and record variations of continuous dependent variables over time – such as the Dow Jones index of stock transactions – and specific events that are deemed to be influential on the dependent variables – such as the announcement of early elections in a country or the publication of the past-quarter statistics on the state of the economy of a country. Event history analysis is often used on this type of data in order to discern whether and to what extent a certain class of events influences the subsequent behaviour of a dependent variable. You will conduct a mini longitudinal study in which you play both the role of the participant and the role of the researcher.

Participant's Phase

As a study participant, you will have to fill in the same set of questionnaires for 14 consecutive days. At the end of each day, you should first recall the most positive and the most negative event of that day, and write them up as two short stories on a sheet of paper or word-processed document, that we will call the *daily report*. Immediately after, you should complete either the PANAS scale or the I-PANAS-SF scale provided in Table 2.1 with reference to the feelings you experienced during that day as a whole, and calculate your positive affect and negative affect scores for that day. Finally, add the date and affect scores to the daily report, and save it for future use.

Researcher's Phase

At the end of the 14 days of data collection in which you served as a study participant, you should as a researcher retrieve all 14 daily reports, and use the information they contain to create a graph in which time (ranging from day 1 to day 14) is the horizontal axis and affect is the vertical axis. For each day, plot the corresponding scores of positive affect and negative affect as two distinct points (e.g., using an asterisk '*' for the positive affect score and a dot '·' for the negative affect score) in the graph, and add labels on top of them to remind you of the most positive and the most negative events of that day. When you have completed the graph answer the following questions:

(a) How stable are your positive and negative affect scores over time?
(b) Which event (either positive or negative) would appear to have had the strongest impact on your affect?
(c) How long did that effect last? For example, did it last only the day it occurred, or also the day after?

(d) Are days with a peak of positive affect followed by particularly positive events the day after?

(e) In all, how much do you think daily events influence your affect, and how much does your affect influence the daily events you encounter? Which of the two effects is stronger?

(f) Finally, how would you go about developing this mini longitudinal study into a real study involving a sample of study participants?

◊ RECOMMENDED WEB RESOURCES AND FURTHER READING ◊

Websites

Sources of worldwide survey data on well-being and socio-economic indicators:

■ World Values Study Association (1981–2013), which is the world's most comprehensive investigation of political and sociocultural change, at: http://www.worldvaluessurvey.org/ You can download data sets and use them for your own research

■ The Gallup Organization (1999–2013), Worldwide Research Methodology, at: http://www.gallup.com/se/128147/Worldwide-Research-Methodology.aspx

Research centres:

■ Barbara Fredrickson's Positive Emotions and Psychophysiology Lab, University of North Carolina, Chapel Hill, at: http://www.unc.edu/peplab/barb_fredrickson_page.html Numerous full-text journal articles co-authored by Fredrickson and co-workers can be downloaded for personal use
  ○ If you are interested in Fredrickson and Losada's (2005) modelling of human flourishing and languishing as nonlinear dynamic processes, you will enjoy browsing through the website of the Society for Chaos Theory in Psychology & Life Sciences (SCTPLS) at: http://www.societyforchaostheory.org/

■ Ed Diener's Website, University of Illinois at Urbana-Champaign, at: http://internal.psychology.illinois.edu/~ediener/ Numerous full-text journal articles co-authored by Diener and co-workers can be downloaded for personal use

Some of the questionnaires reviewed in this chapter can be viewed/downloaded and used freely for your own research:

■ Positive and Negative Affect Schedule (PANAS; Watson, Clark, & Tellegen, 1988) at: http://www.authentichappiness.sas.upenn.edu/questionnaires.aspx

■ Satisfaction with Life Scale (SWLS; Diener et al., 1985) at: http://internal. psychology.illinois.edu/~ediener/SWLS.html
■ Subjective Happiness Scale (SHS; Lyubomirsky & Lepper, 1999) at: http:// www.ppc.sas.upenn.edu/ppquestionnaires.htm
■ Oxford Happiness Questionnaire (OHS; Hills & Argyle, 2002) at: http:// happiness-survey.com/survey/
■ Meaning in Life Questionnaire (MLQ; Steger et al., 2006) at: http://www.ppc. sas.upenn.edu/ppquestionnaires.htm

Reading

Sources on emotions:

■ Russell and Carroll's (1999) circumplex model of emotions that represents positive and negative affect as orthogonal axes
■ Carver and Scheier's (1990) key arguments in support of the cruise control model of affect
■ Fredrickson's (2001) key arguments and empirical findings in support of the broaden-and-build theory of positive emotions
■ Fredrickson and Joiner's (2002) key arguments in support of the build hypothesis within the broaden-and-build theory of positive emotions

Sources on subjective well-being:

■ Diener and co-workers' (1999) review and summary of the findings gathered on subjective well-being
■ Tay and Diener's (2011) investigation of the relationships between human needs and subjective well-being

Sources on psychological well-being:

■ Ryff's (1989) key arguments in support of the independence of the construct of psychological well-being
■ Ryff and Keyes's (1995) presentation of the empirical structure of psychological well-being

Sources on similarities and differences between subjective well-being and psychological well-being:

■ Keyes and co-workers' (2002) empirical assessment
■ Ryan and Deci's (2001) review and meta-analytic assessment

3 Positive Self

INTRODUCTION

There are unique moments in life – when confronting an overwhelming challenge, seeing certainties shattered, or separating from a deeply loved one – when we may feel that we are living in between reality and a dream, and we may become afraid of 'losing it':

> Abruptly, one by one, the windows open. The red curtains, pulled back to the slides, float in the breeze and let him see through to the illuminated white ceiling. What does that mean? The party is over? But no one's come out! A few minutes ago he was searing on the fire of jealousy and now it is only fear he feels, only fear for Chantal. He wants to do everything for her but he does not know what should be done and that's what is intolerable: he does not know how to help her and yet he is the only one who can help her, he, he alone, because she has nobody else in the world, nobody anywhere in the world.
>
> (Kundera, 1998, p. 148)

What, exactly, are we afraid of losing in those moments? What we take for granted in everyday life, sometimes for decades-long periods with no apparent discontinuity: our sense of identity, the 'self'.

What is the self? There is a wide range of conceptions of the self. These can be thought of as a continuum, with poles represented by Immanuel Kant's and David Hume's – arguably the two philosophers who had the most influence in psychology – opposite conceptions of the self. On one hand, Kant (1781/1787/1997) considered the self to be a metaphysical entity, an object that exists in reality as much as our physical bodies do. On the other hand, Hume (1739/1896) considered the perception of the self to be an illusion, a continuous inner construal of reality, but not an object that exists in reality:

> When I turn my reflection on *myself* I never can perceive this *self* without some one or more perceptions; nor can I ever perceive anything but the perceptions. 'Tis the composition of these, therefore, which forms the self.
>
> (Hume, 1739/1896, p. 634)

Kant and Hume fostered two radically different psychological conceptualizations of the self, self as a concept (self-concept) and self as a regulatory process (self-regulation).

The self-concept is an inherently hedonic construct. As for physical appearance, the self-concept can be anything from beautiful to ugly. The implicit hedonic assumption is that the more beautiful our self-concept is, the happier we will be in our lives. Self-regulation, on the other hand, is an inherently eudaimonic construct. As for our physical dexterity, self-regulation can be anything from strong, agile, and coordinated to weak, stiff, and cumbersome. The implicit eudaimonic assumption is that the stronger, the more self-determined, and the more authentic our self-regulation is, the more resilient we will be in face of life difficulties, and the more meaning we will find in our lives.

Chapter 2 presented the hedonic model of subjective well-being (section *The Hedonic Definitional Model of Subjective Well-Being*) and the eudaimonic model of psychological well-being (section *The Eudaimonic Definitional Model of Psychological Well-Being*), which provide conceptually distinct but empirically convergent answers to the question of what constitutes the 'better' for human beings. In either model, the 'better' was defined impersonally, that is, ignoring the representations that people hold about themselves – i.e., their self-concept – as well the dreams, striving, and fears that drive their daily lives – i.e., their self-regulation. In order to gain a better understanding of well-being we now need to personalize it, and to consider explicitly the role played by the self in seeking and sometimes achieving well-being.

This chapter focuses on the 'positivity' of the self, and reviews evidence in favour of the broad hypothesis that a beautiful self-concept and an adaptive self-regulation foster well-being. The first section of this chapter reviews conceptions of the self that fall primarily under the umbrella of self as a concept, whereas the second section reviews conceptions of the self that fall primarily under the umbrella of self as a regulatory process. The third section analyses the relationships between the two conceptions of the self. The final section outlines issues open to discussion, ongoing controversies, and directions for future research.

SELF-CONCEPT

Self-Esteem

Self-esteem has been given a wide range of definitions. James (1892/1963) defined it as the ratio of one's successes over one's attempts to succeed. Consistently, Coopersmith (1967) defined self-esteem as a self-belief of capability, significance, success, and worthiness. Self-esteem can be measured validly and reliably using Rosenberg's (1979) Self-Esteem Scale (available at: http://www.bsos. umd.edu/socy/research/rosenberg.htm). The scale includes ten statements dealing with one's general feelings about oneself (e.g., 'On the whole, I am satisfied with myself') that respondents are asked to rate on a four-point scale with values 1 (*strongly agree*), 2 (*agree*), 3 (*disagree*) and 4 (*strongly disagree*). The scale has been translated into many languages, and it is often used in cross-cultural research. Interestingly, item 8 ('I wish I could have more respect for myself') was excluded from the Chinese version of the scale because it appears to be syntactically problematic in Chinese (Cheng & Hamid, 1995).

Although several psychologists (Harter, 1983; Wylie, 1979) have pointed out that self-esteem is domain-specific to some extent, work with Rosenberg's (1979) Self-Esteem Scale has shown that general self-esteem is a relevant dispositional variable that relates to a wide range of psychological variables (Wylie, 1979). In particular, self-esteem is related to scholastic achievement in children and adolescents. However, Harter (1983) provided evidence that improvements in scholastic achievement anticipate increases in self-esteem, suggesting that success is the determinant of self-esteem, and not the other way around. The scientific community has been divided on self-esteem for decades, with critiques of the concept highlighting its purely descriptive, non-causal nature, and proponents of the concept sustaining its central role in human psychology. Among the latter, Branden (1984) stated:

> [I] Cannot think of a single psychological problem – from anxiety and depression, to fear of intimacy or of success, to spouse battery or child molestation – that is not traceable to the problem of low self-esteem.
>
> (Branden, 1984, p. 12)

After decades of research on self-esteem and attempts to enhance self-esteem in order to foster a wide range of positive outcomes, including academic achievement and mental health, the American Psychological Society Task Force on Self-Esteem published a comprehensive report on the state of the subject (Baumeister et al., 2003). The starting position point of the report was:

> Self-esteem does not carry any definitional requirement of accuracy whatsoever. Thus, high self-esteem may refer to an accurate, justified, balanced appreciation of one's worth as a person and one's successes and competencies, but it can also refer to an inflated, arrogant, grandiose, unwarranted sense of conceited superiority over others. By the same token, low self-esteem can be either an accurate, well-founded understanding of one's shortcomings as a person or a distorted, even pathological sense of insecurity and inferiority.
>
> (Baumeister et al., 2003, p. 2)

In all, self-esteem is perception, not reality.

Baumeister and co-workers (2003) went on by reviewing empirical studies that investigate various causal hypotheses concerning self-esteem. We will consider here a selection of three hypotheses. First, self-esteem was found to correlate as high as .85 with self-ratings of physical attractiveness (Harter, 1993). Given that a correlation of .85 or greater between two variables is generally considered proof that the two variables measure the same construct, one would conclude that self-esteem scales actually measure physical attractiveness. However, given that none of the items used in self-esteem scales refers to appearance, the more likely explanation is that the correlation is boosted by a general tendency to speak highly of oneself no matter what the topic might be. If that were the case, there should be no correlation between self-esteem and other-rated, 'objective' attractiveness. Diener, Wolsic, and Fujita (1995) found that self-esteem correlates as low as .14 with other-ratings of physical attractiveness based on head-and-shoulder pictures, and as low as .06 with other-ratings of physical attractiveness based on full body pictures. These correlations are indeed so low that they compel one to conclude that self-esteem is nearly all about speaking highly about oneself.

Second, self-esteem was found to correlate with happiness as high as .47 in a cross-national study of more than 13,000 undergraduate university students, and it was the best predictor of happiness among all the variables measured in that study (Diener & Diener, 1995). Lyubomirsky, Tkach, and Dimatteo (2006) replicated the findings on a sample of 621 retired employees from a utility company located in Southern California, finding a correlation of .58 between self-esteem and happiness. In all, the correlation between self-esteem and happiness is strong and robust, but there is concern about circular reasoning: is self-esteem causing happiness, or is happiness causing self-esteem?

Finally, the conventional view has been that low self-esteem causes aggressive behaviour, violent behaviour, and other forms of antisocial behaviour. However, Baumeister and co-workers (2003) argued that the empirical evidence overall supports the opposite view: when the self is threatened by others, *narcissism, inflated self-esteem* (i.e., an evaluation of the self that is more positive than one's peers evaluation) and other types of high self-esteem are likely to cause aggressive retaliation. In all, what Baumeister and co-workers defined as *threatened egotism* – i.e., an overly positive view of the self that comes under attack by others – is more commonly linked to aggression than low self-esteem is.

Baumeister and co-workers (2003) concluded their assessment claiming that interventions aimed at boosting self-esteem can foster narcissism and egotism, and hence be as dangerous as a boomerang. Instead, the best for well-being is to achieve accurate and balanced self-esteem, which combines frank appreciation of one's own objective strengths with awareness of one's own limitations. In all, human beings need accurate – not high – self-esteem.

Self-Efficacy

Social Cognitive Theory (Bandura, 1986) provides a comprehensive view of how the self works in interaction with the environment to produce some basic beliefs – called *self-efficacy beliefs* – about one's own capability to handle difficult situations. The theory postulates that self-efficacy beliefs are domain-specific, and that the aggregate self-efficacy across life domains provides an overall assessment of the self. General self-efficacy can be measured validly and reliably using the General Self-Efficacy Scale (GSES; Jerusalem & Schwarzer, 1992; available in numerous language versions at: http://userpage.fu-berlin.de/health/selfscal. htm), which consists of 10 items (e.g., 'I can solve most problems if I invest the necessary effort') to be rated on a four-point scale ranging from 1 (*not at all true of me*) to 4 (*exactly true of me*). The construct of general self-efficacy is conceptually similar to the construct of general self-esteem, in that it consists of positive self-appraisals, but it is different in two important ways. First, the construct of self-efficacy taps beliefs about one's own ability to tackle problems, not the relative frequency of successes over attempts to succeed; thus, one can have high self-efficacy even when losing. Second, the construct of self-efficacy is derived from theory.

All components of Social Cognitive Theory (Bandura, 1986) are purely cognitive: *expectancies*, *beliefs*, *goals*, and *internal standards*.

There are two classes of expectancies, generalized and specific. Generalized expectancies apply to large classes of situations. Specific expectancies apply to small classes of situations or even to one situation only. The theory states that specific expectancies are more important determinants of behaviour than generalized expectancies because persons make a great number of distinctions when they evaluate situations, these distinctions are highly idiosyncratic (i.e., they differ considerably between persons up to becoming nearly person-specific), and persons' behaviour is rooted in their subjective perception of the situation. Expectancies have the form 'if the situation is ___ then I expect that ___ will happen', with fillers to be completed depending on the situation at hand. Based on many such encoded statements, a person develops behavioural patterns matched with specific situations.

Self-efficacy beliefs are persons' beliefs concerning their ability to produce the required behaviour in specific situations and hence to be behaviourally competent in that situation. Self-efficacy beliefs can be captured with questions of the type 'how confident are you that you will be able to ___ in situation ___?', wherein the fillers are to be completed with specific descriptions of the required behaviour and of the situation in which that behaviour is required. Self-efficacy beliefs are thus different from outcome expectancies in that they refer to the preparedness for action, not to the likelihood of success. In practice, however, the difference between self-efficacy beliefs and outcome expectancies is generally small except for those situations in which the outcome is believed to be beyond one's control as, for example, when tossing a coin or throwing dice.

Expectancies and beliefs form matched pairs, in which expectancies refer to specific events, and beliefs refer to one's own capabilities to face those events. These are hypothesized to be the most important determinants of behaviour.

Goals and internal standards form matched pairs, in which goals direct behaviour and standards allow assessing the effectiveness of goal-directed behaviour. Goals allow persons to organize their behaviour over time and delay gratification. Goals differ in time reference (e.g., short-term vs. long-term goals), difficulty level, and specificity. Progress towards achieving a goal is evaluated with reference to internal standards, that is, subjective criteria that people use in evaluating their own behaviour as well as the behaviour of others.

Persons' self-regulatory capabilities follow from two basic types of freedom: (a) freedom to choose and modify goals and internal standards, and (b) freedom to rely on self-reinforcement – self-appraisal of one's own actions – rather than on external reinforcement. Self-reinforcement is essential for maintaining behaviour when one pursues long-term goals.

Self-efficacy beliefs are theorized to influence the choice of goals (people tend to choose goals in the areas in which they feel more efficacious) and the difficulty level of goals (people tend to choose demands that match their self-efficacy). Self-efficacy beliefs are also theorized to influence many facets of behaviour including (a) which activity one chooses to engage in among the available ones, (b) how much effort is devoted to performing the activity, (c) how persistent one is in pursuing the activity, and (d) one's own emotional reactions before engaging in the activity (while anticipating a situation) and while performing the activity. In all, behaviour in every situation is explained by three factors: (a) previous history of situation-specific reinforcements, (b) expectations about the behaviour-reinforcement link, and (c) beliefs on being effective in the required behaviour.

Self-efficacy beliefs are theorized to evolve as a result of a complex, never-ending interaction between person and environment. Four factors influence the self-efficacy level at any given point in time: (a) performance accomplishments (past experience of success/failure in achieving a specific goal in a specific situation), (b) vicarious experience (observation of other persons' success/failure in achieving the same goal in the same situation), (c) emotional arousal during performance (with anxiety and stress hindering self-efficacy), and (d) verbal persuasion (evaluation by others of specific skills).

A large number of empirical studies converged in finding that the effect of self-efficacy beliefs on performance compensates for even large differences in objective skills; they also found that high self-efficacy contributes to a greater sense of control, results in better coping with stressful life events, and is associated with less anxiety and stress while facing difficult tasks (see review by Bandura, 1986). Moreover, self-efficacy was found to correlate with indicators of subjective well-being. For example, Salami (2010) found, on a sample of 242 Nigerian undergraduate university students, that general self-efficacy correlates moderately and positively with measures of life satisfaction ($r = .19$) and happiness ($r = .28$). However, this and other studies are only suggestive of a link between self-efficacy and subjective well-being because they did not control for alternative explanatory factors.

What are the main alternative explanatory factors for the positive associations found between general self-efficacy and subjective well-being? Judge and Hurst (2007) proposed a broad construct – *core self-evaluations* – that includes four components: general self-esteem, general self-efficacy, neuroticism, and *locus of control*. We have considered the first two components in this chapter (section 'Self-Esteem' and the current section). We have encountered the third component in Chapter 2 (section *Origins and Consequences of Affect*), and we will analyse it in greater depth in Chapter 4 (section *The Big Five*). The fourth component – locus of control – signifies individual differences in expectancies across a continuum ranging from *internal* to *external*: people with internal locus of control tend to expect reinforcements to follow from their actions, while people with external locus of control tend to expect reinforcements to come independently of their behaviours (Rotter, 1966). Judge and Hurst reviewed the evidence of numerous correlational studies and concluded that general self-esteem, general self-efficacy, internal locus of control, and emotional stability (i.e., the inverse of neuroticism) correlate strongly with one another to the extent that they lack discriminant validity. The lack of discriminant validity of the components of core self-evaluations in turn implies that associations exhibited by one component (e.g., general self-efficacy) with subjective well-being could equally be attributed to another component (e.g., emotional stability).

Judge and Hurst's analysis implies that (a) there is no strong evidence suggesting that general self-efficacy is a better predictor of subjective well-being than general self-esteem is, and (b) although the concept of self-esteem has no theoretical basis whereas the concept of self-efficacy is grounded in theory, they fundamentally measure the same construct. In all, the criticism Baumeister and co-workers (2003) directed against the construct of general self-esteem also applies to a large extent to the construct of general self-efficacy. In particular, although low self-efficacy is definitely revealing of poor adaptation and low subjective well-being, an unrealistically high level of self-efficacy may represent a flawed, maladaptive, and socially harmful development of the self-concept.

Is there some indicator of eudaimonic well-being that self-efficacy cannot explain? There is one, which is apparently marginal but very important on a closer look. Bandura (1986) found that, up to a threshold, self-efficacy fosters interest and behavioural engagement in a given activity; yet, any increase of self-efficacy past the threshold does not result in more interest and behavioural engagement in that activity. Therefore, feeling very skilful at an activity does not necessarily imply that we are interested in performing that activity or that we will actually engage in that activity. As such, self-efficacy cannot explain why persons develop lifelong interests and pursue their passions persistently and in face of strong difficulties. In order to find an explanation for such a fundamental aspect of eudaimonic well-being we now need to turn attention to the concepts and theories that were developed studying the regulatory processes of the self, that is, self-regulation.

SELF-REGULATION

Ego

Freud (1910) viewed adolescence as the *genital* psychosexual developmental stage that follows the *latency* stage. The latency stage is a long and seemingly quiet period during which the *libido* – i.e., the innate psychosexual energy – expresses itself only indirectly through playing, schooling, and socializing, and the child loses all curiosity and interest in sex. By contrast, the *genital* stage is the period in which the sexual drive returns and transforms itself into a mature form, and the adolescents face increasing societal demands to grow in intellectual and practical abilities. Freud explained the 'storm and stress' of adolescence as the result of the conflict between instinctual strivings and reality demands, and he viewed the end of adolescence and beginning of adulthood as the moment in which the *ego* is fully formed.

In Freud's personality theory the ego is the decision-maker and makes executive decisions based on the reality principle. The main work of the ego is to control the *id*, which seeks immediate gratification based on the pleasure principle. The ego controls the id by delaying gratification until a socially appropriate situation for satisfying a need is encountered. The ego blocks, deviates, or neutralizes unacceptable urges coming from the id by means of defence mechanisms. When the pressure from the id is too strong, the ego produces anxiety. Socialization requires the ego to become strong and hence able to control the id. However, the ego can hardly succeed because it draws its energy entirely from the id; the situation of the ego is thus that of a prison guard who is fed by his prisoner.

Ego psychologists freed the ego from the tyranny of the id. White (1959, 1960, 1963) argued that the ego produces its own independent energy and has its own innate motivation – *effectance motivation* – which is the motivation to master activities and to pursue ever growing competence. Other psychoanalysis-oriented psychologists retained White's argument because the concepts of independent ego energy and effectance motivation accounted for otherwise unexplainable developmental behaviours, such as exploration and the search for tasks that stretch one's own capabilities. Many new self-related constructs were introduced to account for self-integrity and strivings towards its maximization: *ego strength* (Barron, 1953), *ego development* (Loevinger, 1976, 1985, 1993), and *ego resiliency and control* (Block, 1971, 1993; Block & Block, 1980; Funder & Block, 1989). Although there are slight differences in meaning between these concepts, they all highlight the child's or adolescent's tendency to develop a firm sense of self and ability to cope with stress, to delay gratification for achieving distal goals, to dose the level of control over impulses according to the demands of the situation, and to establish and deepen relations with others.

Among the ego psychologists, Erikson (1959, 1963, 1968, 1982) is the one who provided the most articulate explanation of how individuals develop a firm sense of self. Erikson introduced a vision of human development as a life-span journey through eight psychosocial stages. These stages are both maturational and socially determined, are determined both by internal and external forces, are common to all persons (though they are not necessarily the only ones for every person), and are sequential and partially overlapping in that each begins at a specific age and can span beyond the onset of the next stage. In all, the person and the social environment interact in determining an individual lifelong developmental trajectory.

Each stage is characterized by a psychosocial crisis. Each crisis has two possible outcomes – a positive and a negative one – and the outcome of each crisis determines durable positive or negative changes, and hence influences the overall development of the self. The likelihood that the outcome of a crisis is positive depends on whether and to what extent the previous crises were successfully overcome; there is thus a cumulative effect of unsolved crises over future stages. To make things even more complicated for the self, the solution of previous crises does not guarantee a positive outcome of the crisis of the next stage. Figure 3.1 shows the eight psychosocial stages and associated crises, with indicative ages at which they are likely to occur. The positive outcome of each stage is, in this order: (1) trust in oneself and others and hence optimism, (2) volitional self-control and ability to make choices, (3) sense of purpose and initiative, (4) ability to engage in work and derive satisfaction from its completion,

Figure 3.1   *Erikson's taxonomy of psychosocial stages and associated crises in a person's life*

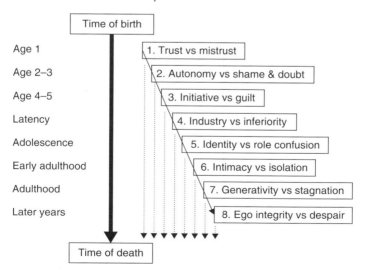

Note: The dotted arrows indicate the potential spanning of a crisis over time; the diagonal arrow indicates the interdependence of stages.

(5) sense of consistent identity across situations and times, (6) ability to unite with others, (7) ability to be absorbed in productive work and relations, and (8) sense of meaning in life and satisfaction with one's own life accomplishments. In particular, Erikson explained the emergence of a strong self in early adulthood as the result of two main strivings: (a) developing competence and proving it to oneself and others, and (b) developing a sense of identity that satisfies one's own need to be unique while obtaining social acceptance and recognition from others.

Given that the only stable thing in life seems to be a state of continuous psychosocial crisis and change, how do people construe the causation of their lives? deCharms (1968) argued that some persons perceive life as if they were 'pawns' – that is, they believe that their behaviour is influenced by external forces – and hence have an *external locus of causation*, whereas other persons perceive life as if they were 'origins' – they believe that they are free to choose, and that they are the prime causes of their own behaviour – and hence have an *internal locus of causation*. Empirical research (e.g., Ryan & Grolnick, 1986) has consistently found that internal (versus external) locus of causation correlates with effectance motivation, self-esteem, and self-efficacy. In all, locus of causation complements both the view of the self as a concept and the view of the self as a regulatory process.

The concepts of effectance motivation, locus of causation, and sense of identity opened a radically new perspective for understanding self-regulation and the differences between healthy and unhealthy functioning of the self. We will see in the next section how the concepts of effectance motivation and locus of causation have been developed into an articulate theoretical framework that is amenable to empirical testing in both laboratory and real-life settings. We will see further ahead in this Chapter (section *The 'I' and the 'Me'*) that the concept of sense of identity inspired the development of a narrative approach to the study of the self that sheds light on the intricate and reciprocal relationships between self-concept and self-regulation.

Intrinsic Motivation, Extrinsic Motivation, and Self-Determination

Intrinsic motivation is the tendency to engage in tasks because one finds them interesting and enjoyable, whereas extrinsic motivation is the tendency to engage in tasks because of task-unrelated factors such as the expectation of reward or punishment (Deci & Ryan, 1985a). Self-Determination Theory (SDT; Deci & Ryan, 1985a; Ryan & Deci, 2000) defines intrinsic motivation as the innate energy source that is central to the active nature of the organism. As it develops in interaction with the environment, intrinsic motivation becomes the natural propensity to engage one's interests, exercise one's capabilities, and seek and conquer *optimal challenges*, that is, challenges that stretch one's capabilities a bit. In all, Self-Determination Theory views intrinsic motivation as the key self-regulatory force underlying the process of learning and psychological adaptation as a whole.

Self-Determination Theory posits that intrinsic motivation and extrinsic motivation are associated with distinct sets of emotions. On the one hand, Izard (1977) advanced that interest is the key promoter of intrinsic motivation as it directs and amplifies attention towards the task and activates exploratory and manipulatory behaviours in novel environments. Csikszentmihalyi (1975/2000) advanced that enjoyment is the key promoter of intrinsic motivation because it provides the inner reward necessary to achieve one-pointedness of mind and task-absorption. Deci and Ryan (1985a, p. 29) concluded that 'interest and enjoyment are the central emotions that accompany intrinsic motivation'. On the other hand, the central emotions that accompany extrinsic motivation are pressure and tension. As anticipated in Chapter 2 (section *Affect and Emotional Complexity*), Self-Determination attributes particular importance to specific emotions: although interest and enjoyment are positive emotions, and pressure and tension are negative emotions, the theory regards the aggregate constructs of positive affect and negative affect too generic for the purpose of understanding the core self-regulatory functions that emotions have on motivation, cognition, and behaviour.

Self-Determination Theory states that when people are driven by intrinsic motivation they tend to enter a state of *task-involvement*, which implies loss of self-consciousness, the feeling that the activity is freely chosen, lack of motives beyond focusing on the interesting aspects of the activity, no feeling of pressure towards particular outcomes that may signify success or failure, and no feeling of tension. We will see in Chapter 6 (section *Self-Determination Theory and Flow*) that, at heightened levels, intrinsic motivation is theorized to make more likely the occurrence of flow, a state of complete absorption in the activity. When instead people are driven by extrinsic motivation they tend to enter a state of *ego-involvement*, which implies heightened self-consciousness, the feeling that the activity is imposed, a focus on the possible outcomes of the activity with emphasis on success or failure, a feeling of pressure towards particular outcomes – such as succeeding at what one is doing or avoiding failure – and a feeling of tension accompanied by lack of interest in and enjoyment of the activity.

Intrinsic motivation was originally measured as a state variable in experimental conditions as free-choice time spent on an interesting task following the departure of the experimenter: the longer the participant keeps working on the task by own choice, the greater intrinsic motivation (Deci, 1971). Nowadays, intrinsic motivation is often measured as an experiential state variable, that is, as the interest and enjoyment experienced in performing experimental or daily tasks (e.g., McAuley, Duncan, & Tammen, 1987).

State intrinsic motivation and state extrinsic motivation are antagonistic to each other at any given point in time. Factors that can turn off intrinsic motivation and promote extrinsic motivation include surveillance, competition, and rewards that do not provide performance feedback, such as paying a person for completing a task irrespectively of the quality of his or her work (Deci & Ryan, 1985a). When these factors are manipulated experimentally to induce temporary states of extrinsic motivation, participants exhibit poorer concept attainment (McCullers & Martin, 1971), impaired problem solving (Glucksberg, 1962), and lower creative output (Amabile, 1979).

Self-Determination Theory postulates the existence of three basic, universal needs: *autonomy*, *competence*, and *relatedness*. Autonomy is rooted in an internal locus of causation (deCharms, 1968), competence is rooted in effectance motivation (White, 1959), and relatedness is rooted in the *need to belong* (Baumeister & Leary, 1995). Activities that satisfy these needs tend to promote intrinsic motivation, whereas activities that do not satisfy these needs tend to hinder intrinsic motivation. Deci and Ryan (1985a) introduced *Cognitive Evaluation Theory* as a sub-theory of Self-Determination Theory to explain specifically how the three needs interact to influence intrinsic motivation. The theory postulates that the satisfaction of the needs for competence and relatedness contributes to intrinsic motivation if and only if the need for autonomy is sufficiently satisfied. Thus, only autonomous, self-determined goals can promote intrinsic motivation. Non-self-determined goals can at times be effective in satisfying the needs for competence and relatedness, but also in those instances they do not promote intrinsic motivation.

Figure 3.2 summarizes the recursive model of how basic needs, intrinsic motivation, and behaviour influence each other when a person is engaging in a task that can satisfy one or more basic needs. The arrows connecting the different variables represent causal paths. The model states that, if satisfied, all three needs

Figure 3.2 *A simplified recursive model of how basic needs, intrinsic motivation, and behaviour influence one another when a person engages in intrinsically motivated behaviour*

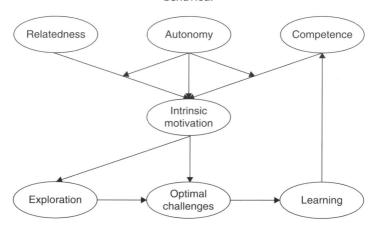

foster intrinsic motivation, with an important caveat. The arrows originating from autonomy and intersecting the arrows originating from relatedness and competence mean that autonomy moderates the effects that relatedness and competence have on intrinsic motivation. In particular, relatedness and competence will foster intrinsic motivation if and only if the need for autonomy is satisfied above a certain threshold. Intrinsic motivation fosters the search for optimal challenges both directly and indirectly, by fostering exploratory behaviour. Insofar as a person actually finds optimal challenges, learning will occur, which will satisfy the need for competence. In turn, the satisfaction of the need for competence will foster intrinsic motivation, so that another loop of intrinsically motivated behaviour will follow. Finally, the emotions of interest and enjoyment accompany every phase of the process, but interest is most salient during exploration and when seeking optimal challenges, whereas enjoyment is most salient when learning occurs and hence the need for competence is satisfied.

Deci and Ryan (1985a) conceptualized the intrinsically motivated behavioural sequence within an O–S–O–R (Organism–Stimulus–Organism–Response) framework. The first 'O' in the acronym signifies that the organism is actively seeking and choosing stimuli based on experiential states such as interest, curiosity, or boredom. The stimuli 'S' are opportunities for action that the organism is relatively free to choose or ignore. The second 'O' signifies that, once it has chosen a stimulus to attend to, the organism is actively processing the stimulus trying to master it. If the selected stimulus is optimally challenging (i.e., if the challenges from the task stretch a bit beyond the organism's capability), the integration will be achieved in a two-step loop: (a) the organism will first have to deal with the stimulus without having adequate structures for the task and hence, in Piaget's (1976) terminology, it will *accommodate* the stimulus and provide a first, fallible response 'R' and (b) through repeated practice with the stimulus, the organism will eventually develop adequate structures to master it and hence, in Piaget's terminology, it will *assimilate* the stimulus and produce a competent response 'R'. The organism will then move to another stimulus that is more challenging than the previous one, and will repeat the accommodation–assimilation steps on the new stimulus. Through several accommodation–assimilation loops the organism exploits the environment for opportunities to learn, and acquires increasingly more complex psychological structures. In all, the O–S–O–R representation of intrinsically motivated behaviour provides a clear explication in terms of competence of the construct of personal growth, which is at the heart of Maslow (1968) and Rogers' (1963) construct of self-actualization.

What happens if a task does not allow satisfying one or more basic needs and hence cannot be intrinsically motivating? In everyday life we encounter plenty of such tasks, such as waking up early to meet a deadline, having to spend hours sitting in our car or standing in a crowded subway train to commute between home and work, or filling in a long and complicated form that the civil servant in front of us deems to be of cosmic importance. That is the domain of extrinsically motivated behaviour, wherein we are apparently condemned to experience tension and pressure with not a blink of interest and enjoyment. Are we? It turns out that there are big individual differences in the way people approach tasks that offer only extrinsic incentives: some fall into an emotional pit of pressure and tension, whereas others seem serene as if they were actually enjoying the activity. It would hence seem that people differ in the ability to self-regulate their extrinsically motivated behaviour.

Deci and Ryan (1985a) introduced *Organismic Integration Theory* (OIT) as a sub-theory of Self-Determination Theory to explain the developmental processes through which individuals learn how to self-regulate extrinsically motivated behaviour. The theory assumes that intrinsic motivation is the energizer of the organismic integration process through which elements of one's internal and external worlds are first differentiated and then integrated harmoniously with one's existing psychological structures. The integrative process requires exploratory behaviours to provide the development of competencies. The exploratory behaviours are typically intrinsically motivated; if they actually lead to the development of competencies, they in turn enhance intrinsic motivation. Environments that provide optimal challenges, support for autonomy, and competence feedback facilitate exploratory behaviour and promote intrinsic motivation, whereas environments that provide excessive or insufficient challenges, penalize autonomy, and provide controlling feedback discourage exploratory behaviour and thwart intrinsic motivation. The theory postulates that the interaction between a child's motivation and the environment has long-lasting, structural effects on psychosocial development.

A ubiquitous problem in psychosocial development is that some behaviours required by society are not interesting per se, and hence cannot be learned through intrinsically motivated processes. These behaviours are initially learned in order to avoid contingent punishment or to obtain contingent reward. Learning then proceeds towards increased levels of *internalization*, which is the process through which the child acquires beliefs and attitudes and transforms them into own goals and values. As learning becomes more internalized, the child develops more self-determination (i.e., autonomy) and more effective functioning (i.e., competence). Internalization is therefore an active, constructive process that is energized by the needs for autonomy and competence.

Internalization becomes possible by the second year of life when children can anticipate events and have some self-control of their own actions. At that point, they encounter impositions by adults, who set limits for children's behaviour and implement reward and punishment schemes. The theory identifies a hierarchy of four stages representing progressive levels of internalization. *External regulation* is the first stage, wherein children's behaviour is only controlled by external contingencies. *Introjection* is the second stage, wherein children construct internal representations of the external controls, and use them to provide themselves with approval or disapproval of their own behaviour. Introjection is more efficient than external regulation but implies emotions of shame and guilt, inner conflict, rigidity, and lack of self-determination. *Identification* is the third stage, wherein children identify in their caretakers and by virtue of such identification they come to accept the set rules of behaviour as if they were their own. Identification is more efficient than introjection at the emotional level, as it implies less inner conflict and pressure and more flexibility of behaviour. *Integration* is the fourth and highest stage, wherein children integrate their identified rules of behaviour with other identifications and hence form a coherent self-regulatory structure. Integration removes the possibility of experiencing inner conflicts and, most important, it allows children to make their own free choices based on their own values and the anticipated consequences of their actions. In all, integration represents the highest level of psychosocial development.

What is the difference, then, between internalization of extrinsic values and integration of capacities that were differentiated through purely intrinsic motivation? The two processes have virtually the same end-point. The end-point of internalization is that the values upheld by a culture become a child's own values, the child understands and accepts that chores are beneficial to one's own goals and applies the internalized values smoothly, with no conflict. As such, the internalized values generate behaviours that are self-determined even if they are not intrinsically motivated. However, internalization is difficult to achieve because it involves conflicts between environmental demands and organismic nature, and hence it requires extensive accommodation, in that the self has to adapt to an external world that would just not change.

Figure 3.3 shows the various types of motivation, with their self-regulatory styles, sorted along the self-determination continuum. On the left end of the continuum, there is a state of *amotivation*, which implies the absence of both intrinsic motivation and extrinsic motivation, the absence of any form of self-regulation, and hence no self-determination. As one moves rightward, there are different states of extrinsic motivation, each associated with a regulatory style corresponding to a stage of the internalization process; within the hierarchy, internalized

Figure 3.3   *The various types of motivation, with their self-regulatory style, organized according to the level of self-determination they allow (adapted from Ryan & Deci, 2000)*

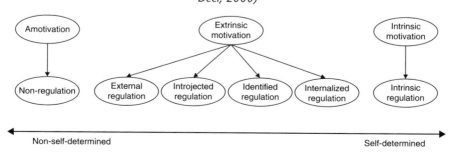

self-regulation constitutes the most self-determined of the extrinsic motivation states. Finally, on the right end of the continuum, there is a state of intrinsic motivation, which is associated with an intrinsic regulatory style, and hence maximal self-determination. Finally, each level of self-determination occurs in correspondence with a locus of causation: the locus of causation is impersonal when there is no self-determination, external for low levels of self-determination, and internal for high levels of self-determination. In all, the theory states that optimal functioning is achieved for high self-determination, that is, when individuals are either intrinsically motivated or are extrinsically motivated and adopt internalized regulation.

Where are we in that continuum? Each one of us is in multiple points depending on the situation, and hence nowhere precisely. An individual in any given situation has the potential of adopting more than one self-regulatory style, sometimes in combination. This implies that the continuum does not represent individual differences, as the same individual may use different self-regulatory styles – as well as different combinations of self-regulatory styles – in different contexts. Yet, as we will see in Chapter 4 (section *Causality Orientations*), the self-determination continuum has been used as a basis for defining and measuring broad individual differences in self-regulatory style across situations and times.

Is self-determination – or autonomy – an indicator of subjective well-being? On one hand, as we have seen in Chapter 2 (section *The Eudaimonic Definitional Model of Psychological Well-Being*), autonomy is one of the six definitional components of Ryff and Keyes' (1995) model of psychological well-being. On the other hand, Deci and Ryan's (1985a) Self-Determination Theory views autonomy as an antecedent of psychological well-being, which implies that high autonomy is a necessary but not sufficient condition for achieving high psychological well-being. We will see in Chapter 4 (section *Causality Orientations*) that, when measured as a trait, autonomy predicts relevant indicators of well-being, and we will see in Chapter 6 (section *Self-Determination Theory and Flow*) that intrinsic motivation and the needs for competence and autonomy explain at the theoretical level the occurrence of flow, a state of one-pointedness of mind and deep task-absorption that represents one of the purest expressions of eudaimonic well-being.

Self-Determination Theory is a universal theory that provides the same explanations no matter what culture a person comes from. Yet, are intrinsic motivation and autonomy equally valued in different cultures? Are they equally positive in terms of their consequences to well-being for members of different cultural groups? The next section presents theoretical arguments and empirical studies that addressed these questions.

Self-Construals and Cross-Cultural Differences in Self-Processes

In the past 25 years, cross-cultural psychologists have challenged the universality of some of the tenets of Self-Determination Theory (Deci & Ryan, 1985a), and claimed the existence of cultural variations in the psychological makeup of the self in Japanese, Chinese and other Asians. In the first phase, researchers questioned the universal relevance of autonomy. In the second phase, researchers defined and measured culture-dependent facets of the self, and used these new variables to test whether and to what extent the predictors of well-being differ between Easterners and Westerners.

Markus and Kitayama (1991) introduced the concept of *self-construals* to represent the complex psychological processes underlying the continuous construction and modification of one's own sense of identity, and differentiated two groups of such processes: *independent self-construal* and *interdependent self-construal*. Independent self-construal is the tendency to construe one's own existence as an individual separate from the social context and relationships entertained with others. Interdependent self-construal is the tendency to construe one's own existence as an integral part of a social group characterized by reciprocal bonds and commitments. They further proposed that independent self-construal and interdependent self-construal are parallel, simultaneous processes in every individual.

How could it be? Imagine you are taking the Twenty Statements Test (TST; Kuhn & McPartland, 1954), which presents you with 20 numbered blanks on a page and asks you 20 answers to the question 'Who am I?' to be written in those blanks. This enables you freely to provide your own self-definitions. For example, you could define yourself as a 'lawyer' – which would signify independent self-construal – in a blank and as a 'mother of two beautiful children' – which would signify an interdependent self-construal – in another blank. The number of 'independent' self-definitions is a measure of independent self-construal, whereas the number of 'interdependent' self-definitions is a measure of interdependent self-construal. As such, you would obtain a score for independent self-construal and a score for interdependent self-construal. Individual differences in self-construals can be more validly and reliably measured using standardized questionnaires, such as Gudykunst and co-workers' (1996) Self-Construal Orientation Scale. The scale includes 29 statements dealing with one's opinions about oneself, of which 14 measure independent self-construal (e.g., 'I should be judged on my own merit') and the remaining 15 measure interdependent self-construal (e.g., 'I consult with others before making important decisions'). Respondents are asked to rate the items on a five-point scale ranging 1 (*strongly agree*) to 5 (*strongly disagree*), with midpoint 3 (*neutral*). The measures of independent self-construal and interdependent self-construal obtained using this and similar scales turned out to be virtually uncorrelated in numerous samples from different cultures (Gudykunst et al., 1996); this robust finding provides support to the hypothesis that the two self-construals are independent processes that coexist within the same individual.

Based on this dual representation of self-construal, Markus and Kitayama (1991) claimed that, compared to Westerners, Easterners have on average less independent self-construal and more interdependent self-construal. Therefore, whereas experienced choice is salient for Westerners because it provides them with the opportunity to pursue consistency with previous behaviour and to fulfil the goal of being unique, experienced choice should be less salient for Easterners because they have a more malleable self-identity across social contexts, and their motivation to be consistent and unique is weaker. From this perspective, Self-Determination Theory would be less applicable to Asians.

Ryan and Deci (2001) rebutted the criticism by pointing out that Markus and Kitayama (1991, 1994) erroneously equated autonomy – meant as free-choice volition – with independence – meant as non-reliance on others or even *reactance*, that is, acting independently as a reaction to conforming pressure exerted by others. Thus, what Markus and Kitayama call autonomy can in some cases be a camouflaged expression of controlled and pressured behaviour. For example, to marry somebody our parents do not like could be as controlled behaviour as it is to marry somebody we do not like because our parents' want us to.

However, irrespective of the controversy on the meaning of autonomy, one should also consider the social consequences of autonomy. Ward and Chang (1997) proposed a *cultural fit* hypothesis stating that strangers adapt better to a host culture the closer their self-construals match the prototypical self-construals of the host culture. The hypothesis predicts that Easterners travelling to the West will adapt better if they emphasize their independent self-construal in interaction with members of the host culture, whereas Westerners travelling to the East will adapt better if they emphasize their interdependent self-construal. In both cases, the stranger–culture matching should help the stranger understand the local perspective and avoid behaviours that clash with the local system of values. Autonomy in an Asian culture may therefore have either positive or negative social consequences, depending on how the environment trades off the value of individual independence against the value of social interdependence. For example, although autonomous functioning is promoted in the Chinese socialization process (Chao, 1995), its role is subordinate to the capacity of developing good interpersonal relations (Guisinger & Blatt, 1994). Therefore, Chinese behavioural expressions of autonomy may receive contrasting feedback in their social environment depending on contextual factors: the feedback will be positive if the autonomous behaviour is well integrated within the value system, and negative if the autonomous behaviour is viewed as disruptive of social harmony. In all, if there are cultural differences in the way the social environment interprets and rewards expressions of autonomy, autonomy might be less conducive to well-being in collectivistic, Eastern cultures.

Empirical research has provided findings in favour and against the universality of the need for autonomy. On one hand, autonomy was found to predict subjective well-being among Bulgarian workers (Deci et al., 2001), and Japanese (Hayamizu, 1997) and Russian undergraduate students (Ryan et al., 1999), and to be equally important for North American and Korean undergraduate students (Sheldon, Elliot, Kim, & Kasser, 2001). On the other hand, it was found that experienced freedom correlates less strongly with subjective well-being in collectivistic cultures relative to individualistic cultures (Oishi, Diener, Lucas, & Suh, 1999), that the subjective well-being of Chinese single mothers (Choy & Moneta, 2002) and undergraduate students (Kwan, Bond & Singelis, 1997) correlates more with dispositions in the domain of interpersonal relatedness than with dispositions in the domain of autonomy, and that the provision of choice in experimental tasks has a stronger motivational effect on North American undergraduate students than on Asian undergraduate students (Iyengar & Lepper, 1999).

These findings indicate that, although the need for autonomy is universal, its satisfaction has a comparatively smaller fostering effect on intrinsic motivation and subjective well-being in Asians. This implies that, for Asians, an activity may be optimal (for the sake of experiencing intrinsic motivation) even if their goals in the activity are not self-determined. Moreover, these findings suggest that intrinsic motivation has a comparatively smaller fostering effect on the need for autonomy in Asians. This implies that, for Asians, a growth in intrinsic motivation does not necessarily lead to a growth in self-determination. In all, the found cultural variations in the role of autonomy imply that intrinsic motivation might be less strongly related to autonomy in Asians than it is in Westerners.

It is theoretically possible to reconcile Self-Determination Theory (Deci & Ryan, 1985a) with cross-cultural conceptions of self-construals (e.g., Markus & Kitayama, 1991; Markus, Kitayama, & Heiman, 1996) if one assumes that both independent self-construal and interdependent self-construal are self-determined processes under some circumstances and non-self-determined processes under others. In particular, in some circumstances interdependent self-construal may be an expression of autonomy embedded within a constellation of relations with others and subject to the ethical constraint of not disrupting social harmony. If this reconciliatory hypothesis holds, then it should be possible to utilize self-construals – which vary across cultures along an individualism–collectivism continuum – as predictors of well-being, and to show that independent self-construal contributes more to well-being in an individualistic culture, whereas interdependent self-construal contributes more to subjective well-being in a collectivistic culture. A study provided support to this reconciliatory hypothesis.

Kwan, Bond, and Singelis (1997) provided interesting evidence indicating that self-construals generate two distinct, parallel paths to life satisfaction, and that members of certain cultures may use one path more than the other. They achieved this result by developing and testing a path model that involves several variables whose effects are chained within each other, creating a domino effect. The definition of the model can be broken down in the following two steps.

In the first step, Kwan and co-workers (1997) hypothesized that independent self-construal promotes self-esteem because it motivates a person's development of the abilities required to become independent and self-actualizing. What, then, is the contribution of interdependent self-construal? They hypothesized that interdependent self-construal promotes *relationship harmony* – the mutuality and quality achieved in relationships – because it motivates a person's development of the abilities required to blend harmoniously with one's own social network. They also developed a short questionnaire – the Interpersonal Relationship Harmony Inventory (IRHI) – to measure relationship harmony. The questionnaire asks participants first to specify the partner's name, gender, and relation for each of the five most significant dyadic social relationships in their lives, and then to score the degree of harmony within each relationship on a seven-point scale with anchors of 1 (*very low*) and 7 (*very high*). The relationship harmony score is calculated as the average of the five relationship harmony ratings.

In the second step, Kwan and co-workers hypothesized that both self-esteem and relationship harmony promote life satisfaction, but they do so differently for members of individualistic and collectivistic cultures. Prior comparisons across nations had revealed that self-esteem correlates fairly with life satisfaction in Western cultures and weakly in Asian cultures (Diener & Diener, 1995), whereas no prior research had been conducted on the link between relationship harmony and life satisfaction. Kwan and co-workers hypothesized that self-esteem and relationship harmony have independent and direct effects on life satisfaction in all cultures, but the effect of self-esteem is stronger in individualistic cultures and the effect of relationship harmony is stronger in collectivistic cultures.

Putting together the hypotheses of step 1 and step 2, Kwan and co-workers proposed the *pancultural model of life satisfaction* shown in Figure 3.4. The model states that independent self-construal and interdependent self-construal generate independent paths towards life satisfaction, an 'individualistic' path energized by feelings and beliefs of self-worth and a 'collectivistic' path energized by feelings and beliefs of connection-worth. The bottom line is that there are two parallel ways of feeling that the glass is full, one based on how good we look as standalone individuals, the other based on how good our closest relationships look.

Figure 3.4 *The pancultural model of life satisfaction (adapted from Kwan et al., 1997)*

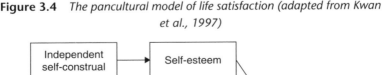
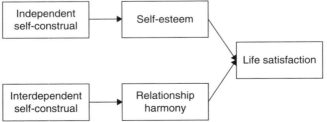

Kwan and co-workers (1997) tested the pancultural model, using structural equation modelling (SEM), on samples of undergraduate students from the US and Hong Kong. The model was supported and shown capable of accounting for some cultural differences in that (a) it had good statistical fit in both samples, (b) all the hypothesized links between variables were statistically significant in both samples, and (c) the path from self-esteem to life satisfaction was stronger in the US sample, whereas the path from relationship harmony to life satisfaction was stronger in the Hong Kong sample. In the Hong Kong sample the paths from self-esteem and relationship harmony to life satisfaction were of virtually equal strength ($\gamma = .45$ and $\gamma = .44$, respectively), whereas in the US sample the path from self-esteem to life satisfaction ($\gamma = .65$) was stronger than the path from relationship harmony to life satisfaction ($\gamma = .23$). In all, these findings indicate that for members of collectivistic cultures self-worth and connection-worth have a balanced influence on life satisfaction, whereas for members of individualistic cultures self-worth has more influence then connection-worth on life satisfaction.

An interesting derivation of the pancultural model is that, because they have less independent self-construal than Westerners, Asians might also have less self-esteem than Westerners. Indeed, cross-cultural studies involving mostly Chinese adolescents and young adults have identified a *self-effacing* tendency that is often interpreted as a strategy for promoting group cohesion and social harmony (Wheeler, Reis, & Bond, 1989). Self-effacement applies to several person perceptions, with the exception of agentic traits like assertiveness and openness to experience (Yik, Bond, & Paulhus, 1998), and results in lower frequency of positive self-statements – such as those contained in self-esteem scales – but not in higher frequency of negative self-statements (Ip & Bond, 1995). Given that a positive self-concept is generally considered a prerequisite of mental health, and that the prevalence of mental disorders does not differ between Asians and Westerners, why do Asians need less self-esteem than Westerners in order to be mentally healthy? Ip and Bond (1995) suggested that the Asian cultural systems offer greater social support and hence Asians may need lower levels of self-approbation to maintain mental health.

Are self-construals cross-sectionally and longitudinally stable to the extent that an individualist will always be individualist and a collectivist will always be collectivist? Interesting evidence against the stability of self-construals across situations and times comes from research on mass emergency behaviour as it occurs when there are natural catastrophes or terrorist attacks. Drury and co-workers (2009) developed a Virtual Reality simulation of an evacuation from an Underground station in London. In Study 2, 40 undergraduate students from the University of Sussex were randomly allocated in equal numbers to either a high identity condition or a low identity condition. The simulation worked exactly the same for both conditions except for in the high identity condition the textual description of the emergency situation emphasized that the participant was together with other fellow students from the same university, and hence was designed to elicit interdependent self-construal. The simulation allowed participants to produce two types of behaviour while moving towards the exit of the Underground station: helping others or pushing others. Compared to participants in the low identity condition, participants in the high identity condition produced more instances of helping behaviour and pushed fewer times. In all, this and other similar studies show that self-construals can change across situations, and that their change exerts formidable influence on interpersonal behaviour.

Are the self-construals of the citizens of a country cross-sectionally and longitudinally stable as a group to the extent that individualistic countries will always be individualistic and collectivistic countries will always be collectivistic? Nations can be allocated to specific points of the individualism–collectivism continuum. Hofstede (2001; see the rankings at The Hofstede Centre: http://www.geert-hofstede.com/geert_hofstede_resources.shtml) ranked 56 countries on individualism. The United States turned out to be first with a score of 91, followed closely by the United Kingdom with a score of 90 and Australia with a score of 89. Countries at the bottom of the ranking included Panama, Ecuador, and Guatemala with scores of 11, 8, and 6, in that order. European Union countries ranked above the median, with France scoring 71 and Germany 67, whereas industrialized Asian countries ranked lower than their European counterparts, with India scoring 48 and Japan 46. Are these rankings stable over time, or can people in a nation become as a group more individualistic or more collectivistic depending on social and historical factors?

Morrison, Tay, and Diener (2011) investigated the relationship between *national satisfaction* – that is, satisfaction with one's country – and life satisfaction using survey data collected by The Gallup Organization (1999–2013; see the used methodology at: http://www.gallup.com/se/128147/Worldwide-Research-Methodology.aspx) on representative samples totalling more than 130,000 participants from 128 countries. National satisfaction correlated fairly with life satisfaction on the whole sample ($r = .47$). Moreover, national satisfaction correlated more strongly with life satisfaction in non-Western, collectivistic countries than it did in Western, individualistic countries; this finding is consistent with the idea that people with more interdependent self-construal evaluate their lives looking more at how well their group is doing, whereas people with more independent self-construal evaluate their lives looking more at how well they are doing as stand-alone individuals. Finally, national satisfaction correlated more strongly with life satisfaction in impoverished countries compared to rich countries, and the difference held after controlling statistically for geographical location (Western vs. non-Western). This finding suggests that, irrespective of the individualism–collectivism of a country, if the economy of that country is doing poorly, collectivism becomes more salient and people will use more interdependent self-construal in appraising their lives; if instead the economy is doing well, individualism becomes more salient and people will use more independent self-construal in appraising their lives. In all, it seems that economical trends can induce changes in the self-construals of entire nations.

Cross-cultural research has provided intriguing evidence that self-processes are multifaceted and malleable, in such a way that a person may simultaneously construe an independent identity and identify with a group, and switch between the two self-identification processes when, for example, interacting with members of a host culture. Is the self capable of even more dramatic and abrupt changes in mode of functioning? The next section presents a view of the self as even more fast-changing. Interestingly, that view links up well with Self-Determination Theory.

Reversals

Reversal Theory (Apter, 1982, 1989; Murgatroyd, 1985) states that people can operate in two metamotivational states – *telic* and *paratelic* – and they switch or reverse between them frequently during an average day. The telic state is goal-oriented and arousal-avoiding, whereas the paratelic state is enjoyment-oriented and arousal-seeking. The telic state tends to occur when people engage in activities they construe as 'work' and deem important, whereas the paratelic state tends to occur when people engage in activities they construe as 'play' and deem unimportant. The two metamotivational states are diametrical ways in which the self relates to the activity one is engaged in, including the goals set and the time framework for achieving them, the perception of choice in engaging in the activity, the perceived importance of the activity, and the source of pleasure derived when the activity goes well.

On one hand, in the telic state people perceive that the goals of the activity they are engaged in are imposed by the situation, the environment, or an inner sense of duty. The person is reactive to the demands of the situation. The activity is construed as being goal-oriented, and the person is geared towards anticipation of the end result. The content of consciousness is thus future oriented, and pleasure is experienced primarily in anticipating a positive end result. On the other hand, in the paratelic state people perceive that they have freely chosen the goals of the activity they are engaged in. The person is proactive and spontaneous in pursuing the activity. The activity is construed as being process oriented, and the person is geared towards the current experience. The content of consciousness is therefore present oriented, and pleasure is experienced primarily in carrying out the activity.

Reversal Theory states that hedonic tone (i.e., the overall pleasantness–unpleasantness of feelings) varies as a function of arousal according to an inverted U curve. In making this assumption, Reversal Theory joins classic theories that postulate concave-down curvilinear relationships involving arousal. Yerkes and Dodson (1908) were the first to propose that learning and performing in any given task is a concave-down function of arousal: performance increases as a function of arousal up to a certain threshold, after which it declines as a function of arousal. In order to perform at one's best one thus needs to have the just-right level of arousal. Is there only one and the same just-right level of arousal for all tasks? Anderson (1994) found that the just-right level of arousal varies as a function of task complexity, in such a way that performance reaches its peak for a high level of arousal if the task is easy, and for a low level of arousal if the task is complex. This implies that there is a continuum of inverted U curves over arousal, wherein each curve applies to a distinct level of task complexity, as shown in Figure 3.5. The leftmost curve represents the Yerkes–Dodson Effect for a very simple task, the rightmost curve represents the Yerkes–Dodson Effect for a very complex task, and the intermediate curves represent the Yerkes–Dodson Effect for tasks at intermediate levels of complexity. The maximum of each curve (m_1, ..., m_n) occurs for a distinct value of arousal (a_1, ..., a_n). The model of one or more inverted U curves, each representing a Yerkes–Dodson Effect, has been applied to explain numerous psychological processes, including the deployment of virtues, as we will see in Chapter 4 (section *Grant and Schwartz: The Inverted U Curve*).

Reversal Theory applies the idea of a variable Yerkes–Dodson Effect to represent the relationship between hedonic tone and arousal, with two important caveats. First, in the initial formulation, the theory considered only two inverted U curves: the leftmost, which applies to telic states, and the rightmost, which applies to paratelic states. Second, which curve applies in any given situation depends primarily on a person's internal state, which can be either telic or paratelic, and secondarily on task characteristics and environmental factors.

Figure 3.5 *The continuum of inverted U curves over arousal, wherein each curve represents an instance of Yerkes–Dodson Effect for a specific context of activity or internal state of the person*

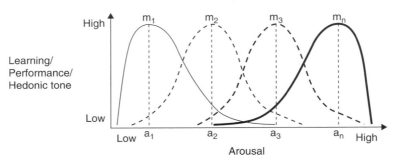

Note: m_1, ..., m_n represent the maximum value of each curve, and a_1, ..., a_n represent the level of arousal for which the maximum value of each curve occurs.

Hedonic tone peaks for low arousal in the telic state and for high arousal in the paratelic state. Moreover, under- and over-arousal determine patterns of feelings that differ between the telic and the paratelic states. In the telic state, insufficient arousal causes a feeling of apathy, and excessive arousal causes anxiety. In the paratelic state, insufficient arousal causes boredom, and excessive arousal causes over excitement. In both metamotivational states, under-arousal fosters arousal-seeking, and over-arousal foster arousal-avoidance. This implies that, if not optimally aroused for an activity, people will try to modify either the activity or their behaviour in order to reach optimal arousal. For example, if a videogame is too easy, a player will select a higher difficulty level, whereas if the videogame is too difficult, a player will select a lower difficulty level. In all, the theory implies that there are two possible optimal arousal levels, one for activities that are conducted in telic mode, the other for activities that are conducted in paratelic mode. Moreover, activities that support both telic and paratelic modes will have an optimal arousal level for telic mode and another optimal arousal level for paratelic mode.

The telic–paratelic distinction can also be interpreted as a matter of degree, that is, as a continuum ranging from completely telic to completely paratelic. A person's momentary standing on the telic–paratelic continuum can be validly and reliably measured using the 12-item Telic/Paratelic State Instrument (T/PSI; O'Connell & Calhoun, 2001; available at: http://reversaltheory.net/org/about-the-theory/research/), with sub-scales Serious-Minded/Playful and Arousal-Seeking/Arousal-Avoidance of seven and five items each, respectively. Items are scored on a six-point scale with anchors that vary depending on the items.

Conceptually, the telic–paratelic continuum is similar to the self-regulatory continuum defined by Self-Determination Theory (Ryan & Deci, 2000), in that low self-determination resembles the telic state and high self-determination resembles the paratelic state. From the description of the two metamotivational states, it is also evident that extrinsic motivation is dominant in the telic state, whereas intrinsic motivation is dominant in the paratelic state. Finally, Reversal Theory and Self-Determination Theory converge in stating that in any given point in time the organism cannot simultaneously be telic and paratelic, non-self-determined and self-determined. Most important, both theories indicate that psychological adjustment would be better and more satisfying if we were living our daily lives in a paratelic and self-determined state.

If there is no problem, just wait a little while and one will present itself. And when it does and it is demanding, are we really free to choose the motivational and metamotivational states we are in? In general, how do we position ourselves and behave when trouble comes? The next section will deal with the self-regulatory processes that are activated when one confronts a problematic situation, experiences stress, and copes with the demands of the situation.

Stress and Coping

Any activity we engage in presents us with demands that, depending on how strong they are relative to our capabilities, can cause stress. Lazarus and Folkman's (1984) transactional model of stress postulates dynamic relationships between potential stressors and psychological stress responses. The person–environment interaction is emphasized by defining stress as 'a particular relationship between the person and the environment that is appraised by the person as taxing or exceeding his or her resources and endangering his or her well-being' (Lazarus & Folkman, 1984, p. 10).

An individual's response to a stressor is theorized to depend on two appraisal processes, *primary appraisal* and *secondary appraisal*. In the primary appraisal process, an event can be perceived as positive, irrelevant, or stressful. If stressful, an event can be further perceived as harmful (i.e., a person believes that psychological and/or physiological damage has already occurred), threatening (i.e., a person anticipates to be harmed), or challenging (i.e., a person is confident to overcome the stressor). In the secondary appraisal process, the demands of the situation are evaluated in respect to one's own coping resources. Coping is defined as 'constantly changing cognitive and behavioural efforts to manage specific external and/or internal demands that are appraised as taxing or exceeding the resources of the person' (Lazarus & Folkman, 1984, p. 141). Coping comprises cognitive, emotional, and behavioural strategies an individual employs to manage a problematic person–environment relationship (Folkman & Lazarus, 1985). In essence, secondary appraisal asks a simple question – can I successfully cope with this stressor? – and provides one of two simple answers: (a) yes, I can, because my coping resources exceed task demands, or (b) no, I cannot, because task demands exceed my coping resources. If the answer is 'yes' then the person will not experience stress, whereas if the answer is 'no' the person will experience stress. In all, perceived stress is the extent to which a stressor is appraised as stressful at the end of the primary and secondary appraisal processes. If the person–stressor interaction goes on for a while, the situation may be reappraised.

What are the emotional outcomes of appraisal? Lazarus (1991) hypothesized that both primary and secondary appraisal processes influence the emotional response to a stressor. Empirical evidence supports this view, with stress having been found to evoke negative emotional responses (e.g., Kamarck, Peterman & Raynor, 1998) and to correlate with anxiety and depression (e.g., Bergdahl & Bergdahl, 2002). This implies that unsuccessful coping will result in negative emotions, whereas successful coping will result in less, or even absence of, negative emotions.

Is there any chance of experiencing positive emotions when coping with a stressor? Initially, Lazarus and Folkman (1984) left this question unaddressed. Subsequently, Lazarus (1993) suggested that positive emotions support the coping effort and that they turn particularly useful when a strong coping effort is required to match a very demanding task. Yet, Lazarus did not suggest that a strong and successful coping effort fosters positive emotions. It was Selye (1983) who theorized this possibility, distinguished healthy from unhealthy forms of stress, and introduced the term *distress* (wherein *dis* is the Greek word for 'bad') to represent the former and the term *eustress* (wherein *eu* is the Greek word for 'good') to represent the latter. Selye briefly described eustress as 'pleasant stress of fulfillment' (p. 20), which is more descriptive of eudaimonic well-being than it is of subjective well-being. In all, strong coping in a high-demand situation is facilitated by positive emotions and, if successful, fosters positive emotions in the realm of sense of fulfilment.

Can we then be in a paratelic, self-determined, and intrinsically motivated state when we cope with a demanding stressor? Yes, eudaimonically, in the sense conveyed by the film *The Gladiator*, when right before engaging in fierce battle the Roman general Maximus Decimus Meridius tells his most loyal troops 'If you find yourself alone riding in green fields with the sun on your face do not be troubled. For you are in Elysium, and you're already dead!', and his soldiers respond with laughter. Not hedonically, though, as we will probably not experience the highest possible levels of pleasantness in the midst of the coping effort. In all, whether we like it or not, there are only two ways out of a difficult spot, either unsuccessful coping accompanied by distress or successful coping accompanied by eustress.

What makes coping successful? Two main classes of coping strategies have been identified: *problem-focused* and *emotion-focused*. Problem-focused coping aims to take direct action for problem solving or seek strategic information about the problem at hand, whereas emotion-focused coping aims to reduce the emotional impact of the problem (Lazarus & Folkman, 1984). Although emotion-focused coping can provide temporary relief from negative emotions, there is consensus that, in the long run, problem-focused coping is adaptive whereas emotion-focused coping is maladaptive (e.g., Zuckerman & Gagne, 2003).

Several questionnaires were developed to measure coping strategies, including the Coping Questionnaire (COPE; Carver, Scheier, & Weintraub, 1989; available at: http://www.psy.miami.edu/faculty/ccarver/sclCOPEF.html) and its short version, the Brief Coping Questionnaire (Brief COPE; Carver, 1997; available at: http://www.psy.miami.edu/faculty/ccarver/sclBrCOPE.html). The most recent and comprehensive conceptualization of coping strategies has lead to the development of the Revised COPE inventory (R-COPE; Zuckerman & Gagne, 2003). The R-COPE measures validly and reliably five main coping strategies defined as individual response tendencies to stressors: *self-help, approach, accommodation, avoidance*, and *self-punishment*. Self-help coping refers to the maintenance of one's emotional well-being when under duress, and includes expressing and understanding emotions, as well as seeking emotional and instrumental support from others. Approach coping represents problem-solving activities that are directed at the source of the stress, and includes active planning and suppression of competing activities. Accommodation coping refers to accepting that the problem cannot be solved but can be reinterpreted in a positive manner, and includes understanding emotion, maintaining optimism, and goal replacement. Avoidance coping drives the person away from the problem, and includes disengagement, denial, and other-blame. Finally, self-punishment coping leads to self-rumination, self-blame, and a pessimistic outlook.

Zuckerman and Gagne (2003) classified the five coping strategies into adaptive (self-help, approach, and accommodation) and maladaptive (avoidance and self-punishment), based on the bidimensional second-order factor structure of the R-COPE and the empirical associations of the two second-order factors with other psychological variables. In particular, adaptive strategies were found to correlate with higher self-esteem and positive mood (Zuckerman & Gagne, 2003), and enhanced academic performance (Cassady & Johnson, 2002), whereas maladaptive strategies were found to correlate with lower self-esteem (Folkman & Lazarus, 1980) and higher anxiety (Muris, Merckelbach, & Bögels, 1995), and reduced academic performance (Zuckerman & Gagne, 2003).

Are adaptive coping strategies always adaptive and maladaptive coping strategies always maladaptive? There are situations in which this is the case. For example, researchers have investigated the coping strategies students use preparing for final academic examinations (Appelhans & Schmeck, 2002; Moneta, Spada, & Rost, 2007): given that the examinations will not magically disappear, there is no doubt that approach coping is adaptive and avoidance coping is maladaptive. Yet, there are situations in which a coping strategy that is adaptive in theory turns out to be maladaptive in practice. Imagine you have an evil boss who is not treating you well: the theoretically adaptive coping strategy would be to approach the boss and explain frankly how bad you feel, but that would reveal your vulnerability and could encourage your evil boss to do more of the same. Moreover, if one is confronting multiple stressors at the same time, it may not be wise to adopt an adaptive coping strategy – such as approach coping – to tackle simultaneously each one of them.

Cheng and Cheung (2005a) argued that every coping strategy has pros and cons that have to be traded off, and each has different degrees of usefulness across situations. For example, monitoring a threat may increase preparedness for a possible attack, but it may also result in more anxiety. By the same token, turning attention away from a threat may decrease preparedness for a possible attack, but it may also result in less anxiety. They argued that people who chose coping strategies flexibly, based on a differentiation of stressors and integration of their trade-offs, are thus more adaptive. They found that individuals with high *coping flexibility* (a) differentiate different stressful situations in terms of how controllable they are, and (b) monitor the controllable stressors more than the uncontrollable stressors (which is a good thing because monitoring and worrying about something uncontrollable is a waste of energy). On the other hand, individuals with low coping flexibility exert the same monitoring effort on controllable and uncontrollable stressors. Coping flexibility was found to prevent negative affect (Fresco, William, & Nugent, 2006), and to buffer the deleterious effects that negative life events have on depression (Lam & McBride-Chang, 2007). In all, coping flexibility fosters both hedonic and eudaimonic well-being.

You must be now tired and perhaps a bit distressed. If so, it is a normal state given that what you have been reading is demanding. The key question is, why did you read up to this point? If you did it only because of a course requirement, then trouble came to you, as stressors often do. If you instead did it mainly as free choice, then you looked for trouble and created your own stressor. Why do we sometimes put ourselves in demanding situations? It must be because we have goals. But are we aware of all of our goals? Could it be that our lives are driven by powerful dreams of which we are not fully aware? The next section will present a view of self-regulatory processes that fall somewhat below the level of consciousness and that explain why people engage in difficult endeavours for extended parts of their lives.

Needs and Motives

Up to this point of the chapter, the workings of the self have been described in quite abstract terms, and some obvious and important questions remain unaddressed. Given that in life we can fight only a limited number of battles, how do we go about choosing them? For example, why do some people spend decades studying to earn a Master degree or a PhD, whereas others dream of the moment in which they finally can get out of compulsory school? Why do some people pursue a career as an artist, accepting long periods in the shade and experiencing the disappointment of not being recognized by others, whereas others seek a safe and somewhat boring job in civil service? Why do some people invest so much energy in maintaining, defending, and enhancing a romantic relationship, while others move effortlessly from one relationship to another? The explanation of the individual differences in the way the self organizes and orients people's lives requires delving into motivational forces that have a *thematic* nature and guide the workings of the self somewhat independently of whether the self is aware of their existence. Murray (1938) was the first psychologist to propose a comprehensive taxonomy of thematic forces.

Murray (1938) argued that, rather than being a unitary and static object, the self is a *congress*, a collection of living and independent characters who – like in a theatre drama – interact with one another in producing a person's unique life narrative. Like in a theatre drama, persons' lives are set in time and are constituted of a sequence of progressively smaller time-units. The person is continuously processing and integrating on-line perceptions with memories of the past and anticipations of the future. The meaning of each action can thus be grasped only in the context of a person's long-term development.

The time-units can be classified from more specific and short-lasting to more general and long-lasting in the following order: *proceedings, durances, serials,* and *serial programs.* A proceeding is an episode representing a single interaction between the person and the environment. Proceedings are unique, and a person may be involved in more than one proceeding at a time. Each proceeding leaves a trace in a person's life history, and the accumulation of proceedings is what makes each person unique. A durance is the class of all overlapping proceedings in a given period of time, and can at times be perceived as a 'life chapter'. A serial is a long-lasting durance that focuses on a single life domain. Finally, a serial program is a person's plan to improve one's own well-being in a specific life domain wherein goals are hierarchically structured and well organized in time.

How is it possible that a person gets into proceedings, durances, serials, and serial programs in a seemingly non-chaotic, idiosyncratic (i.e., somewhat unique to each person), and meaningful way? Murray's answer is that human lives proceed by a never-ending interaction between internal forces (*needs*) and environmental constraints/opportunities (*press*). Needs are the primary determinants of behaviour; yet, whether or not a need will actually drive behaviour depends on the press, the tendency of the environment to encourage or discourage the expression of specific needs. Whenever a specific need and a specific press interact for a sufficiently long period of time, the person will develop a life theme (*thema*). For example, a child with a strong need for achievement who grows in a poor environment may develop a heroic achievement theme. A theme is idiosyncratic and provides a longitudinally stable guidance to a person's action, accounting for the non-chaotic and meaningful – or at least interpretable – development of a person's life. Themes explain why we engage in meaningful sequences of behaviours.

Murray believed that needs and themes are largely unconscious (*implicit* in modern terminology), and he developed a projective test, the Thematic Apperception Test (TAT) to capture them. The TAT presents pictures and asks participants to write imaginative and dramatic stories based on them, explaining what has led up to the event shown in the picture, describing what is happening, and predicting the outcome of the story. Examples of pictures used for research applications include 'architect at a desk', 'two women in lab coats in a laboratory', 'trapeze artists', 'two men (inventors) in a workshop', and 'gymnast on balance beam' (Smith, 1992). The TAT captures themes capitalizing on *apperception,* the process by which one interprets perceptions and 'fills in' ambiguous or incomplete pictures with one's own fantasies and emotions.

By integrating theoretical considerations and data from the application of the TAT Murray identified 20 needs. Of these, four – *achievement, power, intimacy,* and *affiliation* – were researched intensely for decades by McClelland (1985) and other researchers. McClelland redefined the TAT as a technique for assessing *motives* – rather than needs and themes – meant as preferred experiential states that a person is ready to experience or seeks to experience recurrently. Rigorous scoring systems were developed to assess validly and reliably these motives in stories written in response to TAT pictures as well as in any other form of text (Smith, 1992).

Achievement motivation is seeking success in competition with a standard of excellence (McClelland et al., 1953), wherein the standard can be internal (i.e., competition is with self) and/or external (i.e., competition is with others). The achievement motive is the tendency to enjoy the experience of doing better and to look for situations in which to have such experience. Behavioural correlates of high achievement motive include tendencies to have high aims but low risk-taking, to delay gratification for the purpose of achieving goals, to cheat or bend rules in order to cut through the shortest path to a desired goal, and to choose a career in business and entrepreneurial activities (McClelland, 1985). In a pivotal study McClelland (1961) found that achievement themes in textbooks for children in 23 nations predicted nations' economic output 30 years later.

Power motivation is seeking to have impact on others and to control them. The power motive refers to a tendency to enjoy the experience of having impact on and control objects and persons and to look for situations in which to have such experience. Behavioural correlates include tendencies to take high risks in order to become visible, to be an effective organizer of other people's work, to engage in polemic debates, and to choose a career in ruling professions such as executive, teacher, and psychologist (Winter, 1973). In a pivotal study, Winter (1993, 2002) found that the power motive in the United States presidents' inaugural addresses predicted later 'presidential greatness' as rated by political scientists and historians, the number of historically significant decisions made, and the likelihood to lead the country to war.

Intimacy motivation is the desire to experience warm, close, communicative relations with others. The intimacy motive refers to a tendency to enjoy the experience of feeling united with another person, and to look for situations in which to have such experience. Behavioural correlates include tendencies to have more eye contact, self-disclosure, and sharing of secrets in one-on-one conversations, and to think more often of others. In a pivotal study, McAdams, Healy, and Krause (1984) found that the intimacy motive correlates with recollection of meetings with one friend only, recollection of taking a listening role in interactions with friends, and recollection of episodes of self-disclosure in interactions with friends.

Affiliation motivation is seeking to make new acquaintances or to get together with friends and others. Conceptually, the main difference between affiliation and intimacy is that the former refers to establishing positive relations with others, whereas the latter refers to maintaining and deepening a relation once it is established. Empirically, many attempts were made to develop a scoring system for the affiliation motive, but the affiliation and intimacy motives turned out to be highly correlated and difficult to disentangle (Boyatzis, 1973). For this reason, the affiliation motive was no longer investigated.

Are the three thematic motives related to each other within the same person? Emmons and McAdams (1991) found in a sample of 72 US undergraduate students that the three motives correlate from fairly to weakly with one another. In particular, the achievement and power motives are fairly correlated and may be interpreted as expressions of *agency*, whereas the intimacy motive is only weakly correlated to the achievement and power motives, and hence can be regarded as an expression of *communion*, with reference to Bakan's (1966) theory of agency and communion, which will be presented in Chapter 4 (section *The Circumplex of Interpersonal Behaviour and Gender Role Attributes*). Interestingly, McAdams and co-workers (1984) found that both the intimacy motive and the power motive are associated with more recollection of social interactions, but the nature of the recalled interactions differs between the two motives: people high in intimacy motive tend to recall more instances of taking a listening role and engaging in self-disclosure in interactions with others, whereas people high in power motive tend to recall more instances of taking an assertive role in interactions with others. Therefore, both intimacy and power are social motives, but the intimacy motive tends to lead to a communal friendship style, whereas the power motive tends to lead to an agentic friendship style.

Are thematic motives associated with well-being? Conceptually, motives should foster positive emotions if and only if they are satisfied. The satisfaction of a motive requires two conditions. First, a person high on a motive should find contexts that are suitable to the satisfaction of that motive; for example, someone with a strong achievement motive should engage in competitive endeavours in order to experience achievement-related positive emotions. Second, a person high on a motive should also possess the set of abilities required to satisfy that motive; for example, someone with a strong achievement motive who engages in competitive endeavours should possess the abilities required to win competitions in order to experience achievement-related positive emotions. In all, motives are personal assets that can foster positive emotions conditionally on environmental opportunities, proactive seeking of motive-related activities, and individual ability.

Empirical studies support the broad hypothesis that motives and well-being have conditional associations. For example, Hoffer, Bush, and Kiessling (2008) found in a sample of 131 German undergraduate students that life satisfaction is uncorrelated with both the achievement motive and the intimacy-affiliation motive. However, they found that these motives moderate the associations between two indicators of psychological well-being – environmental mastery and positive relations – and life satisfaction. In particular, they found that (a) environmental mastery and positive relations correlate positively with life satisfaction, (b) the achievement motive moderates the association between environmental mastery and life satisfaction in such a way that the association is stronger for individuals with low achievement motive and weaker for individuals with high achievement motive, and (c) the intimacy-affiliation motive moderates the association between positive relations and life satisfaction in such a way that the association is stronger for individuals with high intimacy-affiliation motive, and it is weaker for individuals low in intimacy-affiliation motive. Hoffer and co-workers suggested that the unexpected result (b) might mean that the achievement motive is not facilitating life satisfaction when one has plenty of environmental mastery because life becomes too easy, unchallenging. Moreover, they argued that the expected result (c) means that the intimacy-affiliation motive facilitates life satisfaction when one has plenty of positive relations. In all, the findings from this and other studies indicate that motives have complex, conditional relationships with well-being.

The research on motives was inspired by psychoanalysis and its emphasis on the powerful influence exerted by the unconscious. As scientific psychology as a whole moved progressively from a psychoanalytic to a cognitive perspective, motives began being researched within the framework of cognitive psychology. The next three sections present the cognitive approach to thematic motivation.

Personal Strivings

Stimulated by research findings on implicit motives that are at least in part sub-conscious, psychologists focused on more conscious forms of thematic motivation, which can be investigated simply by asking direct questions of participants. They looked particularly at those clusters of goals that (a) are based on one's anticipation of future outcomes, (b) are purposively oriented towards maximizing future positive outcomes and minimizing future negative outcomes, and (c) are hierarchically organized.

Several similar constructs were proposed. Little (1983, 1987) proposed the construct of *personal projects*, meant as an interrelated sequence of actions intended to achieve a personal goal, such as finding a part-time job or shopping for the holidays, such that people think about them, plan for them, carry them out, and sometimes complete them. Cantor and Kihlstrom (1987) proposed the construct of *life tasks*, meant as problems that people are currently working on, such as preparing for retirement or for a career change, such that they give meaning to one's own everyday life activities, and become more salient during major life transitions. Klinger (1977) proposed the construct of *current concerns*, meant as motivational states in between two points in time – time 1 = identification of a goal, and time 2 = either attainment of the goal or disengagement from the goal, such as losing weight, going for a trip, or keeping a dentist appointment, such that they drive a person's ongoing thoughts, emotions, and behaviours, are highly idiosyncratic, and run in parallel mode in one's everyday life. Life tasks, personal projects, and current concerns are all idiosyncratic (i.e., persons tend to have their own specific lists) and nomothetic (i.e., they can be compared across persons as to value, complexity, and likelihood of success). A problem affecting the use of these constructs in research is that they are open to continuous changes in a person's life (i.e., they are longitudinally unstable) and it is difficult to distinguish them one from the other.

Emmons (1986, 1989) proposed the less contextualized and more longitudinally stable construct of *personal strivings*, meant as idiosyncratic but coherent patterns of goal strivings that represent what an individual is typically trying to do. Strivings are superordinate to goals, in that they can be achieved in different ways by pursuing different specific goals. Emmons developed a valid and reliable procedure to assess strivings thematically. The assessment begins by asking participants to list freely all of their strivings, defined as 'things that you typically or characteristically are trying to do in your everyday behaviour'. Participants are given examples of strivings and explained that the strivings have to refer to a recurring goal, have to be substantiated by actual behaviours, and can be either positive (trying to do something) or negative (trying to avoid something), and are positive or negative regardless of how successful a person is in achieving them.

Besides obtaining an individual list of strivings, several options are available for gaining a deeper understanding of each. For example, a researcher may ask participants to rate each striving on the happiness one would feel upon its successful completion and on the unhappiness one would feel upon failure. Moreover, a researcher may probe the interdependence of strivings by asking for each pair 'does being successful in this striving have a helpful or harmful effect (or no effect at all) on the other striving?' to be answered on a five-point scale ranging from −2 (*very harmful*) to +2 (*very helpful*) with the intermediate 0 value representing no effect at all.

Strivings can also be coded validly and reliably by independent raters according to pre-specified criteria such as the thematic categories of achievement, power, intimacy, and affiliation using the same coding system that was developed for the TAT (Smith, 1992). When coded thematically, personal strivings tend to have weak and negative correlations with each other (McAdams, 1984), suggesting that personal strivings compete with one another in using personal resources; so that, if an individual invests more energy and time in one striving category (e.g., achievement) will tend to invest less energy and time in the other striving categories (e.g., intimacy).

Personal strivings and motives are related but distinct concepts. Strivings refer to what a person is trying to do, with the emphasis on recurrent goal-oriented behaviours. Motives refer to what a person wants to do, enjoys doing, or is concerned with, and the emphasis is on ideation, imagery, and desires rather than behaviours. Thus, strivings are more behavioural and consciously accessed than motives. Moreover, motives are more narrative than strivings, in that they are typically framed as personal stories characterized by an opening, a course of action, and an ending. In all, motives are implicit, whereas strivings are explicit.

Emmons and McAdams (1991) assessed both personal strivings and motives in 72 US undergraduate students and found the correlations between TAT motives and striving categories shown in Table 3.1. In general, strivings and motives belonging to the same thematic category correlate fairly. Moreover, the achievement striving is inversely related to the intimacy motive, suggesting that those who are consciously trying to achieve may do so at least in part because they subconsciously do not seek intimacy. Finally, the affiliation striving is associated with the power motive, suggesting that those who are consciously trying to affiliate with others may do so at least in part because they subconsciously seek power.

Similar to thematic motives, thematic strivings per se do not predict well-being. Yet, Emmons and King (1988) assessed within-person degree of conflict and ambivalence of strivings in 88 US undergraduate students and found that these 'negative' variables correlate in meaningful ways with various measures of subjective well-being and health. In particular, conflict correlates with more health centre visits and greater number of illnesses, whereas ambiguity correlates with less positive affect and more state anxiety and state depression. Moreover, Emmons (1992) assessed level of strivings (ranging from low-concrete to high-abstract) in 100 US couples and found the pattern of correlations with indicators of subjective well-being that is shown in Table 3.2. Interestingly, level is consistently associated with poorer well-being in husbands, whereas it

Table 3.1 *Correlations between striving thematic categories and TAT motives (selected correlation coefficients from Emmons & McAdams, 1991)*

Striving category	TAT motive		
	Achievement	Intimacy	Power
Achievement	.37	−.28	
Affiliation			.28
Intimacy		.42	
Power		.15	.41

Note: Only correlation coefficients significant at least at the $p < .05$ level are included in the table.

Table 3.2 *Correlations between level of strivings (concrete–abstract) and indexes of subjective well-being in couples (selected correlation coefficients from Emmons, 1992)*

Subjective well-being	Husband	Wife
Positive affect	−.22*	.04
Negative affect	.31*	.19
Life satisfaction	−.29*	−.27*
Spouse-rated symptoms	−.33*	−.16

Note: *$p < .05$.

is associated only with less life satisfaction in wives. In all, these studies suggest that the nature and inner relationships of the whole set of strivings impact on subjective well-being.

Goals

Goals are the smallest and simplest cognitive units that enable the self to engage in volitional and directional behaviour. Goals are largely conscious, can range from simple to complex, and often are accompanied by plans, strategies, and techniques that support their achievement. In its simplest form, a goal consists of a cognitive representation of a current situation x and a cognitive representation of a future and desirable situation y. This dual cognitive representation allows the self to frame a goal as a statement of the form 'I want to turn situation x into situation y'.

Carver (2001) proposed that the main classification of goals is between the categories of *approach* and *avoidance*. Approach goals guide the motivation to approach desirable objects, whereas avoidance goals guide the motivation to avoid undesirable objects. Approach motivation is oriented towards incentives and hence energizes and directs behaviour towards desired states, whereas avoidance motivation is oriented towards threats and hence energizes and directs behaviour away from feared states. Every form of motivation reviewed up to this point of the present chapter – such as motives and personal strivings – can be further classified into either approach motivation or avoidance motivation. For example, an intimacy motive or striving may represent either a motivation to seek an intimate relationship with a stranger or a motivation to avoid losing an established intimate relationship: the former represents an instance of approach intimacy motivation, whereas the latter represents an instance of avoidance intimacy motivation.

Carver (2001) proposed that approach and avoidance motivation are functionally independent and influence affect and behaviour according to two different self-regulatory systems. He argued that the circumplex model of emotions (represented in Figure 2.1 of Chapter 2) is incomplete, and should consider two features of emotions in addition to pleasantness and activation: (a) whether an emotion serves the purpose of approaching a desired goal or that of avoiding an undesired goal, and (b) whether or not the goal-directed behaviour is successful. For example, both *elation* and *sadness* pertain to the *approach process*, wherein the former signifies success and the latter failure. By the same token, both *relief* and *fear* pertain to the *avoidance process*, wherein the former signifies success and the latter failure. Therefore, approach–avoidance and success–failure should be considered in addition to pleasantness and activation in order to understand variations of affect. The following studies have consistently corroborated that approach and avoidance motivation influence affect and behaviour in distinct ways: Gable, 2006; Nikitin & Freund, 2010a; Puca, Rinkenauer, & Breidenstein, 2006.

The broad implication of the existence of two separate – approach and avoidance – self-regulatory systems of affect is that the lifelong game of subjective well-being is played simultaneously on two separate tables, and that in order to have overall high hedonic tone one has to succeed in both approach goals and avoidance goals. How is then possible to still be a winner in old age, given that aging is accompanied by a reduced ability to achieve goals? We have seen in Chapter 2 (section *Background Variables and Happiness*) that happiness does not decline with age, and that a possible explanation for the lack of decline is that people adjust their goals as they age, shifting from assimilative coping, in which life conditions are modified to fit personal preferences, to accommodative coping, in which personal preferences are modified to fit constraints. This explanation can now be reinterpreted by stating that with age people shift progressively from approach to avoidance goals. Is there support for such an interpretation? Experimental studies in which participants are shown happy, neutral, and angry faces as stimuli (e.g., Mather & Carstensen, 2003; Nikitin & Freund, 2010b) provided some support, in that (a) participants of all ages equally exhibit gaze preference for positive faces as compared to neutral or negative faces, and (b) older participants are more avoidant of angry faces and hence, compared to younger participants, have more avoidance motivation. Yet, more research is needed for understanding how the approach–avoidance self-regulatory systems change with age, and how their change influences subjective well-being.

Achievement Goals

From the point of view of Self-Determination Theory (Deci & Ryan, 1985a), achievement goals can be regarded as the purpose (Maehr, 1989) and cognitive focus (Elliot, 1997) of behaviour that can satisfy the basic need for competence. Nicholls (1984) and Dwek (1986) advanced that, depending on how an individual construes competence, achievement goals can be divided in *mastery goals* and *performance goals*. The purpose of mastery goals is to learn new skills and strengthen one's own capacity to master the environment, whereas the purpose of performance goals is to produce visible outcomes that attest to one's ability relative to the ability of others. Mastery goals and performance goals thus differ in standards of competence. On one hand, success in the pursuit of mastery goals is evaluated using absolute and intrapersonal standards of competence, that is, the development of competence by attainment of a skill and the improvement of one's own performance and knowledge. On the other hand, success in the pursuit of performance goals is evaluated using relative and interpersonal standards of competence, that is, the display of competence relative to others. In all, *definition of competence* is a dimension that includes on one pole learning goals that focus on the development of competence and on the other pole performance goals that focus on the evaluation of competence.

Elliot and McGregor (2001) extended the taxonomy of achievement goals by introducing a second dimension, *valence of competence*. Competence can be construed by an individual as either success or failure, and achievement goals can hence be divided into approach goals and avoidance goals. The purpose of approach goals is to reach a desirable outcome (i.e., success), whereas the purpose of avoidance goals is to avoid an undesirable outcome (i.e., failure). Valence therefore corresponds to the approach–avoidance distinction that Carver (2001) introduced to explain emotional reactions in response to type of goals, and the perception of progress towards them. In all, *valence of competence* is a dimension that includes on one pole approach goals that focus on attaining success and on the other pole avoidance goals that focus on avoiding failure.

By combining the definition and valence dimensions, Elliot and McGregor (2001) proposed the 2 × 2 classification of achievement goals shown in Table 3.3, and they presented the Achievement Goal Questionnaire to measure validly and reliably the four achievement goals using three items each. Mastery goals can be viewed as expressions of intrinsic motivation, whereas performance goals can be viewed as expressions of extrinsic motivation. Moreover, approach goals can be viewed as the more self-determined side, and avoidance goals as the less self-determined side of both types of motivation. Mastery-approach goals therefore represent the typical expression of intrinsic motivation (e.g., 'It is important for me to understand the content of this course as thoroughly as possible'). Performance-approach goals represent the typical expression of extrinsic motivation (e.g., 'My goal in this course is to get a better grade than most of the other students'). Mastery-avoidance goals represent a diminished expression of intrinsic motivation in that the goal is to sustain an ability or a skill as opposed to acquire a new one (e.g., 'I am often concerned that I may not learn all there is to learn in this course'). Finally, performance-avoidance goals represent a diminished expression of extrinsic motivation that, in the self-determination continuum, sways towards amotivation (e.g., 'My goal in this course is to avoid performing poorly').

Elliot and McGregor (2001) examined the relationship between self-determination and achievement goals in a sample of 148 undergraduate students enrolled in a psychology class (Study 2) and found that self-determination

Table 3.3 *The 2 × 2 classification of achievement goals (adapted from Elliot & McGregor, 2001)*

		Definition	
		Mastery	**Performance**
Valence	Approach	Mastery-approach goals	Performance-approach goals
	Avoidance	Mastery-avoidance goals	Performance-avoidance goals

correlates positively with mastery-approach goals, it is uncorrelated with performance-approach goals, and it correlates negatively with mastery-avoidance and performance-avoidance goals. These findings corroborate the hypothesis that mastery-approach goals are expression of high self-determination, performance-approach goals are expression of medium self-determination, and both types of avoidance goals are expression of low self-determination.

How do achievement goals relate to eudaimonic well-being? Elliot and McGregor (2001) examined the relationships between achievement goals, on one hand, and study strategies, anticipatory test anxiety, and examination performance, on the other, in two samples of 148 and 182 US undergraduate students enrolled in two different psychology courses. They found that mastery-approach goals predicted more deep study strategy, performance-avoidance goals predicted more surface study strategy and more anticipatory test anxiety, and mastery-avoidance goals predicted more disorganized study strategy (Study 2). Moreover, they found that performance-approach goals predicted better examination grades, whereas performance-avoidance goals predicted worse examination grades (Study 3). In all, the findings indicate that approach goals foster cognitive efficiency and performance, and hence represent 'positive' goals in achievement contexts, whereas avoidance goals hinder cognitive efficiency and performance, and hence represent 'negative' goals.

The highest achievement, arguably, is creative achievement. Unlike other forms of achievement – such as earning a good grade, earning a university degree, or earning a promotion at work in competition with other candidates – creative achievement necessarily requires to come up with a novel idea that solves an existing problem that others could not solve. Because many competent and smart people can be found in large numbers in virtually every single field of human endeavour – be it science, arts, business, technology, politics or structured leisure – to be able to come up with something that nobody else had conceived of and that works better than anything existing is definitely not an easy task. The next section reviews what is known about cognitive self-regulation in creative achievement.

The Creative Self

What is creativity? This daunting question can be approached gradually by looking at some recognized examples of creative ideas or products. There is no doubt that Ludwig van Beethoven's *Ninth Symphony* and Albert Einstein's *Theory of Relativity* are model examples of creative achievement. Nevertheless, many products that have become part of our everyday life, and hence go unnoticed, are creative, although to a lesser level. For example, Spencer Silver and Arthur Fry found a use for a faulty glue that would stick feebly and invented *Post-it*, and an unknown inventor found a use for a faulty soap bar that could float on water and invented *Ivory* soap. What is in common to all these different creative ideas and products?

Amabile (1982, 1996) defined creativity as a characteristic of a finished idea or product, not of a person. A finished idea or product is creative if it is new (i.e., nobody has proposed it before) and adaptive (i.e., it works well for a specific purpose). Creativity can be assessed by averaging ratings on a single adjective (e.g., 'creative' or 'original') by domain experts who are independent on each other and blind in respect to the identity and characteristics of the author of the idea or product. Consensus is typically moderate but in line with a wide range of ratings of other properties, such as interpersonal liking and physical attractiveness. By averaging the creativity ratings provided by many judges on the same idea or product one typically achieves a valid assessment of creativity. When major professional achievements are evaluated in the fields of science and the arts, the creativity of ideas and products can be easily assessed using the consensual technique.

How does creative achievement relate to well-being conceptually? There is no doubt that the ability to produce novel and adaptive ideas is a positive personal characteristic, particularly in industrialized countries where innovation plays a fundamental function in the development of the economy in competition with other countries. We have seen in Chapter 2 (point 1 of section *Directions for Future Research*) that the ability and willingness to create has not been included as an indicator of either subjective or psychological well-being. This is indeed odd because through creation and innovation individuals realize their potential as autonomous and mastering agents. Moreover, insofar as some innovations – such as the discovery of a new medical treatment or the development of a new social policy that improves the livelihood of many – contribute to other people's well-being, creativity allows individuals to develop positive relations with others. Therefore, creativity can be regarded as a central – albeit somewhat forgotten – indicator of eudaimonic well-being.

Is creative achievement always possible, no matter what the task is? Amabile (1982, 1996) proposed a distinction between *algorithmic* and *heuristic* tasks. A task is algorithmic if someone is given beforehand a complete set of steps for completing the task, and completing the task is only a question of carrying out the steps. Instead, if discovering the steps is part of the task itself, then the task is heuristic. She then argued that in order to make creative achievement possible a problem must be heuristic, that is, it should not have a clear and readily identifiable path to a solution. The algorithmic–heuristic distinction found strong empirical support in that rewards are positively associated with performance in algorithmic tasks, and negatively associated with both performance and task enjoyment in heuristic tasks (see review by Amabile, 1996). In all, the self can be creative if and only if the task at hand is both demanding and heuristic.

Early research pointed out the cognitive processes that are required to produce novel ideas. Campbell (1960) distinguished two phases in the creative process: *blind variation* and *selective retention*. The first phase is characterized by randomly generated mental experiments, ideas, or recombinations of existing elements to form new ideas (i.e., ideas that were not already possessed by the person). The second phase is characterized by rational evaluation, selection, and retention of those new ideas (which were generated in the blind variation phase) that seem consistent and worthy of further attention. Campbell called the first phase *divergent thinking* and the second phase *convergent thinking*, and these terms entered permanently in the psychological jargon.

Guilford (1962) identified three cognitive components of divergent thinking – *fluency, flexibility,* and *originality* – and developed the Uses Test to measure them. The Uses Test asks participants to list as many uses as possible for a common object (e.g., a brick) in a fixed period of time. The number of uses listed measures fluency. However, the listed uses might fall all in the same semantic category (e.g., construction) or in different semantic categories (e.g., construction, destruction, or artistic composition). The number of different semantic categories measures flexibility. Finally, each listed use can be a more or less common response in the whole sample of participants. The overall uncommonness of responses gathered from an individual measures that individual's originality. In all, Guilford argued that in order to be creative one needs fluency, flexibility, and originality.

Torrance (1965) developed the widely used Torrance Tests of Creative Thinking (TTCT), which measures validly and reliably the dimensions of divergent thinking identified by Guilford (1962) and an additional one, *elaboration*, which is the number of added ideas and represents the extent to which creative ideas are well developed. The original version of the test contained only verbal items, whereas later versions also contain figural items. Verbal items include asking to list as many uses as possible for a common object and asking to find an original way to improve a toy. Figural items include coming up with an interesting and original title for a picture and completing a sketched picture to make it become a picture or object 'no one else would think of'. In a longitudinal study on 46 US high school students, the individual scores of fluency, flexibility, and originality predicted quantity and quality of creative achievements seven years later, and did so better than intelligence, scholastic achievement, and peer nomination (Torrance, 1972). These strong findings point out the practical relevance of divergent thinking skills.

Amabile (1996) proposed a componential model of the creative process that details the alternation and functions of divergent and convergent thinking. The model states that the creative process proceeds in loops of five-stages: *task representation, preparation, response generation, response validation,* and *outcome evaluation.* Task representation involves identifying a problem that would require a creative solution, typically because there is no established way to solve it. Preparation involves acquiring all the relevant information, resources, and skills required for a successful attempt at a solution of the problem. Response generation corresponds to Campbell's blind variation, in which the problem solver plays with ideas and freely generates as many and different possible ways to tackle the problem. Response evaluation is the first sub-phase of Simon's selective retention, in which the problem solver selects one of the generated responses and assesses its feasibility. Finally, outcome evaluation is the second sub-phase of Simon's selective retention, in which the problem solver assesses the validity and effectiveness of the novel idea and answers the bottom line question: does it work better than its competitors? In most real-life situations, a single five-step loop is not sufficient to attain a novel and adaptive idea; so that, the problem solver will typically have to engage in a chain of five-stage loops in order to have a realistic chance of success.

Amabile's (1996) componential model also explains what personal character-istics and resources are required in order to complete each stage of the creative cycle successfully. The model states that a person's task motivation, domain-relevant skills, and creativity-relevant skills – such as fluency and flexibility – influence each stage of the creative cycle. Task intrinsic motivation is useful primarily in the first three stages, as it fosters interest in the problem, learning of required skills, and playing with ideas. Extrinsic motivation is useful prima-rily in the last two stages, as it fosters the development of the novel idea into a product that will sell and hence produce monetary and self-esteem rewards. Domain-relevant skills are useful primarily prior to the response generation stage, in that they restrict preventively the response generation to those ideas that have a realistic chance to be new and adaptive, and in the last two stages, as it provides the standards of reference for evaluating ideas. Finally, creativity-relevant skills are particularly useful in the response generation stage, wherein divergent thinking is required.

Simonton (2000) reviewed decades of research on the nature of creativity and its antecedents and showed how research findings converge in clarifying seven key issues. First, creativity involves normal cognitive processes rather than 'inspiration', as some creative persons describe it. The experience of sudden inspiration is an illusion arising from the fact that a large portion of the cogni-tive work underlying the generation of a novel idea falls below the awareness level. This can be seen with reference to *spreading activation theory* (Anderson, 1983; Collins & Loftus, 1975), which represents memory as an interconnected network of nodes, where each node corresponds to a concept, and each linkage between nodes represents a relationship between concepts. Every response is postulated to involve retrieval of information, a process that is modelled as acti-vation of nodes spreading through the network. For example, in the Uses Test (Guilford, 1967) a participant may be asked to name as many uses as possible for a common brick. Imagine that the concept 'brick' in a participant's semantic network is linked to the concepts 'build' and 'wall'. The test is a stimulus that may activate the concept 'brick'. After 'brick' is activated, activation may spread through the linkages to the concepts 'build' and 'wall' to frame the response 'use the brick to build a wall'. The actual occurrence of this response depends on many factors such as the features of the network, possible alternative responses, and time constraints. The extension and rapidity of activation depends on node-strengths and link-strengths. The strength of a node is its frequency of activation. The strength of a link from node x to node y is the strength of y divided by the sum of all node-strengths in the network, including that of y, that are connected to x (Anderson, 1983). For example, assume that both participant A and participant B have links in their semantic networks from the concept 'brick' to the concepts 'build' and 'wall'. Participant A's links, however, have greater relative strengths than those of participant B's. When both participants are administered the Uses Test, the activation from 'brick' to 'build' and 'wall' spreads faster for participant A. Thus, other things being equal, participant A is more likely than B to respond 'use the brick to build a wall'. In all, persons become aware of a novel association only at the very end of a cognitive process (e.g., when 'use the brick to build a wall' has been construed), which explains the feeling of sudden inspiration. Moreover, differences in creativity between persons can be explained in terms of structural characteristics of their semantic networks.

Second, contrary to popular belief that incompetent people conceive the most creative ideas, creativity requires extensive preparation that, depending on the field, translates on average into at least ten years of apprenticeship in order to build up sufficient domain-relevant knowledge, as required in Amabile's (1996) componential model of the creative process.

Third, high intelligence is not a necessary prerequisite of creativity. This is because beyond a threshold intelligence is no longer associated with creativity.

Fourth, some personality characteristics – independent, nonconformist, unconventional, open to new experiences, and risk-taker – predispose to creativity. We will deal with this issue extensively in Chapter 4 (section *The Big Five and Creative Achievement*).

Fifth, creativity is more likely to occur in environments that support autonomy and hence allow for the expression of intrinsic motivation, and it is less likely to occur in controlling environments that only allow for the expression of extrinsic motivation. This finding is perfectly consistent with the predictions made by Self-Determination Theory (Deci & Ryan, 1985a).

Sixth, culturally heterogeneous and politically fragmented social contexts are conducive to creativity. Arguably, the absence of a firm cultural frame of reference frees people's minds.

Seventh, contrary to popular belief that sees creative genius equivalent to madness, the evidence in favour of a link between creativity and psychological disorders – such as bipolar disorder and schizophrenia – is mixed. Perhaps psychopathology has both positive and negative effects on creativity, which may cancel each other at the aggregate level.

Finally, it is important to note that research in the field of creativity has traditionally adopted the product-oriented definition of creativity, and has hence privileged the judgment of experts over the judgment of peers, discounting the self-perspective. However, some creativity scholars have more recently argued in favour of a process-oriented concept of creativity as a learning process that energizes individual behaviour even when it falls short of producing an output that would be appraised as creative by experts (e.g., Beghetto & Plucker, 2006; Moran & John-Steiner, 2003; Runco, 2005). In particular, Beghetto and Kaufman (2007) advanced that this form of creativity, that they labelled *mini-c*, is necessary in the genesis of any idea that is eventually judged creative by experts. Mini-c creativity is essentially an intra-psychic experience of novelty, sense of ongoing progress, and meaningfulness that might not always be detected and adequately appraised by others. In all, the recognition of the developmental value of an ordinary, mini-c creativity makes the study of everyday life creativity more interesting and worth pursuing. In particular, we will see in Chapter 7 (section *The Inner Work Life, the Progress Principle, and Positive Team Leadership*) that day-to-day mini-c creativity in the work life of the members of project teams is a key to the creative achievement of the team project.

The present and previous three sections reviewed some key contributions of cognitive psychology to the understanding of self-regulation. Is cognitive psychology sufficient for understanding self-regulation in the real world? Arguably, not. This is because the real world involves other people, and hence, in order to achieve in competition with others, exert power on others, or love others, one has to interact with individuals and groups. This is particularly the case for creative achievement. In order to see a novel and good idea recognized as innovative by others the self needs to regulate motivation, emotion, cognition and behaviour in dynamic interaction with the social context. The next section presents the contribution of social psychology to the understanding of the self-regulation required for creative achievement.

The Creative Self in Social Context

Up to this point, the chapter has paid little attention to the social context in which the self works. Findlay and Lumsden (1988) introduced a distinction between two aspects of creativity, *discovery* and *innovation*. Discovery is the production of a novel idea at the individual level, whereas innovation is the social recognition of the novel idea as being both creative and adaptive. This distinction is important, because it points out that creativity is not happening only inside a person's mind, and it involves social processes that only in a limited number of cases end with the recognition of individual creativity. Because creative achievement ultimately requires social approval of a novel idea, the understanding of the creative self requires careful consideration of the social structures and dynamics that allow the self to discover and innovate.

Kuhn (1969) investigated the social dynamics of discovery and innovation in the sciences. He proposed that science proceeds by alternating long periods of *normal science* followed by sudden *scientific revolutions*. In its normal phase, a scientific field is organized in a *paradigm*. A paradigm dictates the scientific goals and the methods to be used for their achievement. Sooner or later, every paradigm encounters falsifications and unexplainable findings and reaches a stalemate, in which there is no longer significant increase in knowledge. This is the paradigm's moment of weakness, when scientists who are at its margins have a chance to introduce new ideas, which in some cases lead to a revolution, a destruction of the paradigm, and the construction of a new paradigm.

Kuhn (1969) differentiated the work carried out by normal scientists from the work carried out by deviant scientists. The paradigm urges the normal scientists to find solutions that are consistent with its theoretical and methodological vision. Thus, the major activity of the normal scientists is problem solving for the survival of the paradigm. At the same time, deviant scientists see the problems encountered by the paradigm but they do not look for solutions that are consistent with the paradigm. They rather believe that these problems are the consequence of global problems in the theoretical structure of the paradigm that cannot be fixed without changing profoundly the structure of the paradigm. Thus, the major activity of these deviant scientists is the destruction of the paradigm and the foundation of a new perspective. In all, although both normal and deviant scientists can come up with creative ideas, the nature of these ideas will be quite different, with a tendency for normal scientists to come up with 'micro solutions' and for deviant scientists to come up with 'macro solutions'. The deviant scientists are the actors of scientific revolutions, which lead to destruction of the paradigm and foundation of a new paradigm. Therefore, we may conclude that creativity and creative potential should reside more in the deviant scientist than in the normal scientist.

Kuhn (1969) sketches a cognitive/linguistic typology for the normal and the deviant scientists. The normal scientists have read the same literature and have interpreted it in similar ways. Consequently, they are cognitively similar. This similarity allows large agreement on professional issues and fast, uncontroversial communication among them. The deviant scientists may have read similar literature but their interpretation is different. Consequently, they are cognitively different from the normal scientists. This cognitive dissimilarity has two consequences. First, the normal scientists do not consider the deviant scientists to be experts. Second, the communication between the normal and the deviant scientists is fragmented and difficult.

How do the experts of the paradigm react to individual creative contributions? On one hand, 'normal' solutions are obviously welcome because they solve problems of the paradigm without imposing profound changes to the paradigm. On the other hand, 'revolutionary' solutions encounter firm resistance, simply because those scientists who are leaders of the paradigm can be made outdated and marginal by a revolution. Therefore, it is not surprising that until they are in the leadership position they will do whatever it takes to keep potential innovators out of the field. In all, the transformation of a discovery – which takes place inside a person's mind – into an innovation – which takes place in the social and epistemological structure of a paradigm – can be a quite troublesome and uncertain process for all authentically creative ideas.

Csikszentmihalyi (1988, 1996) proposed a systems view of creativity that extends Kuhn's (1969) theory to virtually every field of human endeavour. Creativity simultaneously involves individuals, a domain, and a field of experts of the domain. The field 'selects from the variations produced by individuals those that are worth preserving', and the domain 'will preserve and transmit the selected new ideas or forms to the following generations' (Csikszentmihalyi, 1988, p. 325). The rationale for considering domain and field as integral parts of creativity is that:

Without a culturally defined domain of action in which innovation is possible, the person cannot even get started. And without a group of peers to evaluate and confirm the adaptiveness of innovation, it is impossible to differentiate what is creative from what is simply statistically improbable or bizarre.

(Csikszentmihalyi, 1988, p. 325)

It is important to note that domain and field also play a fundamental role in the psychological processes leading to individual discovery, as it is impossible to come up with a novel and adaptive idea without having acquired sufficient domain-specific competence:

The information that will go into the idea existed long before the creative person arrived on the scene. It had been stored in the symbol system of the culture, in the customary practices, the language, the specific notation of the 'domain'. A person who has no access to this information will not be able to make a creative contribution, no matter how able or skilled the person otherwise is.

(Csikszentmihalyi, 1988, pp. 329–330)

Based on Csikszentmihalyi's (1988, 1996) systems view of creativity, the creative process can be thought of as a continuous information flow among the three systems: domain, field, and person. The information content of the three systems changes over time as a function of their interaction. At any given time, the relationship among the information content of the three systems can be represented by Venn diagrams and mappings from set to set, as shown in Figure 3.6. The field maps onto a subset of the domain. This means that the field selects and retrieves portions of the domain as relevant and worthy working on, directs individuals' work towards the improvement and reorganization of these topics, and stimulates – via education, information, and funding – individuals to become experts in these topics and work on them. The person system maps onto a subset of the domain. A part of this subset overlaps with the information

Figure 3.6   *Csikszentmihalyi's (1988) systems view of creativity and innovation*

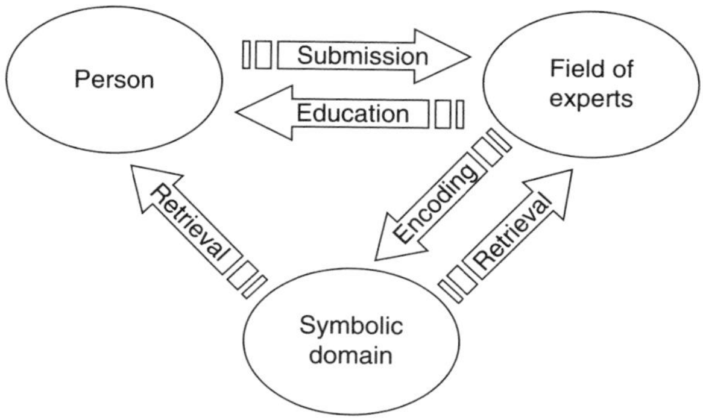

mapped onto by the field (i.e., the prescribed competence); another part is independent on the focus of the field (i.e., the independent knowledge). The person system also maps onto an area of information that is not included in the domain but is a part of other domains. This independent knowledge can contribute to the domain only if it is accepted and encoded by the field. In all, individuals can come up with a novel and adaptive idea only if they have acquired enough domain-specific competence through education together with enough independent knowledge. Moreover, individuals' creative and adaptive ideas will be encoded in the symbolic domain – and hence become innovations – if and only if the field of experts – the gatekeepers – allow it.

Given that the path from discovery to innovation can be a painful one, why do some individuals take it? Sternberg and Lubart (1996) proposed an extrinsic explanation: people invest in creativity in order to earn a profit. In other words, the pain of pushing a novel idea through the gatekeepers is accepted in anticipation of the recognition and monetary reward that an innovation would bring. Such investors look for areas of the domain that do not enjoy popularity among the experts of the field, are somewhat sketchy, and have potential to grow into creative ideas. Therefore, in economical terms, these innovators try to 'buy low and sell high'.

Getzels and Csikszentmihalyi (Getzels, 1964; Getzels & Csikszentmihalyi, 1976) proposed an intrinsic explanation: *problem finding*, a specific exploratory attitude towards the environment aimed at finding a suitable problem to face. Problem solving and problem finding are similar in that they can both initiate and direct exploratory behaviour. Yet, the exploratory behaviours that are generated by problem solving and problem finding differ as to the nature of their goals. In exploration for solving a problem the person has already framed a problem before engaging in exploration, and the goal of exploration is to find a solution to the problem – or at least some cue as to how a solution can be found – in a novel environment. In exploration for finding a problem the person has not yet framed a problem before engaging in exploration, and the goal of exploration is to find a problem that is interesting and worth pursuing. Thus, for Getzels and Csikszentmihalyi the creative process begins when a person who has acquired sufficient domain-specific competence feels dissatisfied with some aspect of the domain and hence finds a problem in it or at least a lead that is worth pursuing. In doing so, the creator-to-be is driven by a mixture of dissatisfaction and interest.

How important is problem finding? Getzels and Csikszentmihalyi (1976) found that there are individual differences in problem finding, and that propensity towards problem finding has long-term implications on artists' career achievement. Students enrolled in a fine arts programme at the Art Institute of Chicago were assigned the task of painting on canvas a three-dimensional object that was placed on a table. Students' problem-finding propensity was assessed using a checklist of exploratory behaviours that they engaged in before and in the course of painting the object, such as walking around the object, handling and lifting the object, and viewing the object from different perspectives. Art students' problem-finding scores predicted their career success, measured as yearly income derived from their artwork at midlife.

How hard is to push an idea through the gatekeepers? A real example may help find the answer. Nadrian Seeman is the pioneer (though he rejects the label) of the field that he created 25 years ago and likes to call 'structural DNA nanotechnology'. We are all aware that the DNA holds the secret of life, but most of us could not even imagine that the DNA can be used to craft minuscule technological objects such as computer chips and nanorobots; that is what exactly structural DNA nanotechnology is all about. In an interview, Seeman explained how he viewed his career: 'After 25 years of one-night stands, suddenly I'm an overnight success' (as cited by Finkbeiner, 2011, p. 36). In those 25 years, Seeman managed with difficulty to earn tenure and little grants that supported his non-mainstream research. When asked whether it now felt good to win prestigious scientific prizes and to see a proliferating new field, he answered: 'It does feel good. It's exciting that there's a whole field based on what I was thinking about, drinking a beer, in 1980' (as cited by Finkbeiner, 2011, p. 37). In all, this example shows that an entire life may be needed to produce a single innovation, and that this type of endeavour can hardly be explained with reference to a 'buy low and sell high' attitude; the creative self is arguably more than that.

In all, decades of research have shown that in order to understand the workings of the creative self one has to consider the social organization of the field, the symbolic domain, and the complex social dynamics that oppose problem finders, on one side, and gatekeepers and their cohorts of problem solvers, on the other side. Only problem finders have a chance to come up with radically new ideas that have the potential to change a domain profoundly. If they do, they will inevitably meet fierce resistance. The next chapter (section *The Big Five and Creative Achievement*) will review what is known about the personal characteristics of those special individuals who succeed and accrue creative achievements in their lives.

THE 'I' AND THE 'ME'

Is there a way to reconcile the two views of the self, self as concept versus self as regulation? What are the relationships between the two? Can one influence the other and, if so, how? This section of the chapter reviews an interesting attempt to answer these questions.

James (1892/1963) introduced a distinction between two aspects of the self, the *I* and the *Me*. McAdams (1996) built on James' distinction and spelled out its meaning with reference to decades of research on the self. The I is the *self-ing*, the endless process of grasping phenomenal experience as one's own and creating a narrative, unified description of one's own experience in time. The Me is the *self*, the product created by the I. In terms of the organization of this chapter, the Me is the self-concept, and includes as key components self-esteem and self-efficacy beliefs, whereas the I is self-regulation, and includes as key components ego strength, self-determination, motives, strivings, goals, and creative processes.

Why does the I construct the Me? According to Erikson (1959, 1968) and McAdams (1996), because we all live immersed in an ideological setting that compels us to construe a Me in order to justify our existence and behaviour in front of others. Ideology is a systematic body of values, beliefs, meanings, and imperatives that are shared or largely agreed upon by the members of a given culture. Ideology can be broad or narrow, strong or weak, depending on the historical juncture:

> At the most it is a militant system with uninformed members and uniform goals; at the least, it is a 'way of life' ... a world view which is consonant with existing theory, available knowledge ... shared as self-evident beyond any need for demonstration.
>
> (Erikson, 1959, p. 41)

Ideology concerns a wide range of questions concerning, for example, truth (e.g., what is true? What is false?), goodness (e.g., what is good? What is bad?), religion (e.g., is there a God? How is he/she?), ethics (e.g., what is right? What is wrong?), ontology (e.g., what is real? What is not real?), aesthetics (e.g., what is beautiful? What is ugly?), politics (e.g., what is good government? What is bad government?), or work (e.g., what is good work? What is bad work?). Ideology may vary considerably across cultures, and may change over time within the same culture.

Erikson (1968) proposed that individuals adopt and personalize ideology, and develop a *personal ideology* that may deviate to some extent from the prevalent one. Personal ideology is the context, the setting wherein persons develop their sense of identity; it constitutes the scene within which the self plays as an actor one or more characters according to a lifelong script. In this connection, Baumeister (1986) sustained that the task of developing a personal ideology and a sense of identity embedded within it first emerged in Western societies in the early 1800s; before then, a person was socially assigned an identity based on fixed status, according to lineage, gender, and social class.

Erikson (1968) thought that ideology is particularly important in adolescence. The adolescent begins construing personal myths as 'first drafts' of a life story on the ideological scenario. Frequent sample statements in a personal life story are 'nobody can truly understand me', 'nobody has done what I did', and 'I am unique'. Adolescents keep probing their personal ideologies to find elements on which to base their identities, and they keep rewriting their identity until they find a version that is realistic – convincing to themselves and others. This explains how the self-concept develops and how things can go terribly wrong when a person develops an unrealistic, delusional, and excessively positive general self-esteem, which, as seen in this chapter (section *Self-Esteem*), can be associated with narcissistic, unempathic, and antisocial tendencies (Baumeister et al., 2003).

Two questions arise: (a) do all teenagers engage in a deep probing of their identities? And (b) what makes them consolidate into one identity? Marcia (1966, 1980) found that adolescents (a) may or may not experience an identity crisis, and (b) may or may not commit themselves to the resolution of the crisis. This leads to four possible identity statuses at the beginning of adulthood. In *diffusion* there is no crisis and no commitment: the young adult has not thought of identity issues and has not charted directions in life. In *moratorium* there is a crisis but no commitment: the young adult is raising questions about identity and is seeking answers. In *foreclosure* there is no crisis and no commitment: the young adult has picked up a ready-made identity without construing it by raising questions and seeking answers. Finally, in *identity achievement* there is a crisis and a commitment: The young adult has sought and found answers, and has construed beliefs, values, and life goals that are identity-consistent. In a seminal study, Meilman (1979) analysed age-trends from early adolescence to early adulthood and found that at age 12 nearly 0 per cent has achieved identity, and by age 24, one of five is still in a state of diffusion. In all, identity construction is not an automatic maturational process, and spans way beyond the adolescent years.

Whereas Erikson (1968) confined the identity psychosocial stage to the adolescent years, McAdams and co-workers (McAdams, 2008; McAdams, Josselson, & Lieblich, 2006) proposed a theory of lifelong identity construction, according to which identity is construed by creating, refining, and integrating *imagoes*. Imagoes are the main characters in our life story, idealized personifications of the self or self-definitions, such as the healer, the teacher, the counsellor, the humanist, the arbiter, the warrior, the lover, and the survivor. Each imago includes and integrates a number of characteristics, roles, and experiences in a person's life. Imagoes are little Mes inside the Me that act, think, and interact with one another like persons do. Imagoes are personifications of aspects of the Me that people believe to be true of themselves concerning the past, the present, and the future; they are the main characters in personal myths that are the building blocks of the narration of one's own life. McAdams' view is that persons change their imagoes at different points of their life, especially in midlife and older age. In all, the I creates a series of Mes, and hence self-concepts, throughout life.

McAdams (1996) also proposed an integrated three-level view of the self. Level 1 contains all unconditional *dispositional signatures*, that is, the decon-textualized characteristics of the Me that are constructed by the I, such as general self-esteem and general self-efficacy – which we reviewed in the present chapter (section *Self-Concept*) – and traits – which will be the subject matter of Chapter 4 (whole chapter). These variables are defined as components of the *psychology of the stranger*, meaning that these are the variables we would like to assess first when we meet a perfect stranger. Level 2 contains all *personal concerns*, that is the contextualized characteristic of the Me where the I asserts its existence in time by directing and energizing behaviour towards the future. These variables include all cognitive-motivational units we reviewed in the present chapter (section *Self-Regulation*) such as goals, personal striv-ings (Emmons, 1986), tasks (Cantor, & Kilhstrom, 1987), projects (Little, 1989), scripts (Demorest, 1995), strategies (Buss, 1987), and current concerns (Cantor, 1990). Finally, level 3 contains all *personal stories*, that is, the explanations that the I relentlessly constructs in order to make sense of one's own life and evolution in time, including updates and modifications of the life story. In agreement with Baumeister (1986), McAdams (1996, 2008) maintains that this level formed only in the past few centuries, as sociocultural environments began pressing individuals to construct a sense of identity that is coherent in expressing the unity of the Me, meaningful, unique, and overall convincing to oneself and the others. All three levels influence one another dynamically so that, for example, a change in life story (e.g., living to become a virtuous person) may prompt consistent changes in the psychology of the stranger (e.g., enhancements of general self-esteem) and in personal concerns (e.g., trying to help others in need).

If indeed the self-concept – the Me – is built by the I through personal con-cerns and life stories, what, if any, are the risks posed by a scientific study of the 'positive self'? Kundera (1988) argued that knowledge, in rational and scientific form, corrodes the self:

> The more he advanced in knowledge, the less clearly could he see either the world as a whole or his own self, and he plunged further into what Husserl's

pupil Heidegger called, in a beautiful and almost magical phrase, 'the forgetting of being'.

(Kundera, 1988, pp. 3–4)

For Kundera, *rationality* and *being* are sharply distinct, and the problem of identity belongs to the former, not the latter. The question of identity is, Who am I? The question of rationality is, How do I get what I want? The answers to these distinct questions may converge in practice, as what one is able to get is a basis to define one's own identity. The problem is that what we get is not in all cases revealing of what we are. For example, a man who gets many women may define himself as a 'Don Juan'. However, in the myth of Don Juan (best known from Mozart's opera *Don Giovanni*) the title character is not just any man who gets many women: here, a terrifying man of stone orders him three times to repent; and three times Don Juan refuses, choosing eternal damnation over repentance. Arguably, not many self-defined Don Juans would have this absolute impenitence and bravery; those who would get cold feet when faced with such a challenge are thus fake Don Juans. In sum, the risk posed by a scientific study of the positive self is that people who read positive psychology may develop 'positive selves' that are as authentic as a cheap imitation Don Juan.

What could be the consequences of developing a non-authentic Me? Imagine a person who is simultaneously very creative and extrinsically motivated for both money and glory, and an extraordinarily skilful manager. He is offered a prestigious job that, however, comes with a huge administrative responsibility. If he has construed his Me based on what is good at getting, he will see himself mostly as a manager and as an ambitious person, and hence will accept the job. Yet, in that job he will hardly have time to do any creative work after attending to the required administrative tasks. Will he be happy in his new job? It depends on whether his Me as a manager and as an ambitious person is authentic or not. In particular, if his authentic self is a creative one, that prestigious job will effectively become the coffin of his creativity. Using the terminology of Self-Determination Theory (Deci & Ryan, 1985a), we could then say that he made a *decision*, not a *choice*, as the latter requires integration of all relevant self-structures and high self-determination. In that case, he might still rate his happiness high consistent with his non-authentic Me – according to the thought chain 'I get what I want', hence 'I feel good about myself', hence 'I am happy' – but his psychological well-being will otherwise be thwarted. In all, the consequences of developing a non-authentic Me are difficult to detect using scales measuring general self-esteem and global happiness, but are potentially dramatic and pervasive.

In all, psychological theories of how the I construes the Me point out that that the self-concept is construed contextually, dynamically, and subjectively. Thus, the self-concept is not always realistic and authentic. To the extent that it is not authentic, the self-concept can hinder rather than foster eudaimonic well-being.

DIRECTIONS FOR FUTURE RESEARCH

The integration of the several points made in this chapter suggests four broad issues that call for debate and empirical research.

1. *Hedonic self: The more the better.*

   The hedonic approach to the self implies – explicitly or implicitly – that the more beautiful, consistent across social roles, and stable in time the self-concept is, the better the self and the person as a whole will be. Empirical studies robustly show that the greater the general self-esteem, the more satisfied one is with life. However, studies also show that some people with high self-esteem have serious problems, are not particularly liked by others, and may even be dangerous to those who threaten their self-esteem. Moreover, a self-concept that is more positive than the evaluation of others is basically a delusion, that is, an inner representation of reality that differs in important ways from reality itself. Therefore, the hedonic assumption on the self-concept is questionable, and future research should identify the specific conditions under which a positive self-concept is truly positive. One can envision at least three directions for future research. First, there might be variables that are important for well-being and that are in conflict with self-esteem. Second, it might be interesting to conceptualize and measure the self-concept as two separate constructs, the first focusing on the positive aspects of the person, and the second focusing on the negative aspects; perhaps the absence of self-criticism is what spoils the positivity of high self-esteem. Finally, researchers might consider the possibility that the relationship between self-esteem and well-being is concave down, so that the highest levels of well-being would be found in correspondence with a level of self-esteem that is positive but not extremely so. In this connection, Grant and Schwartz (2011) proposed a view of 'too much of a good thing' which posits that general self-esteem and numerous other dispositional variables including virtues have positive implications to well-being if they are possessed to a high degree, but have negative implications if they are possessed to an extremely high degree. We will review Grant and Scwhartz' argument applied to the relationship between eudaimonic well-being and virtues in Chapter 4 (section *Grant and Schwartz: The Inverted U Curve*).

2. *Eudaimonic self: One or many positive selves?*

   The eudaimonic approach to the self is so differentiated that implies that there is not a single end-point for the development of a fully functional self. In other words, a successful self is one that succeeds locally, not globally. This in turn implies that the development of the self necessarily comes with conflicts and trade-offs. For example, a person may be very successful in work-related achievement but, because this success comes with the development of psychological structures that are not functional to romantic relationships, may fall short in realizing success in the interpersonal domain. Future research should investigate whether it is indeed possible to grow in all aspects of psychological well-being, and still be able to achieve full success in a specific lifelong endeavour. If that indeed is not possible, then the trade-offs required to succeed locally should become an integral part of psychological theory. In this connection, we will see in Chapter 4 (section *Personality-Culture Matching and Subjective Well-Being*) that there is no single pattern of personality traits leading to highest well-being in all cultures, and hence there are different optimal personalities for different cultures. Moreover, we will see in Chapter 4 (section *The Big Five and Creative Achievement*) that a pattern of personality traits that maximizes subjective well-being would not maximize creative achievement, and vice versa. By analogy, one wonders if the same happens with the various self-regulation processes studied in this chapter: could it be that a self-regulation pattern is optimal in one context, one life, and a different self-regulation pattern is optimal in another context, another life?

3. *Integrating the I and the Me.*
   The theories explaining how the I construes the Me by writing and rewriting one's own life narrative are fascinating. However, there is limited empirical and longitudinal evidence showing that the self-concept changes in important ways following a change in one's own life narrative; we cannot yet rule out the opposite view that it is the self-concept that drives the writing of one's own life narrative. Moreover, future research should investigate how applicable the construct of life narrative is to people who lack literary interest and to members of cultures that emphasize less the need for an individual to write a distinguishing life narrative; to put it simply, it might be that quite a number of people go on with their lives without really writing any long and articulate life narrative.

4. *What else do we need to self-regulate?*
   The self appears to have quite a complex regulatory job to do, particularly when it comes to making an important discovery and innovation in business, the arts, and the sciences. The concepts reviewed

in this chapter are not sufficient to explain such level of complexity and why we do not eventually fall into the dissolution of the self as described in Kundera's words in the introduction of this chapter. Therefore, other factors must play a role in helping the self to do its difficult job. We will see in the following chapters that a wealth of additional constructs should be invoked to explain self-regulation in demanding and long-lasting endeavours. In particular, Chapter 4 will consider the self-regulatory role played by personality traits. Moreover, Chapter 5 (section *Self-Regulation of Emotions*) will consider the self-regulatory role played by special types of traits, such as met-acognitions (section *Adaptive and Maladaptive Metacognitions*), that is, beliefs about one's own cognitive and emotional processes. These special traits, unlike the ordinary personality traits, are amenable to change: we will see in Chapter 8 (section *Mindfulness-Based Cognitive Therapy and Metacognitive Therapy*) that new psychotherapies that target specifically these special traits appear to be remarkably effective in repairing and enhancing a client's ability to self-regulate negative emotions.

SELF-DEVELOPMENT AND UNDERSTANDING EXERCISE

This exercise consists of 'playing' with your self-construals and studying their changes across situations and their consequences to your self-concept. You will conduct a mini longitudinal study in which you play both the role of the participant and the role of the researcher.

Participant's Phase

As a study participant, you will have to fill in the same set of questionnaires in two separate occasions – which we will call session A and session B – at least a week apart, so that the second time you fill in the questionnaires you will not remember well the answers you provided the first time. *Session A.* First, recall a personal, study, or work project on which you worked *all by yourself* that started with profound difficulties and ended successfully. Write it up as a short story – as if you were writing a letter or an email message to a friend – emphasizing your thoughts, emotions, and behaviour when dealing with the challenges of the project, and the emotions you felt upon *succeeding as a sole winner*. Second, complete the Twenty Statements Test – which was presented in the *Self-Construals and Cross-Cultural Differences in Self-Processes* section of this chapter – and calculate your independent and interdependent self-construal scores. Finally, complete Rosenberg's Self-Esteem Scale (available at: http://www.bsos.umd.edu/socy/research/rosenberg.htm) and calculate your self-esteem score.

Session B. First, recall a personal, study, or work project on which you worked as a *member of a team* that started with profound difficulties and ended successfully. Write it up as a short story – as if you were writing a letter or email message to a friend – emphasizing the thoughts, emotions and behaviour of the team when dealing with the challenges of the project, and the emotions the team felt and shared upon *succeeding as a united group.* Second, complete the Twenty Statements Test and calculate your independent and inter-dependent self-construal scores. Finally, complete Rosenberg's Self-Esteem Scale and calculate your self-esteem score.

Researcher's Phase

Once you have completed both data collection sessions as a participant, you should, as a researcher, compare your self-construal and self-esteem scores across the two sessions and answer the following questions:

(a) Was your independent self-construal score greater in session A than in session B?
(b) Was your interdependent self-construal score greater in session B than in session A?
(c) Was your self-esteem score greater in session A than in session B?
(d) Depending on your answers to the previous questions, how can the observed changes be explained using psychological theories of self-construals?
(e) Finally, how would you go about developing this mini longitudinal study into a real study involving a sample of study participants?

◊ RECOMMENDED WEB RESOURCES AND FURTHER READING ◊

Websites

Research organizations:

- Self-Determination Theory at: http://www.selfdeterminationtheory.org/
- Reversal Theory Society at: http://www.reversaltheory.net/org/
- International Center for Studies in Creativity, The State University of New York, Buffalo, at: http://www.buffalostate.edu/creativity/

Some of the questionnaires reviewed in this chapter can be viewed/downloaded and used freely for your own research:

■ Rosenberg's (1979) Self-Esteem Scale at: http://www.bsos.umd.edu/socy/research/rosenberg.htm
■ General Self-Efficacy Scale (GSES; Jerusalem & Schwarzer, 1992), which is available in numerous language versions at: http://userpage.fu-berlin.de/health/selfscal.htm)
■ Telic-Paratelic State Instrument (T/PSI; O'Connell & Calhoun, 2001) at: http://reversaltheory.net/org/about-the-theory/research/
■ Coping Questionnaire (COPE; Carver et al., 1989) at: http://www.psy.miami.edu/faculty/ccarver/sclCOPEF.html
■ Brief Coping Questionnaire (Brief COPE; Carver, 1997) at: http://www.psy.miami.edu/faculty/ccarver/sclBrCOPE.html

Reading

■ Baumeister and co-workers' (2003) critical meta-analysis of research conducted on the construct of self-esteem
■ Ryan and Deci's (2000) succinct presentation of Self-Determination Theory
■ Oishi and co-workers' (1999) investigation on cross-cultural differences in the predictors of life satisfaction
■ Chao's (1995) qualitative study on Chinese and American mothers' child-rearing practices and effects on their children's self-construals
■ Elliot and McGregor's (2001) empirical validation of the 2 × 2 achievement goals model
■ Simonton's (2000) analysis of the multifactorial aetiology of creativity
■ McAdams' (1996) taxonomy of psychological constructs in the domain of personality research (this may help you making sense of the various constructs that will be reviewed in the following chapters)

4 Positive Traits

INTRODUCTION

According to Allport (1961) traits tell us what a person generally does over many situations, and what type of situations a person generally selects. For example, a conscientious person will tend to be organized, punctual, and reliable at work, as well as when interacting with family, friends, and extraneous persons, and will seek a job and acquaintances that appreciate and reward conscientious behaviour. The key features of a personality trait are frequency, intensity, and range of situations wherein a set of behaviours are produced and a set of emotions are experienced. People are thus said to be high on a trait if they produce trait-relevant behaviours and experience trait-relevant emotions frequently, intensely, and across life domains. A trait is an inner disposition that is relatively stable over time (longitudinally) and across situations (cross-situationally).

One trait is more general than another trait if the range of behaviours and emotions to which it refers is larger and if the range of real-life situations to which it applies is larger. For example, one can say that 'extraversion' is more general than 'talkativeness' because: (a) extraversion includes other behaviours or emotions beyond talkativeness, such as sociability, affection, friendliness, and spontaneity, and (b) extraversion tends to 'come out' in all situations, while talkativeness may be expressed only in situations wherein verbal interaction is the main issue. Naturally, the ambition of trait researchers has always been that of identifying and measuring a limited set of most general traits from which all more specific traits can be derived.

A trait can be viewed as a continuum ranging from a 'negative' pole to a 'positive' pole, for example, introverted–extraverted, aggressive–peaceful, and stingy–generous. Individuals can be placed at different points of such continua, so that traits allow for the representation of individual uniqueness (as one point in the continuum) and individual differences (as distance between two points in the continuum). Most trait psychologists think that knowing a person's standing on only one trait is not sufficient for understanding a person: the pattern of distinct traits within a person is fundamental for understanding the whole functioning of the person.

Chapter 3 focused on the two conceptions of the self – self as concept and self as regulation – and analysed how self-concept and self-regulation influence subjective and psychological well-being, and how the two self constructs might be dynamically intertwined. Both conceptions of the self, however, do not explicitly consider personality traits. While self-regulatory processes can be fast-changing either autonomously or in response to changing situations, traits are stable individual tendencies that provide guidance and constraint to self-regulation. In order to gain a better understanding of well-being we now need to look specifically at how traits foster or hinder well-being over and above the fast and malleable workings of the self.

Until the advent of positive psychology, trait psychologists never really asked themselves whether some traits are consistently 'positive' and other traits are consistently 'negative'. Had they been asked the question, most of them would have probably answered 'every trait can have either positive or negative consequences for the person and for others depending on the situation'. For example, the trait of extraversion undoubtedly gives a hedonic advantage to a person who possesses it to a high extent because, as seen in Chapter 2 (section *Origins and Consequences of Affect*), it brings consistently more pleasant affect in everyday life. However, imagine if an extraverted person were sent alone on a space mission to planet Pluto: without Internet access to email and social networks, the extraverted astronaut would experience a living hell all the way to Pluto and back to planet Earth. As such, most trait psychologists would argue that there could not possibly be a trait that is consistently positive or consistently negative across situations and times.

Peterson and Seligman (2004) introduced a whole new set of traits – 24 *character strengths* grouped into six *virtues* – that they claimed are consistently positive in a specific sense of the term: if we use them in our everyday life – be it at work, in relationships, or when engaged in leisure activities – they will consistently foster pleasant affect and *authentic happiness*, a type of happiness that goes beyond the mere experience of pleasure and stems from a sense of engagement in life and meaningfulness. Moreover, Peterson and Seligman claimed that, unlike other personality traits, one's own *signature strengths* – i.e., the set of character strengths one possesses the most – can change over time if a person identifies them and cultivates them in everyday life. Finally, Peterson and Seligman claimed that the cultivation of one's own signature strengths is the golden route to authentic happiness. This development brings ethics right at the heart of psychology, and could create a bridge between scientific psychology and religious traditions.

This chapter focuses on the 'positivity' of traits, and reviews evidence in favour and against the hypothesis that some traits are consistently positive. The first section of this chapter reviews what we know about the Big Five personality traits, and how they influence well-being. The second section reviews what we know about more specific traits that were derived from psychological theory and how they influence well-being. The third section reviews the progress done in developing and applying the constructs of character strengths and virtues. The fourth section reviews ancient and contemporary conceptions of virtues that state the existence of trade-offs between different virtues, as well between virtues and well-being, according to which no single trait can truly be consistently positive. The final section outlines issues open to discussion, ongoing controversies, and directions for future research.

THE BIG FIVE

A Brief History of Trait Research

The nearly 80-year long history of trait research has its beginnings in the United States, moves to England, where it gains in simplicity and clarity, and eventually returns to the United States, where it reaches consolidation and large consensus. In order to identify and interpret traits, researchers relied heavily on factor analysis. Once construct validity had been achieved, researchers looked for evidence of predictive validity, that is, they tested if the scores of the identified traits predicted relevant psychological phenomena.

In the United States, Allport and Odbert (1936) started identifying human traits by looking at the adjectives and short descriptions of the English language, and found more than 18,000 candidate trait-terms. By content analysis, they brought the figure down to about 4,500 terms denoting relatively stable traits. By eliminating redundant terms and metaphors, Cattell (1943) reduced the list to 171 terms. He then asked people to rate others on those terms, obtaining so-called *O-ratings*. By analysing the inter-term correlations of the O-ratings he identified about 40 clusters of traits. By factor analyses on numerous data sets he eventually nailed down 16 fundamental traits that he named *source traits*. In England, by factor analysing his own selection of items, Eysenck (Eysenck & Eysenck, 1975; Eysenck, Eysenck, & Barrett, 1985) brought the total number of personality traits down to just three, which he called *super factors*. In the United States, by means of massive applications of factor analysis on large and representative samples Costa and McCrae (1992) brought the total number of personality traits to just five – these, they claimed, are both necessary and sufficient, and their claim has to date encountered large consensus.

The Big Five

The traits included in the Big Five personality model or Five Factor Model (FFM; Costa & McCrae, 1992) are extraversion, neuroticism, openness to experience, conscientiousness, and agreeableness.

Extraversion is a broad tendency to be sociable and impulsive, and to experience positive affectivity, surgency, and self-confidence. For example, compared to introverts, extraverts enjoy more talking to people, perceive life as faster paced, and more often feel like bursting with energy. In general, extraversion implies friendliness, affection, and spontaneity.

Neuroticism is a broad tendency to experience anxiety, moodiness, depression, vulnerability, and self-consciousness. For example, compared to emotionally stable individuals, neurotics more frequently feel worthless, sad or depressed. In general, neuroticism implies nervousness, insecurity, and vulnerability.

Openness to experience is a broad tendency towards unconventionality, intellectual curiosity, imaginativeness, aesthetic sensitivity, cognitive/emotional differentiation, and engagement of experience. For example, compared to individuals who are closed to experience, individuals who are open to experience are more likely to engage in daydreaming and like it, more likely to play with abstract ideas, and more likely to try out new ways to solve problems, even when they could stick to an approach that had worked well in the past. In general, openness to experience implies originality, imaginativeness, curiosity, and breadth of interests.

Conscientiousness is a broad tendency to be self-disciplined, hardworking, and 'down to earth'. For example, compared to unconscientious individuals, conscientious individuals keep their belongings neater and more organized, and they are more likely to strive for excellence in their study and work endeavours. In general, conscientiousness implies self-discipline, reliability, and perseverance.

Agreeableness is a broad tendency to be altruistic, empathic, warm, accommodating, and helpful to others. For example, compared to disagreeable individuals, agreeable individuals are more likely to cooperate and less likely to compete with others, and are less likely to manipulate others to reach their desired targets. In general, agreeableness implies soft heartedness, kindness, and forgiveness.

How deeply are personality traits rooted in our genetic make-up? Researchers addressed this question by estimating the *heritability* – i.e., the percentage of inter-individual variance in a trait that is attributable to genes as opposed to environment – of each of the Big Five personality traits using as study participants identical twins and fraternal twins (e.g., Bloom, 1964; Loehlin, 1992). In a study based on the entire Swedish Twin Registry, totalling 12,898 twin pairs, heritability estimates exceeded 50 per cent for both extraversion and neuroticism, while were negligible for the other Big Five traits (Floderhus-Myrhed, Pedersen, & Rasmuson, 1980). These results were substantially replicated in the University of Minnesota Twin Study (Tellegen et al., 1988). A more valid estimation of heritability was eventually obtained by examining twins data coming from a wide range of countries. Loehlin (1992) produced aggregate cross-national estimates of heritability and found evidence of significant genetic determination for each of the five traits. In particular, openness had the highest heritability coefficient (46 per cent), followed by extraversion (36 per cent), neuroticism (31 per cent), agreeableness (28 per cent), and conscientiousness (28 per cent). By means of a meta-analysis conducted over a large number of studies, Plomin, Chipuer, and Loehlin (1990) concluded that the total variance (100 per cent) in Big Five personality traits can be decomposed as follows: 40 per cent due to genes, 40 per cent due to environment, and the remaining 20 per cent due to unknown factors. In all, the Big Five personality traits are deeply rooted in our genetic make-up.

The relatively strong genetic determination of traits has led researchers to postulate that traits evolved through evolutionary processes. In particular, traits may have evolved because they support those adaptive behaviours that prolong survival of individuals and groups and enhance reproduction. Goldberg (1990, 1993) advanced a bio-linguistic justification – labelled the *fundamental lexical hypothesis* – of the Big Five personality traits articulated in three points. First, the Big Five traits are crucial for the survival of our species as they enable cooperation within a group. Second, a group's ability to assess its members on the Big Five traits gives an evolutionary advantage to the group. For this reason, all languages must have developed adjectives that tap the Big Five traits.

When and how do the Big Five traits support survival? We have seen in Chapter 3 (section *The 'I' and the 'Me'*) that McAdams (1996) proposed to view the Big Five personality model as the 'psychology of the stranger': a person's standing on the Big Five dimensions is the piece of information that one would like to gather first when dealing with an unknown person. Thus, McAdams' interpretation suggests that the evolutionary advantage of being able to assess people on the Big Five dimensions is confined to the situation of initial familiarization with new acquaintances. More specifically, Kenrick and co-workers (1990) argued that traits such as extraversion and emotional stability – which is the opposite of neuroticism – are likely to foster mating and reproduction, whereas traits like conscientiousness and agreeableness are likely to foster cooperation and group survival. In all, the Big Five traits have survival value and hence ethical value in all cultures.

The Big Five and Subjective Well-Being

How predictive are the Big Five traits of subjective well-being, meant as the combination of high happiness and trait positive affect, and low trait negative affect? As anticipated in Chapter 2 (section *Origins and Consequences of Affect*), controlling for measurement error, trait positive affect has a strong correlation with the trait of extraversion, whereas trait negative affect is virtually undistinguishable from the trait of neuroticism. Two questions arise. First, are extraversion and neuroticism associated with life satisfaction? Second, are there specific sub-components of extraversion and neuroticism that are more specifically related to subjective well-being?

Emmons and Diener (1985) investigated in detail the relationships between personality traits and all three components of subjective well-being on two samples of 74 and 62 US undergraduate students. Personality was measured using the

Eysenck Personality Inventory (EPI; Eysenck & Eysenck, 1975) – which measures extraversion as two separate sub-scales, *sociability* and *impulsivity* – the 16PF (Cattell, Eber, & Tatsuoka, 1970) – which measures personality as 16 traits that map onto the Big Five dimensions; in particular, the 16PF measures neuroticism as *anxiety* with the three sub-components of *tense*, *tender-mindedness*, and *guilt proneness*. Subjective well-being was measured using the Satisfaction with Life Scale (Diener et al., 1985) and trait affect using the PANAS (Watson et al., 1988) as end-of-day diary for 86 consecutive days in sample 1 and 56 consecutive days in sample 2. The traits most strongly associated with subjective well-being were extraversion and neuroticism, and their sub-scales. Table 4.1 shows the most relevant correlation coefficients. Every shown coefficient greater in absolute value than .19 in sample S1 and .22 in sample S2 was statistically significant at least at the $p < .05$ level.

Concerning the first research question, the table shows that extraversion and life satisfaction were moderately and positively correlated in the range .29–.35 across the scales used to measure extraversion and the two study samples,

Table 4.1 *Correlations between different measures of extraversion and neuroticism, on the one hand, and components of subjective well-being, on the other hand, in two samples (S1 and S2) of US undergraduate students (selected correlation coefficients from Emmons & Diener, 1985)*

Questionnaire/Factor/Scale	Subjective well-being					
	Positive affect		Negative affect		Life satisfaction	
	S1	S2	S1	S2	S1	S2
EPI						
Extraversion	.31	.32	−.05	−.01	.29	.30
Sociability	.29	.49	−.08	−.10	.34	.40
Impulsivity	.05	.08	.18	.30	.01	−.07
Neuroticism	−.31	−.14	.61	.33	−.31	−.08
16PF						
Extraversion	.55	.28	−.08	.17	.35	.33
Warmth	.34	.39	−.31	−.20	.21	.18
Surgency	.52	.22	.01	.23	.39	.23
Social boldness	.48	.33	−.10	−.02	.38	.22
Anxiety	−.36	−.02	.54	.44	−.23	−.13
Tense	−.24	.00	.46	.28	−.20	−.16
Tender-mindedness	−.14	.06	.34	.26	−.17	.02
Guilt proneness	−.31	−.06	.48	.43	−.07	−.15

whereas neuroticism and life satisfaction were weakly and negatively correlated in the range −.31–.02 across the scales measuring neuroticism and the two study samples. Therefore, life satisfaction is predicted by extraversion and to a lesser extent by emotional stability.

Concerning the second research question, the table shows that the sociability component of extraversion is the one most strongly associated with positive affect and life satisfaction, whereas there are no marked differences in the associations between the different components of neuroticism and life satisfaction. Therefore, sociability appears to be the key component of extraversion that fosters positive affect and life satisfaction.

Perhaps the most interesting result from Emmons and Diener's (1985) study is the negative finding that all other personality traits were not associated with subjective well-being. Diener and Lucas (1999) reviewed various studies showing that indeed the associations between the other Big Five personality traits and subjective well-being are weak and inconsistent, and advanced that whether or not openness, conscientiousness, and agreeableness foster subjective well-being depends on how the environment rewards behaviours that stem from those traits. In particular, Diener, Suh, and Oishi (1997) suggested that agreeableness and conscientiousness might have indirect effects on subjective well-being because in most social environments they increase the likelihood of receiving reinforcement. Finally, Larsen and Diener (1987) advanced that openness may influence the degree of reactivity to events: persons who are high in openness may have greater intensity in both positive and negative emotions. In all, two of the Big Five personality traits – extraversion and neuroticism – are robustly linked to subjective well-being, and the other three traits may become relevant in interaction with the environment.

The Big Five and Psychological Well-Being

Schmutte and Ryff (1997) investigated the relationships between the Big Five personality traits and the six components of psychological well-being on a sample of 215 US parents. Table 4.2 shows the correlation coefficients of the two sets of variables. Every shown coefficient greater than .15 was statistically significant at least at the $p < .05$ level. Each component of psychological well-being was associated with at least three traits. Purpose in life and personal growth were associated with all five traits. Neuroticism was negatively associated, and extraversion and conscientiousness were positively associated with all six components of psychological well-being. Agreeableness was positively associated with all components of psychological well-being except autonomy. Finally, openness was positively associated with personal growth.

On one hand, the models of psychological and subjective well-being converge, in that neuroticism is a consistently negative predictor and extraversion is a consistently positive predictor of both psychological and subjective well-being.

Table 4.2 *Correlations between Big Five personality traits and components of psychological well-being (selected correlation coefficients from Schmutte & Ryff, 1997)*

Personality traits	Psychological well-being					
	SA	PR	AU	EM	PL	PG
Neuroticism	−.70	−.45	−.48	−.70	−.54	−.20
Extraversion	.43	.44	.24	.31	.38	.43
Openness	.03	.06	.17	.04	.16	.42
Agreeableness	.37	.52	.14	.35	.28	.32
Conscientiousness	.52	.38	.39	.67	.54	.31

Note: SA = Self-Acceptance; PR = Positive Relations; AU = Autonomy; EM = Environmental Mastery; PL = Purpose in Life; PG = Personal Growth.

On the other hand, the patterns of associations for psychological and subjective well-being differ, in that the remaining three traits – openness, agreeableness, and conscientiousness – are more strongly and consistently associated with psychological well-being than they are with subjective well-being. On the whole, the Big Five traits are more consistently associated with indicators of psychological well-being than they are with indicators of subjective well-being.

The Big Five and Consonant–Dissonant Well-Being

We have seen in Chapter 2 (section *Empirical Comparison of Subjective and Psychological Well-Being*) that, once measurement error is controlled for, subjective well-being and psychological well-being as whole latent constructs are strongly correlated to the extent that one wonders if the two constructs are one and the same. Given that the two types of well-being have somewhat different relationships with the Big Five Personality traits, it is interesting to focus on the somewhat rare individuals who have a dissonant well-being – that is those who are high in psychological well-being and low in subjective well-being (high PWB/low SWB) and those who are low in psychological well-being and high in subjective well-being (low PWB/high SWB). How do traits differentiate these two types of dissonant individuals?

Keyes, Shmotkin, and Ryff (2002) investigated this issue on a sample of 3,032 US adults from 48 states. First, they classified the participants in four groups: low PWB/low SWB, low PWB/high SWB, high PWB/low SWB, and high PWB/high SWB. Then, they used discriminant analysis – a statistical technique that helps to identify those factors that discriminate the most members of different groups – to test whether the Big Five personality traits predict membership in the four groups. The comparison between consonant individuals revealed that people in the high PWB/high SWB group tend to have less neuroticism and more extraversion and conscientiousness than do people in the low PWB/low

SWB group. The comparison between dissonant individuals revealed that people in the high PWB/low SWB group tend to have more openness and slightly more neuroticism and conscientiousness than do people in the low PWB/high SWB group. In all, these findings indicate that neuroticism has a consistently negative effect on both types of well-being, whereas extraversion and conscientiousness have consistently positive effects on both types of well-being, and agreeableness is unrelated to both types of well-being. Interestingly, openness to experience seem to foster psychological well-being at the expense of subjective well-being, suggesting that imaginative day dreamers are at risk of emotional drawbacks, perhaps when they wake up to harsh reality.

Personality–Culture Matching and Subjective Well-Being

Although there is substantial evidence that the Big Five personality model holds as a whole across cultures, and that each trait has similar connotations in different cultures, the average standing on the Big Five traits varies somewhat across cultures, and these variations go hand in hand with cultural differences in values (Hofstede & McCrae, 2004). For example, on average (White) North Americans score higher on extraversion than Chinese do, arguably because the values of assertiveness, positive emotionality, and sociability are more upheld in Western, individualistic countries (e.g., McCrae & Allik, 2002). Interesting questions arise: do the relationships between traits and well-being differ across cultures? Could it be that the more a trait is valued in a culture and the more strongly it is related to well-being? More broadly, how do personality and culture interact with each other in influencing subjective well-being?

Fulmer and co-workers (2010) hypothesized that if a trait is highly valued in a culture, members of that culture will tend to score higher on that trait. In turn, somebody in the culture who possesses that trait to a high level will engage in social comparisons and feel to be 'just right' in context. Therefore, in that culture that trait will be more strongly associated with subjective well-being. Fulmer and co-workers tested this personality–culture matching hypothesis on undergraduate student samples from 26 countries totalling 6,224 participants (Study 1). They found that the association between extraversion, on one hand, and general life happiness and positive affect during the past week, on the other hand, was stronger in countries higher on extraversion relative to countries lower in extraversion. These findings support the hypothesis that the matching between the personality trait of extraversion and cultural context moderates the relationship between extraversion and subjective well-being.

Based on the personality–culture matching hypothesis, the best for each of us would be to move to a country wherein our personality is a perfect match with the average personality. In that culture, our 'positive' traits (e.g., extraversion) would more effectively foster subjective well-being, and our 'negative' traits (e.g., neuroticism) would less effectively hinder subjective well-being. So, should we pack and go to a country wherein our personality is a perfect cultural match?

An alternative – albeit not much less laborious – possibility might be to become bilingual. Becoming bilingual requires internalizing the values of two cultures, and hence implies becoming bicultural (LaFromboise et al., 1993). Hong, Chiu, and Kung (1997) proposed that biculturalism carries the potential for *cultural frame switching*, meaning that bicultural individuals may suddenly shift values in the presence of culturally salient stimuli. Perhaps the most culturally salient stimulus is language itself: is it then possible that bilinguals enact a personality when they speak one language, and enact another personality when they speak the other language? This fascinating hypothesis extends the concept of reversals and multiple Yerkes–Dodson Effects, which we reviewed in Chapter 3 (section *Reversals*), to cultures.

Ramírez-Esparza and co-workers (2006) investigated this research question on Spanish–English bilinguals from the United States and Mexico. In Study 1, they assessed cultural differences in Big Five traits between US ($n = 168,451$) and Mexican ($n = 1,031$) monolinguals, and found that, on average, the former scored lower than the latter on neuroticism and higher on the remaining traits. In Studies 2–4, they assessed the Big Five personality traits of 249 bilinguals using both the English and Spanish versions of the same questionnaire, and compared the scores of the traits assessed using the two versions of the questionnaire within participants. They found that, on average, bilinguals scored higher on extraversion, conscientiousness, and agreeableness when answering the English questionnaire, and scored higher on neuroticism and openness when answering the Spanish questionnaire. Therefore, with the exception of openness, language appears to trigger a cultural frame switching in such a way that bilinguals tend to show a Mexican-like personality when they use Spanish and a US-like personality when they use English. In all, these preliminary findings suggest that people can develop, through learning and acculturation, multiple personality profiles, each matching a specific culture, and can suddenly shift between them to optimize their fitness in cultural context.

The Big Five and Creative Achievement

How does personality relate to creative achievement? We have seen in Chapter 3 (section *The Creative Self in Social Context*) that to generate a creative idea inside one's head is amazingly difficult, and that to get that idea recognized by the experts of the field as innovative is even more difficult. We would therefore expect the most creative individuals to have a personality that is an odd mix of imaginativeness and hardiness.

Barron and Harrington (1981) conducted a qualitative review of the creativity literature and concluded that the 'creative personality' is a set of relatively stable characteristics, including broad interests, high valuation of aesthetic qualities in experience, attraction to complexity, intuition, ability to resolve antinomies, high energy, self-confidence, a firm sense of self as 'creative', autonomy, and independence of judgment. This description is suggestive, albeit vaguely, of relationships between the Big Five personality traits and creativity.

On purely theoretical grounds, McCrae (1987) argued that openness to experience should foster creative achievement for two reasons: (a) openness promotes engagement with open-ended tasks and thus increases the likelihood of creative accomplishment, and (b) openness motivates a person to acquire intellectual and divergent thinking skills through practice and, in turn, the acquired skills increase the likelihood of creative accomplishment at a later time. Moreover, McCrae argued that extraversion increases the likelihood of being perceived as creative because extraverted people more readily exhibit their creative achievements, but it does not influence actual creative achievement. In contrast, King and co-workers (King, McKee Walker, & Broyles, 1996) suggested that the surgency component of extraversion facilitates engagement and effectiveness in creative work. Moreover, they proposed that agreeableness hinders creativity because it is a disposition to cooperate with others and to avoid conflict, thus increasing the likelihood of conforming behaviour. McCrae (1987) proposed that conscientiousness increases the likelihood of completing a creative project, whereas King, McKee Walker, and Broyles (1996) contended that conscientiousness has contrasting effects on creative achievement: (a) a positive effect because it leads to perseverance, and (b) a negative effect because it discourages playing with ideas. Finally, McCrae (1987) maintained that neuroticism disrupts engagement in creative work.

Feist (1998) tested these hypotheses conducting a meta-analysis of 83 empirical studies that assessed the relationships between the Big Five personality traits and creative accomplishment, contrasting scientists versus non-scientists, more creative scientists versus less creative scientists, and artists versus non-artists. He found that, compared to less creative individuals, more creative individuals had more openness to experience and extraversion and less conscientiousness and agreeableness, whereas they did not differ in neuroticism. Openness to experience was the trait most robustly related to creativity across studies, followed by extraversion. The effect of extraversion on creative achievement was entirely attributable to the confidence component, and there was no effect involving sociability.

Three findings from Feist's (1998) study are particularly interesting for the goal of this chapter. First, creative achievement – a 'positive' outcome – is maximized by the combination of two 'positive' traits (openness and extraversion-confidence) and two 'negative' traits (lack of conscientiousness and lack of agreeableness). Second, the combination of low conscientiousness and disagreeableness corresponds to a high level of *psychoticism* – definitely not a good trait – in Eysenck's (Eysenck & Eysenck, 1975) personality model. In turn, the fact that psychoticism fosters creative achievement suggests that creative individuals are a bit evil, so to speak, and hence it lends support to the broad principle that the negative can at times foster the positive. Finally, neuroticism – which was found to be the 'black sheep' of both subjective well-being and psychological well-being – is irrelevant to creative achievement, lending support to the broad principle that not all negative hinders the positive. In all, based on Kuhn's (1969) analysis of how scientific paradigms change, insofar as creative achievement requires a certain degree of toughness when facing resistance from others to one's own novel ideas, low conscientiousness and disagreeableness, although they are 'negative' in absolute terms, may turn out to be contextually 'positive', in that they help shield the potential innovator from social pressure to conform.

Are creative individuals perceived as somewhat evil in society? In the United States, Getzels and Jackson (1962) compared sixth–twelfth graders in a high-creative group with students in a high-IQ group, and found that the former believed themselves to be less approved of by teachers than the latter did. In Hong Kong, Spinks, Mei-Oi Lam, and Van Lingen (1996) investigated the implicit views that teachers hold of their ideal and creative pupil. The ideal pupil matched closely the everyday representation of the good Chinese child, characterized by adjectives such as self-disciplined, respectful of parents, and diligent, whereas the creative pupil matched closely the universal definition of creative person (Torrance, 1965), characterized by adjectives such as curious, assertive, and independent. These studies suggest that in both the West and the East teachers like creative children a bit less than they like intelligent and conforming children. This is not to say that creative children are deemed evil – they are just deemed a bit less good.

In all, Feist's (1998) findings suggest that creativity requires trade-offs between socially desirable and socially undesirable traits. The bottom line is that the employer who hires a 'creative personality' will be likely to end up with an open-minded (high openness), self-confident (high extraversion-confidence), not-so-hard-working, disorganized, unreliable (low conscientiousness), unkind, disobedient, and competitive (low agreeableness) employee – that is, definitely not somebody with a 'happy personality'. The bottom line is that creativity costs, and an employer who wants it, has to pay for it.

Are there Consistently Positive and Consistently Negative Traits?

This section has reviewed what is known about the relationships between the Big Five personality traits, on one hand, and subjective well-being, psychological well-being, and creative achievement – meant as realization of eudaimonic potential – on the other hand. We have also touched upon evidence suggesting that the relationships between traits and subjective well-being are moderated by culture in such a way that subjective well-being reaches its maximum when there is a perfect matching between personality and culture. Throughout these analyses, a hierarchical order of traits emerged with reference to how positive or negative they are.

Extraversion predicts more of all six indicators of psychological well-being. Either the sociability component or the reward sensitivity component of extraversion predicts more trait positive affect, life satisfaction, and happiness. Finally, the confidence component of extraversion predicts more lifetime creative achievement. In all, extraversion emerged as a consistently positive trait and the most positive of the Big Five traits.

Neuroticism predicts consistently less subjective well-being and less psychological well-being, but it does not exert an influence on lifetime creative achievement. In all, neuroticism emerged as an inconsistently negative trait and the most negative of the Big Five traits.

The remaining three traits fall in between extraversion and neuroticism, and their relative ordering depends on the weights one assigns to the different indicators of well-being. Openness to experience is virtually unrelated to subjective well-being; it predicts more personal growth, but is unrelated to the other indicators of psychological well-being; and it is the main predictor of lifetime creative achievement. Conscientiousness and agreeableness are similar, in that they are both virtually unrelated to subjective well-being, and they predict consistently more psychological well-being but less lifetime creative achievement. In all, openness, conscientiousness, and agreeableness are not consistently positive or consistently negative traits because they are not consistently related to the various indicators of well-being.

Is there a combination of Big Five traits that would give us simultaneously highest subjective well-being, highest psychological well-being, and highest creativity? You can find the answer by playing a game. Imagine being in the ideal situation of freely choosing your personality: what pattern of Big Five traits would you choose? For example, my dream is to have highest happiness and highest creativity. Therefore, I would choose to be very extraverted, very stable emotionally, very open to experience, very unconscientious, and very disagreeable: with such a combination I would maximize both happiness and creativity, and hence I would have it all. Would I? What about the side effects of low conscientiousness and low agreeableness? Surely that would be detrimental to my psychological well-being, and it would perhaps hinder my chances of establishing and maintaining good relations with others and of finding a partner with whom to share my life. It looks as if I would not actually have it all. What about you?

SPECIAL TRAITS

Five or More?

The Big Five personality model is the most-used in personality research. Does this mean that there are only five traits that deserve attention? Perhaps the best way to approach this question is to look back at how the Big Five model was developed.

We have seen that trait research has been descriptive and exploratory. The conceptual interpretation of each trait has been an 'add-on', in response to the need to explain why a trait was associated with certain psychological variables. For example, the discovery of the association between extraversion and positive affect prompted interpretations and further research. It was then found that only the sociability component of extraversion is associated with positive affect (Emmons & Diener, 1985). That finding prompted more interpretations and research, which eventually led to the discovery that positive affect is actually associated with reward sensitivity, which in turn is the core component of extraversion; sociability therefore turned out to be a by-product of extraversion rather than its core component (Lucas et al., 2000). In all, the Big Five personality model is the apex of the descriptive approach to personality.

A wide range of personality traits was instead identified starting from theory and then moving down to data. This section reviews three sets of theory-driven traits that are particularly relevant to positive psychology. We will try to determine whether some of those traits are consistently 'positive'.

The Circumplex of Interpersonal Behaviour and Gender Role Attributes

From an evolutionary perspective, the most basic animal and human traits are those linked to biological sex: masculinity and femininity. In humans, masculinity and femininity are, of course, also influenced by social factors, including the gender roles upheld in a culture and the way children are socialized to fit those roles. For example, in Western countries boys are typically encouraged to play with toy weapons and girls with baby dolls, with the usual exceptions. In this way, whatever the inborn sex-linked potential is, culture exerts a powerful influence on the way individuals develop their gender role attributes. The gender role attributes of adults are complex and pervasive traits that have the potential to influence a wide range of behaviours over and above mating and reproduction.

Bakan (1966) sustained that gender differences in internalized psychological make-up should be conceptualized as relative individual differences in two distinct and general tendencies to approach the physical and social environment: *agency* and *communion*. Agency implies a separation between the self and the environment finalized to acting on, and modifying the environment. The cause of agency is dissatisfaction with the environment as it is, or with a change that occurred in the environment. The aim of agency is tension-reduction. Tension-reduction is achieved by modifying the environment in order to remove or attenuate its dissatisfying aspects. Communion, instead, implies a lack of separation between the self and the environment finalized to merging with the environment as it is. The cause of communion is acceptance and love for the environment. The aim of communion is union. Union is achieved by connecting the self to objects in the environment and in particular to other persons, establishing relationships wherein the personal self can no longer be perceived as distinguishable from the other selves.

Wiggins and co-workers (Trapnell & Wiggins, 1990; Wiggins & Broughton, 1985, 1991) used Bakan's (1966) conceptualization to create a circumplex model of interpersonal behaviour, which is shown in Figure 4.1. Agency (or dominance) is the vertical axis, and communion (or nurturance) is the horizontal axis. Extraversion and agreeableness can be represented in the model as orthogonal axes that are rotated clockwise of 45 degrees in respect to the agency axis. The eight points in the figure represent specific combinations of agency and communion. The circumplex model interprets the Big Five personality model assigning a primary role to agency and communion – and hence to extraversion and agreeableness – and a secondary role to the remaining three factors of the Big Five personality model. In this sense, the circumplex model can be viewed as an attempt to provide a theoretical foundation to the Big Five personality model.

The circumplex model of interpersonal behaviour has also been used to define and interpret gender role attributes as expressive and instrumental dispositions that correspond to socially defined masculine-agentic and feminine-communal ways of thinking, feeling, and acting. The instrumental component of masculinity and the expressive component of femininity can be represented

Figure 4.1 *The circumplex model of interpersonal behaviour*

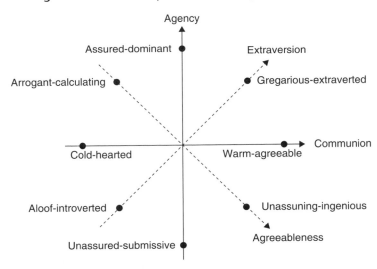

Source: Adapted from Wiggins and Broughton, 1991, *European Journal of Personality, 5*, 343–365, John Wiley & Sons Ltd.

as two independent traits – *instrumentality* and *expressivity* – that are indicators of agency and communion, respectively, in the circumplex model of interpersonal behaviour. Instrumentality and expressivity can be measured validly and reliably as two independent traits by the Personal Attributes Questionnaire (PAQ; Spence, Helmreich, & Stapp, 1974, 1975; Spence & Helmreich, 1978; available at: http://www.utexas.edu/courses/pair/CaseStudy/PPB5c1.html) and the Bem Sex-Role Inventory (BSRI; Bem, 1974). By applying the BSRI, Wiggins and Broughton (1985) found that instrumentality strongly correlates with agency, whereas expressivity strongly correlates with communion.

Do gender role attributes vary across cultures? Several studies indicated that, although many attributes of instrumentality and expressivity have semantic equivalents in all cultures, some traits that distinguish men and women in Western, individualistic cultures are less strongly related, or are even unrelated to gender in Eastern, collectivistic cultures (Brannon, 2005; Costa, Terraciano, & McCrae, 2001; Sugihara & Katsurada, 2002; Ward & Sethi, 1986). For example, a stream of studies on Chinese children and university students indicated that the Chinese expressivity is less gender differentiated, in that the difference in expressivity between males and females is less strong in Chinese than it is in Westerners (Chang & Holt, 1994; Cheung, 1996; Moneta, 2010; Wong, Tinsley, Law, & Mobley, 2003); this finding has been attributed to the high value that the Chinese attach to interrelatedness for both men and women.

Are gender role attributes 'positive'? Cross-cultural studies reveal that, even if there are cultural differences in the definition of gender role attributes and in the degree of differentiation between men and women, gender role attributes are socially desirable in all cultures. In particular, expressive attributes like 'kind' and 'gentle' are desirable for both men and women, and in individualistic cultures they are more desirable for women than they are for men, whereas in some collectivistic cultures such as the Chinese culture they are equally desirable for men and women. Instrumental attributes like 'active' and 'self-confident' are desirable for both men and women, and in both individualistic and collectivistic cultures they are more desirable for men than they are for women. This suggests that both instrumentality and expressivity foster adaptive behaviour.

What about the combination of the two gender role attributes? There are two main groups of individuals to be compared: gender-typed and androgynous. The gender-typed group includes (a) men who are high in instrumentality and low in expressivity, and (b) women who are high in expressivity and low in instrumentality; these individuals match the gender stereotype reciting that men are masculine and women are feminine. The androgynous group includes individuals of both genders who are high in both instrumentality and expressivity; these individuals depart from the gender stereotype. Bem (1974) argued that androgynous individuals should be more adaptive than gender-typed individuals.

The eudaimonic 'positivity' of instrumentality and expressivity was tested using two main competing models, *additive* and *interactive*. The additive model assumes that both instrumentality and expressivity contribute to psychological adjustment independently of each other, so that psychological adjustment is just the sum of the effect of instrumentality and the effect of expressivity. The interactive model assumes, in addition, that instrumentality and expressivity have a synergistic effect on psychological adjustment, so that psychological adjustment is the sum of the effect of instrumentality, the effect of expressivity, and the effect of being instrumentality and expressivity simultaneously high. Neither model has yet been found to be superior to the other (e.g., Francis & Wilcox, 1998; Hall & Taylor, 1985; Shifren & Bauserman, 1996). In all, the evidence indicates that instrumentality and expressivity are consistently positive traits, and that they might be even more positive if an individual possesses both to a high extent.

Two studies supporting the androgyny hypothesis shed light on the reason why the combination of instrumentality and expressivity offers advantages. Cheng and Cheung (2005b) found that Hong Kong Chinese undergraduates with an androgynous gender role orientation have more coping flexibility than their gender-typed counterparts; in this connection, we have seen in Chapter 3 (section *Stress and Coping*) that coping flexibility appears to be the most adaptive coping meta-strategy. Csikszentmihalyi (1996) interviewed very creative individuals asking them to report their experience and behaviour prior to a major creative achievement of their life. He found that they were markedly androgynous, but expressed their instrumentality and expressivity in alternation. For example, in some phases of their work they were meditative, receptive, or even idling, whereas in other phases they were assertive, engaged, and fully engrossed in their work. These two studies together suggest that the advantage of being androgynous does not stem from the simultaneous application of instrumentality and expressivity to a single situation, but rather from the ability to shift from an instrumental mode of functioning to an expressive mode of functioning, and vice versa, depending on what the situation requires.

How do we know when it is best to act in a masculine way and when it is best to act in a feminine way? Cheng and Cheung (2005a) suggested that flexible coping requires some kind of metacognitive self-regulation, and Csikszentmihalyi's (1996) account suggests that creative and androgynous individuals have a keen metacognitive awareness and self-regulation: they know when it is time to stop agency and shift to communion, and vice versa, in order to optimize their work performance. But if indeed metacognition and self-regulation are the key, can we truly say that gender role attributes are consistently positive traits? Could it be instead that gender role attributes are necessary but not sufficient personal resources, and that the metacognition required to use those resources is the authentically positive eudaimonic factor? You may like to read Chapter 5 (sections *Mindfulness* and *Adaptive and Maladaptive Metacognitions*) and find your own answer.

Causality Orientations

As we have seen in Chapter 3 (section *Intrinsic Motivation, Extrinsic Motivation, and Self-Determination*), Deci and Ryan's (1985a) Organismic Developmental Theory explains the developmental processes through which children learn how to self-regulate their behaviour when they are intrinsically or extrinsically motivated. The full range of developmental outcomes occurs between two extremes. On one hand, children who grow in autonomy-supporting and optimally challenging environments tend to develop strong intrinsic motivation, strong self-determination, high internalization of values that originally were not intrinsically motivated, and hence high integration of needs in their self-structure. On the other hand, children who grow in controlling and either unchallenging or threatening environments tend to develop weak intrinsic motivation, weak self-determination, and incomplete internalization of social values, and hence low integration of needs in their self-structure. The theory was then used to define and measure broad orientations towards specific regulatory styles – called *causality orientations* – that capture the overall outcome of psychosocial development in adults.

Causality orientations are three general motivational orientations – *autonomy*, *control*, and *impersonal* – that represent distinct and coexisting personal tendencies to perceive the locus of causation of one's own actions and to adopt a corresponding self-regulatory style. Causality orientations represent people's explicit or implicit understanding of the causation of their behaviours. The autonomy orientation involves a high degree of experienced choice and freedom in activities, as well as a tendency to interpret the environment as informational and to seek out opportunities for autonomy. The control orientation involves experiencing one's own behaviour as being pushed or controlled by external forces or by internal imperatives. The impersonal orientation involves experiencing a sense of incompetence and lack of control when trying to master one's own actions. With respect to motivation, the autonomy orientation is theorized to foster intrinsic motivation, the control orientation is theorized to foster extrinsic motivation, and the impersonal orientation is theorized to foster amotivation, that is, states characterized by absence of both types of motivation. All three orientations can coexist in the same person, and all three can be simultaneously enacted in a given situation. How can it be?

Imagine you accidentally learned that your partner has established communication with an important ex from the past via an Internet-based social network, and you are not happy about it. What would you do? Consider the following three options: (a) you approach your partner openly, explain that you are bothered by this, and ask what such a reunion might mean; (b) you confront your partner and threaten to leave unless the reunion is terminated at once; (c) you do nothing, and hope that your partner will eventually cease chatting with the ex. Option (a) is an indicator of autonomy orientation, option (b) is an indicator of control orientation, and option (c) is an indicator of impersonal orientation.

Of course, if asked in public, we would all chose option (a) because it is the most politically correct and the most self-enhancing. Yet, in our private chambers, we would probably consider all three options. So the question is, what is the probability that you will enact each of these options? For example, the pattern of response (a) = very likely, (b) = very unlikely, and (c) = somewhat likely would indicate that you are high in autonomy orientation, low in control orientation, and medium in impersonal orientation. The three orientations coexist in the same person, and they can be activated simultaneously as potential responses in the same context.

The three causality orientations can be measured validly and reliably using the General Causality Orientations Scale (GCOS; Deci & Ryan, 1985b; extended by Hodgins, Koestner, & Duncan, 1996; available at: http://www.selfdetermi-nationtheory.org/questionnaires/10-questionnaires/46). The extended version of the GCOS consists of 17 hypothetical situations followed by descriptions of three possible ways of reacting to them, each one expressing one of the three causality orientations. Respondents are asked to rate their propensity towards each of the three possible reactions on a seven-point scale ranging from 1 (*very likely*) to 7 (*very unlikely*). A sample vignette is: 'Within your circle of friends, the one with whom you choose to spend the most time is: (a) the one with whom you spend the most time exchanging ideas and feelings, (b) the one who is the most popular of them, (c) the one who needs you the most as a friend'. Response (a) measures autonomy, (b) impersonal, and (c) control orientation. In US samples of undergraduate students, the three scales were found to be relatively independent of one another (Deci & Ryan, 1985b).

Are the causality orientations redundant of the Big Five personality traits? Deponte (2004) investigated the relationships between the causality orientations and the Big Five personality traits on a sample of 101 Italian undergraduate students. Autonomy orientation correlated moderately with agreeableness ($r = .27$) and extraversion ($r = .29$), suggesting that – counter to the stereotype that equates autonomy with selfishness and rebelliousness – the flexible and conflict-free nature of autonomous self-regulation predisposes a person to warm and positive relations with others. Control orientation correlated fairly negatively with agreeableness ($r = -.47$), suggesting that the rigid and conflict-prone nature of controlled self-regulation predisposes a person to be unempathic and cold in relation with others. Finally, impersonal orientation had a fair correlation with neuroticism ($r = .48$) and weak and negative correlations with extraversion ($r = -.33$) and conscientiousness ($r = -.26$), suggesting that lack of self-regulation undermines emotional stability, the ability to have warm relations with others, and productivity in achievement contexts. In all, the relationships between causality orientations and Big Five traits are only moderate, suggesting that causality orientations constitute a set of distinct traits.

Are causality orientations predictive of well-being? Deci and Ryan (1985b) investigated the relationships between the three autonomy orientations and a wide range of psychological variables that tap well-being, in sub-samples of a mixed sample totalling more than 1,000 US undergraduate students and workers. We will consider here only three indicators of well-being. Self-esteem had a weak and positive correlation with autonomy orientation ($r = .35$) and a strong and negative correlation with impersonal orientation ($r = -.61$), and was uncorrelated with control orientation ($r = .01$). External locus of control had a weak and negative correlation with autonomy orientation ($r = -.16$), a weak and positive correlation with control orientation ($r = .29$), and a fair and positive correlation with impersonal orientation ($r = .52$). Finally, ego development had a moderate and positive correlation with autonomy orientation ($r = .43$), a weak and negative correlation with control orientation ($r = -.22$), and a weak and negative correlation with impersonal orientation ($r = -.32$). These findings confirm that the autonomy orientation is a consistently positive trait, the impersonal orientation is a consistently negative trait, and the control orientation is a mixed-value trait. In particular, Deci and Ryan (1985a, 1985b) suggested that whether the control orientation leads to more self-esteem depends on whether the behaviour it fosters is valued positively by others and is rewarded.

In all, the autonomy orientation is consistently associated with positive traits and adaptive behaviours that enable a person to cope flexibly with environmental demands, maintaining a positive sense of self and warm relationships with others; it is thus a consistently positive trait. The impersonal orientation is consistently associated with negative traits and maladaptive behaviour and is thus a consistently negative trait. Finally, the control orientation is basically associated with disagreeableness, and may foster adaptive or maladaptive behaviour depending on the situation; it is neither a positive nor a negative trait.

Trait Intrinsic and Extrinsic Motivation

As we have seen in Chapter 3 (section *Intrinsic Motivation, Extrinsic Motivation, and Self-Determination*), intrinsic motivation and extrinsic motivation were originally defined as state variables that can rapidly change across situations and times, and are antagonistic at any single point in time. Amabile and co-workers (1994) defined intrinsic motivation and extrinsic motivation as trait-like orientations to be driven either by the engagement of work or by a means to some end that is external to the work itself. The rationale is that, although a person's intrinsic and extrinsic motivations vary across situations and times during daily activities as a function of environmental stimuli and opportunities, persons differ in their general, average tendencies to be intrinsically and extrinsically motivated across situations and times.

Trait intrinsic motivation and trait extrinsic motivation in the study or work domains can be measured validly and reliably using the Work Preference Inventory (WPI; Amabile et al., 1994), a 30-item inventory, in which the two types of motivation are measured by 15 items each. Intrinsic motivation is subdivided into *enjoyment*, the tendency to engage in activities because they are interesting or satisfying (e.g., 'It is important for me to be able to do what I most enjoy') and *challenge*, the self-rewarding tendency to tackle and master complex tasks (e.g., 'I enjoy tackling problems that are completely new to me'). Extrinsic motivation is subdivided into *outward*, that is, the tendency to engage in activities because of the dictates of others or of the potential recognition by others (e.g., 'I am concerned about how other people are going to react to my ideas') and *compensation*, the tendency to engage in activities with the purpose of obtaining a reward proportional to the effort made (e.g., 'I am keenly aware of the goals I have for getting good grades'). Items are scored on a four-point scale ranging from 1 (*never or almost never true for me*) to 4 (*always or almost always true for me*).

As state variables, intrinsic motivation and extrinsic motivation have been traditionally considered to be opposites. In particular, the introduction of extrinsic incentives, such as money and praise, into interesting tasks has been systematically found to reduce intrinsic motivation (see review by Deci & Ryan, 1985a). However, as trait variables, intrinsic motivation and extrinsic motivation are reciprocally independent (Amabile et al., 1994): some individuals are high in both, others low in both, and some high in one and low in the other one.

Are motivational traits redundant of causality orientations? Amabile and co-workers (1994) administered the WPI and the GCOS (Deci & Ryan, 1985b) to a sample of 500 US undergraduate students and found that trait intrinsic motivation has the strongest correlation with the autonomy orientation ($r = .36$), and trait extrinsic motivation has the strongest correlation with the control orientation ($r = .39$). These findings are consistent with the idea that autonomy fosters intrinsic motivation, whereas control fosters extrinsic motivation. However, the correlations are weak, and hence trait motivations and causality orientations can be regarded as distinct constructs.

Are motivational traits redundant of the Big Five traits? Interestingly, to date no published research has addressed this question (incidentally, if you are looking for a topic for your undergraduate thesis, this would make a good one). However, Amabile and co-workers (1994) investigated the relationships between motivational traits and the four main *psychological types – introverted–extraverted, intuitive–sensing, feeling–thinking, perceiving–judging* – measured by the Myers–Briggs Type Indicator (MBTI; Myers, 1962; Myers & McCaulley, 1985) in a sample of 60 undergraduate students. Trait intrinsic motivation was uncorrelated with all psychological types, whereas trait extrinsic motivation correlated moderately and positively with all four psychological types, indicating that the extrinsically motivated person is outward oriented, down to earth, and attracted to structures and rewards that are set by others. Because psychological types map well onto the Big Five personality traits excluding neuroticism (McCrae & Costa, 1989), one can reach the indirect conclusion that trait extrinsic motivation is potentially related to all Big Five personality traits excluding neuroticism, whereas trait intrinsic motivation is a quite distinct trait.

Do motivational traits relate to eudaimonic well-being? As we have seen in Chapter 3 (section *The Creative Self*), it has been consistently found that a state of intrinsic motivation facilitates creativity, while a state of extrinsic motivation hinders it (see reviews by Deci & Ryan, 1985a, and Amabile, 1996). Amabile and co-workers (1994) extended the investigation by looking at the relationship between trait motivations and creativity. They assessed creativity using Kirton Adaptation–Innovation Inventory (KAI; Kirton, 1976) in a sample of 284 undergraduate students and in a sample of 268 workers. Trait intrinsic motivation had a positive and moderate correlation with creativity in both samples ($r = .38$ and $r = .41$, respectively), whereas trait extrinsic motivation had a negative and moderate correlation with creativity in both samples ($r = -.39$ and $r = -.18$, respectively). Amabile and co-workers also assessed creativity of final products – such as poems and drawings – using the consensual assessment technique (i.e., creativity ratings made by experts) on various samples of undergraduate students. Trait intrinsic motivation had from weak to fair and positive correlations with rated creativity, whereas trait extrinsic motivation had weak and negative correlations with rated creativity. In all, trait intrinsic motivation appears to foster creativity, whereas trait extrinsic motivation appears to hinder it.

A number of studies investigated the effects that trait intrinsic motivation and trait extrinsic motivation might have on undergraduate students' academic achievement. Amabile and co-workers (1994) found that trait intrinsic motivation correlates modestly with the verbal and mathematical scores of the Scholastic Achievement Test (SAT), which are measures of academic ability and intelligence, and with midterm marks attained in introduction to psychology classes, whereas trait extrinsic motivation is unrelated to both SAT scores and midterm marks. Yet, a previous study (Kahoe & McFarland, 1975) had revealed a somewhat more complex pattern: trait intrinsic and extrinsic motivation interact with perceived difficulty of a course in predicting grade in the course, in such a way that intrinsic motivation predicts higher grades in high challenge courses, whereas extrinsic motivation predicts higher grades in low challenge courses. In, all these findings indicate that intrinsic motivation fosters academic performance at least when students face complex learning tasks. However, because trait intrinsic motivation is related to intelligence, which influences both past and future academic achievement, it is methodologically appropriate to estimate the effects that motivational traits have on future academic performance controlling statistically for students' past academic performance. This was done in two studies, one conducted in Hong Kong in 1998–2001, the other conducted in London in 2011.

The Hong Kong study was conducted on 204 first-year undergraduate students from a wide range of study programmes. It looked specifically at semester Grade Point Average until completion of the study programme, and controlled for the average mark attained in the Hong Kong Advanced Level Examination (HKALE), a pre-enrolment, academic ability test, which can be considered equivalent to the British A-Level Examination and the North American SAT (Moneta & Siu, 2002).

Trait intrinsic motivation predicted worse marks, whereas trait extrinsic motivation predicted better marks. Moreover, the relationships between motivational traits and overall academic performance did not change throughout the three-year study programme. In all, the Hong Kong study indicates that trait extrinsic motivation fosters academic achievement, whereas trait intrinsic motivation hinders it.

The London study was conducted on 101 undergraduate students from a wide range of study programmes in the sciences, social sciences, business, and humanities. It looked specifically at the average mark – expressed in percentage points – attained on all the examinations taken at the end of semester, and controlled for the average mark attained on all the examinations taken in the previous semester (Spada & Moneta, in press). Motivational traits did not have direct effects on academic examination performance, but they did have significant indirect effects through a number of mediating variables. On one hand, trait intrinsic motivation predicted less evaluation anxiety, less avoidance coping in studying, less reliance on a surface, rote approach to studying, and, via these factors, better grades. On the other hand, trait extrinsic motivation predicted more evaluation anxiety, more avoidance coping in studying, more reliance on a surface, rote approach to studying, and, via these factors, worse grades. In all, the London study indicates that trait intrinsic motivation fosters academic achievement, whereas trait extrinsic motivation hinders it.

Why do the two studies provide diametrical results and conclusions? Many factors differed between the two studies, including culture, historical time, and more specific differences in teaching style and student assessment. Biggs (1992) and Salili (1994) depicted the Hong Kong education system of the 1980s and early 1990s as highly competitive and examination oriented, and characterized by large classes, expository teaching, and excessive amounts of homework – definitely not an environment wherein intrinsically motivated students would strive, express creative ideas in coursework and examinations, and see their creativity being rewarded by grades. Therefore, it is possible that at the end of the millennium, when the Hong Kong study was conducted, the overall teaching environment was still geared towards rewarding the extrinsically motivated student.

The interesting contradiction of findings between the Hong Kong and London studies points out that, although trait intrinsic motivation has a positive connotation and trait extrinsic motivation has a negative connotation, whether these traits turn out to foster or hinder performance – meant as an indicator of eudaimonic well-being – depends heavily on context. Therefore, it would seem that motivational traits cannot be regarded as consistently positive or consistently negative traits.

Are there Consistently Positive and Consistently Negative Traits?

This section has reviewed what is known about the relationships between gender role attributes, general causality orientations, and intrinsic and extrinsic motivational orientations, on one hand, and eudaimonic well-being, on the other hand. Throughout these analyses, a hierarchical order of traits emerges with reference to how positive or negative they are. Gender role attributes are consistently positive traits, with the only uncertainty being whether they provide an extra boost of adaptiveness when possessed simultaneously to a high extent, as it happens for androgynous individuals. Of the three causality orientations, autonomy emerges as a consistently positive trait, impersonal orientation emerges as a consistently negative trait, and control emerges as a two-edged sword, which can turn out to foster adaptiveness in controlling environments and to hinder it in informational, autonomy-supporting environments. Finally, trait intrinsic motivation has reasonably consistent positive effects on performance, and trait extrinsic motivation has reasonably consistent negative effects, with the caveat that contextual factors can dramatically reverse the positivity–negativity of these traits.

CHARACTER STRENGTHS AND VIRTUES

Virtues, Strengths, and Authentic Happiness

Clinical psychology has progressed tremendously in the past decades, arguably because it has been able to create an evidence-based, consensual, and comprehensive classification system of mental disorders that can be effectively applied for the purpose of diagnosing, preventing, and treating mental disorders. The classification system of mental disorders is presented with only slight differences in two widely recognized manuals: the American Psychiatric Association's (1994) *Diagnostic and Statistical Manual of Mental Disorders* (*DSM-IV*) and the World Health Organization's (2010) *International Classification of Diseases (ICD)*. The DSM-IV and the ICD can be thought of classification systems of what is wrong with people. Peterson and Seligman (2004) have developed what they claim to be an equivalent classification system of what is right with people. This was needed in order to provide a foundation for positive psychology and, in particular, to support its primary mission of guiding people – through education, coaching, and psychotherapy – towards authentic happiness.

Peterson and Seligman (2004) conceptualized their research goal as one of identifying longitudinally and cross-situationally stable *character strengths* that could be grouped by similarity or synergism into higher order factors called *virtues*. Every time we call a trait a 'strength', we implicitly make an ethical judgment on it. Because ethical values differ both between cultures and within the same culture across historical times, Peterson and Seligman looked specifically at ubiquitous character strengths, that is, traits that are recognized as valuable and ethical in every cultural and historical setting. They pursued this goal by analysing ancient philosophical and religious conceptions of human character that grew and spread over centuries to become pervasive cultural resources in contemporary societies. They considered both traditions from the East – Confucianism, Taoism, Buddhism and Hinduism – and from the West – Greek philosophy, Judaism, Christianity, and Islam.

In their search, Peterson and Seligman (2004) retained only those character strengths that satisfied the criteria summarized in Table 4.3. The first and most important criterion is that in order to be a character strength, a trait must contribute, through the mediation of fulfilments, to the *good life*. What is the good life? Nakamura and Csikszentmihalyi (2005) provided a simple and specific answer: 'the good life is one that is characterized by complete absorption in what one does' (p. 89). Seligman (2002) provided a broad and articulate answer. According to him, there are three different types of happiness whose pursuit leads to three different types of lives: the *pleasant life*, the *engaged (good) life*, and the *meaningful (good) life*. In the pleasant life, happiness is achieved through satisfaction of basic pleasures such as sex, companionship, and good food. In the engaged life, happiness is achieved through a three-step process: (a) identifying ones' own strengths and virtues – the values within ourselves – (b) strengthening them further, and (c) using them to enhance one's own life. Finally, in the meaningful life, happiness is pursued by using one's own strengths and virtues for a purpose that transcends the self. Therefore, the first and most important

Table 4.3 *The ten criteria that Peterson and Seligman (2004) used to identify character strengths and virtues*

1	A strength contributes to one's own and others' fulfilments that constitute the good life	Compulsory
2	A strength is ethically valued independently of the positive effects it might have	Compulsory
3	The display of a strength does not diminish other people's strengths	Compulsory
4	The opposite of a strength does not have a positive connotation	Compulsory
5	A strength is a trait, and hence manifests itself in feelings, thoughts, and behaviours	Compulsory
6	A strength is independent of the other strengths included in the classification system	Compulsory
7	A strength is consensually recognized	Compulsory
8	A strength is championed by one or more individuals	Optional
9	The absence of a strength is championed by one or more individuals	Optional
10	A strength is supported in its development by social institutions	Compulsory

definitional criterion for a strength is that its pursuit will foster authentic happiness, that is, a type of happiness that goes beyond the simplest version of the hedonic principle of maximizing any type of pleasure and minimizing any type of pain.

Peterson and Seligman (2004) identified 24 character strengths grouped by six virtues, as shown in Table 4.4. Dahlsgaard, Peterson, and Seligman (2005) probed

Table 4.4 *Virtues and their constituent character strengths identified by Peterson and Seligman (2004)*

Virtue	Character strength
Wisdom	▪ Creativity (originality and ingenuity) ▪ Curiosity (interest in new things) ▪ Open-mindedness (critical thinking and ability to change one's mind based on evidence) ▪ Love of learning (systematic and beyond curiosity) ▪ Perspective (being able to make sense of the world)
Courage	▪ Bravery (physical and moral) ▪ Persistence (resilience and endurance until completion) ▪ Integrity (honesty and authenticity) ▪ Vitality (enthusiasm and vigour)
Humanity	▪ Love (being able to establish close and reciprocal relations) ▪ Kindness (compassion and nurturance) ▪ Social intelligence (emotional intelligence)
Justice	▪ Citizenship (social responsibility and teamwork) ▪ Fairness (giving everybody a fair chance) ▪ Leadership (organizing groups efficiently and fairly)
Temperance	▪ Forgiveness and mercy (not being vengeful and offering second chances) ▪ Humility/Modesty (maintaining a realistic self-concept) ▪ Prudence (validly assessing risks and not taking undue risks) ▪ Self-regulation (discipline and self-control)
Transcendence	▪ Appreciation of beauty and excellence (in all fields of human endeavour) ▪ Gratitude (being aware of help received and expressing gratitude) ▪ Hope (expecting the best and working to make it happen) ▪ Humour (playfulness and seeing the light side of things) ▪ Spirituality (holding coherent and firm beliefs about the meaning of life)

the completeness and universality of the high six classification, and found surprising commonalities of each identified virtue across cultures. Nevertheless, Peterson and Seligman (2004) warned that the grouping of strengths within virtues has to be taken somewhat prudently, as some character strengths could conceptually be allocated to more than one virtue. For example, a prosecutor investigating organized crime may well need bravery – which is classified under the courage virtue – in order to exert the justice virtue; more broadly, one could argue that justice will always require bravery in consideration of the risks of retaliation that are implicit in administering it, not to mention the social consequences of being considered 'rigorous'.

Seligman (2002) and Peterson and Seligman (2004) proposed that strengths are 'routes' to virtues, in that if one works hard and for long periods of time to improve one or more strengths that are grouped within the same virtue, one will eventually enhance that virtue. This implies that the model of virtues differs from the classic componential models that are validated using factor analysis. In a classic componential model, the factors (in this case the virtues) are thought to cause the facets (in this case the strengths). In Seligman and Peterson's model, instead, the facets (strengths) are thought to cause the factors (virtues), and this is the conceptual basis for arguing that a change in strengths will cause a change in virtues.

The six virtues differ from one another as to the psychological processes they involve. Wisdom involves primarily cognitive strengths that support the acquisition, analysis, and integration of information. Courage involves primarily emotional strengths that support goal-directed behaviour in face of challenge and risk. Humanity involves primarily interpersonal strengths that support understanding, empathizing, and caring about others. Justice involves primarily moral strengths applied to the concept of common good. Temperance involves primarily metacognitive strengths that support emotional and behavioural inhibition. Finally, transcendence involves primarily existential strengths that support inner exploration. In all, each virtue involves quite distinct psychological processes.

What should we do with our strengths and virtues? Peterson and Seligman (2004) maintain that we should identify them and cultivate them. They consider the various strengths and virtues as functionally independent from each other, although they may be empirically correlated, so that each person will have distinct signature strengths. For example, a person may be strong in justice and weak in courage, whereas another person may be strong in courage and weak in justice. What should these persons do in order to pursue the engaged life? Seligman (2002) and Peterson and Seligman (2004) maintain that they should cultivate their signature strengths. This in turn implies that the successful pursuit of the engaged life does not require one to develop all the strengths and virtues; one can be successful just by developing those character strengths that one possessed the most at the onset of the engaged life.

The six virtues and 24 character strengths can be measured using the Values in Action Inventory of Strengths (VIA-IS; Peterson & Seligman, 2001; Peterson, Park, & Seligman, 2006), which can be taken and scored online at: http://www.authentichappiness.sas.upenn.edu/questionnaires.aspx). The questionnaire asks respondents to endorse 240 items – 10 for each of the 24 strengths – on a five-point scale with anchors 1 (*not at all like me*) and 5 (*very much like me*).

Park, Peterson, and Seligman (2004) administered an online survey including both the VIA-IS and the Satisfaction with Life Scale (Diener et al., 1985) to three samples totalling 5,299 adult participants, and estimated in various ways the correlations between character strengths and life satisfaction. As expected, all 24 strengths were found to correlate positively with life satisfaction. Interestingly, hope, zest, gratitude, curiosity, and love were the strengths most strongly associated with life satisfaction, whereas love of learning, judgment, appreciation of beauty, creativity, and modesty/humility were the strengths least strongly associated with life satisfaction. A second study substantially confirmed these findings (Peterson et al., 2007). In all, these findings indicate that the strengths in the interpersonal domain are more conducive to life satisfaction than are the strengths in the achievement domain.

Empirical Assessment of the Strengths and Virtues Classification System

The classification system of strengths and virtues was developed purely on conceptual ground and by identifying similarities and differences in the philosophical teachings of different cultures. It is therefore meaningful to ask whether the VIA-IS – which was designed to measure the identified strengths and virtues – actually measures what is supposed to measure. This question was addressed by testing whether the 24 character strengths measured using the VIA-IS have the hypothesized six-factor structure, wherein each factor represents a virtue.

Macdonald, Bore, and Munro (2008) investigated the factor structure of the VIA-IS on 123 undergraduate students at an Australian university, and found that the 24 strengths did not conform to the hypothesized six-factor structure, whereas they conformed equally well to a single-factor representation and to a four-factor representation. Singh and Choubisa (2010) performed similar analyses on data gathered from 123 undergraduate students at an Indian university, and found that the 24 strengths conformed well to a five-factor representation. Finally, Brdar and Kashdan (2010) performed similar analyses on data collected from 881 undergraduate students at Croatian universities and found that the 24 strengths had a four-factor structure, and that the main factor explained nearly 50 per cent of the total variance in item scores, which suggests that the VIA-IS measures mostly a single virtue superfactor. In all, these studies show that the VIA-IS does not measure well Peterson and Seligman's (2004) classification system of strengths and virtues, and that the latter may need re-elaboration, modification, and probably simplification in the form of reduction of the number of virtues.

Brdar and Kashdan's (2010) classification of the 24 virtues measured using the VIA-IS is based on the following four factors: interpersonal strengths (lead by fairness, teamwork, kindness, forgiveness, and love), fortitude (led by perspective, judgement, originality, intelligence, and valour), conscientiousness (led by zest, hope, curiosity, humour, and perseverance), and vitality (led by prudence, self-regulation, perseverance, humility/modesty, and spirituality). The correlations between the four factors ranged from .61 to .73 and hence were strong. Therefore, it is not surprising to learn that Brdar and Kashdan found that the four virtues have virtually the same patterns of correlations with measures of well-being. In particular, all four virtues correlated with life satisfaction (range of r = .34–.49), the needs for autonomy, competence, and relatedness (range of r = .26–.47), and the orientations to happiness of pleasant life, engaged life, and meaningful life (range of r = .17–.48). In all, these findings indicate that the VIA-IS measures mostly a single, super virtue, which in turn is positively related to a range of indicators of hedonic and eudaimonic well-being.

Are virtues any different from the Big Five personality traits? Perusing the list of character strengths shown in Table 4.4 one can easily spot correspondences between the two trait models. For example, all three strengths of humanity would seem to fall under the agreeableness umbrella, and specific strengths of courage (persistence and integrity) and temperance (self-regulation) would seem to fall under the conscientiousness umbrella. Turning attention to the four virtues identified by Brdar and Kashdan's (2010), interpersonal strengths would seem to imply a combination of extraversion and agreeableness, fortitude is remarkably close to openness to experience, and conscientiousness naturally is a carbon copy of conscientiousness, whereas vitality does not appear to have a correspondence in the Big Five personality model. Empirically, strengths were found to correlate with the Big Five traits (Macdonald et al., 2008), and Park and co-workers (2004) reported in the discussion section of their paper that they had data showing that strengths predict life satisfaction over and above the contributions of the Big Five personality traits. In all, it is likely that strengths can add predictive power to the regression equation of subjective well-being, but given the uncertainties on the overall organization of strengths into virtues, this research issue needs further conceptual and empirical study.

Empirical Identification of Strengths and Virtues

What if character strengths and virtues had been researched empirically, using the same psycholexical approach pioneered by Allport and Odbert (1936), which eventually led to the identification and validation of the Big Five personality model? Somewhat paradoxically, Allport and Odbert when looking at the adjectives and short descriptions of the English language had encountered many 'character evaluations' – such as 'immoral' and 'generous' – that could have been useful for identifying character strengths; yet, they ruled them out as inapt for personality description. Since then personality psychology has largely ignored character strengths and virtues with a few exceptions (e.g., Cawley III, Martin, & Johnson, 2000; De Raad & Van Oudenhoven, 2011).

De Raad and Van Oudenhoven (2011) applied the psycholexical approach to the Dutch language, administered a previously selected list of 153 virtue descriptors to 200 pairs of participants, mostly university students, and asked them to produce both self-ratings and ratings of their partner. Principal component analysis (a statistical technique similar to exploratory factor analysis) of the combined self- and other-ratings revealed the existence of six components or virtues, which are shown in Table 4.5. Based on the labels and the descriptions

Table 4.5 *Virtues identified by De Raad and Van Ouden-hoven (2011), applying the psycholexical approach to the Dutch language and their descriptions*

Virtue	Characteristic
Sociability	■ Love
	■ Friendship
	■ Happiness
	■ Support
	■ Empathy
	■ Caring about others
Achievement	■ Ambition
	■ Dutifulness
	■ Consistency
	■ Agency
Respectfulness	■ Civilized
	■ Good
	■ Modest
	■ Law-abiding
Vigour	■ Certain
	■ Courageous
	■ Resourceful
Altruism	■ Merciful
	■ Big-hearted
Prudence	■ Integrity
	■ Subtle
	■ Discrete
	■ Philosophical

of the virtues, De Raad and Van Oudenhoven's sociability and vigour virtues correspond very well with Peterson and Seligman's (2004) humanity and courage virtues, respectively. Moreover, De Raad and Van Oudenhoven's achievement and respectfulness virtues correspond fairly well with Peterson and Seligman's wisdom and temperance virtues, respectively. Finally, De Raad and Van Oudenhoven's altruism and prudence virtues seem not to have correspondents in Peterson and Seligman's system. At face value, altruism and prudence appear to be ubiquitous virtues, which apply to many cultures beyond the Dutch culture, but they were missed in Peterson and Seligman's system. Therefore, the findings suggest that the psycholexical approach applied to the Dutch culture has produced a broader, more comprehensive classification system of virtues.

Are There Consistently Positive and Consistently Negative Traits?

This section has reviewed what is known about character strengths and virtues, and their relationships with the Big Five personality traits, subjective well-being, and psychological well-being. We have seen that Peterson and Seligman's (2004) conceptual approach and De Raad and Van Oudenhoven's (2011) empirical approach have produced partially overlapping six-virtue classification systems. Therefore, more research is needed to identify a comprehensive and agreed upon classification system for virtues and their underlying character strengths.

Although research on virtues and strengths is still work in progress, there is no doubt that the character strengths and virtues identified to date are all positive traits, with no exception. They are actually more than just 'positive traits'; they are *ethical traits*, that is, positive traits that also constitute markers of moral behaviour and guides for the ethical development of personality. The same could not be said of the positive traits analysed in the previous sections of this chapter. For example, trait intrinsic motivation can be regarded as a positive trait – in that it fosters cognitions, emotions, and behaviours that support psychological well-being – but not as an ethical trait, as there is no social institution that depicts the intrinsically motivated individual as an ethical model for others to follow. In all, character strengths and virtues are positive traits by 'socially-agreed definition'.

Although there is uncertainty about the exact number, meaning, and structure of character strengths and virtues, empirical evidence (Park, Peterson, & Seligman, 2004) suggests that strengths and virtues (a) are related to but somewhat distinct from the Big Five personality traits, and (b) predict life satisfaction and possibly other indicators of well-being over and above the effects that the Big Five personality traits have on the same outcome variables. Therefore, although more research is needed, character strengths and virtues are positive traits because of the unique empirical relationships they have with subjective well-being and psychological well-being.

Are character strengths and virtues consistently positive traits? This is a more complex question that needs to be decomposed into two separate questions. First, is it possible that possessing too much of a strength or virtue hinders well-being? For example, could it be that too much humanity or love could lead to self-destruction? Second, is it possible that possessing too much of a strength or virtue hinders another strength or virtue? For example, could it be that too much humanity or love could hinder creativity or achievement? In order to explore these possibilities, we will next consider some ancient and contemporary conceptions of virtues that state the ubiquitous presence of trade-offs, and hence the broad principle that we cannot have it all.

FROM CONFUCIUS AND ARISTOTLE TO SCHWARTZ, SHARPE, AND GRANT

Confucius

Confucius was born near the city of Qufu in China in or about 551 BC. He is universally recognized as the main Chinese philosopher. He did not write books on his own, but the *Analects* (Leys, 1997) narrate his life and contain verbatim reports of some sharp exchanges he had with disciples and visitors, which provide a lively picture of Confucius' conception of character strengths and virtues. Given that the *Analects* focus entirely on ethics, one would expect Confucius to be a somewhat boring person. Yet, his self-concept speaks to the contrary:

> The Governor of She asked Zilu about Confucius. Zilu did not reply. The Master said: 'Why did you not say "He is the sort of man who, in his enthusiasm, forgets to eat, in his joy forgets to worry, and who ignores the approach of old age"?'
>
> (Leys, 1997, p. 31)

Not surprisingly, when Confucius turns his attention to how people strive for virtue, he warns, 'I have never seen anyone who loved virtue as much as sex' (p. 41), which would seem to suggest that the first core virtue in Confucius' classification system is not to take oneself too seriously. In what follows, we will consider five important ways in which Confucius differs from Peterson and Seligman's (2004) conceptualization of virtues.

Confucius was chiefly concerned with politics, meant as the relentless and flexible striving towards a harmonious society. For Confucius social harmony is 'the better', so that every attempt to change human beings for the better consists of enhancing social harmony. For Confucius ethics should drive politics to the extent that politics becomes a natural extension of ethics. As such, Confucius' conception of well-being is inherently society oriented. Whereas for Western psychologists well-being resides primarily in the person and secondarily in the quality of the relationships one has with others, for Confucius well-being resides primarily in the relationships a person has with others and in the capacity to fulfil one's social roles.

The key social roles are government and family roles. In each role, Confucius emphasizes the dyadic relation between two persons, wherein generally one member of the dyad is subordinate to the other member. The five *cardinal* dyadic relations are the ones between minister and emperor, son and father, wife and husband, brother and brother, and friend and friend (Yang, 1993). Irrespective of its importance or position in the power hierarchy, every role is equal in that it allows the person who fulfils it to excel in the exercise of the role and hence to contribute to social harmony. At the person level, the key virtue required to fulfil one's own role as a human being is humanity, from which all other core virtues derive. Therefore, the first important way Confucius differs from Peterson and Seligman's (2004) conceptualization is that he considers humanity essential for the existence of any other virtue, whereas in Peterson and Seligman's conceptualization it is possible for a person with no humanity to possess other virtues to a high extent.

Surprisingly, neither Peterson and Seligman's (2004) conceptual classification of virtues nor De Raad and Van Oudenhoven's (2011) empirical classification of virtues includes the virtue of goodness, which arguably is the simplest and most referred to by parents and tutors around the globe when they try to socialize their children. Instead, Confucius provides a precise and down-to-earth definition of goodness:

> Zigong said: 'What would you say of a man who showers the people with blessings and who could save the multitude? Could he be called good?' The Master said: 'What has this to do with goodness? He would be a Saint! Even Yao and Shun would be found deficient in this respect. As for the good man: what he wishes to achieve for himself, he helps others to achieve; what he wishes to obtain for himself, he enables others to obtain – the ability simply to take one's own aspirations as a guide is the recipe for goodness'.
>
> (Leys, 1997, p. 28)

Therefore, the second important way Confucius differs from Peterson and Seligman's (2004) conceptualization is that he includes goodness among the core virtues that stem from humanity.

In agreement with Peterson and Seligman (2004), Confucius regards wisdom as a core virtue stemming from humanity. Moreover, Confucius compares wisdom with goodness:

> A man without humanity cannot long bear adversity and cannot long know joy. A good man rests in his humanity, a wise man profits from his humanity.
>
> (Leys, 1997, p. 15)

Although both wisdom and goodness are expressions of humanity – so that absence of humanity entails absence of both virtues – they differ sharply in the way they relate to humanity: the former 'uses' it to achieve, the latter 'resides' in it. In terms of Bakan's (1966) theory, Confucius could be said to view wisdom as an agentic virtue and goodness as a communal virtue. This in turn implies a certain degree of incompatibility between wisdom and goodness, as in any relation with others wisdom fosters achievement whereas goodness fosters union. Therefore, the third important way Confucius differs from Peterson and Seligman's (2004) conceptualization is that he includes potential trade-offs between core virtues across contexts of activity and social roles.

The potential trade-offs between different virtues can be seen in Confucius' conception of teaching, which he represents as a dyadic and hierarchical relation between teacher and student. Given that the context of teaching involves both achievement and relatedness, who is the ideal teacher, a good teacher or a wise teacher? Confucius' position is unequivocal:

> When dealing with a man who is capable of understanding your teaching, if you do not teach him, you waste the man. When dealing with a man who is incapable of understanding your teaching, if you do teach him, you waste your teaching. A wise teacher wastes no man and wastes no teaching.
>
> (Leys, 1997, p. 75)

Unlimited goodness, instead, would lead a teacher to teach every student no matter what. Confucius' idea that wisdom is primary in teaching has probably influenced the Chinese proverb 'Teachers open the door, but you must enter by yourself', which again establishes sharp boundaries to a teacher's goodness. Therefore, the fourth important way Confucius differs from Peterson and Seligman's (2004) conceptualization is that – with the exception of humanity, which is the overarching and necessary virtue – the various core virtues are not equally valuable across all contexts and social roles: some virtues – like respectfulness and obedience – are primary in some contexts – e.g., when fulfilling the role of son – and other virtues – such as wisdom – are primary in other contexts – e.g., when fulfilling the role of teacher. In turn, this implies that for Confucius there is only one virtue – humanity – that one should seek to maximize, whereas all the other virtues have to be evaluated and pursued accordingly in their due degrees in context. In all, for Confucius it is not sensible to develop only one's own signature strengths, as there will be situations in which those strengths are useless or even harmful, whereas other strengths are useful.

The *Analects* often use the concept of harmony, and various sentences suggest that a virtuous person can foster social harmony by developing inner balance, avoiding the extremes of 'going beyond' and 'falling short'. The concept of inner balance is the main theme of *The Doctrine of the Mean*, a book attributed either to Tsze-sze, Confucius' grandson, or to anonymous Confucian scholars.

The doctrine of the mean states that the perfectly virtuous person will strike a balance between opposing emotions and strivings, and by doing so will be able to influence favourably the course of events:

> While there are no stirrings of pleasure, anger, sorrow, or joy, the mind may be said to be in the state of Equilibrium. When those feelings have been stirred, and they act in their due degree, there ensues what may be called the state of Harmony. This Equilibrium is the great root from which grow all the human actings in the world, and this Harmony is the universal path which they all should pursue. Let the states of equilibrium and harmony exist in perfection, and a happy order will prevail throughout heaven and earth, and all things will be nourished and flourish.
>
> (The Internet Classics Archive by Daniel C. Stevenson, Web Atomics, 1994–2009a, Chapter 1)

Perhaps the strongest psychological and testable argument Confucius raises in favour of equilibrium over 'going beyond' and 'falling short' is that equilibrium fosters resilience in face of enduring challenges:

> The Master said 'Men all say, "We are wise"; but being driven forward and taken in a net, a trap, or a pitfall, they know not how to escape. Men all say, "We are wise"; but happening to choose the course of the Mean, they are not able to keep it for a round month'.
>
> (The Internet Classics Archive by Daniel C. Stevenson, Web Atomics, 1994–2009a, Chapter 7)

Therefore, the fifth important way Confucius differs from Peterson and Seligman's (2004) conceptualization is that he defines the ideal moral development of the person as one in which the various virtues are possessed and enacted in their due degrees.

Aristotle

Aristotle was born in Greece in 384 BC. He is universally recognized as one of the main ancient Greek philosophers and a founder of Western philosophical thought. He wrote numerous books on a wide range of topics, and condensed his conception of ethics and virtues in the *Nicomachean Ethics* (The Internet Classics Archive by Daniel C. Stevenson, Web Atomics, 1994–2009b). He viewed virtues as expressions of the proper functioning of the individual, and hence as the way towards *eudaimonia*, which can be regarded as a type of happiness that is very akin to Seligman's (2002) concept of authentic happiness. He also viewed virtues as the necessary complement of intellect, and thought that the highest eudaimonic level is achieved when both virtues and intellect are developed. Aristotle was thus interested in ethics and virtues primarily because he wanted to identify the type of character that is most conducive to eudaimonic well-being.

In what follows, we will consider four important ways in which Aristotle differs from Peterson and Seligman's (2004) conceptualization of virtues.

Aristotle considered *practical wisdom* paramount for virtues to the extent that, if it is absent, the benefits of all virtues will be wasted: 'for the one determines the end and the other makes us do the things that lead to the end' (The Internet Classics Archive by Daniel C. Stevenson, Web Atomics, 1994–2009b, IV 13). For example, a person with good character who sees somebody in danger will try to help, but without practical wisdom, may do so by running unnecessary risk to nobody's advantage, and hence will act recklessly, not courageously. Therefore, the virtue of courage, as well as any other virtue, requires practical wisdom in order to exist and manifest itself in virtuous behaviour. By the same token, practical wisdom is of no use in itself; in order to be useful practical wisdom requires virtue. As Moss (2011) argued, for Aristotle virtue is a non-intellectual state, whose function is to provide the content of goals; in that specific sense, only virtue can make the goal right. Practical wisdom and virtue are thus necessary conditions for each other: 'It is not possible to be good in the strict sense without practical wisdom, nor practically wise without moral virtue' (The Internet Classics Archive by Daniel C. Stevenson, Web Atomics, 1994–2009b, IV 13). In all, practical wisdom is not a virtue in itself, but it determines the appropriate virtue for the situation at hand and its appropriate level, and guides the virtue towards its end.

The first important way Aristotle differs from Peterson and Seligman's (2004) conceptualization of virtues is that (a) he disentangles practical and theoretical wisdom, (b) he does not consider practical wisdom to be a virtue, and (c) he considers practical wisdom essential to the same existence of all virtues. Aristotle would therefore criticize Peterson and Seligman's (2004) model of virtues by pointing out that, for example, humanity with no practical wisdom is just a vague, unsubstantiated longing for something one might do to help others – a virtue 'in theory' – without a chance to become a real virtue and to produce effective virtuous behaviour.

Aristotle believed that every virtue has its own due degree of existence and expression, that is, every virtue has a 'golden mean':

> There are three kinds of disposition, then, two of them vices, involving excess and deficiency respectively, and one a virtue, viz. the mean, and all are in a sense opposed to all; for the extreme states are contrary both to the intermediate state and to each other, and the intermediate to the extremes; as the equal is greater relatively to the less, less relatively to the greater, so the middle states are excessive relatively to the deficiencies, deficient relatively to the excesses, both in passions and in actions.
>
> (The Internet Classics Archive by Daniel C. Stevenson, Web Atomics, 1994–2009b, II 8)

The mean is virtue in itself, and it manifests itself both as a state of character and as virtuous behaviour. Therefore, the second important way Aristotle differs from Peterson and Seligman's (2004) conceptualization of virtues is that he states that possessing too much of a virtue will foster non-virtuous behaviour and will hinder eudaimonic well-being. In particular, Aristotle would criticize Peterson and Seligman's prescription to cultivate one's own signature strengths on the ground that excess development of a virtue will not lead to virtuous behaviour.

For Aristotle every virtue is important, and virtuous behaviour requires the development of all virtues, in addition to the development of practical wisdom. Therefore, the third important way Aristotle differs from Peterson and Seligman's (2004) conceptualization of virtues is that virtuous behaviour requires an all-rounded ethical development of character. As such, Aristotle would criticize Peterson and Seligman's prescription to cultivate only one's own signature strengths on the ground that the development of only a small set of strengths will lead to a deformed character, analogous to a body with long arms and short legs.

In conclusion, Aristotle believed that all virtues are important and hence should be developed. Moreover, all virtues should be developed to their due degrees and should be deployed in context to their due degrees. For each virtue, he prescribed to develop an internal golden mean in character and an external golden mean in action. He believed that one learns the external mean by practicing the internal mean through habits. Once the internal mean eventually becomes a settled state, a person has acquired highest moral virtue as second nature. In all, Aristotle's conceptualization of virtues is more similar to Confucius' – in particular with reference to an optimal mean development of each virtue as well as to the need of cultivating all virtues – than it is to Peterson and Seligman's (2004). The next section will focus on how Aristotle's conception has influenced the conceptualizations of contemporary psychologists.

Schwartz and Sharpe: The Psychological View of Practical Wisdom

In a position paper, Schwartz and Sharpe (2006) recognized the importance of the character strengths and virtues identified by Peterson and Seligman (2004), but expressed their disagreement with the underlying conceptual model on three grounds: (a) strengths and virtues should be considered functionally interdependent, (b) the Aristotelian principle of moderation should be applied to the overall development of all the strengths and virtues by pursuing their relative balance, and (c) the Aristotelian concept of practical wisdom should be regarded as the fundamental precondition for the proper deployment of strengths and virtues in context.

Building on Aristotle's arguments, Schwartz and Sharpe (2006) argued that 'strengths do not come with their conditions of application attached to them' (p. 382), and hence in every situation one has to determine the relative relevance of virtues (i.e., which virtues are most applicable to this situation?), the possible conflicts between relevant virtues, and the specific ways the relevant virtues should be deployed in order to achieve a positive outcome. They argue that these three problems – relevance, conflict, and specificity – can only be tackled using practical wisdom.

The need for practical wisdom can be best illustrated with reference to moral dilemmas. Aristotle recognized that in every specific context of activity, different virtues apply, and they often are in conflict with each other. For example, consider a judge who has to decide the sentence for someone who was found guilty beyond a reasonable doubt by a jury of peers. Two conflicting virtues apply to that context: justice and mercy. Should the judge apply the law by the book – and hence deploy the virtue of justice – or forgive and let the offender walk free from court – and hence deploy the virtue of mercy? What might the consequences of either action be? If the offender committed the crime by sheer error of judgment, a strict sentence may be an excessive punishment that may destroy the life of an otherwise good person. If instead the offender committed the crime by deliberate and callous determination, a merciful sentence may reinforce the offender's sense of impunity and determination to reiterate the crime. Is there any straightforward, 'procedural', or administrative way to calculate the average between the virtues of justice and mercy? No, because, according to Aristotle, justice and mercy are not completely opposite virtues. In particular, justice is the virtue that lies between the vices of cruelty and softness, whereas mercy is the virtue that lies between the vices of cruelty and uncaring. Therefore, justice and mercy share only one referent vice, and hence they are only partially opposite to each other. This in turn implies that in order to find the 'golden mean' between justice and mercy, the judge of this example will have to resort to practical wisdom; without it, justice and mercy will be useless in context, and the sentence will more likely be wrong. In all, this example shows that, no matter how good one's intentions are, mere intentions do not help much when deciding one's course of action in a specific context.

Schwartz and Sharpe (2006) argued that a proper deployment of virtues in a specific context requires three components of practical wisdom – discernment, perceptiveness, and imagination – and that these personal assets are not included in the virtue of wisdom nor in any other virtue of Peterson and Seligman's (2004) classification system. Moreover, they argued that practical wisdom does not include only the skills needed to achieve one's own goals; it also includes the will to do good, that is, the will to act in order to foster the common good, and not just one's own good. Therefore, Grant and Sharpe view practical wisdom as an executive function that guides the deployment of virtues in context towards the common good. We will review in Chapter 6 theories that might capture some aspects of this complex and potentially relevant executive function.

Grant and Schwartz: The Inverted U Curve

What does 'too much of a good thing' mean? The expression 'good thing' implies that the 'thing' is a variable that predicts some positive outcome, and as such can be called a 'positive thing'. The expression 'too much of' implies that, passed a certain threshold, the 'positive thing' no longer predicts the positive outcome or even predicts less of it, and hence becomes a 'neutral thing' or even a 'negative thing'. Graphically, 'too much of a good thing' implies that the relationship between the positive outcome (e.g., happiness), plotted on the vertical axis, and the 'thing' (e.g., the virtue of justice), plotted on the horizontal axis, is concave-down or has an inverted U shape, such that happiness grows as a function of justice up to a certain threshold value of justice, beyond which it decreases as a function of justice. Whenever there is an inverted U relationship, the optimal outcome (i.e., the most positive value of the outcome variable) is attained for the threshold value of the predictor variable; any increment of the predictor variable passed the threshold will result in a sub-optimal outcome. In all, the inverted U relationship is a mathematical and graphical representation of the Aristotelian moderation claim. This mathematical representation is the same as the Yerkes–Dodson Effect that we have reviewed in Chapter 3 (section *Reversals*) with reference to the relationships between learning, performance, and hedonic tone, on one hand, and arousal on the other.

In a position paper, Grant and Schwartz (2011) reviewed empirical studies pointing out that the relationships between four of the virtues identified by Peterson and Seligman (2004) – wisdom, courage, humanity and justice – and well-being is concave-down, as one would expect based on Aristotelian principles. For example, high levels of *learning orientation* – a construct akin to love for learning within the virtue of wisdom – were found to reduce the business performance of teams (Bunderson & Sutcliffe, 2003), arguably because learning takes attentional resources away from task focus and may lead to exploratory behaviours that have a small probability to yield a return. High levels of persistence – a character strength within the virtue of courage – in the form of task practice were found to reduce individual work performance (Langer & Imber, 1979), arguably because it leads to overlearning and inflexible thinking. High levels of time spent volunteering – a behaviour consistent with the virtue of humanity – were found to reduce psychological well-being (Windsor, Anstey, & Rodgers, 2008), arguably because it increases work overload and takes time and energy away from other activities that promote one's own well-being. Finally, high levels of commitment to a work organization – an expression of the loyalty strength within the virtue of justice – were found to reduce intention to report illegal practices within the organization (Somers & Casal, 1994) – a behaviour opposite to fairness within the virtue of justice – arguably because loyalty and fairness can easily be in conflict with each other.

In all, Grant and Schwartz (2011) concluded that a wealth of empirical evidence indicates that the inverted U model represents faithfully the relationships between eudaimonic well-being, on one hand, and character strengths and virtues, on the other hand, as well the relationships between virtues and those between strengths within the same virtue. This pattern is consistent with the broad Aristotelian proposition that virtues become vices if they are possessed and deployed at excessive levels. From this perspective, character strengths and virtues are 'positive within a range', and hence cannot be regarded as consistently positive traits.

DIRECTIONS FOR FUTURE RESEARCH

The integration of the several points made in this chapter suggests four broad issues that call for debate and empirical research.

1. *How many virtues and which ones?*
   It is somewhat disturbing that there is limited overlap between Peterson and Seligman's classification system of virtues and the empirical factor structure identified using the VIA-IS. Moreover, it is puzzling that there is limited overlap between Peterson and Seligman's classification system and the classification systems that have been developed using the psycholexical approach. Future research should reach broad consensus on the structure and meaning of universal virtues.
2. *Trade-offs between virtues and the deformed body model.*
   Critics point out that Peterson and Seligman's classification system ignores the functional trade-offs between different virtues, and that Peterson and Seligman's prescription to cultivate primarily one's own signature strengths can create monstrous characters, similar to deformed bodies. Once the number and nature of strengths and virtues is ascertained, researchers will have to assess the extent to which virtues are interdependent, and base on that assessment any plan for possible interventions aiming at enhancing character. In this connection, we have seen in Chapter 2 (point 1 of section *Directions for Future Research*) that the models of psychological and subjective well-being can be criticized for being 'bodybuilder models', as they advocate a complete and unconstrained development of all components of well-being. Here, Peterson and Seligman's model is being criticized for being a 'deformed body model', as it advocates the unconstrained development of a limited set of character strengths and virtues. What is in common about the two

criticisms? Both point out the need of considering constraints in future research in the form of (a) possible trade-offs between well-being indicators and between predictors of well-being, and (b) possible curvilinear relationships between well-being indicators and their predictors.

3. *Context dependence of virtues and practical wisdom.*

The analysis of ethical dilemmas in everyday life reveals that, no matter how good one's intentions are, it is incredibly difficult to act in such a way that (a) competing moral imperatives are smoothly weighed one against the other, and (b) the effects of one's action are the best possible in that context. This, according to Aristotle and some contemporary psychologists, can only be achieved if the agent possesses plenty of practical wisdom. Future research should identify the key components of practical wisdom, and the mechanisms through which they guide the deployment of virtues. Chapter 5 will consider some personal assets – such as optimism, attentional control, and metacognition – that capture facets of the complex construct of practical wisdom.

4. *Can we truly change strengths and virtues and at what risk?*

Irrespective of whether Peterson and Seligman are right in prescribing cultivation of one's own signature strengths, it is unclear if indeed it is possible to change one's character strengths and virtues. Aristotle thought that it is possible if one adopts the habit of internal and external moderation in everyday life. However, as it is the case for all socially desirable traits, there is a risk that character enhancement efforts may turn into a self-deceiving journey towards a condition of grandiosity. Future research should determine both the feasibility of character interventions, and their possible side effects. Chapter 8 (section *Happiness-Enhancing Interventions*) will examine preliminary intervention studies that tried to enhance well-being by intervening on character strengths.

SELF-DEVELOPMENT AND UNDERSTANDING EXERCISE

This preferably is a group exercise. The group task is to discuss and reach consensual answers to the following questions (there are no right or wrong answers). For each of the Big Five traits:

(a) State what could be the evolutionary and/or social advantage to a person for being high or low in that dimension. For example, what could be the benefit of being low in extraversion (i.e., high in intro-version) or high in neuroticism (i.e., low in emotional stability)?

(b) State what could be the evolutionary and/or social advantage to a group for having a certain distribution of individual differences along that dimension among its members. For example, what could be the benefit of having members that are high in neuroticism or low in agreeableness? Is there an 'optimal' percentage of emotion-ally unstable individuals in a group?

(c) What are the ethical implications of your answers to the previous questions? In particular, is there a trait that is definitely and consist-ently unethical and hence socially undesirable? If yes, why do you think that trait 'survived' in the evolutionary process?

◊ RECOMMENDED WEB RESOURCES AND FURTHER READING ◊

Websites

Websites for reading and consultation:

- Great Ideas in Personality reviews promising research developments in the field of personality psychology at: http://www.personalityresearch.org/
- The Internet Classics Archive by Daniel C. Stevenson, Web Atomics (1994–2009a, 1994–2009b) features the *Nicomachean Ethics by Aristotle, The Doctrine of the Mean by Confucius* and many other classics at: http://classics.mit.edu/

Some of the questionnaires reviewed in this chapter can be viewed/downloaded and used freely for your own research:

- Copyright-free bank of items measuring the Big Five personality traits at: http://ipip.ori.org/
- Personal Attributes Questionnaire (PAQ; Spence, Helmreich, & Stapp, 1974, 1975; Spence & Helmreich, 1978) at: http://www.utexas.edu/courses/pair/CaseStudy/PPB5c1.html
- General Causality Orientations Scale (GCOS; Deci & Ryan, 1985b; extended by Hodgins, Koestner, & Duncan, 1996) at: http://www.selfdetermination-theory.org/questionnaires/10-questionnaires/46
- Values in Action Inventory of Strengths (VIA-IS; Peterson & Seligman, 2001; Peterson, Park, & Seligman, 2006) can be taken and scored at: http://www.authentichappiness.sas.upenn.edu/questionnaires.aspx

Reading

- Dahlsgaard and co-workers' (2005) succinct presentation of the theory of virtues and human strengths

- Schwartz and Sharpe's (2006) position paper on the role that the construct of practical wisdom should have in positive psychology
- Grant and Schwartz's (2011) meta-analysis of studies suggesting that possessing too much of a 'positive' trait carries negative consequences
- Feist's (1998) meta-analysis of the relationships between personality traits and creative achievement in the arts and sciences

5 Optimism and Self-Regulation of Emotions

INTRODUCTION

Chapter 3 highlighted that in order to act adaptively in context one needs to activate numerous self-regulatory processes. Moreover, Chapter 4 pointed out that one's personality traits and character strengths will exert an important influence on well-being, by imposing constraints on self-regulatory processes and the way they produce behaviour in context. Finally, in Chapter 4 (section *From Confucius and Aristotle to Schwartz, Sharpe, and Grant*) we reviewed an argument put forth by Aristotle and some contemporary psychologists that boils down to stating that intentions and dispositions are not sufficient to produce the 'just right' behaviour in context; one also needs 'practical wisdom', yet another resource in the psychological arsenal. Aristotle wrote that practical wisdom is not a virtue in itself, but it guides emotions and virtues towards their right end. The present chapter seeks an answer to the question: What are the key components of practical wisdom, and how do they influence well-being?

This chapter will consider selected psychological variables that tap, albeit each imperfectly, the construct of practical wisdom. These are trait-like variables, meaning that their measures look like measures of personality traits, but differ from personality traits because they are more amenable to change. As such, these variables are more appealing than personality traits insofar as one has a realistic chance to change them for the better, and by doing so to enhance well-being. We will see in Chapter 8 (section *Mindfulness-Based Cognitive Therapy and Metacognitive Therapy*) that two of these trait-like facets of practical wisdom – mindfulness and metacognitions – became the primary targets of new forms of psychotherapy that appear to be remarkably effective.

In a seminal study, Seligman, Maier, and Geer (1968) showed that when an intelligent organism is repeatedly inflicted an aversive stimulus, without having the option to escape, it will eventually stop trying to escape and, even if it is given the opportunity, it will not escape; that is, the organism has learned helplessness. The existence of *learned helplessness* demonstrates the basic principle that intelligent organisms will not engage in volitional behaviour unless they have sufficiently positive expectations about the consequences of their actions. This in turn implies that *optimism* is a precondition for volitional, intentional action. Don Quixote had plenty of optimism, but his delusions wasted it. Therefore, volitional control requires more 'muscles for bones', including a realistic cognitive representation of possible pathways leading to success, which are a key component of the broader construct of *hope*. Finally, virtually any pathway to success passes through the interaction with others, and hence success requires the ability to elicit approval and cooperation. This in turn requires accurate understanding of one's own and others' emotions, which is a key component of *emotional intelligence*. The first section of this chapter will review what is known about optimism, hope, and emotional intelligence, and how these variables relate to well-being.

Unlike the ideal world, the real world often presents people with ill-structured problems (e.g., Sternberg, 2006), that is, problems with no clear path to a solution, problems with multiple paths to a solution, problems with no solution, problems with unstated constraints, and problems to which no general rule applies. When confronting such problems, it is inevitable that we experience negative emotions. Primary negative emotions can either hinder or help problem solving depending on how the self regulates and utilizes them. Four main forms of self-regulation of emotions may be required in order to reach and maintain a state that allows adaptive behaviour in context: (a) attentional control (i.e., the ability to focus on the task and to swiftly shift attention away from the task when it is no longer required), (b) mindfulness (i.e., being intentionally and constantly aware of what happens around us and inside as it happens), (c) meta-emotions (i.e., emotions about one's own primary emotions), and (d) metacognitions (i.e., knowledge about one's own cognitive and emotional processes). The second section of this chapter will review what is known about attentional control, mindfulness, meta-emotions, and metacognitions, and how they relate to well-being. The final section outlines issues open to discussion, ongoing controversies, and directions for future research.

OPTIMISM, HOPE, AND EMOTIONAL INTELLIGENCE

Optimism

In natural language optimism represents a feeling that all is going to turn out well. In a large meta-analysis of empirical studies conducted in the field of cognitive psychology Matlin and Stang (1978) concluded that most studies depict human beings as having a natural predisposition towards positivity or, using cognitive terminology, a positive bias in recall and self-evaluation. Moreover, the majority of people expect happiness in the future, and the majority of those who are currently happy expect to be happier in the future. Evolutionary psychologists proposed that optimism is to some extent genetically determined, and became common in the population because of the evolutionary advantages it offers to individuals and groups (e.g., Buss, 1991). In particular, Tiger (1979) proposed that optimism serves the evolutionary purpose of counteracting the anxiety individuals experience when facing risk, hence allowing them to focus on the task at hand and go on with their everyday life activities as usual.

The scientific study of optimism has used two distinct definitions of the construct. Seligman and collaborators defined optimism as an individual *explanatory style* (e.g., Buchanan & Seligman, 1995; Peterson, 2000). People with an optimistic explanatory style tend to explain bad events in their lives with reference to external, unstable, and specific causes, whereas people with a pessimistic explanatory style tend to explain bad events with reference to internal, stable, and general causes. For example, an optimistic soccer player who misses a penalty kick is likely to attribute failure to a strong wind that deflected the ball, hence invoking a cause that is external to the self, temporary, and specific. In contrast, a pessimistic player is likely to attribute failure to a chronic inability to handle pressure, hence invoking a cause that is internal to the self, durable, and general.

Following the discovery of learned helplessness (Seligman, Maier, & Geer, 1968), Seligman and collaborators argued that dogs, rats, and people alike can 'learn' pessimism if, after experiencing repeated and uncontrollable undesirable events, they develop a belief that there is no contingency between their actions and the outcomes of their actions (Maier & Seligman, 1976; Peterson & Park, 1998). If the learned belief of action–outcome independence generalizes across situations, a person will develop a generalized expectancy that future outcomes are unrelated to one's own actions, which is the essence of pessimism (Peterson, 2000). In an important development of the theory of explanatory styles, Seligman (1998) proposed that people can learn optimism by experiencing positive outcomes in response to their actions, developing a belief that there is contingency between their actions and the outcomes of their actions, and generalizing their action-outcome belief across situations.

Individual differences in optimistic and pessimistic explanatory styles can be measured validly and reliably using the Attributional Style Questionnaire (ASQ; Peterson, et al., 1982). The ASQ contains 12 hypothetical scenarios, of which six are negative and six are positive. For each scenario, respondents are asked to imagine that the event described is happening to them, to report what they believe is the main cause of the event, and to rate the main cause on three scales: (a) internal–external, (b) stable–transient, and (c) general–specific. The scores from the 12 X 3 scales are then summed up to provide separate overall scores for optimistic explanatory style and pessimistic explanatory style. The two subscale scores are not perfectly and negatively intercorrelated, which indicates that when measured by the ASQ optimism is not just the opposite of pessimism, and that optimism and pessimism can coexist within the same person.

Empirical research on the consequences of the explanatory styles has focused on academic achievement. Seligman (1998) argued that an optimistic explanatory style is paramount for academic achievement, in that aptitudes and talent are wasted if optimism is absent. The evidence gathered to date is mixed. For example, Peterson and Barrett (1987) found that first-year university students who at the beginning of the year had an optimistic explanatory style performed better than students who had a pessimistic explanatory style, and that the difference in performance held after controlling for measures of academic ability and depression. On the other hand, Bridges (2001) found that explanatory styles were not as good as pre-enrolment academic ability measures in predicting academic performance. In sum, more research is needed to clarify whether indeed an optimistic explanatory style contributes to academic success, and whether interventions aimed at turning a pessimistic explanatory style into an optimistic one are beneficial.

Scheier and Carver (1985; Carver & Scheier, 2003) defined optimism as a tendency to believe that one will experience good rather than bad events in life, or at least more good than bad ones. Moreover, they proposed that this generalized expectancy is cross-situationally and cross-longitudinally stable, that is, it is a trait. Dispositional optimism can be measured validly and reliably using the Life Orientation Test (LOT, Scheier & Carver, 1985) or its revised version (LOT-R; Scheier, Carver, & Bridges, 1994; available at: http://www.psy.miami. edu/faculty/ccarver/sclLOT-R.html). The LOT-R consists of 10 items. Three items are positively worded (e.g., 'In uncertain times, I usually expect the best') and measure the optimism sub-scale; three items are negatively worded and measure the pessimism sub-scale (e.g., 'I hardly ever expect things to go my way'); the remaining four are filler items (e.g., 'I enjoy my friends a lot'). The items are scored on a five-point scale with anchors of 1 (*strongly disagree*) to 5 (*strongly agree*). The scale is treated as unidimensional by, first, reverse scoring the items of the pessimism sub-scale and, then, averaging the six items of the optimism and pessimism sub-scales. The optimism and pessimism sub-scales are not perfectly and negatively intercorrelated, which indicates that also when measured by the LOT-R optimism is not just the opposite of pessimism. Interestingly, the negative correlation between optimism and pessimism is comparatively weaker in the Chinese version of the LOT-R, which suggests that the Western concept of expectancy-value may not fully apply to Chinese and members of other Eastern cultures (Lai et al., 1998). In this connection, we have seen in Chapter 2 (section *Cross-Cultural Differences in Emotions*) that momentary positive affect and negative affect are less strongly correlated in Asians than they are in Westerners, and this cultural difference is attributed to the dialectic conception of opposites that is common across Eastern cultures; the same dialectic conception might be responsible for the weaker correlation between optimism and pessimism found in Chinese.

The LOT and the ASQ provide only weakly correlated scores of optimism (Reilley et al., 2005), which indicates that dispositional optimism and optimistic explanatory style are distinct constructs. Dispositional optimism has been the more widely investigated of the two constructs.

Numerous empirical studies found that dispositional optimism is associated with better health outcomes, health-enhancing habits, and speed of recovery from illness (see review by Scheier & Carver, 1992). For example, Scheier and Carver (1985) found that optimism in undergraduate university students predicted fewer physical symptoms during a stressful academic period. Moreover, Scheier et al. (1989) found that optimism in patients who underwent surgery predicted faster post-surgical progress, such as being able to sit on bed, walking, and resuming normal life. Finally, Shepperd, Maroto, and Ebert (1996) found that optimism in patients with coronary heart disease predicted health-enhancing habits.

Numerous empirical studies found that optimism is associated with psychological adaptation. For example, compared to pessimists, optimists have a more positive self-image (Scheier & Carver, 1992), express more satisfaction with their level of social support (Fontaine & Seal, 1997), are more ready to seek social support when needed (Scheier et al., 1986), and have better adjustment to life changes such as adjustment to college life (Aspinwall & Taylor, 1992). Optimism was also found to correlate negatively with depressive symptoms and distress (Chang, 1998; Schweizer, Beck-Seyffer, & Schneider, 1999; Boland & Cappeliez, 1997; Marshall & Lang, 1990), and positively with life satisfaction (Boland & Cappeliez, 1997; Chang, Maydeu, & D'Zurilla, 1997; Chang, Asakawa, & Sanna, 2001; Myers & Diener, 1995).

The wide-ranging effects of dispositional optimism raised the suspicion that the construct might just be an aggregate of Big Five personality traits. Dispositional optimism was indeed found to correlate strongly with emotional stability and extraversion; moreover, agreeableness and conscientiousness explained additional variance in optimism over and above the variance explained by emotional stability and extraversion (Sharpe, Martin, & Roth, 2011). Despite the strong links with other traits, optimism and depression were found to be good predictors of happiness and life satisfaction controlling statistically for the Big Five personality traits (Quevedo & Abella, 2011). In sum, although related to four of the Big Five personality traits, dispositional optimism contributes uniquely to happiness and life satisfaction.

Numerous empirical studies (see reviews by Scheier & Carver, 1992 and by Scheier, Carver, & Bridges, 2001) have found that dispositional optimism is associated with more use of adaptive coping strategies – such as acceptance, positive reinterpretation of negative events, and humour – and less use of maladaptive coping strategies – such as denial, wishful thinking, and disengagement (the concepts of adaptive and maladaptive coping are reviewed in Chapter 3, section *Stress and Coping*). In general, optimism is associated with approach coping, whereas pessimism is associated with avoidance coping. This supports the broad proposition that people who are confident about eventual success will keep trying no matter how difficult the problem is, whereas people who are doubtful about the outcome of an endeavour will seek distraction, engage in wishful thinking, and eventually stop trying.

Coping was found to be the key mediator of the relationship between optimism and adaptation (Scheier & Carver, 1992). Three complementary explanations of the mediation process have been proposed. First, optimists view life problems as less severe than pessimists do (Blankstein, Flett, & Koledin, 1991). Second, positive expectations lead to more effective problem solving and, in turn, fewer adverse consequences (Scheier & Carver, 1992). Third, optimism leads to more positive affect that, in turn, reduces depressive symptoms (Chang & Sanna, 2001; Peterson, 2000). The rationale for these explanations is grounded in Carver and Scheier's (1981, 1990, 2000) cruise control model, which was reviewed in Chapter 2 (sections *Origins and Consequences of Affect* and *The Dual Nature of Affect: Signal and Cause of Progress*), according to which people keep trying to achieve goals only if their expectancies of success are sufficiently positive. In turn, if movement towards the goals is sufficient, then affect will be positive; otherwise, if progress is insufficient, affect will be negative. Therefore, because they have comparatively more expectations of success, optimists are theorized to cope more adaptively, to make more rapid progress towards their goals, and hence to experience more positive affect and less negative affect throughout their endeavours.

The empirical evidence overwhelmingly shows that dispositional optimism is a positive trait, as it correlates with a wide range of indicators of health, resilience, and well-being. However, a number of researchers pointed out the risks associated with extremely high levels of optimism. For example, Haaga and Stewart (1992) argued that extreme optimism might lead to overestimation of one's own skills to cope with a challenge. Milam and co-workers (2004) added that extreme optimism might lead to expectations that cannot be met, and suggested that 'there could be an "optimal" margin of optimism' (p. 177). In this vein, Seligman and co-workers (1995) prescribed to teach children 'accurate optimism' (p. 298), not extreme optimism. Carver, Sheier, and Segerstrom (2010) acknowledged that optimism may have drawbacks in contexts wherein the stronger goal persistence of the optimist backfires, but concluded that optimism offers overwhelmingly more benefits than costs. Yet, if this is indeed the case, one could argue that the link between optimism and success exists because of the beneficial effects of other variables that help to convert wishful and positive thinking into winning behaviour.

Hope

Snyder and co-workers (1991; Snyder, 2000) proposed a theory of *hope* in an attempt to explain how the wishful and positive thinking inherent in optimism can, under some circumstances, become volitional thinking that leads to adaptive, goal-directed behaviour. They defined hope as a positive trait constituted of three components of thinking: (a) *goal thinking* (i.e., the ability and willingness to set clear goals for one's own action), (b) *pathways thinking* (i.e., the ability and willingness to develop viable strategies to achieve the set goals), and (c) *agency thinking* (i.e., the ability and willingness to deploy the strategies and to sustain one's own motivation in using them until the goals are fully achieved). Goals must be interesting in order to provide the target for volitional behaviour; in general, goals of moderate difficulty are more suitable for pathways and agency thinking than easy goals are (Snyder, 2002). Pathways are viable routes to goals, and to have many such routes to choose from is particularly important in ill-structured and difficult situations, wherein there are many impediments (Snyder, Rand, & Sigmon, 2005). Agency is the motivational component of goal-directed behaviour, and represents the confidence in one's ability to initiate and sustain goal-directed behaviour (Snyder et al., 2003).

Hope theory states that all three components of thinking are necessary in order for a person to possess hope and to engage in adaptive, goal-directed behaviour (Snyder, 2002). In particular, absence of clear and interesting goals makes strategies and agency utterly useless. Moreover, strategic thinking without agency has no chance to produce goal-directed behaviour. Finally, agency without valid strategies can produce behaviour but it can hardly produce organized and adaptive behaviour. Pathways thinking and agency thinking go hand in hand, and are often correlated within the same person, but they are not the same variable, and both are needed in order to produce adaptive, goal-directed behaviour.

Individual differences in pathway thinking and agency thinking can be measured validly and reliably using the Adult Hope Scale (AHS; Snyder et al., 1991), a 12-item questionnaire which uses four items to measure pathways thinking (e.g., 'There are lots of ways around any problem'), four items to measure agency thinking (e.g., 'I've been pretty successful in life'), and the remaining four items as fillers (e.g., 'I feel tired most of the time'). Moreover, an unpublished manuscript presents a Revised Snyder Hope Scale (RHS; Shorey et al., 2007).

Hope theory states that, compared to people with less dispositional hope, people with more dispositional hope tend to be more successful in goal pursuit, and hence experience more positive emotions and fewer negative emotions (Snyder, 2002). Several studies found that hope is associated with better academic and sport performance (e.g., Marques, Pais-Ribeiro, & Lopez, 2009; Snyder, 2002), supporting the hypothesis that hope facilitates goal attainment in achievement contexts. Moreover, some studies found that hope is associated with life satisfaction (e.g., Gilman, Dooley, & Florell, 2006) and, among adolescents, buffers the effects of negative life events on life satisfaction (Valle, Huebner, & Suldo, 2006), supporting the hypothesis that hope fosters subjective well-being.

However, these findings are somewhat inconclusive because they were not obtained controlling for dispositional optimism, which arguably is the main competing explanatory factor for the effects of dispositional hope. Carver and Sheier's (2003) theory of optimism and Snyder's (2002) hope theory are similar in that they both provide explanations for why generalized positive expectancies foster well-being. Yet, the two theories differ in focus: the former focuses on generalized expectancies of positive outcomes, whereas the latter focuses on positive evaluations of personal agency in goal-pursuit situations. The key questions are (a) are optimism and hope distinct variables? and (b) if yes, are they both needed as explanatory factors of subjective and psychological well-being?

Gallagher and Lopez (2009) tackled comprehensively these questions by measuring optimism, hope, subjective well-being, and psychological well-being on a sample of 591 undergraduates at a Midwestern university in the United States. First, using confirmatory factor analysis to control for measurement error, they obtained an estimated correlation of .66 between the optimism factor and the hope factor; this means that optimism and hope overlap to some extent but are nonetheless distinct variables. Then, using SEM to control for measurement error, they obtained the estimated standardized regression effects of the two variables on well-being indicators that are shown in Table 5.1. In general, optimism is more strongly related to subjective well-being, whereas hope is more strongly related to psychological well-being. More specifically, optimism is a very good predictor of self-acceptance and life satisfaction, whereas hope is a very good predictor of purpose in life and personal growth. In sum, dispositional hope is a novel and powerful addition to the class of predictors of psychological well-being.

Table 5.1 *Structural regression of well-being indicators (criterion variables) on optimism and hope (predictor variables) (selected standardized regression coefficients from Gallagher & Lopez, 2009)*

Well-being	Positive expectancies	
	Optimism	Hope
Psychological well-being		
Self-acceptance	.68	.26
Positive relations	.47	.30
Autonomy	.07	.49
Environmental mastery	.51	.44
Purpose in life	.23	.73
Personal growth	.09	.70
Subjective well-being		
Life satisfaction	.66	.14
Positive affect	.24	.54
Negative affect	−.15	−.12

Emotional Intelligence

Emotions have often been considered distinct from, and sometimes even opposite to reason. Mowrer (1960) countered sharply this view and argued that emotions are 'a high order of intelligence' (p. 308). Salovey and Mayer (1990) were the first to build on this notion, and proposed a conceptual definition of emotional intelligence as the ability (a) to appraise and express emotions, (b) to regulate emotions, and (c) to utilize emotions to enhance reasoning. As a whole, Salovey and Mayer viewed emotional intelligence as the ability to understand emotions in self and others, and to utilize this emotional understanding as information that contributes to thinking and acting. Numerous researchers then proposed their own definitions of emotional intelligence (e.g., Bar-On, 1997; Epstein, 1998; Goleman, 1995). All these new definitions portrayed emotional intelligence as a personality trait that should be assessed using self-report questionnaires, and not as an ability that should be assessed using objective performance tests, as maintained by Salovey and Mayer (1990).

Goleman's (1995) conception of emotional intelligence had the strongest impact on the general public, and sparkled endless controversies. He defined emotional intelligence as a personality trait with five interrelated components: (1) *emotional self-awareness* (i.e., knowing one's own true emotions), (2) *managing one's own emotions* (e.g., reducing anxiety and regaining a good mood after a negative experience), (3) *using emotions for self-motivation* (e.g., being able to delay gratification), (4) *recognizing emotions in others* (i.e., being empathic), and (5) *managing emotions in others* (e.g., supporting and motivating others). He argued that emotional self-awareness helps to make good decisions, managing one's own emotions helps to cope with stress, using emotions for self-motivation helps to achieve, recognizing emotions in others helps to establish and maintain good relations with others, and managing emotions in others helps to lead others effectively. Finally, he claimed that emotional intelligence predicts academic, occupational, and relational success better than general intelligence does. This claim was deemed speculative by many researchers (e.g., Roberts, Zeidner, & Matthews, 2001), as it went well beyond the data available at that time.

In a seminal paper, Davies, Stankov, and Roberts (1998, Study 2) administered 10 emotional intelligence measurement instruments (including both ability tests and self-report questionnaires) and a self-report questionnaire measuring the Big Five personality traits to 300 US Air Force recruits. Factor analysis of the whole set of measured variables revealed that:

> Self-report measures of emotional intelligence ... are related to neuroticism, extraversion, agreeableness, and verbal ability ... [and] the linkage between cognitive abilities and emotional intelligence is weak.
>
> (Davies et al., 1998, p. 1005)

In sum, 'little remains of emotional intelligence that is unique and psycho-metrically sound' (p. 1013). From the ashes Davies and co-workers left behind, new efforts have been made to develop psychometrically sound measures of emotional intelligence. We will next focus on two research approaches: Mayer and Salovey's (1997) work on emotional intelligence as an ability and Schutte and co-workers' (1998) work on emotional intelligence as a personality trait.

Mayer, Salovey and co-workers (Mayer, Caruso, & Salovey, 1999; Mayer, & Salovey, 1997; Salovey, Bedell, Detweiler, & Mayer, 2000; Salovey, Mayer, & Caruso, 2005) proposed a four-branch definitional model of emotional intel-ligence, which is summarized in Table 5.2. Each branch of emotional intel-ligence requires a set of distinct abilities. *Emotional perception and expression* requires the ability to read and express accurately one's own feelings; this is

Table 5.2 *The four-branch ability model of emotional intelligence developed by Salovey and co-workers (2005)*

Branch	Ability
Emotional perception and expression	■ To identify emotions in one's own physical and psychological states ■ To identify emotions in other people ■ To express emotions accurately and to express needs related to them ■ To discriminate between accurate/honest and inaccurate/dishonest feelings
Emotional facilitation of thought	■ To redirect and prioritize thinking on the basis of associated feelings ■ To generate emotions to facilitate judgment and memory ■ To capitalize on mood changes to appreciate multiple points of view ■ To use emotional states to facilitate problem solving and creativity
Emotional understanding	■ To understand relationships among various emotions ■ To perceive the causes and consequences of emotions ■ To understand complex feelings, emotional blends, and contradictory states ■ To understand transitions among emotions
Emotional management	■ To be open to feelings, both pleasant and unpleasant ■ To monitor and reflect on emotions ■ To engage, prolong, or detach from an emotional state ■ To manage emotions in oneself ■ To manage emotions in others

a necessary branch for emotional intelligence to exist. *Emotional facilitation of thought* requires the ability to use emotional intelligence in thinking processes; in particular, this involves an understanding that emotions influence thinking, and that one can thus self-regulate emotions in order to approach a problem from different perspectives. *Emotional understanding* requires the ability to analyse, interpret, and express in words one's own emotions and those of others; in particular, this involves understanding complex emotions, their meaning, and their dynamics. Finally, *emotional management* requires the ability to self-regulate emotions and to regulate others' emotions; in particular, this involves the proper use of strategies to restore a positive mental state after an unpleasant experience, such as engaging in physical exercise, relaxation, or emotional disclosure in writing (e.g., Pennebaker, 1997).

Mayer, Salovey, and Caruso (2002a, 2002b) developed the Mayer–Salovey–Caruso Emotional Intelligence Test (MSCEIT) to measure individual differences in the four branches of emotional intelligence. The MSCEIT is an objective performance test, wherein participants are given problems to solve and their answers are scored as either correct or incorrect. The correctness of an answer is determined with reference to either the most common answer in the pool of respondents or the answer provided by experts. The MSCEIT contains 141 problems. Emotional perception and expression is measured by asking participants to identify correctly emotions conveyed through facial expressions (Scale A) and abstract pictures (Scale E). Emotional facilitation of thoughts is measured by asking participants how certain emotions facilitate thinking (Scale B) and how they relate to sensations of, for example, heat and light (Scale F). Emotional understanding is measured by asking participants to associate emotions with situations (Scale G) and to explain how emotions change over time (Scale C). Finally, emotional management is measured by asking participants to rate emotions on their appropriateness to handle certain situations (Scale H) and on their effectiveness for self-regulation (Scale D).

Mayer, Salovey, and Caruso (2002b) regard the MSCEIT as a unidimensional instrument, and hence recommend using the MSCEIT total score in research and application. However, a series of studies indicated that the MSCEIT total score and the branch scores lack reliability (e.g., Føllesdal & Hagtvet, 2009), and that the eight sub-scales of the MSCEIT do not conform well to the theoretical factor structure (e.g., Keele & Bell, 2008). Moreover, the MSCEIT is strongly predicted by the Big Five personality traits and general intelligence, leading to the conclusion: 'Emotional intelligence: Not much more than g and personality' (Schulte, Ree, & Carretta, 2004, p. 1059; also see the same conclusion in Fiori & Antonakis, 2011). Finally, the four branches of MSCEIT correlate in different ways with general intelligence and the Big Five personality traits, to the extent that Fiori and Antonakis recommended using branch scores in lieu of the total score, and testing any hypothesis concerning emotional intelligence controlling for general intelligence and personality.

Shutte and co-workers (1998) developed the Emotional Intelligence Scale – which is often called Shutte Self-Report Inventory (SSRI) – to measure individual differences in emotional intelligence meant as a personality trait. The SSRI contains 33 items measuring the extent to which individuals identify and understand emotions (e.g., 'I know why my emotions change'), cultivate and regulate their own and other people's emotions (e.g., 'I help other people feel better when they are down'). Participants record their responses on a five-point scale ranging from 1 (*strongly disagree*) to 5 (*strongly agree*).

Shutte and co-workers regard the SSRI as a unidimensional scale and hence recommend using the SSRI total score in research and application. However, a series of studies indicated that the SSRI has a multifactorial structure (e.g., Davies et al., 2010; Ferrándiz et al., 2006; Petrides & Furnham, 2000), and that the SSRI total score correlates from moderately to strongly across studies with the Big Five personality traits (e.g., Brackett & Mayer, 2003; Ferrándiz et al., 2006; Saklofske, Austin, & Minski, 2003); for example, Ferrándiz and co-workers found on a sample of 115 Spanish university students that emotional intelligence correlates with extraversion ($r = .43$), openness to experience ($r = .39$), and neuroticism ($r = -.29$). In all, it seems advisable to test any hypothesis concerning self-reported emotional intelligence controlling for personality.

What is the unique contribution of emotional intelligence to well-being? Brackett and Mayer (2003) found on a sample of 207 US undergraduate students that the MSCEIT total score and the SSRI total score correlated weakly ($r = .18$), indicating that the two scales measure distinct constructs. The MSCEIT total score correlated weakly with an aggregate measure of psychological well-being ($r = .28$) and was uncorrelated with an aggregate measure of subjective well-being ($r = -.05$), whereas the SSRI total score correlated strongly with psychological well-being ($r = .69$) and correlated weakly with subjective well-being ($r = .22$), indicating that trait emotional intelligence is a better predictor of well-being than ability emotional intelligence is. Yet, this conclusion is tentative, as Brackett and Mayer did not test the relationships between emotional intelligence and well-being controlling statistically for personality traits, even if they had measures of the Big Five personality traits in their data set. Extremera and co-workers (2011) tested the relationships between ability emotional intelligence and well-being, controlling for the Big Five personality traits on a sample of 349 Spanish undergraduate students. They found that the MSCEIT total score predicted both subjective well-being and psychological well-being 12 weeks after measuring emotional intelligence and controlling statistically for the effects of personality. The unique contribution of ability emotional intelligence to well-being was modest but nonetheless statistically significant. In all, these studies suggest that emotional intelligence might play some unique, albeit limited, role in promoting hedonic and eudaimonic well-being. However, given the uncertainty about the psychometric properties of the available measures of emotional intelligence, this conclusion is tentative.

SELF-REGULATION OF EMOTIONS

Attentional Control

The theories of emotions reviewed in Chapter 2 explain the origin and consequences of emotions, but do not explicitly consider whether and how individuals regulate their own emotions. The term self-regulation of emotions refers to individuals' ability to willingly tune – either by enhancing or by suppressing – their own emotional responses. The simplest form of self-regulation of emotions is behavioural, and consists of deliberately avoiding stimuli that were previously experienced as either aversive or pleasant. For example, one can down-regulate negative emotions about rats by not engaging in speleological missions, and hence reducing the likelihood of encountering rats. By the same token, a student who needs to concentrate on exam preparation can down-regulate positive emotions that would interfere with the task by switching off mobile phone and tablet, and hence preventing any arousal from social interaction.

A more sophisticated form of self-regulation of emotions is attentional, and consists of focusing on, or shifting attention away from emotion-arousing stimuli. For example, one can down-regulate negative emotions about rats by shifting attention away from rats and internal representations of rats. By the same token, students can energize their exam preparation efforts by focusing on the prospect of earning good grades in the upcoming exams. The ability to deliberately focus and shift attention in order to regulate one's own emotions is called *attentional control*.

When experiencing negative emotions, attentional control is the ability to inhibit automatic fight-or-flee responses and to foster the exploration of more elaborate and more potentially adaptive responses to a perceived challenge or threat (Derryberry & Reed, 2002). Specifically, attentional control includes the ability to process and organize stimuli in order to maintain a positive emotional state, the ability to delay gratification, and the ability to cope with environmental change (Rothbart et al., 2004). As a whole, attentional control is theorized to be a dispositional component of executive functioning (Mathews, Yiend, & Lawrence, 2004), the large class of cognitive abilities that help organize information, generate plans, coordinate thinking and action towards goal achievement, and hence support volitional control.

Individual differences in attentional control were identified in children (Rothbart & Derryberry, 1981), and can be measured validly and reliably in adults in laboratory settings and using self-report questionnaires (Derryberry & Reed, 2002, 2009). Three facets of attentional control have been identified to date: (a) *attention focusing* (i.e., the ability to hold concentration on the task at hand), (b) *attention shifting* (i.e., the ability to swiftly switch attention from one task to another), and (c) *flexible control of thought* (i.e., the ability to rapidly focus attention on a novel task or on a known task but from a new perspective) (Derryberry, 2002).

Individual differences in the three facets of attentional control can be measured validly and reliably using the Attentional Control Scale (ACS; Derryberry & Reed, 2002; available at: http://dionysus.psych.wisc.edu/Wiki/index.php?title=Attention_Control_Scale_%28ATTC%29), a 20-item self-report inventory that uses nine items to measure attentional focus (e.g., 'When trying to focus my attention on something, I have difficulty blocking out distracting thoughts', reverse scored), seven items to measure attentional shift (e.g., 'I can quickly switch from one task to another'), and four items measuring attentional flexibility (e.g., 'I can become interested in a new topic very quickly when I need to'). Participants record their responses on a four-point scale ranging from 1 (*always*) to 4 (*almost never*).

Does attentional control influence hedonic well-being? Derryberry & Reed (2002) found that attentional control, measured as a single construct using the ACS, correlates positively with extraversion ($r = .40$) and negatively with trait anxiety ($r = -.55$), consistent with the hypothesis that attentional control has a dual effect on emotions: it fosters positive emotions and it prevents negative emotions. Moreover, research on adolescents has robustly shown that self-reported attentional control is negatively associated with a range of psychopathological symptoms, including anxiety, depression, and aggression (e.g., Muris, Mayer, van Lint, & Hofman, 2008; Muris, Meesters, & Rompelberg, 2007). Finally, Spada, Georgiou, and Wells (2010) found on a sample of 142 undergraduate students at a British university that both attentional focus and attentional shift correlate negatively with state anxiety ($r = -.40, -.38$, respectively). In sum, attentional control and some of its facets appear to foster hedonic well-being.

Does attentional control influence eudaimonic well-being? Theoretically, it should. A substantial body of evidence from cognitive neuroscience research identified a goal-directed and a stimulus-driven attentional system (Posner & Rothbart, 1998; see review by Pashler, Johnston, and Ruthroff, 2001). The goal-directed attentional system exerts top-down control of attention directed by knowledge, expectation, and current goals. The stimulus-driven attentional system exerts bottom-up control of attention responding to salient stimuli. Attentional control should allow a person facing a difficult situation to shift more easily from the stimulus-driven attentional system to the goal-directed attentional system, and hence increase the processing capacity of working memory and improve cognitive efficiency meant as the ratio between quality of performance and effort or resources needed in the task. Some empirical support to this prediction comes from a study (Cermakova, Moneta, & Spada, 2010) that found, on a sample of 240 undergraduate students at a British university, that attentional control predicts more deep approach to studying and less surface approach to studying during the week before end-of-semester examinations, when presumably students experience overload on both attentional systems. In all, although the evidence is preliminary, attentional control is likely to play a role in the processes leading to eudaimonic well-being.

Mindfulness

In Chapter 2 (section *Emotions, Feelings, and Moods*) we encountered the distinction between emotions and feelings, wherein feelings are perceptions of those emotions that pass the threshold of consciousness. The idea that emotions – particularly those that are disturbing and threaten the self – do not necessarily surface to consciousness dates back to Freud's psychoanalysis. Freud (1925) thought that ego-threatening impulses coming from the id cause anxiety, which in turn may activate *defence mechanisms*. Defence mechanisms are ego functions finalized to protect the person from real or imaginary threats. The most primitive defence mechanism is *repression*, in which disturbing thoughts and desires are buried altogether in the unconscious. Concurring to some extent with Freud, Rogers (1963) believed that the person seeks *congruence* – that is, the absence of difference and conflict between self-perceptions and reality. Whenever a specific experience challenges one's own self-structure – the self-concept and its valuing system – a conflict arises and anxiety is experienced, which in turn may activate the defences of *denial* (of the existence of the experience) and *distortion* (of the meaning of the experience). Both Freud and Rogers believed that suppression of emotions offers short-term benefits but leads to neuroticism and hence is taxing in the long run.

Gross and John (2003) developed a short questionnaire to measure individual differences in the suppression of emotions (e.g., 'I keep my emotions to myself') and conducted a series of studies on samples of US undergraduate students to examine the consequences of suppression to subjective well-being. In Study 2, they found that suppression correlates negatively with coping through venting ($r = -.43$), confirming that suppressors express their upset comparatively less and are probably less aware of it. In Study 3, they found that suppression correlates negatively with positive affect ($r = -.33$) and positively with negative affect ($r = .39$). Moreover, compared to non-suppressors, suppressors express less their positive emotions with others, whereas they do not differ from non-suppressors in the expression of negative emotions. In all, Freud's and Rogers' predictions that suppression hinders well-being is supported.

Mindfulness can be broadly viewed as opposite to suppression. Mindfulness is being intentionally and constantly aware of ongoing experience (e.g., Brown & Ryan, 2003), and hence its essence is captured in the expression 'being there', with reference to the film directed by Hal Ashby. The concept has its roots in the Eastern Buddhist traditions, which with some differences all prescribe to cultivate present-moment awareness through meditation (Baer, Smith, & Allen, 2004). Present-moment awareness is generally thought to help prevent perseverative thinking – including heightened self-consciousness, over monitoring, and rumination about upsetting events and associated negative emotions – and hence to help restore and maintain a positive state of mind in face of challenges. In sum, mindfulness is thought to provide a third important way to self-regulate negative emotions, in addition to behavioural and attentional self-regulation.

Several conceptualizations of mindfulness have been proposed. Originally, researchers treated mindfulness as a unidimensional construct. The Mindful Attention Awareness Scale (MAAS; Brown & Ryan, 2003; available at: http:// www.selfdeterminationtheory.org/questionnaires/10-questionnaires/61) measures mindfulness validly and reliably as a single construct using 15 items (e.g., 'I find myself doing things without paying attention', reverse scored) that are scored on a six-point scale with anchors of 1 (*almost always*) to 6 (*almost never*).

Researchers then began developing multidimensional conceptions of mindfulness. Bishop and co-workers (2004) proposed to distinguish two components of mindfulness: *attention regulation* and *non-judgmental attitude of acceptance*. Attention regulation is the process of directing attention towards ongoing experience without suppressing emotions and without getting trapped by the content of those emotions. Non-judgmental attitude of acceptance is the process of accepting the identified experiences with openness, detachment, acceptance, and even curiosity. Underlying both components of mindfulness is the belief that no matter how bad thoughts, emotions, and situations may look at first glance, they are transient events that signal something about reality but they are not reality itself.

Even more complex multidimensional representations were proposed in conjunction with the development of the main questionnaire that measures mindfulness. The Kentucky Inventory of Mindfulness Skills (KIMS; Baer et al., 2004) measures four components of mindfulness: (a) *observing* (i.e., the extent to which a person pays close attention to ongoing thoughts and feelings), (b) *acting with awareness* (i.e., the opposite of doing activities on 'automatic pilot'), (c) *accepting without judgment* (i.e., the openness to experience thoughts and feelings with acceptance), and (d) *describing* (i.e., the ability to express experience into words). The KIMS was subsequently developed into the Five Facet Mindfulness Questionnaire (FFMQ) (Baer et al., 2006), which splits 'accepting without judgment' into two components: (a) *non-judging of inner experience* (i.e., refraining from evaluating one's own thoughts and feelings), and (b) *non-reactivity to inner experience* (i.e., allowing thoughts and feelings to flow freely without 'locking' on them or getting caught up with them). The FFMQ measures individual differences in the five components of mindfulness validly and reliably using 39 items that are scored on a five-point scale with anchors of 1 (*never or very rarely true*) to 5 (*very often or always true*).

Brown and Ryan (2003) stated two main reasons why mindfulness should foster well-being. First, a state of keen awareness may facilitate the choice of behaviours that satisfy the basic needs for autonomy, competence, and relatedness, which were reviewed in Chapter 3 (section *Intrinsic Motivation, Extrinsic Motivation, and Self-Determination*). Second, awareness may enhance the enjoyment of the activity one is engaged in. Brown and Ryan examined the relationships between their unidimensional MAAS measure of mindfulness and a wide range of indicators of well-being in samples of US undergraduate students and adults from the general population. They found that mindfulness correlates negatively with neuroticism, negative affect, state anxiety, and state depression, and positively with positive affect, self-esteem, optimism, life satisfaction, self-actualization, and all three basic needs.

Baer and co-workers (2006) administered the five main questionnaires measuring mindfulness – including the MAAS and KIMS described above – to a sample of 613 US undergraduate students, and found strong convergence between the different measures of the same construct. Moreover, they found that all the single-construct measures of mindfulness correlate positively with emotional intelligence and openness to experience, and negatively with neuroticism. Finally, they investigated the correlations that the FFMQ facets of mindfulness have with emotional intelligence, openness to experience, and neuroticism. Of the five facets, describing was the most strongly correlated with emotional intelligence ($r = .60$), observing was the most strongly correlated with openness ($r = .42$), and non-judging of inner experience was the most strongly correlated with neuroticism ($r = -.55$).

Brown and Ryan (2003) and Bishop and co-workers (2004) warned about the risk of confusing components or facets of mindfulness with consequences of mindfulness. Baer and co-workers (2006) admitted that their five-facet conception of mindfulness is open to such risk, but they argued that two definition components of mindfulness stand firm: avoiding automatic plot and observing experience without judgment and reactivity. In all, the empirical evidence gathered to date indicates that mindfulness and some of its components are likely to play a relevant role in the processes leading to both hedonic well-being and eudaimonic well-being.

Meta-Emotions

Up to this point we have implicitly assumed that emotions are either positive or negative. According to that seemingly obvious principle, the emotion of fear should always be negative, and the emotion of joy should always be positive. Yet, riding a rollercoaster can elicit an amazingly exciting fear, and seeing the picture of a loved one we have lost can elicit a dramatically saddened joy. These and other emotional paradoxes show that the positivity and negativity of emotions is a tricky issue, and that under some circumstances unpleasant emotions can be positive and pleasant emotions can be negative. Therefore, the hedonic view of 'the better' as a state of highest positive emotionality and lowest negative emotionality might be too simple.

In recent years, philosophers approached the explanation of emotional paradoxes invoking the new concept of meta-emotions (e.g., Jäger & Bartsch, 2006), that is, emotions about one's own emotions. Gottman, Katz, and Hooven (1997) introduced the concept of meta-emotions in psychology to represent parents' emotional reactions to their children's display of emotions. Greenberg (2002) defined meta-emotions as a sub-set of secondary emotions (i.e., emotions that follow in time primary emotions), that is, secondary emotions that have as object primary emotions, such as being angry about having felt ashamed in a given situation. Most recently, Mitmansgruber and co-workers (2009) proposed that meta-emotions explain both *emotional avoidance* – a willingness not to experience emotions and alter them (Hayes et al., 2004) – and lack of mindfulness, and that they constitute yet another form of self-regulation of emotions. They also hypothesized that recurrent, trait-like meta-emotions influence well-being.

In order to test their predictions, Mitmansgruber and co-workers (2009) first developed the Meta-Emotions Scale (MES), a questionnaire of 28 items to be scored on a six-point scale ranging from 1 (*is not at all true for me*) to 6 (*is completely true for me*). The MES measures validly and reliably individual differences in four negative meta-emotions – *anger* (e.g., 'Repeatedly, I am irritated by my stupid emotional reactions'), *contempt/shame* (e.g., 'I cannot forgive myself for a long time when I have done something wrong'), *tough control* (e.g., 'I repeatedly force myself to pull myself together'), and *suppression* (e.g., 'I fight strongly against my emotions') – and two positive meta-emotions – *interest* (e.g., 'Negative emotions provide me with interesting information about myself') and *compassionate care* (e.g., 'When I experience strong negative emotions, I comfort and encourage myself').

Then, they examined on a sample of 334 undergraduate students at an Austrian university and a sample of 297 inpatients in a psychosomatic clinic in Germany the relationships between the six meta-emotions, on one hand, and life satisfaction and psychological well-being, on the other hand. In both samples negative meta-emotions correlated negatively with life satisfaction and the components of psychological well-being except for purpose in life, whereas positive meta-emotions correlated positively with life satisfaction and the components of psychological well-being except for purpose in life. Moreover, these correlations held in regression analyses controlling for experiential avoidance and mindfulness. Finally, they examined on a sample of 222 medical students at an Austrian university the relationships between meta-emotions and the Big Five personality traits. Negative meta-emotions correlated positively with neuroticism and negatively with extraversion. Positive meta-emotions correlated negatively with neuroticism and positively with extraversion, openness to experience, and agreeableness. In all, positive and negative meta-emotional traits are meaningfully related to the Big Five personality traits and are strong predictors of both subjective and psychological well-being, except for purpose in life.

The study of meta-emotions is in its early stages, but the initial findings are promising. The concept of meta-emotion is theoretically interesting because it can explain why negative emotions are not universally negative. For example, a person high in the meta-emotion of interest will respond to primary negative emotions in a more philosophical way, reacting to the incident that caused the primary negative emotions as if it contained a lesson to learn. In turn, if the meta-emotion of interest becomes a habit in one's own life, it could down-regulate or even undo primary negative emotions as they occur; so that, the person will eventually experience lower levels of negative affect throughout everyday life activities. In all, the concept of meta-emotion has the potential to explain that primary emotions do not dominate the self, and that experiencing primary negative emotions is not a hindrance to well-being if one possesses positive meta-emotions to counter them.

Adaptive and Maladaptive Metacognitions

Metacognition refers to the knowledge and beliefs about one's own cognitive regulation and the capability to deconstruct and understand them through reflection and problem solving (Flavell, 1979); it is often defined as 'cognition about cognition'. The study of metacognitions was pioneered in the field of developmental and educational psychology (Flavell, 1979; Nelson & Narens, 1990), and has been applied in the field of clinical psychology (Wells & Matthews, 1994; Wells, 2000, 2009) and more recently in the field of positive psychology (Beer & Moneta, 2010).

Wells and Matthews' (1994) and Wells' (2000, 2009) theory of psychological dysfunction focuses on maladaptive metacognitions and posits that they drive coping in response to external stimuli and to one's own internal states. The theory defines metacognitive beliefs as information about one's own cognition and internal states, and about coping strategies that can influence both. The theory states that psychological dysfunction is maintained by (a) perseverative thinking, (b) maladaptive use of attention, and (c) maladaptive coping, which conjointly constitute a *cognitive-attentional syndrome* (CAS; Wells, 2000). Maladaptive metacognitions are theorized to maintain the CAS, and to become active whenever an individual encounters a problematic situation.

Wells and Matthews' (1994) theory posits that when facing a problematic situation, an individual can operate in two distinct modes: *object mode* and *metacognitive mode*. In the object mode an individual interprets thoughts as facts, whereas in the metacognitive mode an individual interprets thoughts as cues that have to be subsequently evaluated. The object mode is theorized to be functional only in genuinely threatening situations, and to be dysfunctional in all other situations because it fosters perseverative thinking and hence maladaptive coping. The metacognitive mode is theorized to be functional across the board because it enhances evidence-based belief elaboration and hence adaptive coping. A key prediction of the theory is that, compared with individuals who score high on maladaptive metacognitive traits, individuals who score low on maladaptive metacognitive traits are more likely to operate in metacognitive mode when facing a problematic situation.

Maladaptive metacognitive traits have been studied using the Meta-Cognitions Questionnaire (MCQ; Cartwright-Hatton & Wells, 1997; available as Appendix 1 at: http://onlinelibrary.wiley.com/book/10.1002/9780470713662) or its shorter form (MCQ-30; Wells & Cartwright-Hatton, 2004; available at: http://www.mct-institute.com/therapist-resources.html) to measure five interrelated traits: (1) *positive beliefs about worry*, i.e., the extent to which a person believes that worrying is useful (e.g., 'I need to worry in order to remain organized'); (2) *negative beliefs about worry concerning uncontrollability and danger*, i.e., the extent to which a person believes that worrying is uncontrollable and dangerous (e.g., 'I cannot ignore my worrying thoughts'); (3) *cognitive confidence* (lack of), i.e., the extent to which a person lacks confidence in his or her attention and memory (e.g., 'I do not trust my memory'); (4) *beliefs about the need to control thoughts*, i.e., the extent to which a person believes that disturbing thoughts should be suppressed (e.g., 'I should be in control of my thoughts all the time'); and (5) *cognitive self-consciousness*, i.e., the extent to which a person focuses attention inwards to monitor own thoughts (e.g., 'I monitor my thoughts'). The MCQ-30 measures validly and reliably individual differences in the five metacognitive traits, each measured by six items. Items are scored on a four-point scale ranging from 1 (*do not agree*) to 4 (*agree very much*).

Wells and Cartwright-Hatton (2004) found, on a mixed sample of 182 university students and employees in a British University, that all five maladaptive metacognitive traits correlate with measures of perseverative thinking, including worry, obsessive-compulsive symptoms, and trait anxiety. Using SEM, Spada, Mohiyeddini, and Wells (2008) examined, on a mixed sample of 1,304 students and workers in the United Kingdom, the unique relationships between maladaptive metacognitive traits and negative emotions, and found that state anxiety is predicted only by positive beliefs about worry, whereas state depression is predicted only by positive beliefs about worry, (lack of) cognitive confidence, and beliefs about the need to control thoughts. Spada and Moneta (2012) found, on a sample of 528 undergraduate students from a London university, that maladaptive metacognitive traits as a single latent variable predict more evaluation anxiety, more avoidance coping, and more surface approach to studying during the week before end-of-semester examinations. Finally, Beer and Moneta (2012) found, on a mixed sample of 212 workers and university students in London, that maladaptive metacognitive traits as a single latent variable predict more maladaptive coping (i.e., denial, substance use, behavioural disengagement, and self-distraction) in response to everyday life stress. In all, maladaptive metacognitions are good predictors of failure to achieve hedonic and eudaimonic well-being, but they do not seem to predict success indicators of well-being, such as positive emotions, deep approach to studying, or adaptive coping.

Beer and Moneta (2010, 2012) searched for adaptive metacognitions that could predict the success side of well-being. They made two initial assumptions. First, both object and metacognitive modes can contribute to success if they are activated each in an appropriate context and in a strategic sequential order that leads to turning setbacks into opportunities for success. Second, the adaptive use of object and metacognitive modes requires metacognitive beliefs of an agentic type that support identification of alternative pathways and flexible goal restructuring as well as the meta-emotion of interest – identified by Mitmansgruber and co-workers (2009) – in one's own primary emotional responses to challenges. Based on these assumptions and drawing from interview data, they developed the Positive Metacognitions and Positive Meta-Emotions Questionnaire (PMCEQ; Beer & Moneta, 2010) to measure validly and reliably individual differences in three adaptive metacognitive traits, each measured by six items: (1) *confidence in extinguishing perseverative thoughts and emotions* (e.g., 'When the "blues" overcomes me I tend to struggle with controlling my low mood', reverse scored); (2) *confidence in interpreting own emotions as cues, restraining from immediate reaction, and mind setting for problem solving* (e.g., 'I can stop any "negative thinking spirals" and focus on what I can do in the situation'); (3) *confidence in setting flexible and feasible hierarchies of goals* (e.g., 'When progress becomes slow and difficult I can readily adopt a step-by-step approach to remove obstacles'). Items are scored on a four-point scale ranging from 1 (*do not agree*) to 4 (*agree very much*).

Beer and Moneta (2010) found on a sample of 475 undergraduate students from a London university that confidence in extinguishing perseverative thoughts and emotions is inversely related to maladaptive metacognitive traits, and hence does not stand as an independent trait, whereas confidence in interpreting own emotions as cues, restraining from immediate reaction, and mind setting for problem solving and confidence in setting flexible and feasible hierarchies of goals are distinct from maladaptive metacognitive traits, and correlate with trait intrinsic motivation. Moreover, Beer and Moneta (2012) found on a mixed sample of 212 workers and university students in London that these two traits as a single latent variable predict more adaptive coping (i.e., active coping, planning and strategy use, using functional support, and positive reframing) in response to everyday life stress. In all, the initial evidence suggests that adaptive metacognitions might be good predictors of success to achieve hedonic and eudaimonic well-being, and hence to complement maladaptive metacognitive traits as metacognitive predictors of the whole construct of well-being.

DIRECTIONS FOR FUTURE RESEARCH

The integration of the several points made in this chapter suggests five broad issues that call for debate and empirical research.

1. *The core feature of practical wisdom.*
   At its onset, this chapter promised to identify facets of the Aristotelian construct of practical wisdom. We have seen in Chapter 4 (section

Aristotle) that for Aristotle practical wisdom determines the appropriate virtue for the situation at hand and its appropriate level, and hence guides emotions and virtues towards their right end. All the constructs studied in the present chapter do a good job of explaining how some difficult goals can be achieved by regulating and channelling emotions, but fall short of explaining how the right goals are chosen. There is an exception, though. Insofar as mindfulness gives insight into one's own emotions, it may help one choose goals that are consistent with, and promote one's own authentic feelings and basic needs. We may then conclude that goals grounded in authentic feelings are 'right'. Are they? Aristotle – as any other philosopher who does not believe in the intrinsic goodness of uncultured human nature – might argue that in order to be 'right' a goal should promote the common good in context, and that may sometimes require to drive a bulldozer over one's own feelings, whether authentic or not. If this argument is correct, than positive psychology has to date missed perhaps the most positive of human qualities, that is, the ability and determination to choose the goals that maximize the common good in context.

2. *The virtue of quitting.*

With the exception of mindfulness, all the constructs covered in this chapter explain the reasons for success or failure in achieving goals, and hence implicitly assume that quitting is bad. Yet, there are four scenarios in which quitting is the right thing to do. First, quitting is right when the goal is unattainable, as one could save time and energy and move on to the pursuit of another, attainable goal. Second, quitting is right if in the process of approaching the goal one learns more about the goal and realizes that it is not as right as originally thought. Third, quitting is right if in the process of approaching the goal one discovers a better goal. Finally, quitting is right if the context wherein the goal was right changes in such a way that the original goal is no longer right in the changed context. Future research should study the ability and willingness to engage in constant present-moment evaluation of goals with the aim of quitting and changing goals as required.

3. *Accurate optimism or just accuracy?*

Excessive optimism may have drawbacks that are similar to those of excessive self-esteem, which we reviewed in Chapter 3 (section *Self-Esteem*), and excessive virtue, which we reviewed in Chapter 4 (section *Grant and Schwartz: The Inverted U Curve*). For this reason, Seligman proposed teaching children 'accurate optimism'. This leads to the question: can we drop one word and say that we should just teach children 'accuracy'? It is surprising that studies on the effects of optimism on performance and well-being have never controlled for participants' accuracy in evaluating the level of difficulty of the task at hand and the level of their task-related skills. Future research should investigate the effects of a generalized positive bias over and above the effects of accuracy in estimating task difficulty and own skills.

4. *The impact of self-regulation of negative emotions on the quality of relations.*

We will see in Chapter 7 (sections *The Missing Bolt in the Affect-Creativity Yoke: Negative Emotions* and *Extracurricular Activities: Developmental and Negative Experiences*) that negative emotions are a 'necessary evil' of relations, and they may even foster positive outcomes such as creativity at work and the development of hardiness. Thus, constructs representing the ability and willingness to self-regulate negative emotions – chiefly attentional control, mindfulness, meta-emotions, and metacognitions – should be personal resources that foster the adaptive experience and use of negative emotions for the purpose of developing deeper and more successful relations. In sum, research on the contextual effects of the ability to self-regulate emotions looks like a very promising area for future research.

5. *The practical wisdom of feeble emotionality: Flow.*

In Chapter 2, the hedonic model of subjective well-being was criticized for making the assumptions 'the more positive affect, the better' (point 5 of section *Future Research Directions*) and 'the more negative affect, the worse' (point 4 of section *Future Research Directions*). In this chapter we have seen that negative emotions are not necessarily harmful to an individual who has good self-regulation of emotions. As stated in point 4 above, there is evidence that, if properly self-regulated, negative emotions can even foster eudaimonic well-being. Yet, a more fundamental question arises: do we really need all these emotions – no matter if positive or negative – in order to function optimally? I once ended up having emergency surgery in a major city hospital in the middle of the night. The surgeon in charge of the night shift was a man in his late sixties who had seen everything one can possibly see in life, and whose looks showed it all; he displayed surface empathy combined with authentic psychopathy, and his welcoming message to the operating table was: 'Hmm, yes, they just would not retire us'. He remained unemotional and totally absorbed in the task throughout the procedure. Despite the lack of emotions, he patched me beautifully. Could it be that he did such a good job right because he had virtually no emotion? We will consider such a possibility in Chapter 6, which deals with flow, a state of feeble emotionality and intense task focus that is often associated with good work performance.

SELF-DEVELOPMENT AND UNDERSTANDING EXERCISE

This exercise consists of carrying out a not-so-simple qualitative analysis on one of your relevant experiences of success. You will conduct a mini interview study in which you play both the role of the participant and the role of the researcher.

Participant's Phase

Think of a project that started with profound difficulties, which you eventually managed to resolve to score a full success. This can be either a personal or a professional endeavour. You should recall your predominant thoughts, emotions, and behaviour throughout your endeavour. You should also try to identify stages and turning points. In particular, when and how did you realize that you coped successfully or at least came close to achieving your goal(s)? When you feel that you have all the main points of your personal story clear in your mind and well organized, write it up as a 2–5 page long story and store your document for future use.

Researcher's Phase

Two days after writing your personal story, take your written document and analyse it sentence by sentence. For each unit of text, determine whether any of the constructs reviewed in this chapter (i.e., optimism, hope, emotional intelligence, attentional control, mindfulness, meta-emotions, and metacognitions) could be used to explain the thoughts, emotions or behaviours you described in that unit. For example:

- Were you optimistic or pessimistic about the final outcome of your endeavour at that stage, and how did such expectations influence your subsequent thoughts, emotions, and behaviours?

■ Did you use emotional intelligence, and if so in which way(s)?
■ Did you experience meta-emotions, and if so how did they influence your subsequent thoughts, emotions, and behaviours?

If a construct applies to a unit of text, add it as a note or comment to the unit. You are free to apply more than one construct to the same unit of text. When you have interpreted and annotated your entire text, answer the following questions:

(a) What construct did appear most frequently in the annotations of your text?
(b) Is that construct the most important in explaining why you eventually succeeded in your endeavour? If not, which construct was the most relevant in determining your success?
(c) In which way(s) did the most relevant construct influence your behaviour throughout your endeavour?

◊ RECOMMENDED WEB RESOURCES AND FURTHER READING ◊

Websites

Some of the questionnaires reviewed in this chapter can be viewed/downloaded and used freely for your own research:

■ Life Orientation Test Revised (LOT-R; Scheier, Carver, & Bridges, 1994) at: http://www.psy.miami.edu/faculty/ccarver/sclLOT-R.html
■ Attentional Control Scale (ACS; Derryberry & Reed, 2002) at: http://dionysus.psych.wisc.edu/Wiki/index.php?title=Attention_Control_Scale_%28ATTC%29
■ Mindful Attention Awareness Scale (MAAS; Brown & Ryan 2003) at: http://www.selfdeterminationtheory.org/questionnaires/10-questionnaires/61
■ Meta-Cognitions Questionnaire (MCQ; Cartwright-Hatton & Wells, 1997) as Appendix 1 at: http://onlinelibrary.wiley.com/book/10.1002/9780470713662
■ Meta-Cognitions Questionnaire 30 (MCQ-30; Wells & Cartwright-Hatton, 2004) at: http://www.mct-institute.com/therapist-resources.html

Reading

■ Carver and co-workers' (2010) meta-analysis of research conducted on dispositional optimism
■ Gallagher and Lopez' (2009) attempt to disentangle empirically the effects of hope and optimism on well-being

- Schulte and co-workers' (2004) empirical study assessing the extent to which the construct of emotional intelligence is independent of general intelligence and personality
- Brown and Ryan's (2003) validation paper of the Mindful Attention Awareness Scale (MAAS)
- Cartwright-Hatton and Wells' (1997) validation study of the Meta-Cognitions Questionnaire (MCQ)

6 Flow

INTRODUCTION

In the early seventies, Mihaly Csikszentmihalyi interviewed surgeons, rock climbers, composers, dancers, chess players, and athletes, asking them to report their experience when they engaged in the most challenging phases of their preferred endeavours, and he reported the findings in the seminal book *Beyond Boredom and Anxiety* (1975/2000). The interviews produced a wealth of textual descriptions that, although coming from persons with different backgrounds and working in different domains, shared six main themes: (1) focused *concentration* on the present activity, with centring of attention on a narrow stimulus field (e.g., 'When I start, I really do shut out the world'), (2) *merging of action and awareness* ('I am so involved in what I am doing ... I don't see myself as separate from what I am doing'), (3) *loss of self-consciousness* (e.g., 'I am less aware of myself and my problems', (4) *sense of control* over one's own actions (e.g., 'I feel immensely strong'), (5) *unambiguous feedback* from the activity (e.g., 'you don't feel you have all sorts of different kinds of demands, often conflicting, upon you'), and (6) *autotelic experience*, that is, the sense that the activity is an end in itself, and hence runs independently of external rewards (e.g., 'the act of writing justifies poetry') [the word autotelic is the combination of two Greek words, *auto* (self) and *telos* (goal)]. Csikszentmihalyi named *flow* the simultaneous enactment of these six themes, and set out to search for its origins and consequences.

Flow is a state of profound task-absorption, enhanced cognitive efficiency, and deep intrinsic enjoyment that makes a person feel one with the activity. To put it simply, flow is fun, as any everyday life activity – whether it is socially defined as 'work' or 'leisure' – can lead to flow; so that, if we find flow recurrently in daily activities we will live a more enjoyable and fulfilling life.

Yet, is flow any good other than for providing enjoyment and inner fulfilment? Thirty years after introducing the concept of flow, Csikszentmihalyi (1996) interviewed 91 outstanding individuals in the fields of science, business, and the arts, and asked them to report their experience prior to conceiving novel ideas and seeing them recognized by peers as major innovations. Intense and recurrent flow in work emerged as the main theme underlying each innovation.

Flow Theory states that flow has a direct impact on subjective well-being by promoting the experience of happiness in the here and now (Csikszentmihalyi, 1982). Moreover, the theory states that flow has a long-lasting indirect effect on subjective well-being in that it motivates a person to face and master increasingly difficult tasks, thus promoting lifelong organismic growth (Csikszentmihalyi, 1990). Therefore, Flow Theory constitutes a synthesis of hedonic and eudaimonic approaches to subjective well-being, and has the potential to allow for the quadrature of the circle, that is, for enabling to construct a life that combines enjoyment, fulfilment, and achievement with happiness.

In terms of its relationships with other constructs in the field of positive psychology, flow is everywhere and nowhere, so to speak. The concept of flow is related to the concept of intrinsic motivation, which we reviewed in Chapter 3 (section *Intrinsic Motivation, Extrinsic Motivation, and Self-Determination*) and Chapter 4 (section *Trait Intrinsic and Extrinsic Motivation*), but the nature of the relationship is not yet agreed upon. Insofar as flow occurs frequently in an individual's life, it signifies the profound engagement of authentic happiness, which we reviewed in Chapter 4 (section *Virtues, Strengths, and Authentic Happiness*), but it is not clear if flow is an antecedent or a consequence of authentic happiness. Yet, despite these uncertainties, or perhaps because of them, flow is vigorously researched particularly in the fields of organizational psychology and sports psychology, wherein the maximization of human performance is paramount.

The bad news is that, not surprisingly, the operationalization of flow has proved to be a formidably complex task. Therefore, this chapter first reviews the different ways flow has been conceptualized and measured in empirical studies, and then moves on to the analysis and discussion of what we have learned so far about the origins and consequences of flow. The final section outlines issues open to discussion, ongoing controversies, and directions for future research.

MEASUREMENT METHODS AND MODELS OF FLOW

The Flow Questionnaire and the First Model of Flow

By now you have probably asked yourself the question: do I have flow? In order to answer this seemingly simple question Csikszentmihalyi (Csikszentmihalyi & Csikszentmihalyi, 1988) developed the Flow Questionnaire. The questionnaire presents three quotations that vividly describe the flow experience:

1. My mind isn't wandering. I am not thinking of something else. I am totally involved in what I am doing. My body feels good. I don't seem to hear anything. The world seems to be cut off from me. I am less aware of myself and my problems.
2. My concentration is like breathing. I never think of it. I am really quite oblivious to my surroundings after I really get going. I think that the phone could

ring, and the doorbell could ring, or the house burn down or something like that. When I start, I really do shut out the whole world. Once I stop, I can let it back in again.

3. I am so involved in what I am doing. I don't see myself as separate from what I am doing (Csikszentmihalyi & Csikszentmihalyi, 1988, p. 195).

These quotations capture the three core components of flow: *centring of attention* (e.g., 'my concentration is like breathing I never think of it'), *merging of action and awareness* (e.g., 'I don't see myself as separate from what I am doing'), and *loss of self-consciousness* (e.g., 'I am less aware of myself and my problems'). The questionnaire then asks whether one has ever felt similar experiences; this requires just a single yes/no answer to all three flow quotations, and hence allows classifying participants into those who experienced flow in their lives (*flow-ers*) and those who did not (*non-flow-ers*). Next, the questionnaire asks flow-ers to list freely the activities in which they experienced flow; researchers can then code these flow-conducive activities into categories such as 'work activity' or 'leisure activity'. Next, the questionnaire asks flow-ers who reported two or more flow-conducive activities to select the one that best represents the experience described in the quotations, that is, the best flow-conducive activity. Finally, the questionnaire asks participants to rate their subjective experience when they are engaged in the best flow-conducive activity (flow-ers only) and in other activities (both flow-ers and non-flow-ers) – such as studying or spending time with family – using numerical scales that had emerged from interviews (Csikszentmihalyi, 1975/2000), such as 'I get direct clues on how well I am doing' and 'I enjoy the experience and the use of my skills'.

The main strength of the Flow Questionnaire is that it provides a single definition of flow that captures the simultaneous presence of the key components of flow, and hence allows a straightforward estimation of the prevalence of flow, that is, the percentage of people in a population (e.g., students or workers) who have experienced flow in their lives. It also allows breaking down the overall prevalence figure for a population by groups of activities (e.g., work or study) as well as specific activities (e.g., taking an exam or playing soccer).

Researchers at the University of Milan, Italy, used intensely the Flow Questionnaire on samples of adolescents and workers across a wide range of cultures and found that (a) flow is a universal experience, (b) the specific activities that foster flow are shaped by culture and hence differ somewhat across cultures, and (c) in all cultures flow is more likely to occur in work or structured leisure activities (e.g., Delle Fave & Massimini, 2003; Massimini, Inghilleri, & Delle Fave, 1996).

Because flow may be influenced by major historical events, it is interesting to examine data collected after the 2008 onset of the ongoing global economic recession. Figure 6.1 shows the prevalence rates of flow across daily activities estimated on 367 highly educated British workers from a wide range of occupations,

Figure 6.1 *Prevalence rates of flow across daily activities estimated on a sample of 367 highly educated British workers (data from Moneta, 2012b)*

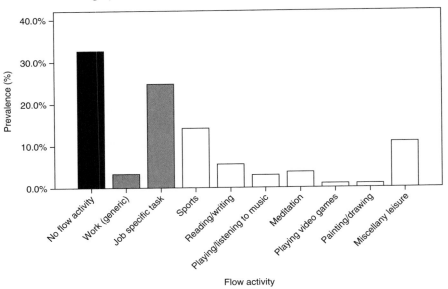

including as main groups 85 managers, 61 health specialists, 61 administrators, 23 IT specialists, 23 consultants, 20 investment bankers, 16 commercial traders, 15 researchers, and 63 participants in miscellaneous occupations (Moneta, 2012b). Thirty-three per cent of participants reported not having experienced flow in their lives (non-flow-ers). The participants who reported having experienced flow and selected a work activity as best representing the quotations of flow experience (work flow-ers) were 28 per cent. The majority of those participants selected a specific activity within work. The specific work activities were so disparate that they could not be further classified. The participants who reported having experienced flow and selected a leisure activity as best representing the quotations of flow experience (leisure flow-ers) were 39 per cent. The range of selected leisure activities was wide, with sports and reading/writing emerging as the most frequent. In all, the findings indicate that flow is common, but not easy to achieve in work, at least in the current historical juncture.

Given that flow can occur in a wide variety of activities, what are the common characteristics that make each of them equally suitable for flow? In an effort to answer this question, Csikszentmihalyi (1975/2000) proposed the first model of the flow state. The model assumes that at any point during a challenging endeavour (e.g., a doctor performing a surgery or a chess master playing a tournament game), people assess the perceived challenges from the activity and the perceived skills in carrying out the activity, and update their perceptions depending on how well the activity is going. The model partitions the experience in the endeavour into three possible states – flow, anxiety, and boredom – that are represented as non-overlapping areas of a challenge by skill Cartesian space. Flow occurs when there is an equivalent ratio of perceived challenges from the activity to perceived skills in carrying out the activity. Anxiety occurs when the perceived challenges from the activity exceed the perceived skills in carrying out the activity, whereas boredom occurs when the perceived skills in carrying out the activity exceed the perceived challenges from the activity.

In order to understand more precisely what the model entails, it must be operationalized. Figure 6.2 shows a plausible operationalization. Imagine that challenge, skill, and flow could each be measured on a ten-point scale ranging from 1 (*low*) to 10 (*high*). The figures inside the cells represent the flow intensity one is expected to experience for the corresponding values of challenge and skill. The shaded cells, wherein challenge equates skill, represent the flow state. The upper diagonal cells, wherein challenge exceeds skills, represent the anxiety state. The lower diagonal cells, wherein skill exceeds challenge, represent the boredom state. It can be seen that flow intensity reaches its maximum value of 10 in the shaded cells. Moreover, flow intensity remains constant across all the shaded cells (e.g., flow intensity equals 10 for challenge = 1 and skill = 1, and it equals 10 for challenge = 10 and skill = 10). This means that the balance

Figure 6.2   *An operationalization of the first model of the flow state*

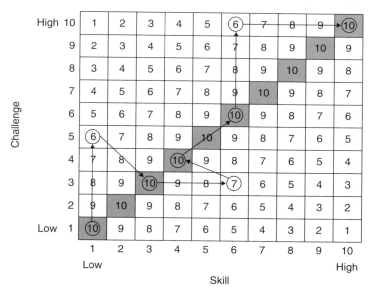

Notes: The figures inside the cells represent the flow intensity (measured on a scale ranging from 1 'low' to 10 'high') one is expected to experience for the corresponding pair of values of challenge and skill. The shaded cells, wherein challenge equates skill, represent the flow state.

of challenge and skill is the only thing that matters in order to get into flow. Finally, an endeavour is represented dynamically as a less-than-perfect 'walk' in quest of flow and towards higher and higher levels of challenge and skill.

The model specifies a causal process leading to flow, anxiety, and boredom, which unveils dynamically as the actor interacts with the activity. The Flow Questionnaire is a good measurement method for the purpose of identifying flow, describing the experience associated with it, and estimating its prevalence. But it is not good for the purpose of testing the hypothesized flow model shown in Figure 6.2 in everyday life. This limitation led to the development of the new measurement method and models that are presented next.

The Experience Sampling Method and the Quadrant and Octant Models

The original version of the Experience Sampling Method (ESM; Csikszentmihalyi, Larson, & Prescott, 1977; Csikszentmihalyi & Larson, 1987) gathers eight self-reports per day in response to electronic signals randomly generated by pagers that respondents wear for a whole week. After each signal, participants provide their answers on the Experience Sampling Form (ESF). The first few questions of the form reconstruct the activity a person was engaged in when beeped and its context. Then, the form presents scaled items designed to measure the intensity of a range of feelings, including core elements of flow (e.g., concentration, self-consciousness, and feeling of control) and the key predictor variables of challenges from the activity and skills in the activity. The main strength of the ESM is that, unlike traditional pen-and-pencil questionnaires, it asks the relevant questions on the spot, when participants are engaged in their daily tasks and in their natural environments, and hence minimizes mnemonic distortions and maximizes ecological validity. The main challenge posed by the ESM is that it produces a huge amount of data that are difficult to analyse and make sense of.

In order to test the prediction that challenges and skills foster flow, Csikszentmihalyi and co-workers had to develop new models of flow – the quadrant (Csikszentmihalyi & LeFevre, 1989) and octant (Massimini, Csikszentmihalyi, & Carli, 1987; Delle Fave & Massimini, 2005) models – and new ingenious ways to summarize and analyse the data gathered using the ESM. The *quadrant model*, which is shown in Figure 6.3, partitions the world of experience in four main states – flow, anxiety, boredom, and apathy – that are represented as quadrants of a challenge by skill Cartesian space in which both axis variables are standardized for each participant separately, with the 0 value representing the mean calculated over all the observations gathered during the week of the study.

The *octant model*, which is shown in Figure 6.4, partitions experience in eight states that are represented as arc-sectors ('channels') of 45 degrees each of a challenge by skill Cartesian space in which both axis variables are individually

Figure 6.3 *The quadrant model of the flow state*

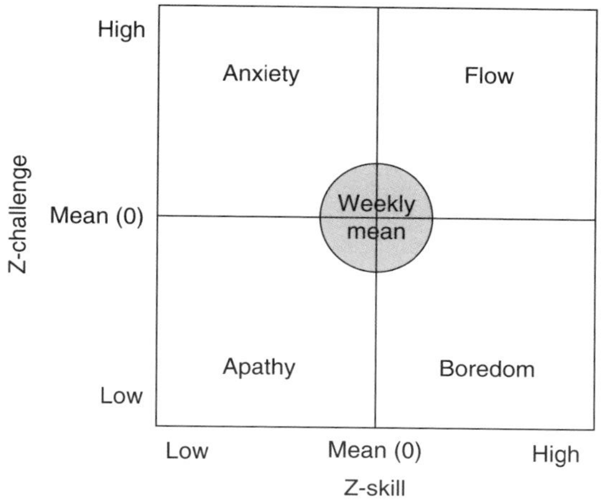

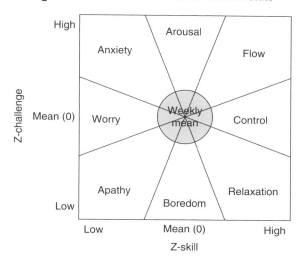

Figure 6.4 *The octant model of the flow state*

Source: Adapted from Delle Fave and Massimini (2005), European Psychologist, *10*(4): 264–274, Hogrefe and Huber Publishers. © 2005 Hogrefe & Huber Publishers (now Hogrefe Publishing), www.hogrefe.com, DOI 10.1027/1016-9040.10.4.264.

standardized as for the quadrant model. The two models are similar in that both represent flow as a state in which a participant perceives challenge and skill greater than the weekly average and in relative balance with each other, and differ in that the octant model provides a more detailed classification of states. Both models differ from the original model shown in Figure 6.2 because they state that if there is a balance of challenge and skill, and both variables score below the weekly average, a person will experience apathy, and not flow as the original model states.

Massimini and co-workers (Massimini & Carli, 1988; Massimini, Csikszent-mihalyi, & Carli, 1987) used the octant model for the first time to analyse ESM data gathered on a sample of 47 Italian high school students in Milan. They found that the mean score of numerous facets of subjective experience – such as concentration and feeling strong – was highest in the flow channel (high-challenge/high-skill) and lowest in the apathy channel (low-challenge/low-skill). The findings were replicated in numerous samples of different age and culture (Carli, Delle Fave, & Massimini, 1988; Csikszentmihalyi, 1990, 1997; Delle Fave & Bassi, 2000; Delle Fave & Massimini, 2005; Haworth & Evans, 1995). The findings of those studies are consistent with the hypothesis that challenges and skills foster flow.

What about the effect of challenges being in relative balance with skills? The term 'balance' implies that something special happens when the variables equal each other. Consider for example a two-component glue: if only one component is applied on the surfaces to be glued together, the glue will be ineffective; the glue will be most effective if you use both components in equal amounts. Do the findings suggest that anything like that happened? Not quite: the findings obtained using the quadrant and octant models could be obtained if simply challenge and skill had separate and independent effects on experience. Recognition of this led the researchers to develop statistical regression models (see review in Moneta, 2012a) to disentangle the effects of challenge and skill from the effect of their balance. Studies on different samples and different facets of experience found that balance has an effect on the quality of experience over and above the effects of challenge and skill, although the effect of balance is small compared to the independent effects of challenge and skill (Ellis, Voelkl, & Morris, 1994; Moneta & Csikszentmihalyi, 1996, 1999; Pfister, 2002).

In sum, the use of the ESM in combination with the development of new models of flow allowed investigating the flow state in daily life, and testing the effects that perceived challenges and skills and their balance have on flow. Yet, the studies carried out to date are affected by two problems. First, as Ellis and co-workers (1994) pointed out, many of the investigated facets of experience are not clearly connected to the flow construct, and hence cannot be regarded as indicators of flow. In particular, variables like 'alert–drowsy', 'active–passive', or 'sad–happy' have never been theorized to be an integral part of flow. Second, the construct validity of the scales used to tap the investigated facets of experience has never been assessed by standard psychometric methods, such as exploratory and confirmatory factor analysis. This limitation led to the development of the new measurement methods and models that are presented in the next section.

The Standardized Flow Scales and the Componential Model

Several standardized scales were developed to measure flow (Bakker, 2008; Engeser & Rheinberg 2008; Keller & Bless, 2008; Schüler, 2010). Two scales – the Flow State Scale-2 (FSS-2) and the Dispositional Flow Scale-2 (DFS-2) developed by Jackson and Eklund (2002, 2004) – are selected here because they are consistent with Csikszentmihalyi's (Jackson & Csikszentmihalyi, 1999) latest conception of flow, they measure flow both as a state and as a trait, and they are the most frequently used in research.

Jackson and Csikszenmihalyi (1999) described flow as a state characterized by nine components. Six of them are components that Csikszentmihalyi (1975/2000) identified from the onset of flow research and that were listed at the beginning of this chapter: concentration, merging of action and awareness, loss of self-consciousness, sense of control, unambiguous feedback, and autotelic experience. The remaining three components have emerged in more recent research: *dynamic balance between challenge and skill, clear proximal goals,* and *loss of time-awareness or time acceleration.* Experiencing a dynamic balance between challenge and skill means that, when in flow, people typically perceive that the activity is demanding but that they possess the skills required to meet its demands. Moreover, having clear and proximal goals means that, when in flow, people have a strong sense of what they want to do and achieve every step of the way. Finally, the experience of loss of time-awareness or time acceleration means that, when in flow, people become unaware of time passing or perceive that time either speeds up or slows down.

Jackson and Csikszentmihalyi (1999) regarded these nine components as correlated dimensions of the flow construct that can trade-off in determining the intensity or level of flow. If the level of all components is highest, a person will be in a most intense, complex, and ordered flow state. If some components reach highest level whereas others reach only medium or low levels, the contributions to flow of the different components will sum up in producing a flow state that will be overall less intense, complex, and ordered than the ideal flow state.

Jackson and Eklund (2002, 2004) applied the nine-component view of flow to measure flow as a state, a broad trait (i.e., the tendency to experience flow frequently and intensely across a wide range of situations), and a domain-specific trait (i.e., the tendency to experience flow frequently and intensely in specific contexts of activity such as study, sports, work or leisure). In this way, flow is similar to intrinsic motivation in that both variables can be studied as either states or traits (see the definition of intrinsic motivation as a state in Chapter 3, section *Intrinsic Motivation, Extrinsic Motivation, and Self-Determination,* and as a trait in Chapter 4, section *Trait Intrinsic and Extrinsic Motivation*). They developed, refined, and validated two standardized questionnaires: the Flow State

Scale-2, which measures intensity of flow as a state, and the Dispositional Flow Scale-2, which measures intensity of flow as either a general trait or as a domain-specific trait (Jackson & Eklund, 2002, 2004). In all, the componential approach provides a comprehensive definition of flow, and has generated measures of flow – both as a state and as a trait – that are psychometrically more valid and reliable than those provided by the Flow Questionnaire and the ESM. Yet the componential approach is affected by two problems.

First, the componential model contradicts the models that researchers developed in conjunction with the Flow Questionnaire and the ESM, in that it ignores altogether the distinction between antecedents of flow (i.e., factors that can, under some circumstances, cause flow) and indicators of flow (i.e., experiences and behaviours that are, under some circumstances, caused by flow). In particular, the dynamic balance between challenge and skill was regarded as a predictor of flow (i.e., a factor that increases the likelihood that a person will experience flow in a given situation) in all the ESM studies reviewed in the previous section of this chapter. A similar argument applies to other components of flow. For example, clear proximal goals and unambiguous feedback can be regarded as factors that increase the likelihood of experiencing flow, rather than expressions of flow itself. Therefore, there is the need of more conceptual work in order to classify the nine components of flow into antecedents of flow and indicators of flow.

Second, even if the number of components of flow is restricted to the three key components – concentration, merging of action and awareness, and loss of self-consciousness – the componential approach will encounter paradoxes. For example, assume that the three key components are each measured on a five-point scale ranging from 1 (*low*) to 5 (*high*), and that the overall flow score is calculated as the arithmetic mean of the scores of the three components. Jimmy has just encountered a snake in the wild, and he scores 5 on concentration and 1 on both merging of action and awareness and loss of self-consciousness, earning an overall flow score of 2.33, which is slightly below the mid-point of the scale. Does it mean that Jimmy has a bit of flow? Perhaps, but it is more likely that he is in a state of anxiety. Helen is just approaching bedtime, and she scores 1 on concentration and 5 on both merging of action and awareness and loss of self-consciousness, earning an overall flow score of 2.33. Does it mean that Helen has a bit of flow? Perhaps, but it is more likely that she is in a state of boredom or relaxation, as she hugs a fluffy pillow. Generalizing beyond the cases of Jimmy and Helen, the componential approach will give a flow score to everybody in virtually every situation, except for when they are unconscious. This is in striking contrast with the operationalization of flow carried out by the Flow Questionnaire, which requires that all three key components of flow – concentration, merging of action and awareness, and loss of self-consciousness – be simultaneously present in order to define a mental state as flow.

Overall Assessment

This section introduced in chronological order the models – original, quadrant, octant, and componential models – and measurement methods – the Flow Questionnaire, the Experience Sampling Method, and the standardized scales of the componential approach – that researchers developed and used in conducting research on flow. The analysis reveals that, although the concept of flow has remained relatively stable since its first formulation, the models and operationalizations of flow have changed substantially over time, and are not perfectly consistent with one another. For what concerns measurement methods, the Flow Questionnaire is the best method for measuring prevalence of flow, the EXM is the best method for measuring subjective experience and flow in daily activities, and the standardized scales of the componential model are the best methods for measuring intensity of flow upon completion of an activity or as a trait. No single model-method pair emerges as the overall winner. In all, there is enough convergence of views to conclude that flow is a real and relevant phenomenon, but researchers will have to work harder in order to have a firm grip on it.

THE ORIGINS OF FLOW

Self-Determination Theory and Flow

Where does flow come from? As we have seen in Chapters 3 (section *Intrinsic Motivation, Extrinsic Motivation, and Self-Determination*) and 4 (section *Causality Orientations*), Self-Determination Theory (Deci & Ryan, 1985a; Ryan & Deci, 2000) provides a comprehensive framework within which a wide range of positive phenomena – including flow – can be explained in terms of intrinsic motivation, basic needs that are common to all human beings, person-environment interactions, and developmental processes. Specifically, Self-Determination Theory postulates that the flow state is a key indicator of intrinsically motivated behaviour: 'the concept of flow represents a descriptive dimension that may signify some of the purer instances of intrinsic motivation' (Deci & Ryan, 1985a, p. 29).

Both Self-Determination Theory and Flow Theory highlight the keyness of the need for competence in intrinsically motivated behaviour, with a caveat: the former postulates that intrinsic motivation requires *optimal challenges* (i.e., challenges that stretch slightly beyond one's skills), whereas the latter postulates that flow requires that challenges and skills be both high and in relative balance with each other. Drawing from Self-Determination Theory, the experience of flow in a self-determined task can be hypothetically explained as the recursive five-step process shown in Figure 6.5: (1) intrinsic motivation drives the individual towards high-challenge/high-skill tasks that provide maximal opportunity for learning; (2) the co-occurrence of high challenges and high

Figure 6.5   *A hypothetical recursive model of how basic needs, intrinsic motivation, flow, and behaviour influence one another when a person engages in intrinsically motivated behaviour*

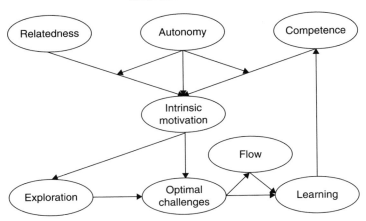

Note: This figure is an extension of Figure 3.2.

skills fosters flow in the task; (3) flow fosters learning; (4) learning satisfies the need for competence; and (5) the satisfaction of the need for competence fosters intrinsic motivation. The model shows that optimal challenges foster learning both directly and indirectly, through the mediation of flow. This in turn implies that, if flow occurs, there will be more or higher quality learning.

Yet, a disarmingly simple question can put this whole chapter in question: are intrinsic motivation and flow one and the same variable? The potential overlap between the two constructs can be assessed with reference to the nine-component model of flow. Among the indicators of flow, only autotelic experience – representing the intrinsic drive of the activity irrespective of goals and rewards external to the activity itself – overlaps conceptually with intrinsic motivation. Therefore, the two constructs are distinct if autotelic experience is not included among the indicators of flow.

Should autotelic experience be regarded as a definitional component of flow? Rheinberg (2008) and Engeser and Schiepe-Tiska (2012) argued it should not, because in some instances flow can be triggered by external goals and can occur in activities that have no obvious intrinsic connotation. This position can be viewed as a specific instance of Allport's (1961) concept of *functional autonomy*, according to which an activity can start because of extrinsic reasons and then become self-rewarding and hence intrinsically motivated. In sum, if the autotelic component is not included in the conceptualization and measurement of flow, intrinsic motivation and flow are different variables, and Self-Determination Theory provides an elegant explanation of the relationships between the two variables.

The Teleonomy of the Self and the Autotelic Personality

Flow Theory represents the person as a system that acts according to three integrated teleonomies: the *genetic teleonomy*, the *cultural teleonomy*, and the *teleonomy of the self* (Csikszentmihalyi, 1982). The genetic teleonomy is a drive to seek pleasures and goals that are genetically programmed in the person's organism, such as eating and being healthy or sexually satisfied. The cultural teleonomy is a drive to seek and maintain social and economical success. The teleonomy of the self is a drive to increase *psychic negentropy*, that is, reorganization and growth in the order and complexity of consciousness, which people experience as enjoyable and rewarding regardless of any concomitant genetic and cultural prompt or reinforcement. Flow Theory postulates that the optimal conditions for subjective experience – which are conducive to flow – occur when the person is driven by the teleonomy of the self.

The teleonomy of the self is characterized as a two-step cyclical process (Csikszentmihalyi & Massimini, 1985): (a) if the perceived skills are less than the perceived challenges in a given task, a person experiences anxiety and will try to restore balance by learning new skills, and (b) if the perceived skills are greater than the perceived challenges, a person experiences boredom and will try to restore balance by increasing the level of challenge of the task or by seeking a more challenging task. While the genetic and cultural teleonomies are homeostatic processes, oriented towards stationary states, the teleonomy of the self is an endless maximization process towards higher and higher levels of perceived challenges and skills.

Flow Theory posits that there are strong individual differences in how the three teleonomies are hierarchically ordered. Some persons are mainly driven by cultural and biological motivations, while others are driven primarily by the teleonomy of the self and develop an *autotelic personality*. Those with an autotelic personality have a greater predisposition and ability in finding challenges and developing skills, and hence in finding flow in their daily lives.

No standardized scale has yet been developed to measure the autotelic personality as a trait or set of traits. The ESM was used to operationalize the construct of autotelic person as one who spends lots of time in high-challenge/high-skill situations, and found that, compared to non-autotelic persons, autotelic persons have higher quality of experience in those situations (Asakawa, 2004, 2010). These findings suggest that high-challenge/high-skill situations work as an attractor state for autotelic persons. Rathunde (1988) observed that autotelic persons are more likely to grow in 'complex families', which provide their children with a combination of high challenge and high support. In all, Nakamura and Csikszentmihalyi (2005) list the construct of autotelic personality among the most promising ones in flow research, but conclude that very little is known about the conditions that foster the development of the autotelic personality or about the dispositions that allow some people to find flow systematically in their lives.

Cultural Influence on Flow

Funder (2001) pointed out that flow describes 'a rather solitary kind of happiness' (p. 356) in which the individual is isolated from others, and argued that the optimal experience of, for example, a Zen Buddhist would definitely require 'a sense of one's relationships to other people' and 'an awareness of the whole universe of interconnections' (Funder, 2001, p. 357). This observation questions the cultural invariance of flow with regard to members of collectivist cultures, who value interconnectedness more than members of individualistic cultures do. Some researchers followed this lead and examined three forms of cultural difference: (a) difference in the prevalence of flow, (b) difference in the activities associated with flow, and (c) difference in the challenge/skill ratio that is most conducive to flow and hence can be named *optimal challenge/ skill ratio*.

Two studies used the Flow Questionnaire to address research questions (a) and (b) on differences in flow prevalence and differences in the activities wherein flow is experienced. In the first study, Delle Fave and Massimini (2004) investigated flow prevalence among 52 Walser people living in Northern Italy, 50 villagers from Southern Italy, 60 Gypsy (Roma) people living in Italian camps, 63 Indonesian people from Java, 27 Iranian people from Tehran. The prevalence of flow was 92 per cent for the whole sample, and did not vary significantly across sub-samples. However, there were marked cultural differences in the best flow-conducive activities. Notably, flow in work was more prevalent in Italians and Indonesians, flow in studying was more prevalent in Iranians, flow in family and social interactions were more prevalent in Roma, and flow in religious practices was reported as a flow-conducive activity only by Indonesians and Iranians. In all, these findings suggest that culture does not influence the probability of experiencing flow, but it does influence the social contexts and types of activities in which flow is more likely to occur. In particular, contrary to Funder's (2001) argument, Roma apparently have no problem in experiencing flow while interacting and feeling connected with others.

In the second study, Asakawa investigated flow prevalence in 315 Japanese undergraduate students and found that 73 per cent of them experienced flow. This prevalence estimate is less than that reported by Delle Fave and Massimini (2004) on a mixed culture sample, but greater than the estimate reported by Moneta (2012b) on a British worker sample (67 per cent) studied in the same historical period. Therefore, the findings from this study also do not support the hypothesis that flow is less prevalent in a collectivist culture.

Two studies used the ESM to address the research question c on differences in the optimal challenge/skill ratio. In the first study, Asakawa (2004) used the quadrant model to classify scores gathered on 102 Japanese undergraduate students on concentration, happiness, enjoyment, activation, satisfaction, perceived control over the activity, perceived importance of the activity for future goals, and *Jujitsu-kan*, a Japanese word meaning a sense of fulfilment. He found that each of these facets of subjective experience reached their maximum when challenges and skills were simultaneously high. Therefore, Japanese students would appear to have the same 1:1 optimal challenge/skill ratio as North American and European students do.

In the second study, Moneta (2004) used a dedicated regression model to estimate the optimal challenge/skill ratio of enjoyment of the activity and interest in the activity for 269 Hong Kong Chinese undergraduate students and 573 US twelfth graders, which was a sub-sample of the 1,309 high school students engaged in the Alfred P. Sloan Longitudinal Study of Youth and Social Development (Csikszentmihalyi & Schneider, 2000). Enjoyment and interest were highest in the high-challenge/high-skill condition for the US sample, whereas these emotions were highest in the low-challenge/high skill condition for the Chinese sample. Therefore, Hong Kong Chinese undergraduate students have an optimal challenge/skill ratio for interest and enjoyment that is biased towards skills, so that one can infer that they are more likely to reach flow when they perceive their skills to exceed the demands of the activity.

Asakawa (2004) and Moneta's (2004) findings prompt two questions. First, why do Hong Kong Chinese differ in optimal challenge/skill ratio from Japanese undergraduate students, given that they are both Asians and hence share collectivistic values? A plausible answer is that there are cultural factors other than individualism–collectivism that influence the optimal ratio. Second, why should a state of high skills and low challenge – which has a slightly negative connotation in Flow Theory as a state of boredom or relaxation – be positive for Hong Kong Chinese and possibly other Asian students? A plausible answer is that such a state may – within certain cultures that are informed by Taoist and Confucianist principles prescribing prudence, attention to detail, balance between proactivity and receptiveness, and interconnectedness with others – foster a more prudent, master-practice path towards flow.

In sum, the evidence in support of or against cultural differences in flow is scanty and mixed. Flow is a universal experience, and its prevalence seems not to differ markedly across cultures. Culture does influence the type of activities wherein people are more likely to experience flow or to experience it with greater intensity. Some cultural factors that include but go beyond the individualism–collectivism dimension seem to influence the optimal challenge/skill ratio, that is, the ratio that is most likely to foster flow. Two important research questions have not yet been addressed: (1) Is the flow state perceived and described differently by people from different cultures? And (2) Do people from different cultures attribute the same significance to flow? There are therefore plenty of things to do in this promising area of research.

CONSEQUENCES OF FLOW

Flow and Creativity

As reported at the beginning of this chapter, Csikszenmihalyi's (1996) interviews with innovators in a wide range of endeavours revealed that frequent and intense flow in work is a universal antecedent of every creative idea that grows into a fully fledged innovation. But what about 'small creativity', that is, that more ordinary and common form of creativity that characterizes the lives of most us?

A direct link from flow to creativity is documented in a study on music students (MacDonald, Byrne, & Carlton, 2006). Forty-five undergraduate students were divided in groups of three members each to produce a music composition as a group project. At each group meeting, students completed an ESF designed to measure flow intensity during the meeting. When all the groups completed the assignment, 24 composition specialists rated the creativity of each composition. The group mean score of flow intensity correlated positively with mean rated creativity of composition.

Indirect support to the flow–creativity link comes from a seminal ESM study conducted on 208 teenagers who were nominated by their teachers as showing talent in mathematics, science, music, athletics, or arts (Csikszentmihalyi, Rathunde, & Whalen, 1993). The percentage of time teenagers were found in the high-challenge/high-skill condition during talent-related activities predicted whether these teenagers were still engaged in their talent area four years later, that is, in their early adulthood. No other study variable predicted talent engagement, including grades in talent class, subjective commitment, highest talent level reached, and teacher's ratings of the student. Scholastic Aptitude Test (SAT) scores were the best predictors of grades and teacher's ratings of the student, whereas frequency of engagement in the high-challenge/high-skill condition was the only predictor of progress in the school curriculum in one's talent area, leading to the conclusion: 'A talent will be developed if it produces optimal experiences' (Csikszentmihalyi et al., 1993, p. 252). Given that talent in a subject area is a premise for contributing creatively to that area, the study also suggests that flow in adolescence will foster lifetime creative achievement through the mediation of talent development.

Flow and Sport Performance

Jackson and Roberts (1992) investigated the association between flow intensity and performance during competition in 200 undergraduate athletes from a wide range of individual sports, including swimming, athletics, gymnastics, and tennis. The athletes completed a precursor of the FSS-2 three times, the first time thinking of their general experience when they compete (average performance), the second time thinking of their best performance, and the third time thinking of their worst performance. Flow was more intense in the best performance than in the average and worst performances. These findings indicate that flow contributes to performance, with the caveat that they may be affected by the methodological problems typical of correlational and retrospective studies, which assess the independent variable – in this instance flow intensity – by asking people to remember how they felt in specific occasions. In particular, the association found between flow and performance might also be explained with reference to a memory bias; for example, athletes may recall more intense flow in their best performance because success sheds a rosy light on their recollection of the event.

Other correlational and retrospective studies found indirect effects of flow on individual performance. Two studies on marathon runners found no association between flow during the race and running time (Stoll & Lau, 2005; Schüler & Brunner, 2009). Yet, Schüler and Brunner found that flow during training was associated with more intense training prior to the race, which in turn was associated with better performance. These findings suggest that flow fosters performance indirectly, by fostering task motivation.

One study provides strong evidence in support of the flow–performance link in team sports (Bakker et al., 2011). The study participants were 398 soccer players from 45 talented teams in The Netherlands and their coaches. The soccer players completed the Flow State Scale with reference to a specific match, and the coaches rated the performance of each of their players in that match. The average flow score in a team (i.e., flow at the team level) was higher in drawn and won matches than it was in lost matches, and it correlated with the average coach rating of performance in the team (i.e., performance at the team level). Therefore, flow – although it is commonly viewed as a solitary experience – appears to be a team resource and a promoter of team performance in competition with other teams.

Flow and Work Performance

Bakker (2008) investigated the relationship between intensity of flow at work, on one hand, and peer-rated in-role performance (e.g., 'Achieves the objectives of the job') and extra-role performance (e.g., 'Willingly attends functions not required by the organization, but helps in its overall image') in a sample of 147 Dutch human service professionals. He assessed intensity of flow using his Work-Related Flow Inventory (WOLF; Bakker, 2008), which measures three correlated factors: *absorption*, *work enjoyment*, and *intrinsic work motivation*. Work enjoyment correlated with in-role performance, and intrinsic work motivation correlated with extra-role performance. These findings suggest that flow fosters work performance, with the caveat that it is not clear whether the WOLF measures flow or intrinsic motivation, so that it is possible that intrinsic motivation, rather than flow, is the promoter of job performance.

Flow and Academic Performance

Engeser and Rheinberg (2008) conducted two longitudinal studies on under-graduate students to test the hypothesis that flow in studying, measured using their Flow Short Scale (FSS; Rheinberg, Vollmeyer, & Engeser, 2003), predicts better academic performance as measured at the end of the semester. In the first study, conducted on 246 students taking a statistics course, flow experienced while solving a revision problem one week prior to the final examination correlated with final examination mark. In the second study, conducted on 61 students taking a voluntary French course, flow in class measured in two occasions during the semester correlated with the final course mark, which combined a mark for in-class participation with a mark for the final examination. In both studies, the flow-performance link held significant when the researchers controlled statistically for baseline knowledge in the subject as measured before enrolling in the course. Therefore, flow in studying appears to have a positive causal effect on academic performance, with a caveat. We have seen in Chapter 2 (section *The Dual Nature of Affect: Signal and Cause of Progress*) that positive affect experienced in study activities in the mid of a semester predicts better end-of-semester grades across the board, controlling for previous semester grades. It is therefore possible that positive affect, rather than flow, is the promoter of academic performance.

Flow and Emotions

Does flow make us feel happier? As simple as it may seem, this question has proven to be an extremely difficult one to answer. Two problems inherent to the research question need to be acknowledged. First, when in a deep flow, study participants do not fill in any questionnaire – they are simply too busy dealing with their 'flowing tasks'. Participants normally answer questions about flow minutes or even hours after the moment they came out from flow and let the ordinary world of experience back in again. As a consequence, it is not clear if the answers provided to a flow scale refer to the flow experience or to its aftermath. Therefore, we should distinguish sharply the positive affect experienced whilst in flow from the positive affect experienced before and after flow.

Second, flow proceeds by increasing levels of absorption in the task and, in turn, isolation from the sensory and social environment. Moneta and Csikszentmihalyi (1999) proposed that the task-absorption of flow reduces the rate by which emotions gain access to consciousness. For some the reduction may be moderate, so that a substantial flow of feelings to consciousness is still possible, while for others the reduction may be so drastic that hedonic tone cannot be experienced. In the first case, a person has the resources for experiencing and expressing a full range of feelings, while in the second case a person would be in a virtually unemotional state. Only in the first case would flow be contingent with an overall high level of positive affect. Therefore, when using the ESM to assess subjective experience in high-challenge/high-skills situations we should not expect to observe 'explosions' of positive affect.

Early ESM studies found – using either the quadrant model or the octant model – that facets of positive affect (e.g., feeling happy, feeling strong, and wishing to do the activity) generally peak in the high-challenge/high-skill condition (e.g., Massimini & Carli, 1988; Csikszentmihalyi & LeFevre, 1989). Two studies conducted on a sample of 208 talented US teenagers (Csikszentmihalyi, Rathunde, & Whalen, 1993) delved deeper into the issue. In the first study, Csikszentmihalyi and Rathunde (1993) examined the happiness scores across 20 daily activities and found that for only seven of them the maximum score of happiness occurred in the high-challenge/high-skill quadrant. Therefore, happiness is not maximized in the conditions that are most likely to conduce to flow. In the second study, Moneta and Csikszentmihalyi (1996) used a dedicated regression model to estimate the optimal challenge/skill ratio for four facets of experience: concentration, involvement, happiness, and wish to do the activity. They found that the optimal ratio for concentration and involvement is close to the theoretical 1:1 ratio, whereas the optimal ratio for happiness and wish to the activity is biased towards skills in such a way that these facets of experience are maximized when skills exceed challenges. Therefore, there is no universally optimal challenge/skill ratio that would allow maximizing simultaneously all facets of subjective experience. The bottom line is that we cannot have it all: if we follow the challenge = skill path towards flow, we will lose some happiness along the way.

What about the link between flow and happiness after flow? Could it be that once we return from flow we feel happier than before entering flow? Only one experimental study tested the link between intensity of flow whilst engaged in an experimental task and positive affect experienced afterwards controlling for baseline positive affect, and it failed to support the hypothesis (Keller, Bless et al., 2011, experiment 2). As a single experiment is not sufficient to draw a firm conclusion, this important issue awaits for more attempts.

Frequency of Flow and Well-Being

Asakawa's (2010) study on a sample of 315 Japanese undergraduate students provides insightful evidence on the relationship between frequency of flow in daily life, on one hand, and indicators of hedonic and eudaimonic well-being. He used an enhanced version of the Flow Questionnaire which, after asking whether one has had flow experiences, also asks how frequently one had those experiences on a seven-point scale ranging from 1 (*a few times a year*) to 7 (*a few times a day*). This measure of frequency of flow correlated positively with life satisfaction, self-esteem, will for meaningful life, problem-focused and emotion-focused strategies, and negatively with trait anxiety, problem-avoidance coping, disengagement from college life, and psychological moratorium in career decision making. In all, frequency of flow appears to foster a range of positive outcomes and prevent a range of negative outcomes. Nevertheless, prudence is in order because the identified associations might reflect, at least in part, reversed causation (e.g., the use of problem-focused coping strategies may foster flow).

Negative Consequences of Flow

Up to this point, the present chapter has focused on the positive consequences of flow. Yet, Csikszentmihalyi and Rathunde (1993) argued that, as any other form of energy, flow can be directed towards either positive or negative ends, and hence that flow can be experienced in antisocial activities. The potential for a maladaptive or even evil use of flow is inherent in the definition of flow. The tunnelling of attention that is core to flow implies a reduced capacity for monitoring one's own behaviour, including the risks it may pose to oneself and the others and its ethical score. Once in flow, then, individuals have a reduced capability to detect and interpret potentially relevant contextual cues, and to inhibit potentially harmful behaviour. A small number of studies identified maladaptive uses of flow in three domains: flow was found to be implicated in Internet and online gaming addiction (e.g., Chen, 2006; Thatcher, Wretschko, & Fridjhon, 2008), risk-taking behaviour (e.g., Sato, 1988; Schüler & Pfenninger, 2011), and killing in combat (Harari, 2008). This interesting area of research should be developed because it has great potential for application.

DIRECTIONS FOR FUTURE RESEARCH

The integration of the several points made in this chapter suggests eight broad issues that call for debate and empirical research.

1. *Studying frequency and level of flow simultaneously.*
   Most of the reviewed studies investigated either prevalence of flow or intensity of flow. Yet, there are at least two good reasons for studying frequency and intensity of flow in combination. First, assessing intensity of flow on a person who does not experience flow in the first place is as meaningful as assessing number of cigarettes smoked per day on a non-smoker. Second, having both a measure of frequency and a measure of intensity would allow answering a whole new range of relevant research questions. For example, is it better – for persons, their employers, or society as whole – to experience intense flow in a single activity or to experience a less intense flow in many different activities? In turn, should we expose our children

to just one or two extracurricular developmental activities (such as those that we will review in Chapter 7, section *Extracurricular Activities: Developmental and Negative Experiences*), in order to help them experience a deep flow in those activities, or should we expose them to numerous extracurricular activities in order to help them experience many different instances of 'mini flow'? These and many other relevant questions require designing studies in such a way that one can test the specific effects of frequency of flow, intensity of flow, and the interaction of the two.

2. *Controlling for confounding by intrinsic motivation.*

   If intrinsic motivation and flow are one and the same variable, then there will be no point in using different names. Yet, if one believes that they are related but distinct constructs, then there will be the need to disentangle their effects in every empirical study. For example, consider the reviewed studies that found that flow fosters performance. Is it truly flow the cause of better performance or could it be that intrinsic motivation causes better performance? Could it be that intrinsic motivation contributes to some aspects of performance and flow to other aspects of performance? These and many other relevant questions require designing studies in such a way that one can test the specific effects of flow over and above those of intrinsic motivation.

3. *Identifying environmental factors for flow.*

   One strength of Flow Theory is that it posits a minimal number of explanatory variables for flow, chiefly challenges and skills. Yet, because both challenges and skills are defined as inherently subjective variables, the theory says little about the environmental factors that foster or hinder perceptions of challenges and skills, and hence flow. This has at least two negative consequences. First, it is difficult to figure out how environments, such as schools and work places, should be structured and managed in order to foster flow. Second, it is difficult to study the effects that the interaction of personal and environmental factors has on flow. There is thus a wealth of research questions that wait for an answer. For example, is there one 'optimal' work environment that fosters flow for all employees, or do different employees have different, personalized optimal environments? Depending on the answer, how should managers shape the work environment to foster their subordinates' flow? In order to answer this type of questions research should identify environmental factors for flow and test whether they have different effects on different individuals.

4. *Examining the effects of flow on relations.*

   Flow has been studied mostly at the individual level. Yet, people conduct most study and work activities in groups and teams, and when they are finished with work they join partners, families, and friends. Therefore, there are many interesting and unanswered questions on how people deal with each other's flow states. For example, is your partner an autotelic person? If yes, how does it feel to live with somebody who spends hours in what looks like a quasi-coma state, forgets appointments, and misses meals, but is indeed very fulfilled? How do work teams function when some team members are in flow and others are not? In order to answer this type of questions research should focus on dyads and groups.

5. *Identifying the self-regulation of flow.*

   Until now, flow has been studied as a naturally occurring phenomenon, neglecting that in some instances it occurs because a person is aware of its usefulness and makes it happen almost at will. For example, in *A Moveable Feast* Hemingway (2009) described a highly productive phase of his life in which he allocated each morning to the writing of no more than a single paragraph, and spent the rest of the day enjoying Parisian bars and boulevards. Based on his description of the experience of writing a paragraph and the extraordinary quality of the product, there is little doubt that he experienced flow in each morning-paragraph, and used flow profitably. Future research should investigate the metacognitive self-regulatory process of flow in exceptional individuals in order to extract the principles that could be used to coach people for flow.

6. *Studying the cultural, indigenous influence on the definition of flow.*

   Only a few cross-cultural studies of flow have been conducted. Although these studies suggest that cultural variation is small, a more basic test has not yet been conducted. The key question is: if we were to repeat the whole process that led to the componential model of flow – starting with interviews and proceeding to the construction of the measurement scales – in a new culture (e.g., the Chinese or Indian cultures), would we identify exactly the same facets of flow and antecedents of flow?

7. *Seeking the ultimate answer: Can we have it all?*

   Flow Theory is most ambitious in that it posits that it is possible to maximize simultaneously eudaimonic and hedonic well-being. Yet, research so far suggests that maximizing flow results in a loss of happiness, and maximizing happiness results in a loss of flow. Future research should test this trade-off comprehensively, and if it is confirmed, should incorporate a trade-off construct in Flow Theory and other theories of subjective and psychological well-being.

8. *Flow: Panacea or uninvited guest?* As anticipated at the beginning of this chapter, the construct of flow is everywhere and nowhere precisely in the field of positive psychology. As I write, a team of researchers of which I am a member has finalized a contract for publishing a book on flow at work. Commenting on the original book proposal, the publisher specifically asked to ensure that each chapter of the book positions flow research in the broader context of positive psychology research. How should this be done? My own idea can be best conveyed by an example. I once designed and assembled a huge kitchen (yes, one of those that requires thousands of nuts and bolts and infinite patience) for my house. It took a month, which is more or less the time I need to write a paper. The question is: in the overall economy of my life, was it wise to use a month for assembling a kitchen instead of writing a paper? I had flow in carrying out the kitchen project as much as I have in writing up a paper, so flow tells me nothing about the wisdom of my choice. This illustrates that flow has no wisdom in its DNA; to paraphrase Aristotle and Moss, flow does not 'make the goal right'. All the virtue and practical wisdom comes into play before getting into flow – when one decides which endeavour to engage in (the domain of virtue) and how to approach it (the domain of practical wisdom) – and after having experienced flow – when one assesses the quality and meaning of the work done and decides whether to further pursue that endeavour or to move to another one. Therefore, in future research it would be appropriate to link the concept of flow to virtues, which we reviewed in Chapter 4 (section *From Confucius and Aristotle to Schwartz, Sharpe, and Grant*), and to those self-regulatory variables in the realm of practical wisdom that we reviewed in Chapter 5 (section *Self-Regulation of Emotions*).

SELF-DEVELOPMENT AND UNDERSTANDING EXERCISE

Do you experience flow? (You can use the three flow quotations of the Flow Questionnaire, which are shown in the first section of the present chapter, to answer the question). If your answer is 'yes', think of the activity in which you feel flow with the highest intensity and answer the following questions, which were adapted from the Flow Questionnaire:

1. While you were carrying out that activity, for what percentage of time did you have flow?
2. While you were carrying out that activity and you had flow, how long did flow last on average?
3. Try to imagine yourself when you are doing the activity you selected and when this activity is going well.
   a. When does flow happen during the activity?
   b. How does it feel?
   c. How does this feeling get started?
   d. What do you do (if anything) to get it started?
   e. Can it happen anywhere, anytime?
   f. What keeps it going, once it starts?
   g. How do you feel before having flow?
   h. How do you feel after having flow?

Analyse your answers and check whether and to what extent they fit the concepts and findings presented in this chapter. If there are some discrepancies, figure out possible explanations.

◊ RECOMMENDED WEB RESOURCES AND FURTHER READING ◊

Websites

Curiously enough, there seem to be no website devoted to flow from a research perspective. Could it be that flow researchers are so absorbed in their work that find it hard to communicate with other members of the human species? In any case, there is a light at the end of the tunnel: I found the European Flow-Researcher Network on Facebook. The timeline says it was created on December 12, 2012, that is, shortly after Corinna Peifer (contact details available at: http://www.uni-trier.de/index.php?id=28908) and Stefan Engeser (contact details available at: http://www.uni-trier.de/index.php?id=34268) hosted a meeting of the network members at the University of Trier, Germany. I attended that meeting together with 24 other researchers (yes, we worked, dined together, and had social interactions like ordinary human beings do) and learned that many others who could not attend expressed interest in joining the network activities in the future.

Reading

- Engeser and Schiepe-Tiska's (2012) succinct and comprehensive historical review of research on flow, as well as the other chapters in Engeser's (2012) edited book
- Bakker and co-workers' (2011) study on the flow of talented soccer players
- Moneta's (2012b) study of how dispositional intrinsic motivation and opportunity for creativity in the job conjointly influence flow at work
- Asakawa's (2010) study on autotelic Japanese undergraduate students

7 Positive Relationships

INTRODUCTION

A robust finding is that successful, satisfying, harmonious, or otherwise fulfilling close relations with others are the best predictor of life satisfaction (e.g., Myers, 1999; Sears, 1977). The previous chapters focused primarily on the person and marginally on the 'close others'. We analysed relational constructs – such as the traits of extraversion and agreeableness, and the indicator of eudaimonic well-being called positive relations with others – but we did it primarily from the point of view of the person, focusing on one's inner representation of the relationships held with others. The perhaps excessive focus on the person is due to the fact that positive psychology originates historically and conceptually from personality psychology. Nevertheless, a growing number of researchers in the field of positive psychology have developed an authentic interest in social relationships as the units of analysis, and their interest is generating non-obvious findings that have the potential to put what we know about the person in a new perspective.

This chapter builds on prior chapters but goes beyond in two specific ways. First, although the constructs of subjective and psychological well-being introduced in Chapter 1 remain important indicators of the goodness of a relationship when one looks at the individual in isolation, inherently relational constructs of well-being must also be considered. For example, it is theoretically possible to have a team of workers who individually are all happy people, whereas their team is unadulterated hell. In order to study the 'positivity' of a relationship one therefore needs to introduce relationship-level indicators of well-being. Second, although it would be tempting to consider dyads and groups as simply aggregates of selves and personalities as defined in Chapters 3 and 4, dyads and groups have a power structure, in which a weaker member is subordinate to a stronger member; examples of this are child–parent, child–teacher, and subordinate–manager relationships. In order to study the 'positivity' of a relationship one therefore needs to focus primarily on how well the stronger member fulfils the leading role; as we have seen in Chapter 4 (section *Confucius*) Confucius would have certainly endorsed such a perspective of analysis.

The study of positive relationships is still too scattered to allow for a comprehensive review. Therefore, this chapter will focus on a restricted set of topics with the goal of providing cues as to what lies ahead in the field. We will review selected research findings on (a) romantic relationships, (b) work relationships, and (c) parenting, teacher–student and child–other relationships. For each of the three types of relationships, we will first review the relationship-specific indicators of well-being that reveal the extent to which a relationship is positive. We will then see what factors seem to influence the 'positivity' of that type of relationship. The final section outlines issues open to discussion, ongoing controversies, and directions for future research.

ROMANTIC LOVE

Well-Being in Love

Virtual social networks offer the opportunity to declare one's relationship status. In addition to the obvious options – single, in a relationship, and married with _____ – one sometimes encounters the novel 'it's complicated' option, which is an expression that an evolutionary psychologist might find hard to understand. As we have seen in Chapter 2 (sections *Emotions, Feelings, and Moods* and *Origins and Consequences of Affect*), positive emotions are universally believed to have emerged in the evolutionary process because they support interpersonal relationships and mating in particular. So, what complication there could possibly be in a romantic relationship? The complication stems from the fact that – according to Hatfield (1988) – the complex link passion–love–marriage emerged in the Western world only in the 18th century. Before then there was just a passion–love link, and that was typically pursued outside of marriage; marriage was decided purely on social conventions. Hendrick and Hendrick (2005) proposed that the passion–love–marriage link is growing stronger:

> (...) we believe that love, sex, marriage (or cohabitation), and friendship are increasingly being linked in romantic relationships. This cohesion is a powerful 'bundling' of four of the most positive facets of life. Today, people generally should find more joy in their romantic relationships than was possible in previous centuries. There is a price, however, in that the expectations of these relationships are also much higher.
>
> (Hendrick & Hendrick, 2005, p. 473)

As the expectations grow, it may become increasingly 'complicated' to find, build, and maintain a romantic relationship that has it all.

Three main indicators of the wellness of a romantic relationship have been used in research. The first and obvious indicator is whether a couple is still together, has split, or is in the process of falling apart.

The second indicator is relationship satisfaction, which, similar to life satisfaction, is based on a mixture of feelings and cognitive appraisals. Individual differences in global relationship satisfaction can be measured validly and reliably by various scales. For example, the Satisfaction Level sub-scale of the Investment Model Scale (IMS; Rusbult, Martz, & Agnew, 1998; available at: http://carylrusbult.com/) consists of five items (e.g., 'I feel satisfied with our relationship') to be scored on a nine-point scale ranging from 1 (*don't agree at all*) to 9 (*agree completely*). The Relationship Assessment Scale (RAS; Hendrick, 1988) consists of seven items (e.g., 'How well does your partner meet your needs?' and 'In general, how satisfied are you with your relationship?') to be scored on a five-point scale ranging from 1 (*not at all*) to 5 (*extremely*). The RAS score was found to correlate strongly between the two members of a couple, and to predict well whether a couple will stay together or will separate (Hendrick, 1988).

The third and final indicator is sexual satisfaction, which can be measured validly and reliably by various scales. For example, the Sexual Satisfaction Inventory (SSI; Whitley, 1998) measures the average level of satisfaction with 32 sexual activities one may engage in, to be scored on a 5-point scale ranging from 1 (*no satisfaction*) to 5 (*maximum satisfaction*), with 'N/A' option in case the respondent does not practice a specific activity. The Index of Sexual Satisfaction (ISS; Hudson, 1998; Hudson, Harrison, & Crosscup, 1981) measures general satisfaction with the sexual component of one's current relationship on 25 items (e.g., 'I feel that my partner enjoys our sex life') to be scored on a five-point scale ranging from 1 (*rarely or none of the time*) to 5 (*most or all of the time*). The Sexual Attitudes Scale (SAS; Hendrick & Hendrick, 1987) is a 51-item questionnaire measuring four attitudes towards sex: *permissiveness* (26 items, e.g., 'Casual sex is acceptable'), *sex practices* (8 items, e.g., 'Masturbation is all right'), *communion* (11 items, e.g., 'Orgasm is the greatest experience in the world'), and *instrumentality* (6 items, e.g., 'Sex is primarily physical'). Items are scored on a five-point scale ranging from 1 (*strongly agree*) to 5 (*strongly disagree*).

Components of Love

Several componential definitions of love have been proposed. We will consider three that are very popular and of increasing levels of complexity: passionate and companionate love, triangular theory of love, and love styles.

Berscheid and Walster (1969) introduced a distinction between *passionate love* and *companionate love*. The former is a state of emotional involvement between lovers that is characterized by strong passion, mood swings, and fear of losing the other, whereas the latter is a state of affection and intimacy that is characterized by mutual self-disclosure and intertwining. Berscheid and Walster proposed that a successful relationship typically starts with passionate love and, in due course, settles in companionate love. Hatfield (1988), instead, argued that people want to experience both components of love at all times in a relationship, and that the two can coexist over time.

Sternberg (1988) proposed the *triangular theory of love*, according to which love consists of three components that together can be viewed as forming the vertices of a triangle: intimacy, passion, and commitment. These components are distinct but one can have all of them ('consummate love'), only one or two of them, or none at all ('nonlove') while still being in a relationship. Intimacy refers to feelings of bonding leading to self-disclosure and sharing, and is theorized to build up over a long period of time. Passion refers to the emotions that energize romance, attraction, and sex, and is theorized to be most intense in the early stages of a relationship. Commitment refers to both the initial decision to love someone and the lasting determination to maintain that love. Individual differences in the three components of love can be measured validly and reliably using the Triangular Love Scale (TLS; Sternberg, 1998; available at: http://articles.dailypress.com/1998-03-01/features/9802270261_1_romantic-relationship-intimacy-and-commitment), which consists of 15 items measuring intimacy (e.g., 'I have a warm relationship with ____'), 15 items measuring passion (e.g., 'I idealize ____'), and 15 items measuring commitment (e.g., 'I plan to continue my relationship with ____') to be scored on a nine-point scale ranging from 1 (*not at all*) to 9 (*extremely*).

Hendrick and Hendrick (1986) proposed a definition of love in six components and developed the Love Attitude Scale (LAS) to measure validly and reliably each component with four items to be scored on a five-point scale ranging from 1 (*strongly agree*) to 5 (*strongly disagree*). *Eros* is passionate love with a focus on idealization of one's partner more than on sexual excitement (e.g., 'I feel that my partner and I were meant for each other'). *Ludus* is love as playing, with a focus on enjoyment and lack of commitment (e.g., 'I have sometimes had to keep my partner from finding out about other partners'). *Storge* is companionate love as defined by Berscheid and Walster (1969) (e.g., 'Our love is really a deep friendship, not a mysterious, mystical emotion'). *Pragma* is love for a practical reason, with a focus on the usefulness of partner's characteristics (e.g., 'An important factor in choosing my partner was whether or not he/she would be a good parent'). *Mania* is desperate and painful love, with a focus on jealousy (e.g., 'I cannot relax if I suspect that my partner is with someone else'). Finally, *agape* is love, with a focus on fostering the partner's well-being and with a hint of dramatic self-sacrificing tendency (e.g., 'I would rather suffer myself than let my partner suffer').

Are the components of love the same across cultures? Hatfield and Rapson (1996) reviewed the studies conducted using the LAS with participants from different cultures and concluded that there is much more similarity than difference between cultures. An interesting, albeit small, difference was detected between Taiwanese university students living in the United States and local students: in the former, agape and pragma formed a single factor, which was labelled *obligatory love* to reflect the combination of altruism and utilitarianism (Cho & Cross, 1995). Although empirically there seem to be only small cross-cultural differences in the structure of love components, a number of researchers argued that there should be cross-cultural differences in the love components that lead to choosing a partner for marriage. In particular, passionate love is thought to be more salient in Western, individualistic cultures that emphasize the need for positive emotions in a romantic relationship, whereas companionate love is thought to be more salient in Eastern, collectivistic cultures that emphasize the need to integrate a romantic relationship within an extended kinship network (e.g., Ho, 1986; Moore, 1998).

Types of Love and Relationship Well-Being

Hendrick (1988, Study 1) investigated the associations between components of love, measured using the LAS, and relationship satisfaction, measured using the total RAS score, on 125 undergraduate students at a university in the southwestern United States who reported to be 'in love'. Relationship satisfaction correlated most strongly with eros ($r = .60$), followed by agape ($r = .36$) and, negatively, ludus ($r = -.30$), whereas it did not correlate significantly with storge, pragma, and mania. In all, unsurprisingly, erotic and altruistic love foster wellness of a relationship, whereas game-playing love hinders it.

Hendrick and Hendrick (1987) investigated the associations between sexual attitudes, measured using the SAS, and the components of love, measured using the LAS, on three undergraduate student samples from different universities in the United States totalling 1,592 participants. The strongest correlations were found between permissiveness and ludus (range of $r = .46–.52$), between communion and eros (range of $r = .20–.42$), and between instrumentality and ludus (range of $r = .32–.37$), and communion and agape (range of $r = .01–.25$). In all, the findings indicate that a preference for promiscuous sexuality is associated with game-playing love, whereas a preference for communal sexuality is associated with erotic and altruistic love.

Two interesting questions remain unanswered. First, how do components of love and sexual attitudes conjointly influence relationship satisfaction? In particular, it would be interesting to know whether mismatches between sexual preferences and love components (e.g., permissiveness and agape, or communion and pragma) negatively influence relationship satisfaction. Second, do dyadic differences matter? In particular, it would be interesting to know whether mismatches in sexual preferences and love components between the two members of a dyad negatively influence relationship satisfaction.

Love and Subjective Well-Being

Hendrick and Hendrick (2005) summarized the findings from two unpublished studies they conducted on US undergraduate student samples showing positive associations between love and a single-item measure of happiness. In particular, students in love were on average happier than students not in love. Among those in love, happiness correlated positively with relationship satisfaction, companionate love, and passionate love, with the caveat that passionate love was not related to happiness in one of the two studies. These summary findings suggest that love and some of its components foster well-being.

Kim and Hatfield (2004) investigated the associations between two components of love – passionate love and companionate love – and two component of subjective well-being – life satisfaction and affect operationalized as the combination of positive affect and reverse scored negative affect – on 217 American students at the University of Hawaii and 182 Korean students at Korea University. They measured passionate love using the Passionate Love Scale (PLS; Hatfield & Rapson, 1993), which consist of 15 items (e.g., 'I would feel deep despair if ____ left me') to be scored on a nine-point scale ranging from 1 (*not all true*) to 9 (*definitely true*), and companionate love using the Companionate Love Scale (CLS; Sternberg, 1986), which contains five intimacy items and five commitment items from the TLS (Sternberg, 1998). Companionate love was the best predictor of life satisfaction, whereas passionate love was the best predictor of affect in both samples. Moreover, some interesting gender differences were found: the correlation between passionate love and affect was statistically significant for males only, and the correlation between companionate love and life satisfaction was stronger for females than it was for males. In all, these findings support the popular view that intimacy and commitment are conducive to happiness particularly in women, passion boosts emotions particularly in men, and this pattern is not influenced by culture, at least in university student samples.

We have seen in Chapter 2 (section *The Ratio of Positive to Negative Emotions*) that Fredrickson and Losada (2005) extended broaden-and-build theory adopting a nonlinear dynamic model of human flourishing, according to which a critical positivity ratio – a ratio of positive over negative emotions – of 2.9 separates flourishing from languishing. Is there a critical positivity ratio for romantic relationships and, if so, is it 2.9? Gottman (1994) videotaped 77 couples discussing a relationship problem, and estimated the positivity ratio of each couple separately on speech acts and observed emotions. In couples wherein both partners were satisfied with their relationship – and hence the relationship was flourishing – the mean positivity ratio was 5.1 for speech acts and 4.7 for observed emotions, whereas in languishing couples the corresponding figures were 0.9 and 0.7, respectively. In all, it appears that there is a critical positivity ratio that needs to be exceeded in order for a romantic relationship to flourish.

RELATIONSHIPS IN WORK ENVIRONMENTS

Well-Being at Work

It might seem odd to discuss work in the context of relationships. Yet, with very few exceptions, work is carried out in interaction with others, wherein 'the others' are an integral part of work itself. The social interaction of work can be real, as in the service sector, or symbolic. For example, I am writing this paragraph in total isolation – except that I am listening with the back of my mind to a boring political debate on TV – but I do so thinking of you who will be reading it, even if I do not know you and perhaps I never will. Thus, even writing in isolation is an inherently social activity that implies a relationship with others. In most of jobs, work relationships involve relationships with individuals (e.g., boss or colleague), teams, and the organization as a whole. If we consider all the relationships in the work environment in aggregate, we can study the wellness of a work relationship as much as we can study the wellness of a romantic relationship.

Six main indicators of the wellness of a work relationship have been used in research. The first and obvious indicator is whether a worker is still employed with a work organization, has quit, or is in the process of leaving.

The second and 'negative' indicator is *intention to quit* or *intention to leave* one's job or profession. Individual differences in intention to leave can be measured validly and reliably using the Intention to Leave Scale (ILS; Weisberg, 1994), which consists of only three items. The scale was originally developed for teachers: (1) 'I have considered leaving teaching', (2) 'I think that if I was choosing my career again, I would choose teaching' (reverse scored), and (3) 'I think in the near future I will leave teaching'. The scale can be adapted to other jobs or professions just by substituting the word 'teaching' with an appropriate word in all three items. Items are scored on a five-point scale ranging from 1 (*very little*) to 5 (*very much*). Many different intention to quit scales – ranging from two (e.g., Firth, Mellor, Moore, & Loquet, 2004) to five items (e.g., Elangovan, 2001) – have been used in organizational research.

The third indicator – and perhaps the most important from an employee's perspective – is *job satisfaction*, which, similar to life satisfaction and relationship satisfaction, is based on a mixture of feelings and cognitive appraisals. Job satisfaction can be measured validly and reliably using the global job satisfaction scale included in the Job Diagnostic Survey (JDS; Hackman & Oldham, 1974), which consists of three items: (1) 'Generally speaking, I am satisfied with my job', (2) 'I frequently think of quitting this job' (reverse scored), and (3) 'I am generally satisfied with the kind of work I do in this job'. The second item can be dropped if one wants to avoid confounding with intention to leave. The items are scored on a seven-point scale ranging from 1 (*disagree strongly*) to 7 (*agree strongly*).

The fourth and 'negative' indicator is *burnout*. Freudenberger (1974) introduced the construct of burnout to describe a stable pattern of work-related stress. Maslach and Jackson (1981) developed the construct to depict a crisis in one's relationship with work that comprises three correlated but distinct components: (a) *emotional exhaustion*, which represents a prolonged emotional draining experienced in connection with work activities; (b) *cynicism*, which represents a loss of interest and belief in the job and the organization; (c) *reduced personal efficacy*, which represents a perception of inability to perform as required by the job. Individual differences in the three components of burnout can be measured validly and reliably using the Maslach Burnout Inventory (MBI; Maslach, Jackson, & Leiter, 1996): emotional exhaustion (five items), cynicism (four items), and reduced personal efficacy (six items). Items are scored on a seven-point scale ranging from 0 (*never*) to 6 (*always*).

The fifth indicator is *work engagement*. Kahn (1990) introduced the construct as 'harnessing of organization members' selves to their work roles: in engagement, people employ and express themselves physically, cognitively, emotionally and mentally during in role performances' (p. 694). Schaufeli and co-workers (2002) provided a componential definition of work engagement as 'positive, fulfilling, work-related state of mind that is characterised by vigour, dedication, and absorption' (p. 74). *Vigour* represents energy, persistence, and resilience in one's work. *Dedication* represents enthusiasm and pride for one's work. Finally, *absorption* represents concentration and engrossment in one's work, and hence is similar to the construct of flow in work as defined in Chapter 6. Individual differences in the three components of work engagement can be measured validly and reliably using the Utrecht Work Engagement Scale (UWES; Schaufeli et al., 2002) or its short nine-item form UWES-9 (Schaufeli, Bakker, & Salanova, 2006): vigour (three items, e.g., 'At my work, I feel bursting with energy'), dedication (three items, e.g., 'I am enthusiastic about my job'), and absorption (three items, e.g., 'I am immersed in my work'). Items are scored on a seven-point scale ranging from 0 (*never*) to 6 (*every day*).

The final indicator – and obviously the most important from an employer's perspective – is *job performance*. In a limited number of jobs performance can be measured objectively. For example, a surgeon's performance can be measured using indicators such as number of surgical operations of a certain type performed, percentage of patients who survived the surgery, and percentage of patients who did not develop post-surgery complications. By the same token, investment bankers' performance can be measured by the growth of their clients' portfolios relative to the growth of the average portfolio in a given span of time. In the majority of jobs, however, performance can only be measured using subjective ratings provided by supervisors, peers, and the employee. In a meta-analysis of such performance ratings, Harris and Schaubroeck (1988) found fair correlations between peer ratings and supervisor ratings of employees ($r = .62$), and moderate correlations between self ratings and supervisor ratings ($r = .35$) and between self ratings and peer ratings ($r = .36$). These figures were moderated neither by type of rating – i.e., trait-like assessment of overall employee's performance over a long period of time versus behavioural assessment of employee's performance in a specific task over a short period of time – nor by scale format – i.e., using items that measure overall performance as a single factor versus using items that measure performance as a set of distinct aspects, such as in-role performance and extra-role performance. A subsequent meta-analysis (Conway & Huffcutt, 1997) confirmed that supervisor and peer ratings converge more strongly than either does with self ratings. In all, job performance can be measured validly and reliably with the caveat that the self perspective may differ from the supervisor and peers' perspectives.

Among all facets of job performance, creativity is becoming increasingly important for organizations (Bharadwaj & Menon, 2000; Amabile & Khaire, 2008), to the extent that the term *organizational creativity* has become ubiquitous in organizational research. Organizational creativity refers to the generation of novel and useful ideas or products within an organization, including processes, procedures and services (e.g., Woodman, Sawyer, & Griffin, 1993). Individual and team creativity are at the heart of entrepreneurial business whenever a new enterprise is launched or an established business seeks expansion into a new and competitive market (e.g., Amabile & Khaire, 2008), and foster other facets of performance such as product quality and financial gain (e.g., Huth, 2008). In a small but fast growing number of jobs creative job performance can be measured objectively. For example, an applied scientist's creative performance can be measured using indicators such as number of authored patents and number of patents that were sold to third parties or progressed to industrial production. In the majority of jobs, creative performance in both individual and team work projects can be measured using supervisor, peer, and self ratings, and the degree of convergence between the three different types of ratings is comparable to that achieved on other facets of job performance (Moneta et al., 2010).

Relationships between Indicators of Wellness

If the Earth were a simple planet, all the indicators of wellness at work would be strongly intercorrelated; for example, workers who are very satisfied with their job would also be strong performers, and vice versa. In reality, the various indicators of wellness are only moderately intercorrelated, and their relationships involve non-obvious psychological processes. Some of these processes are outlined here.

First of all, what is the origin of job satisfaction? The person or the job? Ilies and Judge (2002) administered first the NEO Five-Factor Inventory (NEO-FFI) to measure the Big Five personality traits (which were reviewed in Chapter 4, section *The Big Five*) and then the ESM (which was reviewed in Chapter 6, section *The Experience Sampling Method and the Quadrant and Octant Models*) to 27 employees from the Midwest of the United States for a period of four consecutive weeks. At each signal, the ESM measured momentary job satisfaction (e.g., 'at this very moment I am fairly satisfied with my job') and positive and negative affect (which were reviewed in Chapter 2, section *Positive and Negative Affect*). Positive and negative affect conjointly explained 29 per cent of intra-individual variation of job satisfaction. Moreover, the trait of neuroticism explained 14 per cent of the intra-individual variation in negative affect and 31 per cent of the intra-individual variation in job satisfaction. Finally, there was an indication – albeit not statistically significant – that neuroticism exacerbates the association between negative affect and job satisfaction, in such a way that the association is stronger for employees who score high on neuroticism. In all, these findings indicate that job satisfaction is influenced by the emotions experienced at work and by an employee's level of neuroticism.

Based on the definitions of the constructs, one would infer that work engagement is just the opposite of burnout. Yet, empirically the two constructs turned out to be negatively but not perfectly correlated. For example, in a multi-nation sample of 11,152 employees the correlations – corrected for measurement error – between the facets of one of the two constructs and the other construct as a whole ranged from –.45 to –.64. This implies that engagement and burnout are inversely related but distinct constructs. It is possible, therefore, for a worker to be both engaged and burned out at a given point in time, as may happen to a workaholic. This implies that in order to identify the unique effects that each construct has on relevant outcome variables – such as job performance – a researcher needs to assess both variables on the study participants and control one for the other in the statistical analysis.

What are the best predictors of intention to leave one's job or profession? Emotional burnout has been theorized to be the best predictor. In particular, Leiter's (1993) model of burnout and coping characterizes emotional exhaustion and cynicism as the affective components of burnout, and reduced efficacy as the cognitive component of burnout. The model posits that the affective components of burnout promote avoidant coping, or escaping from the stressors at work, whereas the cognitive component of burnout promotes approach coping, or directly tackling the stressors. The model thus predicts that emotional exhaustion and cynicism will foster intention to leave, whereas reduced efficacy will lead to less approach coping. Empirical studies confirmed that emotional exhaustion and cynicism are the main predictors of intention to leave (see review by Lee and Ashforth, 1996). Yet, a Web survey of 1,475 Belgian workers found a negative and fairly strong correlation ($r = -.47$) between work engagement and turnover intention (De Cuyper, Notelaers, & De Witte, 2009). Therefore, both emotional burnout and lack of work engagement appear to be strong predictors of intention to leave.

Does job satisfaction predict job performance? For many years, organizational researchers sought evidence in support of an association between the two variables. Meta-analytic studies (Judge et al., 2001; Wright, 2005) concluded that, whether job satisfaction is measured as a single global construct or as a multifaceted construct (e.g., by separating factors such as satisfaction with pay and satisfaction with social support), it has a modest correlation of .30 or slightly higher with measures of job performance. However, given that job satisfaction is heavily influenced by affect (e.g., Ilies & Judge, 2002), Wright (2005) argued that the association between job satisfaction and performance is confounded by subjective well-being. Consistent with this hypothesis, Zelenski, Murphy, and Jenkins (2008), using the ESM, found that positive affect is more strongly linked to self-rated performance than job satisfaction is. In all, it seems that 'happy workers' (i.e., those who experience much positive affect and little negative affect at work), rather than 'satisfied with the job workers', are more productive at work.

Is work engagement a predictor of job performance? Schaufeli, Taris, and Bakker (2006) conducted a survey on a sample of 2,165 Dutch workers from a wide range of occupations and found that both in-role performance ($r = .37$) and extra-role performance ($r = .32$) correlated with work engagement. Christian, Garza, and Slaughter's (2011) meta-analysis of 91 studies produced mean correlation coefficients corrected for measurement error that are a bit stronger: work engagement correlated with both in-role performance ($r = .43$) and extra-role performance ($r = .34$). Moreover, Christian and co-workers found that work engagement mediates completely the effects that attitudes towards work (e.g., task significance), personality traits (e.g., conscientiousness), and positive affect have on job performance. The last finding is crucial because work engagement involves positive affect (particularly in the vigour component), and hence the association between work engagement and job performance might be due to a 'happy worker' effect. The finding that positive affect at work influences in-role and extra-role performance entirely through the mediation of work engagement effectively rules out the possibility that the association between work engagement and performance is spurious. In all, work engagement emerges as the main personal factor influencing job performance.

Positive Work Environment Factors

Over the past thirty years, organizational researchers have been looking for work environment factors that foster or hinder employees' well-being and productivity. These studies can be conveniently grouped into studies of job characteristics, team characteristics, and broader organizational characteristics.

Research on job characteristics emphasized the role played by the incentives that are inherent to the tasks carried out at work. For example, Hackman and Oldham (1974, 1980) proposed that internal work motivation, 'growth satisfaction', and work effectiveness are fostered by five core job characteristics: (1) skill variety (i.e., working on a range of tasks that utilize distinct skills), (2) task identity (i.e., seeing the overall meaning of one's work), (3) task significance (i.e., attributing importance to one's work), (4) autonomy (i.e., experiencing freedom in the way one carries out work tasks), and (5) feedback from the job (i.e., working on tasks that have a built-in feedback mechanism). These predictions were substantially supported in empirical research (e.g., Loher et al., 1985).

Research on team characteristics has emphasized the role of supervisors and the specific behaviours they engage in with their subordinates. For example, Hackman (2002) found evidence supporting the idea that *expert coaching* – the responsive and proactive interaction with team members aimed at enabling them to use collective resources in accomplishing team project work – fosters both individual well-being and team performance.

Finally, research on organizational characteristics has focused on workers' perception of organizational support. Eisenberger and co-workers (1986) defined *perceived organizational support* as the extent to which workers perceive their organizations as caring and nurturing of its work force, whereas Hackman (1987) emphasized the resource-providing role of organizations, including the provision of materials, information, training, and rewards. Keenan and Newton (1985) found evidence that perceptions of shortness of materials and of impediments in the production process are associated with less employee's job satisfaction.

Amabile and co-workers (1996) proposed a comprehensive classification system of perceived work environment factors, and developed a valid and reliable questionnaire – the KEYS – to measure them. Their primary goal in constructing and validating the KEYS was to identify factors that promote the creative achievement of individuals, teams, and entire organizations. The KEYS consists of 78 items measuring eight scales, each tapping a distinct dimension of perceived work environment. All eight scales were found to differ significantly – and in the expected directions – in mean between work projects that were rated by experts as either 'high-creativity' or 'low-creativity'. The eight perceived work environment factors can be conveniently divided in three groups: job characteristics, team characteristics, and organizational characteristics.

Four KEYS scales measure job characteristics: *challenging work, freedom, sufficient resources*, and *workload pressure*. Challenging work represents the perception that one is working on relevant projects, and that the tasks in one's work are challenging and require the best use of one's own skills. Freedom represents the perception of being free in choosing one's work projects and the way one carries them out. Sufficient resources represents the perception of being provided with the materials, facilities, budget, information, and data that are required to carry out one's work. Finally, workload pressure represents the perception that one is given too much work in respect to the allocated time.

Two KEYS scales measure team characteristics: *supervisory encouragement* and *work group supports*. Supervisory encouragement represents the perception that one's supervisor is open to subordinates' ideas, values their contributions, provides constructive feedback about their work, supports the work group or team within the organization, sets clear overall goals for work, plans work effectively, is a good work role model, and has good interpersonal skills. Work group supports represents a perception that the people with whom one works closely are

committed to work, contribute the right mix of competencies, and communicate openly with, support, and provide constructive criticism to one another.

Finally, two KEYS scales measure organizational characteristics: *organizational
encouragement* and *organizational impediments*. Organizational encouragement
represents a perception that one's organization is open to ideas, encourages taking
risk, and expects, supports, and rewards its employees' creative work. Organizational impediments represent a perception that the organization is afflicted by
territorial behaviour and excessive competitiveness, is risk-avoidant and too critical of new ideas, and exerts strict control and pressure on its employees.

Because most creative work being done in contemporary organizations occurs
in team projects, the figure of the project supervisor becomes increasingly salient. Project supervisors can be viewed as sergeants, leading a platoon in the midst
of the battlefield and facing two fronts simultaneously. On one hand, they have
to stay in touch with the team members, providing guidance and emotional support. On the other hand, they have to stay in touch with the upper management,
providing project results and negotiating resources for the project and the team.
The next two sections will expand on the work of team managers and its impact
on the wellness of both the team members and the team project.

Positive Management

Fleishman (1953) initiated the systematic study of leader behaviours, meant as
the class of activities that managers engage in when carrying out their leadership functions, and, in particular, the class of behaviours they should engage
in to be good managers. Fleishman proposed a two-factor behavioural theory
of leadership, which specifies that all leader behaviours can be characterized as
either task-oriented or relationship-oriented. He called the first factor *initiating
structure* and the second *consideration*. Initiating structure aims at successfully
completing the assigned work project, and includes such behaviours as clarifying roles and responsibilities, planning, monitoring progress, and managing
time and resources. Consideration aims at supporting subordinates' well-being,
and includes such behaviours as showing consideration for their feelings, acting
friendly, and supporting them in difficult moments.

Yukl (2002) provided a more fine-grained taxonomy of leadership behaviours.
The taxonomy includes 14 leader behaviours: (1) planning and organizing, (2)
problem solving, (3) clarifying roles and objectives, (4) informing, (5) monitoring, (6) motivating and inspiring, (7) consulting, (8) delegating, (9) supporting, (10) developing and mentoring, (11) managing conflict and team building,
(12) networking, (13) recognizing, and (14) rewarding. These can be broadly
interpreted with reference to Fleishman's (1953) factors of initiating structure
and consideration, with a caveat. Behaviours 1 through 6 and 8 in Yukl's classification system appear to tap only initiating structure; behaviours 11 and 12
appear to tap only consideration; all the remaining behaviours appear to tap a
mixture of initiating structure and consideration. For example, consulting (7)

serves both the function of getting the job done well (initiating structure) and the function of making subordinates feel valued (consideration). By the same token, developing and mentoring (10) serves both the function of improving performance in future projects (initiating structure) and the function of making subordinates feel that they are worth investing on (consideration). Finally, even those leader behaviours that obviously belong to the initiating structure factor contain elements of the consideration factor. For example, a manager could not monitor (5) subordinates' work progress without interacting with them and providing – either explicitly or implicitly – personal feedback; so that, monitoring can be perceived by a subordinate in different ways, ranging from a controlling use of authority to an interesting and motivating exchange. In all, to varying degrees, each of the leader behaviours implies a combination of initiating structure and consideration.

Looking at Yukl's (2002) taxonomy one would naturally conclude that managing people is a complex job, and that many managers must fall short of performing all 14 behavioural tasks and performing each every time they should. Amabile and co-workers (2004) pointed out an additional complication: managers who perform a required leader behaviour may do so ineffectively and sometimes even cause more harm than good. As such, they identified three ways a leader behaviour can fail: the required leader behaviour (1) was not performed when the subordinates expected it (e.g., failing to provide requested information in a timely fashion), (2) was intrinsically negative (e.g., being harsh), or (3) was done poorly (e.g., being unclear when clarifying goals). Of course, whether a leader behaviour actually turns out to be faulty, ultimately depends on whether it causes the target subordinate(s) to feel bad about it. Amabile and co-workers provided evidence of leader behaviours that can be classified as 'good' or 'bad' based on their subordinates' accounts of the incident in end-of-day diaries. An example of good monitoring from a subordinate's perspective is 'Received a call from Aaron [the team leader] who is in Italy. Just checking up on things and giving an encouraging word on progress and that we are doing the right things' (p. 17), whereas an example of bad monitoring is '[My team leader] mentioned this morning that he wanted to review my presentation w/ me sometime today – again – he needs to be in control!!' (p. 19). In all, in order to understand what distinguishes good from bad managers one needs to probe the *inner work life* of their subordinates.

The Inner Work Life, the Progress Principle, and Positive Team Leadership

Amabile and Kramer (2011) conducted a unique longitudinal study of teams in corporations in the United States. They selected 26 project teams from seven companies within three industries (consumer products, chemicals, and high-tech) specifically because, according to top managers in the companies, creativity was both possible and desirable in the teams' projects. Most of the members of each team had the team's project as their main work assignment. The total number of team members was 238. All teams had a management-designated supervisor who was also an active member of the team. Data were collected from the onset to the end of each project, with a mean of 123.7 days and a range of 57–256 days. Every day for the whole duration of the projects, participants completed an end-of-day diary, which asked them to report freely on the most project-relevant event from the day, describing their work on the project, their own feelings about the project, and teammates' feelings about the project. The rich textual data, together with a wealth of standardized quantitative measures of personal and team characteristics, allowed the researchers to triangulate information coming from different members of each team and hence gain a deep understanding of the complex day-to-day dynamics that led some teams to strive and others to struggle.

Amabile and Kramer (2011) proposed a dynamic model of individual performance in team project work that they called *the inner work life stream*. The model posits that individual performance in every workday is a function of workday events. Workday events influence perceptions about the organization, its managers, the work being done, and the extent to which work is accomplished, and foster positive or negative emotions. Perceptions and emotions go hand in hand and influence each other; for example, an instance of positive leader behaviour may foster positive affect, which in turn may foster a positive appraisal of management. Perceptions and emotions conjointly influence work motivation, including the identification of goals, the determination to pursue them, and the way they are pursued. Finally, the whole workday inner life – including the perceptions, emotions, and motivation lived in the course of a workday – determines the individual performance on that workday.

How does good performance on a single workday evolve into good long-term performance? By focusing on a specific project team that demonstrated remarkable resilience and performance, Amabile and Kramer (2011) discovered that making real, meaningful progress in the team project day after day boosts long-term performance by enhancing work-related emotions, perceptions of the team and the organization, and hence work motivation, to create that virtuous cycle that exemplifies the *progress principle*. The progress principle essentially states that uninterrupted, stepwise progress feeds inner work life, which in turn fosters more progress, leading to an upward spiral. The perception of progress includes breakthroughs, small wins, goal completion, and demonstrable progress towards goal completion. There might be many different kinds of positive events in a workday; but what the progress principle states is that only the perception that real and meaningful progress was made in the team project work has the power to boost long-term performance. The bottom line is that, what matters is progress, not just pleasant emotions.

Amabile and Kramer (2011) investigated the influence that positive and negative events at work have on inner work life and performance, and discovered a marked asymmetry: setbacks are more powerful, and their effect more durable in hindering inner work life, than incidents of progress are in fostering inner work life. How do setbacks influence inner work life? A single diary report from a study participant is sufficient to describe the effects:

> I don't understand why R&D kills so many of my projects, yet I am supposedly measured on new product development! Dean Fisher [VP of R&D] killed my new handheld mixer three times before it was approved a couple of weeks ago. Very conflicting goals, causing us to start, stop, restart, etc.
>
> (Amabile & Kramer, 2011, p. 101)

Obviously, team leaders should act promptly on setbacks like this in order to prevent a vicious cycle that runs opposite to the progress principle, but Amabile and Kramer found that few do it and even fewer do it well.

What should team leaders do in order to keep their team on a continuing progress path towards goal accomplishment? Amabile and Kramer (2011) classified good team-leader actions into *catalysts* and *nourishments*. The former include leader behaviours that support the project, whereas the latter include leader behaviours that support the people working on the project. Catalysts include (1) setting clear short-term and long-term goals, including both direction and meaning of work, (2) allowing autonomy, with the aim of supporting intrinsic motivation and creativity, (3) providing resources, (4) giving just enough time to complete the work (but not too much time), (5) helping with work when one needs it, (6) learning from both problems and successes, and (7) allowing ideas to flow freely within the team. Nourishments include: (1) respecting people, (2) encouraging people, (3) giving emotional support by acknowledging people's negative and positive emotions, and (4) establishing affiliation with people, which is particularly important when people work and communicate from remote locations.

In all, Amabile and Kramer's (2011) study found that what drives individual contributions to a team project is the inner work life of the team members. Moreover, the study found that the inner work life follows the progress principle, and that the team leader plays a fundamental role in facilitating continuing individual and team progress by providing catalysts and nourishments. The unique contribution of Amabile and Kramer's study is that it validates certain classes of leader behaviours not because of their inherent goodness, but because they specifically foster the inner work life of their team members and, via the progress principle, both individual and team performance.

The Missing Bolt in the Affect–Creativity Yoke: Negative Emotions

The studies reviewed in this section of the chapter point out that the positive emotions experienced when engaging in work activities are conducive to better performance, in general, and to increased creativity, in particular. This is consistent with the study reviewed in Chapter 2 (section *Origins and Consequences of Affect*) by Amabile and co-workers (2005), which found that positive affect experienced in any given workday results in more creative work being completed the following workday. This also is consistent with the study reviewed in Chapter 2 (section *The Dual Nature of Affect: Signal and Cause of Progress*) by Rogaten and co-workers (in press), which found that undergraduate students' positive affect in studying predicts better end-of-semester grades, controlling statistically for the grades they received in the previous semester. Finally, this is consistent with studies that manipulated emotions in experimental settings and found that induced positive moods result in more flexible thinking (Hirt et al., 1997), more unusual and possibly original word associations in verbal tasks (Isen, Daubman, & Nowicki, 1987), and more divergent thinking (Vosburg, 1998) in the context of short experimental follow-ups. In all, both longitudinal studies and experimental studies support the hypothesis that positive affect fosters performance and creativity.

What about negative emotions? The studies reviewed in this section of the chapter acknowledge that the real work environments are no paradise (with the obvious two exceptions of your work environment and mine). Problems occur in direct interaction with peers and managers, in failure to solve problems as a consequence of competition with other companies or market downfalls, and indirectly as a result of conflicts between managers at various levels of an organization. All these factors mean that workers are bound to experience negative affect in their average workday. The reviewed studies point out that negative affect can have deleterious effects on work performance and can sometimes even make creative work impossible. Yet, good management nourishes and informs workers to such an extent that they can overcome their negative emotions and remain engaged and productive in their daily work. In all, the reviewed studies support the hypothesis that negative affect hinders performance and creativity, and that even the best management can only offset the negative consequences of negative emotions. Is it true that negative emotions have no positive effect whatsoever on performance and creativity at work?

Studies that we reviewed in previous chapters offer clues to an answer. The study reviewed in Chapter 3 (section *The Creative Self in Social Context*) by Getzels and Csikszentmihalyi (1976) indicate that problem-finding is a necessary component of any creative endeavour. Problem-finding begins with a feeling of dissatisfaction with how things are currently done in a given domain of activity, and ends with the identification of a problem. For example, a banker may discover a certain internal procedure that leads to unnecessary loss of profit for the bank. Both the discovery of the problem and the preceding phase of actively looking for a problem are bound to elicit some negative emotionality. Moreover, the historical reconstruction of scientific discovery and innovation reviewed in Chapter 3 (section *The Creative Self in Social Context*) by Kuhn (1969) indicates that, in order to be successful, discoverers typically need to endure long and dark periods in which they face denial and opposition from their peers before seeing their novel idea recognized as an innovation. In this connection, we have also seen in Chapter 4 (section *The Big Five and Creative Achievement*) that the most creative scientists and artists tend to score quite low on the Big Five trait of agreeableness and mildly low on conscientiousness, which in combination makes them somewhat 'callous', and hence more resistant to opposition by peers. In sum, negative emotions appear to be a 'necessary evil' for any authentically creative endeavour, and the ability and willingness to withstand negative emotions is paramount to success.

Is it possible that negative emotions actually fuel problem-finding and discovery? Anecdotally, this seems to happen with Dr House, the main character of a popular television series *House*. Every episode follows the same two-step script. In the first step, as soon as his colleagues agree and settle on a diagnosis, Dr House sets out to prove them wrong; he does seem to do so driven by negative affect and the desire to humiliate them. In the second step, as he accrues evidence disproving his colleagues' initial diagnosis, Dr House identifies a possible alternative diagnosis and starts following that lead; he does seem to do so driven by positive affect and the desire of finding out the truth (albeit he does not seem to empathize much with the to-be-diagnosed patient). If this account were descriptive of real life, negative emotions would foster performance and creativity at the start of an endeavour, when a problem has to be identified and framed, and positive emotions would foster performance in a subsequent phase of the endeavour, when the identified problem undergoes reality tests and a solution to it is sought. Could the Dr House effect be defined theoretically and tested empirically? Two studies fly counter to the flock and propose that negative affect plays specific and key positive roles in the genesis of creative work.

Martin and co-workers (1993) proposed the *mood-as-input model* to posit that mood influences task motivation in subtle and relevant ways. In general, Martin and co-workers assumed that when people are in a positive mood they tend to process information heuristically, whereas when they are in a negative mood they tend to process information systematically. Thus, people tend to be more analytic when they are in a negative mood compared to when they are in a positive mood. However, Martin and co-workers argued that the effects of mood on information processing are not direct, but are mediated by people's interpretations of their own mood. In any goal-directed activity there are two key questions that determine whether and how to continue the activity: (1) Have I achieved my goal? (2) Am I enjoying the activity? If the first question is raised, people in a positive mood are more likely than those in a negative mood to answer 'yes' and hence process information less systematically, or even stop the activity altogether. If the second question is raised, people in a positive mood are more likely to answer 'yes' than people in a negative mood are; moreover, if they interpret their positive mood as a sign that they are enjoying the activity, they are more likely than people in a negative mood to process information systematically, and hence persist longer in the activity.

Martin and co-workers (1993) tested their hypotheses in two experiments. In experiment 1, participants were shown a list of behaviours to form an impression, and were asked to stop when they felt they had enough information (the experimenter's goal, here, is to elicit the 'have I achieved my goal?' question). As expected, people in a positive mood stopped earlier, on average, than people in a negative mood did. In experiment 2, participants were asked to generate freely a list of bird names. In the first experimental condition participants were told to stop when they thought 'it was a good time to stop' (in order to elicit the 'have I achieved my goal?' question). In the second experimental condition participants were told to stop when they felt 'like stopping' (this is aimed at eliciting the 'am I enjoying the activity?' question). As expected, people in a positive mood stopped earlier in the first condition and later in the second condition than people in a negative mood did. In all, both positive emotions and negative emotions can foster systematic information processing and exertion of effort towards goal achievement, but they do it in distinct contexts depending on which of the two key stop-or-go rules is adopted and on how people interpret their own mood in relation to the adopted rule.

Based on the mood-as-input model, in which contexts are positive affect and negative affect likely to foster performance at work? On one hand, positive affect will foster performance when the stop-or-go rule inherent to the task is the answer to the 'am I enjoying the activity?' question, the worker's answer is 'yes', and he or she interprets his or her positive mood as a sign that the task is enjoyable. In that context, the worker is more likely to process information systematically and to persist in pursuing the activity for its own sake. On the other hand, negative affect will foster performance when the stop-or-go rule inherent to the task is the answer to the 'have I achieved my goal?' question, the worker's answer is 'no', and he or she interprets his or her negative mood as a sign that the goal was not achieved. In that context, the worker is more likely to process information systematically and to persist in pursuing the goal until there is hope.

Given that both can be useful, what is the best way to combine positive affect and negative affect in order to foster creativity at work? We have seen in Chapter 2 (section *Positive and Negative Affect*) that, although it is possible in some circumstances to experience positive and negative affect simultaneously, in general positive and negative affect inhibit each other in any given moment, so that the moment-to-moment variation of affect resembles the movement of a pendulum, alternating phases of positive affect with phases of negative affect. As such, the optimal combination of positive and negative affect can hardly be a constant neutral state. By exclusion, if there is an optimal way to combine positive affect and negative affect at work it should be an optimal sequencing of work phases in which one experiences primarily negative affect followed by work phases in which one experiences primarily positive affect.

Bledow and co-workers (2013) developed and tested a specific model of optimal alternation of affective states that is inspired by the phoenix, the mythological colourful bird that burns to and then rises from ashes, repeating this shocking death–life cycle indefinitely. They based their model on the basic assumption that positive affect fosters creativity at work, and focused on the influence that the affect experienced in one workday (time 1) influences the creativity at work on the same day (time 1) and on the day after (time 2). In these settings they formulated two novel hypotheses.

First, they acknowledged that the negative affect experienced at time 1 hinders creativity at time 1 because it narrows attention down to the details of the problem at hand, fosters slow analytical thinking, and hence can hardly lead to a novel solution to the problem. However, they argued that negative affect helps to build a knowledge structure of incongruous information about the problem. Such a knowledge structure built at time 1 can, under some circumstances, foster creativity at time 2 by strengthening the link between time-2 positive affect and time-2 creativity. Thus, positive affect at time 2 is more likely to generate new mental associations that are specifically about the structure of incongruent information about the problem that was built at time 1, while the worker was driven by negative affect. Therefore, they hypothesized that negative affect at time 1 will moderate the association between positive affect at time 2 and creativity at time 2, in such a way that the higher negative affect is at time 1 the stronger the association between positive affect at time 2 and creativity at time 2 will be.

Second, they argued that, once the structure of incongruous information about the problem has been built, negative affect would cease being useful for the purpose of finding a creative solution to the problem. In particular, a continuing state of heightened negative affect would undermine the cognitive processes that lead from positive affect to a creative solution of the problem. Therefore, they hypothesized that the change of negative affect occurring from time 1 to time 2 will moderate the association between positive affect at time 2 and creativity at time 2, in such a way that the stronger the drop of negative affect is, the stronger the association between positive affect and creativity will be.

The two moderation hypotheses conjointly capture a pattern of change of internal states that Bledow and co-workers (2013) labelled *affective shift*. An affective shift begins with a state of heightened negative affect and ends with a state of heightened positive affect and lowered negative affect. Positive affect at the beginning of the process is beneficial for creativity, but what really matter are the growth of positive affect and the decline of negative affect occurring from the beginning to the end of the process. Bledow and co-workers found evidence supporting the research hypotheses in a longitudinal field study in which participants' affect and self-reported creativity were measured at the beginning and end of a workday for a week, and in an experimental study that induced an affective shift. Although still preliminary, the findings support the idea that negative emotions are not just a 'necessary evil', they are an essential factor of creativity at work. In particular, negative emotions do not seem to have a direct impact on creativity, but they seem to have an indirect impact by activating self-regulatory processes that foster creativity.

PARENTING, TEACHER–STUDENT, AND CHILD–OTHER RELATIONSHIPS

Well-Being Indicators

Parenting and teaching share one important goal: to promote children's psychological growth and socialization in such a way that they will become mentally healthy, competent, socially engaged and responsible, and resilient, and will have an overall high level of well-being. The difference between good and bad parenting or teaching can thus ultimately be seen only when children have become adults. There also are intermediate indicators of positive development, such as how well children are doing in school and whether or not they engage in risky or socially deviant behaviours.

This section will first consider one end-point indicator – creativity in the teenage years – and one intermediate indicator – engagement in classroom activities. A teenager's creativity – or, more precisely, potential to be creative – is a key indicator of eudaimonic well-being. A child's proactive engagement in classroom activities channels motivation into learning, which eventually leads to both the development of competencies and good grades; classroom engagement can therefore be considered an indicator of eudaimonic well-being.

This section will then focus on a somewhat less researched but practically important area of children's lives: the interactions they have with their peers and mentors in the context of structured extracurricular activities, such as sports and group religious activities, that are typically conducted after school and without direct parental supervision. This 'universe' of experiences lies somewhere in between parenting and schooling, and it may have independent effects on children's well-being. A new indicator of well-being will be considered: the extent to which extracurricular activities foster developmental (i.e., positive) and negative experiences in the here and now.

Positive Parenting

Rogers (1954) developed a comprehensive theory of how the self develops in childhood, and of how its development is influenced by parents or tutors. In early childhood, the self becomes a separate part of the *phenomenal field*, that is, the continuous flow of perceptions. At the birth of the self, a child develops a need for positive regard that will last for the entire life, and will always be potentially in conflict with the need for remaining in touch with one's own feelings. Rogers posited that if something goes systematically wrong in parent–child interactions, then the need for positive regard will become too dominant and lead a child to develop systematic patterns of denial and distortion of feelings in adulthood.

The key construct for child–parent interaction is the distinction between acceptant, democratic parental attitudes versus rejecting, authoritarian parental attitudes. On one hand, democratic parents establish an extensive set of rules for child's behaviour, enforce the rules firmly using rewards and praises more than punishments, establish a liberal, non-coercive atmosphere within the boundary of the rules (so that, the child has an autonomous space of action), recognize fully the child's rights and opinions and hence accept the child as a person, and give the child unconditional positive regard, that is, a totally positive appraisal independently of how compliant a child's behaviour is. In this ideal situation, whenever the child violates the set rules, the specific behaviour will be reprehended but the positive regard for the child as a whole will not be put in question. For example, the democratic parent will say 'your action was bad' or 'you did the wrong thing', and not 'you are bad' or 'there is something wrong with you'. On the other hand, authoritarian parents establish incomplete and ambiguous sets of rules, enforce the rules only at times and inconsistently, enforce the rules using punishments more than rewards and praises, establish a coercive atmosphere over all domains of the child's action (so that, the child has no autonomous space of action), consider the child as an incomplete human being who has no meaningful opinions and deserves no rights of expression and decision making, and give the child positive regard conditionally on whether the child behaves the way the parents want.

What is wrong with conditional positive regard? Rogers contended that conditional positive regard is harmful because it leads to the apprehension (learning) of conditions of worth, that is, conditions under which the child is loved, such as 'if I do well in school I am worth loving'. In turn, either implicitly or after receiving punishments, a child will form conditions of not-worth, such as (for a girl) 'if I play soccer with boys I am not worth loving'. By this process what the parents think is worthy and not worthy is *introjected* – through self-reflected appraisal – by the child and becomes a child's own judgment, the phenomenal field begins splitting into aspects of experience that are worthy and aspects of experience that are not worthy, the self begins splitting into aspects that are worthy and aspects that are not worthy, the not-worthy aspects of the self begin being denied or distorted, experience in conflict with the conditions of worth is denied or distorted, and self incongruence settles in. In all, receiving plenty of conditional regard in childhood is a recipe for languishing mental health in adult life.

In sum, democratic parenting is characterized by support for autonomy, structure, and unconditional regard, whereas authoritarian parenting is characterized by control, lack of structure, and conditional regard. Rogers predicted that democratic parenting would lead a child to healthy psychological development, including self-actualization, self-consistency, congruence, lack of defensiveness, and creativity, whereas authoritarian parenting would lead a child to unhealthy psychological development, including lack of self-actualization, inconsistency of the self, incongruence, defensiveness, and lack of creativity.

Harrington, Block, and Block (1987) tested Rogers' (1954) prediction that democratic parenting would foster creativity on a sample of 106 3- and 4-year-olds in California using a longitudinal study design. They assessed the child-rearing attitudes and practices of both parents of each child using two methods. First, mothers and fathers separately answered a questionnaire listing 91 child-rearing-practices items; the set of items that were consensually judged most typical of Rogers' creativity-fostering environment are shown in the upper part of Table 7.1. About a year later, mothers and fathers were asked separately to teach their children a battery of two convergent thinking tasks and two divergent

Table 7.1 *Child-rearing practices self-report items and teaching strategies rating items that were consensually judged as most typical of Rogers' creativity-fostering environment (adapted from Harrington et al., 1987)*

Measure	Item
Child-rearing practices self-report items	▦ I respect my child's opinions and encourage him to express them
	▦ I feel a child should have time to think, day dream, and even loaf
	▦ I let my child make many decisions for himself
	▦ My child and I have warm, intimate times together
	▦ I encourage my child to be curious, to explore and question things
	▦ I make sure my child knows I appreciate what s/he tries or accomplishes
Teaching strategies rating items	▦ Parent encouraged the child
	▦ Parent was warm and supportive
	▦ Parent reacted to the child in an ego-enhancing manner
	▦ Child appeared to enjoy the situation
	▦ Adult derived pleasure from being with the child
	▦ Parent was supportive and encouraging of the child
	▦ Parent praised the child
	▦ Parent was able to establish a good working relationship with the child
	▦ Parent encouraged child to proceed independently

thinking tasks in the presence of an observer who, immediately after the teaching session, rated the parent-teacher on 49 teaching strategies items; the set of items that were consensually judged most typical of Rogers' creativity-fostering environment are shown in the lower part of Table 7.1. Self-report and observer data were then combined to create indices of creativity-fostering child-rearing index for mother, father, and the two in combination for each child. Finally, children's creative potential was comprehensively assessed, by schoolteachers and examiners, in early adolescence, from 7 to 11 years after having measured their parents' child-rearing practices.

Harrington and co-workers (1987) found that creative potential in adolescence correlated with the combined parents' child-rearing index ($r = .46$), mother's child-rearing index ($r = .44$), and father's child-rearing index ($r = .38$). Moreover, regression analyses revealed that parents' child-rearing behaviour in the pre-school years predicted creative potential in adolescence after controlling for, gender, preschool general intelligence, and preschool creative potential. In all, the findings provide full support to Rogers' prediction that democratic parenting fosters children's development of creativity.

Positive Teaching: Autonomy and Structure

The previous section pointed out that positive parenting requires providing children with both support for autonomy and structure. Does this apply to positive teaching as well? Jang, Reeve, and Deci (2010) investigated whether teachers need to provide children with both support for autonomy and structure in order to foster children's engagement in learning activities. They used trained observers to rate the instructional styles of 133 teachers and the behavioural engagement during in-classroom teaching of their 2,533 students in public high school classrooms in the Midwest of the United States. Autonomy supporting instructional style was operationalized using three categories of behaviours: (1) nurturing students' motivation to learn (e.g., stimulating interest and a sense of challenge versus using incentives and seeking compliance), (2) refraining from using controlling language (e.g., providing choices versus stating 'musts'), and (3) acknowledging students' perceptions and feelings (e.g., accepting the expression of negative affect versus prohibiting it). The degree of structure in instructional style was operationalized using three categories of behaviours: (1) making the goals and directions of the learning activities clear, (2) proposing strategies and plans for students to achieve the set goals, and (3) providing constructive feedback in order to help students to develop competencies and good grades. Finally, the collective student engagement of a whole classroom was operationalized using six behavioural indicators: (1) attention, (2) effort, (3) verbal participation, (4) persistence, (5) positive emotions, and (6) voice. Students' collective behavioural engagement correlated strongly with both teacher-provided autonomy support ($r = .70$) and teacher-provided structure ($r = .76$). Moreover, regression analyses revealed that both teacher-provided autonomy support and teacher-provided structure predicted unique portions of variance in students' collective behavioural engagement. In all, the findings provide full support to the broad hypothesis – that can be traced back to Rogers' theory – stating that positive teaching requires providing children with both support for autonomy and structure.

Extracurricular Activities: Developmental and Negative Experiences

What do children and adolescents do beyond spending time in school or with their parents and siblings? Besides spending time alone and hanging out with friends, they typically engage in one or more structured extracurricular activities, such as practicing sports or participating in religious group activities. Structured extracurricular activities are generally viewed as learning environments that offer unique developmental opportunities. But are all extracurricular activities equally good in providing such opportunities? If you have already chosen an extracurricular activity for your child, which guiding principle did you follow? If you still have to make such a choice, how will you go about picking one among the many available in your community? A study addressed the issue by assessing the developmental experiences and the negative experiences that children tend to have when they engage in specific classes of extracurricular and community-based activities.

Larson, Hansen, and Moneta (2006) administered an electronic version of the Youth Activity Inventory and the Youth Experiences Survey (YES 2.0; available at: http://youthdev.illinois.edu/yes.htm) to a sample of 2,280 eleventh graders from 19 high schools in the US state of Illinois. The sample was representative, in terms of demographic figures, of the youth in the United States at that time. In the first step of the survey, the Youth Activity Inventory presented students with a list of 67 activities that are grouped into six categories – sports, performance and fine arts, academic clubs and organizations, community-oriented activities (e.g., Boy Scouts and Girl Scouts), service activities, and faith-based youth groups – and asked to check all the activities in the list they had practiced in the past three months. In the second step of the survey, participants were asked to complete the YES 2.0 survey for only two of the checked activities. The YES 2.0 contains 70 questions tapping three domains of personal development experiences, three domains of interpersonal development experiences, and five domains of negative experiences, as shown in Table 7.2. Students are asked to rate each question on a four-point scale ranging from 1 (*not at all*) to 4 (*yes, definitely*). This methodology allowed for comparison of the six categories of extracurricular activities on each of the 11 YES 2.0 domains of experience; it thus was possible to rank the six activities on 'positivity' and 'negativity'.

Table 7.2 *The types and domains of experiences in extracurricular activities measured by the Youth Experiences Survey (YES 2.0; adapted from Larson et al., 2006)*

Type of experience	Domain of experience
Personal development	▪ Identity work ▪ Initiative ▪ Emotional regulation
Interpersonal development	▪ Teamwork and social skills ▪ Positive relations ▪ Adult networks and social capital
Negative	▪ Stress ▪ Inappropriate adult behaviour ▪ Negative influences ▪ Social exclusion ▪ Negative group dynamics

Larson and co-workers' study (2006) generated three key findings, each holding after controlling statistically for gender, ethnicity, socioeconomic status, and region. First, compared to the mean scores calculated over the six extracurricular activities, attending school classes yielded lower levels of personal and interpersonal development experiences in all domains (particularly so in the domain of emotional regulation), and higher levels of negative experiences in the domain of stress; school classes thus appear to be overall less 'positive' and more 'negative' than extracurricular activities in general. Second, compared to the mean scores calculated over the other five extracurricular activities, participation in faith-based youth groups yielded higher levels of personal and interpersonal development experiences in all domains (particularly so in the domain of positive relations), and lower levels of negative experiences in the domain of stress; thus, faith-based youth groups appear to be the overall most 'positive' and least 'negative' of the six extracurricular activities. Finally, compared to the mean scores calculated over the other five extracurricular activities, sports participation yielded higher levels of personal and interpersonal development experiences in all domains, but also higher levels of negative experiences in the domains of stress and social exclusion; sports therefore appear to be the overall most 'mixed' (i.e., most 'positive' and most 'negative' at the same time) of the six extracurricular activities.

Taken at face value, these findings would suggest that schools are not doing a good job, that sports are dangerous, and that faith-based youth groups are the *panacea*, that is, all the nourishment children need and the total remedy to the developmental problems they may ever encounter. Following this inference, one would then simply send children to faith-based youth group activities, keeping them away from school and sports. What is wrong with this seemingly logical reasoning? First, its collective end-result would definitely not be 'the achieving society' as viewed by McClelland (1961). Second, it disregards entirely the 'no pain, no gain' principle. The main strength of Larson and co-workers' (2006) study is that it compels us to raise some key questions: are negative experiences altogether 'negative'? Or are some negative experiences 'positive', insofar as they provide children with anticipations of real-life challenges and the opportunity to build up personal resources and hardiness to overcome them? More precisely, could it be that the path to adult well-being requires an optimal combination and alternation of developmental and 'negative' experiences? Because Larson and co-workers (2006) assessed the 'positivity' and 'negativity' of experiences only in the here and now, their study cannot answer those exquisitely longitudinal questions.

DIRECTIONS FOR FUTURE RESEARCH

The integration of the several points made in this chapter suggests five broad issues that call for debate and empirical research.

1. *Looking beyond a single romantic relationship.*
   As whole, the study of romantic relationships is still in the early stages. Researchers have focused primarily on factors that influence relationship well-being and its effects on overall subjective well-being, and mostly in the here and now. However, the majority of people engage in various relationships in their lives, sometimes sequentially, other times simultaneously or in partially overlapping sequences. The bottom line is that the majority of dyadic romantic relationships ends well before one of the two partners dies, and some individuals accrue a 'curriculum vitae' of relationships that is much longer than their official CV. Therefore, many questions remain unanswered concerning the dynamics, sequencing, and long-term effects of relationships. For example, how do components of love influence subjective well-being and psychological well-being in the long run, and particularly after a relationship ends? Who is better off, someone who went for passionate love or someone who went for companionate love? More broadly, are persons who privilege passionate love in their multiple relationships better off in the long run than persons who privilege companionate love, or vice versa? These and many other interesting questions wait for an answer.

2. *Individually tailored person–environment matching.*

Research on students and workers appears to make the implicit assumption that there is just one optimal path towards learning, engagement, and performance that works equally well for everybody. This perspective ignores that the various models used to test hypotheses about the relationships between environmental factors and individual well-being indicators generally explain only a relatively small percentage of variance in individual well-being indicators, and hence work only for the average person. It is therefore possible that optimal learning and optimal working require individualized optimal paths. For example, could it be that some students engage the most with the study material if they are given high autonomy and low structure, whereas others engage the most if they are given low autonomy and high structure? By the same token, could it be that some workers need plenty of catalysts and nourishments from their team leader in order to maintain a positive inner work life, whereas others feel somewhat suffocated by plenty of team leader's support? In particular, could it be that some more motivated, autonomous, and creative individuals perceive high structure and high support as spoon-feeding, and hence function better when structure and support are low or even absent? Future research should investigate individual differences in the 'positivity' of 'positive' environmental factors with the purpose of identifying individually tailored person-environment matching.

3. *The progress principle versus the cruise control model.*

On one hand, the progress principle states that experiencing meaningful positive affect every workday fosters work engagement and performance. On the other hand, the cruise control model (which we reviewed in Chapter 2, section *Origins and Consequences of Affect*) states that if people make fast progress in an endeavour, they will experience positive affect and reduce effort. Therefore, the two models make opposite predictions on the link between positive affect in work and work engagement. However, Carver and Scheier (2000) argued that people sometimes avoid 'coasting' by *recalibrating* the speed of progress towards goals that they deem satisfactory. For example, if you have made fast progress in your work today, you may set a faster standard in your work tomorrow: this makes it more difficult for you to experience positive affect tomorrow, and hence keeps you motivated to achieve. Although the concept of recalibration reduces the conflict between the progress principle and the cruise control model, future research should clarify the conditions under which either model applies.

4. *The role of negative emotions and negative experiences in fostering personal growth and well-being.*

   We have seen that Bledow and co-workers (2013) developed an affective shift model of creativity at work that points out the essential role played by the negative emotions experienced in the initial approach to a problem: those seem to drive the construal of a knowledge base of incongruous information about the problem that in a subsequent phase can feed the creative process driven by positive affect. We have also seen that Larson and co-workers (2006) found that sports as an extracurricular activity tend to elicit both developmental and negative experiences in young people. Because sports are universally recognized as offering unique opportunities for personal growth, one naturally wonders if those 'negative' experiences are negative in all instances or whether they may, under some circumstances, turn out to be useful for building up hardiness and hence be 'positive' after all. Finally, we have seen no reference whatsoever to the possible usefulness of negative emotions in romantic relations. This raises the question of whether research on romantic relations has been too rosy and edulcorated, and overlooked the potential goodness inherent in a frank and direct – yet civilized – confrontation between two adults who plan to share a life together. In sum, whether the context is romance, work or school, a key question that awaits for an answer is whether negative experiences and negative emotions are just a necessary evil or, in addition, key ingredients of deep, fulfilling, and successful relations.

5. *The role of trait-like variables that support the self-regulation of emotions.* We reviewed in Chapter 5 (section *Self-Regulation of Emotions*) a number of constructs – attentional control, mindfulness, meta-emotions, and metacognitions – that represent convergent but somewhat distinct trait-like characteristics that allow the individual to self-regulate the negative emotions experienced in challenging contexts, and even turn them into opportunities for enhanced problem solving and achievement. In connection to the previous point, if negative emotions are useful for developing better relations, the ability and willingness to self-regulate negative emotions should be paramount. Future research on relations should assess whether and to what extent mindfulness and adaptive metacognitions, for example, facilitate the affective shift that Bledow and co-workers (2013) regard as the golden route to creative achievement at work.

SELF-DEVELOPMENT AND UNDERSTANDING EXERCISE

This is a group exercise. The task is to discuss and reach consensual answers to the simple problem of promoting life satisfaction in a nation. You as a group are the government of the country in which you reside. In order to make the exercise more real, you should now decide who will play the role of the prime minister (or president) and who will play the role of the various ministers (or secretaries) in the key areas of internal affairs, education, health care, social security, justice, and so on, depending on how many you are.

Your mission is to come up with a governmental strategy to promote the global life satisfaction of your fellow citizens. Identify the main problems faced by your country, paying attention specifically to the economical trends. Is your country getting poorer or richer in these days? How do you expect the economy of your country to fare in the next two years? Based on this assessment, you should decide what messages to give to the population in public speeches, brochures, ads, and behaviours produced by civil servants as they interact with the general public. In other words, how are you going to improve the relationship between the nation – as it is represented by its institutions and the civil servants working for them – and the general public with the aim of fostering peoples' life satisfaction?

In particular, consider the following starting point for your group discussion. We have seen in Chapter 3 (section *Self-Construals and Cross-Cultural Differences in Self-Processes*) that if the economy of a country is doing poorly, collectivism becomes more salient and people will use more interdependent self-construal in evaluating one's own global life satisfaction; if instead the economy is doing well, individualism becomes more salient and people will use more independent self-construal. This means that when the economy goes poorly national satisfaction is more conducive to life satisfaction, so that improvement of the former may prove very useful to sustain the life satisfaction of your fellow citizens in taxing times. How would you then go about improving national satisfaction?

You may draw ideas by perusing the web site of the Office of National Statistics (http://www.ons.gov.uk/ons/guide-method/user-guidance/well-being/index.html), which outlines a research project undertaken by the British Government, under the supervision of Prime Minister David Cameron, to assess validly and reliably national happiness in the United Kingdom. Finally, if you run a web search on expressions like 'national happiness index' you will find numerous articles from major newspapers commenting on this and other countries' similar endeavours.

◊ RECOMMENDED WEB RESOURCES AND FURTHER READING ◊

Websites

Some of the questionnaires reviewed in this chapter can be viewed/downloaded and used freely for your own research:

- Investment Model Scale (IMS; Rusbult et al., 1998) at: http://carylrusbult.com/
- Triangular Love Scale (TLS; Sternberg, 1998) at: http://articles.dailypress.com/1998-03-01/features/9802270261_1_romantic-relationship-intimacy-and-commitment
- Youth Experiences Survey (YES 2.0; Larson et al., 2006) at: http://youthdev.illinois.edu/yes.htm

Reading

- Hendrick and Hendrick's (2005) book chapter reviewing decades of research on romantic relations
- Yukl's (2002) book introducing his taxonomy of managerial behaviours
- Amabile and Kramer's (2011) investigation on project team work in corporations that led to the identification of the progress principle
- Bledow and co-workers' (2013) development and test of the affective shift model of creativity at work
- Harrington and co-workers' (1987) test of Carl Rogers' theory of democratic and authoritarian parenting and their consequences to children's creativity
- Larson and co-workers' study (2006) on the developmental and negative experiences of youth engaged in extracurricular activities

8   Positive Therapy

INTRODUCTION

Psychotherapy has been traditionally defined as a treatment of mental and/or emotional problems – which are collectively labelled 'mental disorders' – by psychological means, involving interaction between a 'client' and a 'therapist'. The client is a person in need of help, and the therapist is a person trained to help. Psychotherapy can be viewed as a structured relationship between a client and a therapist aimed at solving, or at least reducing, the mental and/or emotional problem affecting the client. In essence, if a client's problem before therapy is given a negative score representing its severity as departure from a neutral point representing absence of mental disorder (e.g., –10), psychotherapy will seek making that score less negative (e.g., –3). The maximal success of psychotherapy hence is to reduce a client's problem to a 0 severity score. In this, the traditional approach to psychotherapy wholly endorses the traditional medical model, according to which the ultimate goal of medical therapy is healing, meant as disappearance of a disease.

A large number of therapies for mental disorders have been developed. These can be conveniently grouped into three main schools of thought. Freud's (e.g., 1925) psychoanalysis focuses on the sexual and aggressive contents of the unconscious, and tries to solve clients' current problems by retrieving and re-enacting memories of events that took place in their early childhoods. In contrast, behaviourist therapies (e.g., Yates, 1970) focus on how problems can be acquired through learning via classic or operant conditioning, and tries to solve clients' current problems by 'unlearning' maladaptive stimulus–response associations, that is, by manipulating the environmental stimuli in such a way that the unwanted symptoms would eventually extinguish, hence making the client 'asymptomatic'. Finally, cognitive therapy (CT) – which was pioneered by Aaron Beck (e.g., 1967) and Albert Ellis (e.g., 1987) – focuses on the identification of dysfunctional thinking, and tries to solve clients' current problems by openly confronting and changing their dysfunctional thinking in order to help them to overcome their symptoms. Although these three broad approaches to psychotherapy differ profoundly in many theoretical aspects, they all share the assumption that the purpose of psychotherapy is the reduction of the severity of a client's problem.

Since the birth of positive psychology, Martin Seligman has frequently stated that the practical goal of positive psychology is to foster health and strength over and above the mere absence of symptoms. Numerically, this means that positive psychology should not be content with reducing the severity of a client's problem from −10 to −3, but rather should seek an improvement passing all the way the 0 severity threshold, such as +5. This raises two related questions: what does lie on the positive range of the scale, and why should one seek an outcome of therapy on the positive range? A brief answer to the first question is that, on the negative side of the scale lies *mental illness*, whereas on the positive side lies *mental health*. The brief answer to the second question is that the key advantage of being on the positive side of the scale is that a state of mental health reduces the risk of developing mental illness in the future. We have anticipated in Chapter 2 (section *The Ratio of Positive to Negative Emotions*) that Corey Keyes developed a novel conception of mental health as a continuum ranging from languishing to flourishing. The first section of this chapter reviews in greater depth the distinction between mental illness and mental health and focuses on the dynamic relation between the two constructs.

Although the goal of positive psychology therapy is clear and distinct from the goal of traditional therapies, there is as yet no systematic and specific positive psychology therapy. Undoubtedly, the most novel and distinct form of positive psychology therapy has been developed by Seligman and collaborators to target virtues and character strengths in order to become authentically happy. Chapter 4 (section *Character Strengths and Virtues*) reviewed the conceptual model guiding interventions aimed at improving one's signature strengths to achieve authentic happiness. The second section of this chapter reviews some of the techniques that have been developed to achieve authentic happiness, and reviews preliminary evidence on their effectiveness.

The broaden-and-build theory of positive emotions, which we reviewed in Chapter 2 (section *The Broaden-and-Build Theory of Positive Emotions*), posits that positive emotions can have a profound and long-lasting healing effect. Positive emotions have never been a popular topic in the field of traditional psychotherapy. Yet, in an interesting conceptual paper Barbara Fredrickson argued that the induction and manipulation of positive emotions occurs in many forms of traditional therapy, and this might be a key reason why those therapies are effective. This in turn implies that a bit of positive psychology has resided in traditional therapies well before the birth of positive psychology as an independent field of psychology. The third section of this chapter reviews Fredrickson's argument.

Although CT has earned a dominant position in the field of psychotherapy, difficulties encountered in the treatment of depression have prompted clinicians to develop two main new brands of cognitive therapy: *mindfulness-based cognitive therapy* (MBCT) and *metacognitive therapy* (MCT). The former is enrooted in theories of mindfulness that we reviewed in Chapter 5 (section *Mindfulness*), whereas the latter is enrooted in the theory of maladaptive metacognitions that we also reviewed in Chapter 5 (section *Adaptive and Maladaptive Metacognitions*). Both forms of therapy can in some ways be viewed as interventions aimed at fostering practical wisdom, as defined in Chapter 4 (section *Aristotle*). Interestingly, both therapies appear to clash with basic principles underlying both CT and character strengths interventions. The fourth section of this chapter reviews MBCT and MCT. The final section outlines issues open to discussion, ongoing controversies, and directions for future research.

MENTAL ILLNESS AND MENTAL HEALTH

The traditional approach to psychotherapy is based on a comprehensive classification system of mental disorders that, with only minor differences, is well operationalized by the American Psychiatric Association's (1994) *Diagnostic and Statistical Manual of Mental Disorders (DSM-IV)* and the World Health Organization's (2010) *International Classification of Diseases (ICD)*. With reference to these classification systems, and with the aid of a variety of standardized questionnaires and clinical interview protocols, clinical psychologists and psychiatrists can ascertain validly and reliably the presence or absence of any mental disorder, and hence determine whether a person is disorder-free or is affected by one or more disorders. The traditional approach to psychotherapy, which is based on the medical model, starts with the assessment of the presence and severity of mental disorders, and has as its key target the reduction of severity and possibly disappearance of all mental disorders affecting a client. In all, the concept of mental illness is clear and operational.

What, then, is mental health? The concept of mental health entered formally in the medical literature through a revolutionary statement made by the World Health Organization:

> Mental health is a state of well-being in which the individual realizes his or her own abilities, can cope with the normal stresses of life, can work productively and fruitfully, and is able to make a contribution to his or her community.
>
> (World Health Organization, 2005, p. 2)

Three features of this statement are striking. First, the definition of mental health contains no reference whatsoever to the presence or absence of mental illness, thus implying that it is possible to be mentally healthy while having a mental illness, and that it is possible to be mentally unhealthy while having no mental illness. The statement thus claims the relative independence of the constructs of mental illness and mental health. Second, the definition of mental health refers to the two main definitions of well-being that have been proposed in the field of positive psychology: hedonic well-being (i.e., 'a state of well-being') and eudaimonic well-being (i.e., 'the individual realizes his or her own abilities, can cope with the normal stresses of life, can work productively and fruitfully'). The statement therefore effectively revolutionizes the traditional medical model by including as prime targets of psychotherapy both hedonic well-being and eudaimonic well-being. Finally, the definition of mental health refers to a third, social component of eudaimonic well-being (i.e., '[the individual] is able to make a contribution to his or her community') that until then had been downplayed by both traditional psychotherapy and positive psychology, with only some exceptions (e.g., Keyes, 1998).

Following the publication of the World Health Organization's definition of mental health, Keyes and co-workers set to develop a comprehensive conceptual model and operationalization of the concept of mental health, which was presented in its most complete form by Westerhof and Keyes (2010). Westerhof and Keyes defined mental health as a dimension characterized by three related but distinct components: hedonic well-being, individual eudaimonic well-being, and social eudaimonic well-being. In accordance with Diener and co-workers (1999), hedonic well-being is characterized by high life satisfaction, high positive affect, and low negative affect. In accordance with Ryff and Keyes' (1995) model of eudaimonic well-being, individual eudaimonic well-being – meant as optimal functioning leading to individual fulfilment – is characterized by self-acceptance, positive relations with others, autonomy, environmental mastery, purpose in life, and personal growth. Finally, consistent with the theories proposed by classic sociologists such as Durkheim and Merton (see the review by Keyes, 1998), social eudaimonic well-being – meant as optimal functioning leading to social fulfilment – is characterized by *social coherence* (i.e., the ability to make sense of the working of one's own society), *social acceptance* (i.e., acceptance of others), *social actualization* (i.e., an optimistic outlook on the potential of one's own community), *social contribution* (i.e., a sense that one's own endeavours contribute to the common good), and *social integration* (i.e., feeling to be an integral part of one's own community). In all, high levels on the dimension of mental health require to achieve hedonic well-being as well as both individual and social eudaimonic well-being.

Is mental health, as defined by Westerhof and Keyes (2010), truly independent of mental illness? Numerous studies have addressed this question by administering measures of both constructs to study participants of different demographic backgrounds and cultures – e.g., US adults (Keyes, 2005), US adolescents (Keyes, 2006), Dutch (Westerhof & Keyes, 2008) and South African adults (Keyes et al., 2008) – and analysing their underlying factorial structure. The results from these studies consistently confirmed that the data have a two-factor structure, and showed that a single latent score for the dimension of mental illness and a single latent score for the dimension of mental health have a moderate and negative intercorrelation of about –.5. This overall estimate has, of course, to be evaluated considering the nature of specific mental disorders. For example, a major depressive episode implies both reduced hedonic well-being (e.g., low positive affect) and reduced eudaimonic well-being (e.g., reduced functioning at work and weak social engagement), and as such is likely to correlate strongly and negatively with mental health. Yet, allowing for variability across specific types of mental disorders, on the whole, mental illness and mental health are relatively independent dimensions, and hence are both potential targets for therapy.

We have briefly seen in Chapter 2 (section *The Ratio of Positive to Negative Emotions*) that Keyes (2002) had introduced the view of mental health as lying along the flourishing–languishing continuum. Keyes, Dhingra, and Simoes (2010) used Westerhof and Keyes' (2010) conceptualization of mental health to provide a tighter operationalization of the constructs of flourishing and languishing. In order to be classified as flourishing in mental health individuals must score in the upper tertile (i.e., the top 33 per cent in the distribution of the population) on the majority of the measures of hedonic well-being and on the majority of the measures of individual and social eudaimonic well-being; for example, if two measures are available for hedonic well-being and 11 measures are available for eudaimonic well-being, flourishing requires to be in the upper tertile of at least one measure of hedonic well-being and at least six measures of eudaimonic well-being. In order to be classified as languishing in mental health individuals must score in the lower tertile on the majority of the measures of hedonic well-being and on the majority of the measures of individual and social eudaimonic well-being. Finally, individuals who fit neither the criteria of flourishing nor those of languishing are classified as having moderate mental health.

Are mental health and mental illness functionally related to each other? In particular, does a state of flourishing mental health prevent future occurrence of mental illness? Keyes and co-workers (2010) addressed this research question using a longitudinal study design. They assessed the mental health and the presence/absence of mental illness (12-month major depressive episode, generalized anxiety disorder, and panic disorder) on a sample of 1,723 US adults in two occasions, first in 1995 and second in 2005. They then estimated the relative risk of having mental illness in 2005 as a function of the mental health status in 1995 and its subsequent change. Compared to people who stayed flourishing (i.e., who were flourishing in both 1995 and 2005), the relative risk of having mental illness in 2005 was 8.2 times greater among those who passed from flourishing or moderate to languishing, 6.6 times greater among those who stayed languishing, 4.4 times greater among those who stayed moderate, 3.7 times greater among those who passed from flourishing to moderate, and 3.4 times greater among those who passed from languishing to moderate. Interestingly, the risk of mental illness in 2005 did not differ between those who stayed flourishing and those who passed from languishing or moderate to flourishing. These findings indicate that mental health predicts future occurrence of mental illness and, in particular, that flourishing prevents mental illness, whereas languishing fosters mental illness. In all, it would appear that what we have studied in this book is of profound theoretical and practical relevance to psychotherapists of all orientations.

HAPPINESS-ENHANCING INTERVENTIONS

We have seen in Chapter 4 (section *Character Strengths and Virtues*) that Peterson and Seligman (2004) introduced a whole new set of traits – 24 character strengths grouped into six virtues – that they claimed foster authentic happiness if deployed in everyday life. Moreover, Peterson and Seligman claimed that one's own signature strengths – the set of character strengths one possesses the most – can change over time if one identifies them and cultivates them in everyday life. Finally, Peterson and Seligman claimed that the cultivation of one's own signature strengths would lead to even greater authentic happiness. This section reviews some of the techniques that have been developed to cultivate the various types of character strengths, and the effects that the use of these techniques have on subjective well-being.

Is it complicated to foster character strengths? Rashid and Anjum (2005; available at: http://www.viastrengths.org/Applications/Exercises/tabid/132/Default. aspx) compiled a list of 340 ways in which character strengths can be practiced and strengthened. Table 8.1 lists selected techniques for a subset of strengths. What is striking about the listed techniques is that they are simple, concrete, and feasible for virtually everyone. Therefore, unlike many traditional psychotherapeutic techniques that require the active involvement and continuous monitoring of a therapist, strength-enhancing techniques can be used in interventions other than one-on-one psychotherapy, such as Internet-based interventions and even self-help practice. Obviously, there is not yet evidence that each of the 340 strength-enhancing techniques is effective, but an evaluation of their effectiveness would require just straightforward intervention studies, and hence is at easy reach.

Seligman and co-workers (2005) conducted the first large randomized clinical trial of happiness-enhancing techniques on an Internet sample of 411 adults. Participants were randomly assigned to one of six treatments. Each treatment lasted one week. The first treatment was a placebo exercise that required participants to write about their early memories at the end of each day ('placebo'). The second treatment required participants to write a letter of gratitude to someone who had been kind to them but they never properly thanked, and to deliver it in person within one week ('gratitude visit'). The third treatment required participants to write down three things that went well during the day, together with a causal explanation for them, at the end of each day ('three good things in life'). The fourth treatment required participants to write about a time in their

Table 8.1 *Selected ways of deploying character strengths proposed by Rashid and Anjum (2005)*

Virtue	Character strength	Way to deploy a character strength
Wisdom	▨ Creativity	▨ Do at least one assignment weekly in a different and creative manner
Courage	▨ Bravery	▨ Ask difficult questions that help you and others face reality
Humanity	▨ Love	▨ Reunite at the end of the day and discuss how it went
Justice	▨ Citizenship	▨ Decorate a communal place
Temperance	▨ Forgiveness and mercy	▨ Evaluate your emotions before and after forgiving someone
Transcendence	▨ Appreciation of beauty and excellence	▨ Make your surroundings aesthetically beautiful

life in which they were at their best, identifying their strengths at that time, and to review their story and reflect on the identified strengths once a day ('you at your best'). The fifth treatment required participants first to identify their signature strengths by completing the VIA-IS (Peterson & Seligman, 2001), and then to deploy one of them in a new way every day ('using signature strengths in a new way'). The sixth and last treatment required participants simply to identify their signature strengths by completing the VIA-IS within one week ('identifying signature strengths'). All participants completed scales measuring happiness and depression before the one-week assignment, immediately after, and one week, one month, three months, and six months after completing the assignment. This study design allowed testing several hypotheses about the relative effectiveness of the different types of interventions.

The first and simplest finding was that all six interventions – including the placebo – resulted in increased mean levels of happiness and decreased mean levels of depression over the six-month follow-up, compared with the pre-test, baseline levels. This means that just being a participant in a happiness-enhancing study has a positive and lasting effect on subjective well-being. The second and more substantial finding was that, compared to the placebo, the 'using signature strengths in a new way' exercise and the 'three good things in life' exercise were the only interventions that resulted in higher mean levels of happiness and lower mean levels of depression at each measurement point throughout the six-month follow-up, and hence emerged as the most consistently effective of the studied interventions. The third finding was that, compared to the placebo, the 'gratitude visit' exercise resulted in higher mean levels of happiness and lower mean levels of depression for the duration of one month only. The final and arguably most interesting finding is that the positive effects of the 'using signature strengths in a new way' exercise and the 'three good things in life' exercise were mediated by their continued practice. In other words, participants continued to practice these exercises beyond the one-week intervention, and this continued practice explains at least in part why those exercises still had a positive effect on subjective well-being six months after the intervention. In sum, at least two of the happiness-enhancing exercises ('using signature strengths in a new way' and 'three good things in life') appear to be effective if practiced with continuity, and hence are candidates for inclusion in any therapeutic intervention.

A following intervention study confirmed that happiness-enhancing techniques are effective particularly if study participants commit to them and keep practicing them after the formal treatment period. Lyubomirsky and co-workers (2011b) conducted a randomized clinical trial on 330 US undergraduate students. Participants were randomly assigned to one of three treatments. Each treatment lasted eight weeks. The first treatment was a placebo exercise that required participants to spend 15 minutes per week remembering their activities over the past week ('placebo'). The second treatment required participants to spend 15 minutes per week remembering instances in which they were grateful to someone who had been kind to them and then write a thank-you letter to that person – but without sending it ('expressing gratitude'). The third and final treatment required participants to spend 15 minutes per week envisioning a life consistent with their ideal self – including the domains of romantic life, educational achievement, personal interests, family life, career opportunities, social life, community involvement, and health – and to write it up ('expressing optimism'). Participants in all three treatment groups completed scales measuring effort put in carrying out the weekly exercise, happiness, life satisfaction, and affect before the eight-week assignment, immediately after, and six months after completing the assignment.

Three findings are of particular importance here. First, compared to the placebo, the 'expressing gratitude' exercise and the 'expressing optimism' exercise did not result in significantly higher mean levels of happiness, life satisfaction, and positive affect, and did not result in significantly lower mean levels of negative affect throughout the six-month follow-up. Second, effort in practicing the assignment during and after the eight-week treatment predicted more subjective well-being throughout the six-month follow-up. Finally, the interaction of treatment and effort was nearly significant, suggesting that effort predicts more future subjective well-being for the 'expressing gratitude' exercise and the 'expressing optimism' exercise but not for the placebo exercise. In all, these findings suggest that in order to have a lasting effect, happiness-enhancing techniques require commitment and continued practice, and hence – so to speak – do not provide immunization by a single inoculation.

POSITIVE EMOTIONS INTERVENTIONS

We have seen in Chapter 2 (section *The Broaden-and-Build Theory of Positive Emotions*) that the broaden-and-build theory of positive emotions states that positive emotions expand the scope of attention and broaden cognitive and behavioural repertoires (broaden hypothesis), may have long-term effects by enhancing cognitive resources (build hypothesis), and diminish or even undo the deleterious influence of negative emotions (undoing hypothesis). In a conceptual paper, Fredrickson (2000) contended that two large groups of psychotherapies are effective because they foster positive emotions, even if the proponents of those psychotherapies hold different explanations for their effectiveness.

The first group consists of relaxation therapies. These therapies are a large and heterogeneous group ranging from the traditional Asian practices of meditation and Yoga to modern techniques like biofeedback (e.g., Blumenthal, 1985) and autogenic training (e.g., Stetter & Kupper, 2002). What is common to all these therapies is that they seek to elicit a measurable psychophysiological relaxation response, and that they are used to treat both psychological disorders (e.g., anxiety disorders, mild-to-moderate depression, and sleep disorders) and physical disorders (e.g., headache, coronary heart disease, and asthma). They generally include one or more of the following exercises: (a) muscle relaxation, (b) imagery of quiet sceneries or pleasant events, and (c) meditation toward present-moment experience (i.e., mindfulness). Two main explanations were put forth for the effectiveness of relaxation therapies. First, the relaxation response is physiologically incompatible with the stress response, and hence the former impedes the latter (e.g., Benson, 1975). Second, relaxation fosters mindfulness and adaptive coping, which in turn foster a more positive re-appraisal of the stressor and hence less perceived stress. Fredrickson (2000) instead posited that relaxation therapies are effective chiefly because they foster the positive emotion of contentment. As such, relaxation therapies are re-conceptualized as emotion induction techniques.

The second group consists of therapies aimed at finding positive meaning in everyday life. These therapies include three distinct approaches that aim at treating depression and dysphoria, which can be viewed as systematic deficit of positive affect throughout everyday life activities (e.g., Watson, Clark, & Carey, 1988). Within the behaviourist tradition, treatment focuses on enhancing a client's engagement in pleasant daily activities, such as socializing, exercising, and inventing (e.g., Lewinsohn & Gotlib, 1995). Within the cognitive tradition treatment focuses on changing a client's explanatory style from an internal, stable, and global causal interpretation of negative events to an external, changeable, and local explanatory style (e.g., Seligman et al., 1988; also see Chapter 5, section *Optimism*). Within the phenomenological tradition, treatment focuses on seeking and finding meaning and purpose in everyday life challenges through, for example, philosophical reflection and religious exploration (e.g., Folkman, 1997). Fredrickson (2000) instead posited that all these three forms of therapy are effective chiefly because they foster positive emotions. Thus, therapies aimed at finding positive meaning in everyday life are re-conceptualized as emotion induction techniques.

Are then positive emotions the panacea for all mental disorders and depression in particular? Fredrickson (2000) invited cautiousness: 'Certainly, momentary relief from sad or depressed mood is not sufficient to prevent or treat depression' (no pagination). Yet, she argued that just one meaningfully positive emotion can increase an individual's receptiveness to future meaningfully positive events, which can foster more meaningfully positive emotions and, hence, trigger an upward spiral.

MINDFULNESS-BASED COGNITIVE THERAPY AND METACOGNITIVE THERAPY

The World Health Organization (2012) reports that depression was the first cause of disability among all physical and mental diseases, and the fourth contributor to the *global burden of disease* (i.e., the sum of years of potential life lost due to premature mortality and the years of productive life lost due to disability) in the year 2000. Moreover, the World Health Organization (2012) deems depression to be on the rise worldwide, and predicts that it will be the second contributor to the global burden of disease by the year 2020. Depression is therefore a major concern for all psychotherapies, and in particular for CT (e.g., Butler et al., 2006).

The CT of depression is grounded in Becks' Cognitive Theory of Depression (Beck, 1967; Clark, Beck, & Alford, 1999). In a nutshell, the theory posits that depression-prone people hold negative beliefs about self (e.g., they perceive themselves as flawed, worthless, and even not worth loving), their environment (e.g., they perceive significant others as hostile, unhelpful, or even harmful), and their future prospects (e.g., they believe that their effort will not pay off, and hence feel helpless). These negative beliefs often form structured schemata, that is, integrated and distorted ways to interpret reality characterized by a core of key negative assumptions that a person will tend not to question and hence will retain 'as is'. Negative schemata are deemed to distort the interpretation of everyday life events through a variety of processes, such as overgeneralization, magnification of negative events, and minimization of positive events. The theory posits that negative schemata are the main cause of dysfunctional mood, dysfunctional behaviour in response to negative events, and ultimately depression. Therefore, the theory prescribes that the treatment of depression should primarily target negative schemata. In accordance with Beck's theory, the CT of depression hinges on identifying a client's negative schemata and challenging them through evidence-based and open discussion. This is typically accomplished by asking clients to test their unquestioned assumptions in order to determine whether they are wrong, unrealistic, or simply self-defeating.

Numerous clinical trials have consistently found that CT has an enduring effect in the treatment of depression (e.g., Butler et al., 2006; Hollon, Stewart, & Strunk, 2006). Yet, if the clients are not closely monitored and supported after the primary treatment, the relapse and reoccurrence rates are remarkably high (e.g., Kupfer et al., 1992). In an attempt to prevent relapse and reoccurrence of primary depressive episodes, researchers have developed MBCT.

As seen in Chapter 5 (section *Mindfulness*), mindfulness essentially means a deliberate attentional focus on ongoing experience and a non-judgmental approach to experience. This in turn implies 'stepping back', not being caught into experience, and accepting experience 'as is' no matter how painful it might be. Although there is no single agreed upon and standardized mindfulness enhancement intervention, any form of MBCT is bound to differ from CT on two key points. First, CT invites the client to engage in self-appraisal and make explicit one's own beliefs about the self, whereas MBCT invites the client to listen to experience directly, without thinking of the self and engaging in self-appraisal. Second, CT challenges client's beliefs in and around schemata, whereas MBCT asks the client to listen to one's own ongoing experience.

Numerous studies have evaluated the effectiveness of MBCT relative to other forms of intervention. We will focus here on a small selection of studies. A clinical trial on clients with recurrent depression found that the relapse rates over 15 months following primary treatment were lower in a MBCT group compared to those in a maintenance anti-depressant medication (m-ADM) group (Kuyken et al., 2008). A clinical trial on adults with a history of depression and current depressive symptoms found, using the Experience Sampling Method, that mindfulness training results in more positive emotion and greater responsiveness to pleasant daily events relative to no training (Geschwind et al., 2011). An eight-week Web-based intervention study on people from the community with mild-to-moderate psychological problems found that mindfulness training resulted in higher positive affect and lower negative affect at post-treatment (Schroevers & Brandsma, 2010). Finally, an eight-week intervention study on a non-clinical sample of people facing stressful circumstances in their daily lives found that those who received mindfulness training experienced less anxiety and depression before, during, and after stressful events than those in a waiting-for-treatment list (Kaviani, Javaheri, & Hatami, 2011). In all, MBCT appears to foster both subjective well-being and psychological well-being in both clinical and non-clinical samples.

MCT is the most recent approach to the prevention of relapse and reoccurrence of depression (Wells, 2009). As seen in Chapter 5 (section *Adaptive and Maladaptive Metacognitions*), maladaptive metacognition essentially means relatively stable beliefs about own cognitive processes that foster maladaptive coping in response to threatening external stimuli and to one's own dysphoric internal states. In particular, Wells and Matthews' (1994) and Wells' (2000, 2009) theory of psychological dysfunction posits that maladaptive metacognitions are dormant in normal times and become active whenever an individual encounters a problematic situation. Through repeated activation, metacognitions maintain psychological dysfunction meant as cognitive-attentional syndrome (CAS) characterized by perseverative thinking, maladaptive use of attention, and maladaptive coping. The primary goal of MCT is to help clients to operate in metacognitive mode, so that, they interpret thoughts as cues that have to be subsequently evaluated, perform evidence-based belief tests and elaboration, and adopt adaptive coping strategies. The successful completion of treatment consists of teaching a client a new and stable way of responding to threatening stimuli and dysphonic feelings that does not involve the activation of the CAS. MCT has been successfully applied to the treatment of many disorders, including depression (Papageorgiou & Wells, 2003), generalized anxiety disorder (Wells & Carter, 2001), and hypochondriasis (Bouman & Meijer, 1999).

The MCT of depression (Wells, 2009) uses four techniques: (a) attention training (designed to foster flexible use of attention and awareness of one's own metacognitive processes), (b) identification of rumination and threat monitoring (designed to foster awareness of perseverative thinking), (c) challenge negative metacognitive beliefs about the uncontrollability of dysphoric feelings (designed to demonstrate that feelings of anxiety and depression often are transient and insignificant), and (d) challenge positive metacognitive beliefs about rumination and threat monitoring (designed to demonstrate that perseverative thinking leads to maladaptive coping).

MCT differs in an important way from CT. The two theories are similar in that they both challenge client's beliefs. However, whereas CT challenges the content of dysphoric thoughts and emotions, MCT challenges the metacognitive beliefs that lead to rumination and threat monitoring. Imagine, for example, the case of Jim, a young man who is slightly overweight, believes he is seen as 'fat' by others, feels bad about it, and hence has a low self-concept. On one hand, CT would challenge Jim's belief that he is fat, for example by referring to population statistics or focusing on daily experience of potential partners demonstrating interest in him. On the other hand, MCT would ignore Jim's belief that he is fat and would instead challenge his belief that ruminating about his looks and monitoring all the time how bad he feels about his looks can be of any help, for example, in finding a partner.

MCT also differs in an important way from MBCT. The two theories are similar in that they both foster a non-judgmental approach to problems and feelings. However, whereas MBCT advocates a global reduction of judgmental processes across the board, MCT advocates a specific reduction of judgmental processes for the purpose of identifying rumination and threat monitoring. Moreover, MCT requires a judgmental approach when challenging metacognitive beliefs.

In all, the key difference is that MCT views mindfulness as a tool and not as an end in itself – as a stepping stone for targeting those specific psychological processes that directly maintain dysphoric feelings.

When comparing the three forms of therapy considered in this section one can easily see that MBCT and MCT are more similar to each other than either is to CT. CT works primarily on self-beliefs in an attempt to improve a compromised self-concept. MBCT works primarily on gaining unconditional, direct access to the flow of momentary experience in an attempt to improve thwarted self-processes. MCT works primarily on changing metacognitive beliefs about rumination and threat monitoring in an attempt to substitute dysfunctional self-processes with adaptive ones. In sum, CT differs from the others in that it focuses on the self-concept, whereas MBCT and MCT are similar in that they both focus on self-processes.

How do the three forms of therapy considered in this section compare with signature strengths enhancing interventions? Strengths interventions differ from CT in that they are not content with making a negative self-concept less negative. They are content only if clients develop character strengths to the extent that their self-concepts will be on the positive side of the scale after treatment. Keeping in mind this difference, CT and strengths interventions are both self-concept treatments. Strengths interventions and CT differ greatly from MBCT and MCT, in that the latter two are both self-process treatments. Given the growing evidence in support of the effectiveness of MBCT and MCT, positive psychologists might consider shifting from interventions that target the self-concept to interventions that target self-regulation.

DIRECTIONS FOR FUTURE RESEARCH

The integration of the several points made in this chapter suggests three broad issues that call for debate and empirical research.

1. *Combining and contrasting 'positive' and 'negative' treatments.* Given that positive psychology therapy is work in progress, it is too early for overall evaluations of its effectiveness. Yet, the preliminary evidence reviewed in this chapter suggests that specific positive psychology interventions are both parsimonious and effective, and hence might complement well-established, traditional therapies at least in some instances. There are many interesting research questions that should be asked about the ancillary use of positive psychology interventions. For example, would gratitude exercises be a useful addition to the CT of depression? Answering that question would require to

conduct a randomized trial in which a group of depressed clients is treated using only CT and another group is treated using both CT and a gratitude exercise. If follow-up measures of subjective well-being and psychological well-being turned out to be higher in the latter group, then the evidence would support the hypothesis that a gratitude exercise contributes over and above CT to recovery from depressive symptoms. In all, humble applications of this kind could provide great insight in the unique contribution of positive psychology interventions.

2. *Should we foster the self-concept or the self-process?*
   We have seen that character strengths based therapies essentially target the self-concept, and hence try to foster a 'thought change' in respect to oneself. On the other hand, the emerging MBCT and MCT emphasize acceptance of internal states rather than their modification. Future research should discern which of the two approaches is better, and whether a combination of the two approaches is feasible and more effective than is either of the two in isolation.

3. *Searching for interventions that foster upward spirals.*
   There is growing evidence that emotion enhancing interventions are effective. Yet, their post-treatment effects (e.g., three and six months after treatment) might be due chiefly to participants continuing the emotion enhancing exercises on their own after the treatment. Is this as good as it gets? Broaden-and-build theory posits that, at least in some circumstances, positive emotions will trigger upward spirals that drive a self-regulated growth in subjective well-being and psychological well-being. As such, positive psychology interventions should perhaps become more ambitious and try to identify emotion-enhancing techniques that have long-term effects without requiring from participants a conscious and continued practice following the intervention.

SELF-DEVELOPMENT AND UNDERSTANDING EXERCISE

This exercise consists of carrying out Seligman's gratitude exercise and assessing the effects it will have on you. You will conduct a mini longitudinal and intervention study in which you play both the role of the participant and the role of the researcher.

Participant's Phase

As a study participant, you will have to fill in the same set of questionnaires in two separate occasions – sessions A and E of the five-session process – at least four weeks apart; so that (a) the second time you fill in the questionnaires you will not remember well the answers you provided the first time, and (b) enough time elapses to allow for the effects of the gratitude exercise to become visible. Session A. First, fill in the Satisfaction with Life Scale (available at: http://internal.psychology.illinois.edu/~ediener/SWLS.html) and the Subjective Happiness Scale (available at: http://www.ppc.sas.upenn.edu/ppquestionnaires.htm), calculate your scores of life satisfaction and happiness, and write them down for future use. Session B. The day after, think of a living person who has been especially kind to you and has had a very positive influence on your life, and whom you have never properly thanked. Write a 300-word testimonial to that person, in which you explain clearly and concretely what they did for you, how their actions have positively influenced you, and how you are and feel now as a result of their influence. You should complete your testimonial in one day. Session C. Call this person and tell him or her 'I want to come visit you within a week'. If the person asks you why you will answer 'I don't want to tell you. It's a surprise'. Session D. On the arranged day and time, show up at his or her door, sit down, and read the testimonial. Session E. After three weeks from your gratitude visit, fill in again the SWLS and the SHS, and calculate your scores of life satisfaction and happiness.

Researcher's Phase

Once you have completed sessions A through E as a participant, you should, as a researcher, compare your scores of life satisfaction and happiness across the sessions A and E (i.e., before and after your gratitude visit) and answer the following questions:

(a) Was your life satisfaction score greater in session E than in session A?
(b) Was your happiness score greater in session E than in session A?
(c) Based on your answer to the previous questions, did the gratitude visit have a positive effect on your subjective well-being?
(d) Depending on your answers to the previous question, how can the observed changes (or lack thereof) be explained using the psychological theories covered in this book?
(e) Finally, how would you go about developing this mini longitudinal study into a real study involving a sample of study participants?

◊ RECOMMENDED WEB RESOURCES AND FURTHER READING ◊

Websites

Associations for psychotherapy, with information on study programmes, research developments and upcoming conferences:

■ Mindfulness-Based Cognitive Therapy at: http://mbct.co.uk/
■ Metacognitive Therapy Institute at: http://www.mct-institute.com/about-metacognitive-therapy.html

The following documents can be freely downloaded:

■ World Health Organization's (2010) *International Classification of Diseases (ICD-10)* at: http://www.who.int/classifications/icd/en/
■ World Health Organization's (2012) *Depression: A global public health concern* at: http://www.who.int/mental_health/management/depression/en/
■ Rashid and Anjum's (2005) *340 ways to use VIA character strengths* at: http://www.viastrengths.org/Applications/Exercises/tabid/132/Default.aspx)

Reading

■ Keyes' (2002) seminal paper introducing the construct of a mental health continuum ranging from languishing to flourishing
■ Butler et al.'s (2006) meta-analysis of empirical studies assessing the effectiveness of cognitive-behavioural therapy (useful to grasp the methodological requirements for the assessment of any form of psychotherapy)
■ Garland and co-workers' (2010) theoretical paper probing the possibility that upward spirals of positive emotions can counter downward spirals of negative emotions, and hence foster human flourishing
■ Geschwind and co-workers' (2011) assessment of the effectiveness of mindfulness training in fostering positive emotions in daily life
■ Papageorgiou and Wells' (2003) assessment of the effectiveness of MCT in reducing rumination and depressive symptoms

9 Future Directions in Positive Psychology

THE THREE APPROACHES TO THE QUESTION

Where is positive psychology going? There are three main ways to address this question. The first approach is to look at what positive psychologists think. Many positive psychologists have tried to answer the question, but the answers differ substantially from one another, as Linley and co-workers (2006) pointed out. Following up on Linley and co-workers, Peterson (2009) argued 'It is of course impossible for me to make predictions about the future say with any certainty – if I could, I'd move to Las Vegas or Wall Street and set up shop ...' (no pagination), but then provided his view and recommendations. If you enter the expression 'the future of positive psychology' in a search engine you will find an unbelievable number of entries – I just did it and found 8,320,000 entries, and I am not sure I used the best search engine! I apologize to you, but my life expectancy is too short to review each one of these Internet sources and integrate them into a consistent pattern for you; not to mention that by when I have completed the task, many new entries will have been made. I can only encourage you to browse the Web and see for yourself.

The second approach to the prediction of the future of positive psychology is to look at historical patterns of emergence, development, and 'death' of scientific endeavours and fields. This approach requires the assumption that history will repeat itself in a cyclical fashion. Simonton (2011) gathered and analyzed relevant historical data on persons and events to make specific predictions on the future development of positive psychology. There is a problem, though: it is not always the case that the past repeats itself. For example, every time I purchase a financial product over the phone, my banker forces me to listen to a long ('it will take about 5 minutes ...') disclaimer and at the end asks 'do you confirm that you understand this?' – and the full exchange between us is recorded. The key point she wants me to confirm that I have understood is that 'past performance is not indicative of future performance'. The pragmatic reason for gathering informed consent from me is to ensure that, if the investment goes wrong and I lose money, I will not be in a position to blame the bank. Nevertheless, she is 'scientifically' right, as Lehman Brothers passed in only three days from being a top rated bank to being an insolvent bank in 2008, and that was the beginning of a long, yet unfinished phase in which the financial markets have proven to be hard to predict. In light of this, I encourage you to read Simonton's (2011) interesting analysis and forecast, but keeping in mind what my banker says.

The third approach to the prediction of the future of positive psychology is to look at what the prominent positive psychologists have to say on the topic. In 2011, Sheldon, Kashdan, and Steger published *Designing Positive Psychology: Taking Stock and Moving Forward*, a collection of contributions from an outstanding group of expert positive psychologists. The book includes a broad introduction by Csikszentmihalyi and Nakamura as well Simonton's historical perspective, mentioned above. At this stage you know enough positive psychology to delve into that book, and to be able to understand and evaluate critically its various arguments and perspectives to shape your own informed opinion.

Given the extensive work referenced above, I will not even try to predict the future of positive psychology or to state normatively what it should be. In what follows, I will just pursue the humble goal of outlining three scientific issues that have emerged through the seven substantive chapters of this book. These I find interesting and challenging, and I propose them to you in a 'try it on for size' spirit, that is, as things that it would be interesting to know better or more.

THE TRADE-OFFS OF HAPPINESS

As Oishi and Kurtz (2011) pointed out, positive psychology has always held the implicit assumption that the happier, the better. This assumption, in turn, rests on two subordinate assumptions. The first subordinate assumption is that individual happiness is paramount. The second subordinate assumption is that nothing else will be harmed if one maximizes one's own happiness. However, both secondary assumptions are open to criticism.

First, is individual happiness truly the most important thing in life? Kundera (1984) answers the question by reflecting on one of his imaginary characters – a dog:

> If Karenin had been a person instead of a dog, he would surely have long since said to Tereza, 'Look, I'm sick and tired of carrying that roll in my mouth every day. Can't you come up with something different?' And therein lies the whole of man's plight. Human time does not turn in a circle; it runs ahead in a straight line. That is why man cannot be happy: happiness is the longing for repetition.
>
> (Kundera, 1984, p. 298)

If we indeed find happiness in repetition, how can we be happy when we venture in unknown territory? When we engage in a new and challenging endeavour, we can feel thrilled, motivated or even enter flow, but can we be happiest at the same time? We have seen in Chapter 6 that flow seems to be an antecedent of subjective well-being; yet, flow per se is a rather unemotional state, as one's cognitive resources are focused on the task at hand. Moreover, we have seen in Chapter 3 that creative achievement typically requires a long-term struggle to see one's novel idea recognized as innovative by a field of experts. As such, a life of creative achievement seems to be somewhat at odds with a life of happiness. Which one is more important, creative achievement or happiness? Perhaps happiness is not the only thing that matters after all.

Second, as we have seen in Chapter 3, all persons construe their selves both as individual beings and as members of a group, and individuals from Western cultures tend to have a more individualist self whereas individuals from Eastern cultures tend to have a more collectivist self. By definition, individual happiness should be consistent with the individual self, but not necessarily with the collective self. Therefore, there is a risk that anything that fosters individual happiness may at the same time reduce collective happiness within the mind of the same individual. Moreover, what promotes individual happiness may make other people feel miserable. For example, if one of my speculative investments gives me a high yield I will certainly be happy; at the same time, that speculation may result in other investors' financial loss and hence unhappiness. As such, a life of individual happiness seems to be somewhat at odds with a life of collective happiness, and might even endanger the common good. Perhaps the unconditional pursuit of individual happiness is harmful to both the individual and the others.

In sum, the assumption 'the happier, the better' rests on two shaky underlying assumptions. Although it is obvious that a stable condition of unhappiness is dangerous, unconstrained and unconditional pursuit of individual happiness can have a boomerang effect on both the individual and the community. The challenge for future research is to develop and test conceptual models in which individual happiness enters as one variable – not as the only one – which interacts and trades off with other competing variables in determining the overall wellness of single individuals and of their communities. Based on Grant and Schwartz's (2011) view of 'too much of a good thing', which was reviewed in Chapter 4, it is possible that once all the relevant variables are factored in the model, the relationship between the overall wellness of an individual and his or her individual happiness will look like an inverted U curve, such that overall wellness is maximized for a value of individual happiness which is high but not extremely so.

NEGATIVE EMOTIONS AS SIGNALS

Are negative emotions always bad for an individual? As Oishi and Kurtz (2011) pointed out, positive psychology has always held the implicit assumption that negative emotions are unconditionally bad for an individual. Contrary to this assumption, they argued that negative emotions play an important role in any well-lived life. Consistent with Oishi and Kurtz's view, some of the theories reviewed in Chapter 5 claim that there is nothing inherently wrong with negative emotions, and that much depends on how an individual attends to them. Individuals with strong attentional control are able to respond to negative emotions by exploring potentially adaptive responses to the perceived problem. Likewise, individuals who experience meta-emotions of interest for their primary negative emotions are able to down-regulate their primary emotions. Finally, mindfulness, which implies a non-judgmental opening to experience no matter how painful it might be, fosters resilience in face of negative emotions. In all, there is plenty of theoretical and empirical work indicating that negative emotions are not necessarily bad for an individual.

Are negative emotions a necessary evil? Probably yes, not only because life is not always beautiful, but also because any endeavour encounters some degree of resistance, particularly if it involves creativity. We have seen in Chapter 3 that problem-finding appears to be a necessary component of any creative endeavour. Problem-finding begins with a feeling of dissatisfaction with how things are currently done in a given domain of activity, and ends with the identification of a problem. Both the looking for and the discovery of the problem are bound to be accompanied, and perhaps even fuelled, by negative emotionality. Finding true problems is an important social function. If we want to exert that function we need to accept that negative emotions are necessary.

Finally, can negative emotions be good for an individual? This is a difficult one. We know that in the early stages of a challenging endeavour individuals typically engage in perseverative thinking, characterized by excessive threat monitoring and fight-or-flee responses. We know that those who succeed in their endeavours eventually snap out of perseverative thinking, make a feasible plan of action, and pursue it until they achieve the set goals. What we do not know is if the initial perseverative phase, with all the negative emotions associated with it, is useful for motivating the person to take active steps toward success. To put it simply, we need to know if getting justifiably upset is actually good for us, or if we instead should live through any downturn in a permanent state of mindfulness.

Preliminary evidence suggests that being in or getting into a negative mood at the onset of a challenging endeavour is paramount to produce a novel and adaptive solution to a problem. We have seen in Chapter 7 that Bledow and co-workers (2013) developed an affective shift model of creativity at work that points out the essential role played by the negative emotions experienced in the initial approach to a problem. Those emotions seem to drive the systematic construal of a knowledge base of incongruous information about the problem that in a subsequent phase of the endeavour can feed the creative process under two conditions: (a) negative affect decreases, and (b) positive affect increases. If both conditions are satisfied, positive affect will foster mental associations that are likely to be about the knowledge base of incongruous information, and hence lead to a creative solution of the problem.

If indeed negative emotions have an important, albeit yet insufficiently under-stood, role in the genesis of eudaimonic well-being, the ability and willingness to self-regulate one's own emotions should play an equally important role. We reviewed in Chapter 5 a number of constructs – such as attentional control, mindfulness, meta-emotions, and adaptive and maladaptive metacognitions – that represent convergent but distinct trait-like characteristics that allow the individual to self-regulate the negative emotions experienced in challenging endeavours and even turn them into a propeller of enhanced problem-solving and achievement. These constructs have earned prominent positions in applied fields of psychology, and they wait only to be further developed and applied in the field of positive psychology.

OPTIMAL STATES VERSUS OPTIMAL SEQUENCING OF STATES

We have seen throughout this book that positive psychologists have identified various optimal states, such as a state of heightened intrinsic motivation, a state of mindfulness, and a state of flow. These and other states are considered optimal because of their positive consequences to subjective well-being and psychological well-being. There is some uncertainty as to whether optimal states differ from one another or are different names for essentially a single optimal state. There is even greater uncertainty as to how optimal states should be managed in daily life in order to be authentically optimal. Research to date has looked at this issue by implicitly adopting the assumption 'the more, the better', so that, for example, the more frequently students experience flow, the better they cope with stress. Some outstanding questions are: when should we stop prac-ticing mindfulness and engage in daily life like 'normal' human beings do? Is there any risk associated with excessive flow? When should we stop pursuing an intrinsically motivated engagement – such as writing a book – and do some trading in the stock markets? More broadly, how should we combine the dif-ferent optimal states in our daily life? Addressing these types of questions will require positive psychology to shift from a focus on discrete optimal states to a focus on optimal sequencing of these states.

BEYOND GOOD AND BAD

The three outstanding research issues outlined in this concluding chapter boil down to a single overarching issue. Until recently, positive psychology has proceeded under the simplified assumption that some things (e.g., negative emotions, quitting behaviour, or procrastination) are unconditionally bad for human beings, whereas other things (e.g., positive emotions, perseverance, or task engagement) are unconditionally good. This simplification has helped positive psychology to establish itself as a research endeavour that is distinct from all other areas of psychology. However, the simplified distinction between bad and good is an illusion that masks some of the most intriguing psychological processes that are activated when individuals face challenge and uncertainty. Perhaps, the development and same existence of positive psychology depend on whether it will be able to explain the complex intertwining of 'good' and 'bad' that supports successful adaptation of individuals and groups.

References

Allport, G. W. (1961). *Pattern and growth in personality*. New York: Holt, Rinehart and Winston.

Allport, G. W., & Odbert, H. S. (1936). *Trait-names: A psycho-lexical study*. Albany, New York: Psychological Review Company.

Amabile, T. M. (1979). Effects of external evaluation on artistic creativity. *Journal of Personality and Social Psychology, 37*, 221–233.

Amabile, T. M. (1982). Social psychology of creativity: A consensual assessment technique. *Journal of Personality and Social Psychology, 43*, 997–1013.

Amabile, T. M. (1996). *Creativity in context*. Boulder, CO: Westview Press.

Amabile, T. M., Barsade, S., Mueller, J., & Staw, B. (2005). Affect and creativity at work. *Administrative Science Quarterly, 50*, 367–403.

Amabile, T. M., Conti, R., Coon, H., Lazenby, J., & Herron, M. (1996). Assessing the work environment for creativity. *Academy of Management Journal, 39*, 1154–1184.

Amabile, T. M., Hill, K. G., Hennessey, B. A., & Tighe, E. (1994). The Work Preference Inventory: Assessing intrinsic and extrinsic motivational orientations. *Journal of Personality and Social Psychology, 66*, 950–967.

Amabile, T. M., & Khaire, M. (2008). Creativity and the role of the leader. *Harvard Business Review, 86*, 100–109.

Amabile, T. M., & Kramer, S. J. (2011). *The progress principle: Using small wins to ignite joy, engagement, and creativity at work*. Boston, MA: Harvard Business Review Press.

Amabile, T. M., Schatzel, E., Moneta, G. B., & Kramer, S. J. (2004). Leader behaviors and the work environment for creativity: Perceived leader support. *The Leadership Quarterly, 15*, 5–32.

American Psychiatric Association (1994). *Diagnostic and statistical manual of mental disorders: DSM-IV* (4th ed.). Washington: American Psychiatric Association.

Andersen, P. A., & Guerrero, L. K. (1998). Principles of communication and emotion in social interaction. In P. A. Andersen & L. K. Guerrero (Eds), *Handbook of communication and emotion: Research, theory, applications, and contexts* (pp. 49–96). San Diego: Academic Press.

Anderson, J. R. (1983). *The architecture of cognition*. Cambridge, MA: Harvard University Press.

Anderson, K. J. (1994). Impulsivity, caffeine, and task difficulty: A within-subjects test of the Yerkes–Dodson law. *Personality and Individual Differences, 16*, 813–829.

Andrews, F. M., & Withey, S. B. (1976). *Social indictors of well-being: America's perception of life quality*. New York: Plenum Press.

Appelhans, B. M., & Schmeck, R. R. (2002). Learning styles and approach versus avoidant coping during academic exam preparation. *College Student Journal, 36*, 157–160.

Apter, M. J. (1982). *The experience of motivation: The theory of psychological reversals*. London: Academic Press.

Apter, M. J. (1989). *Reversal theory: Motivation, emotion and personality.* London: Routledge.

Asakawa, K. (2004). Flow experience and autotelic personality in Japanese college students: How do they experience challenges in daily life? *Journal of Happiness Studies, 5,* 123–154.

Asakawa, K. (2010). Flow experience, culture, and well-being: How do autotelic Japanese college students feel, behave, and think in their daily lives? *Journal of Happiness Studies, 11,* 205–223.

Aspinwall, L. G., & Taylor, S. E. (1992). Modeling cognitive adaptation: A longitudinal investigation of the impact of individual differences and coping on college adjustment and performance. *Journal of Personality and Social Psychology, 63,* 989–1003.

Averill, J. (1997). The emotions: An integrative approach. In R. Hogan, J. Johnson, & S. Biggs (Eds), *Handbook of personality psychology* (pp. 513–541). New York: Academic Press.

Baer, R. A., Smith, G. T., & Allen, K. B. (2004). Assessment of mindfulness by self-report: The Kentucky inventory of mindfulness skills. *Assessment, 11,* 191–206.

Baer, R. A., Smith, G. T., Hopkins, J., Krietemeyer, J., & Toney, L. (2006). Using self-report assessment methods to explore facets of mindfulness. *Assessment, 13,* 27–45.

Bagozzi, R. P., Wong, N., & Yi, Y. (1999). The role of culture and gender in the relationship between positive and negative affect. *Cognition and Emotion, 13,* 641–672.

Bakan, D. (1966). *The duality of human existence.* Chicago: Rand McNally.

Bakker, A. B. (2008). The Work-Related Flow Inventory: Construction and initial validation of the WOLF. *Journal of Vocational Behavior, 72,* 400–414.

Bakker, A. B., Oerlemans, W., Demerouti, E., Bruins Slot, B., & Karamat Ali, D. (2011). Flow and performance: A study among talented Dutch soccer players. *Psychology of Sport and Exercise, 12,* 442–450.

Bandura, A. (1986). *Social foundations of thought and action: A social cognitive theory.* Englewood Cliffs, NJ: Prentice-Hall.

Bar-On, R. (1997). *Bar-On Emotional Quotient Inventory: User's manual.* Toronto, Canada: Multi-Health Systems.

Barron, F. (1953). An ego-strength scale which predicts response to psychotherapy. *Journal of Consulting Psychology, 17,* 327–333.

Barron, F. X., & Harrington, D. M. (1981). Creativity, intelligence, and personality. *Annual Review of Psychology, 32,* 439–476.

Batson, C. D. (1990). Affect and altruism. In B. S. Moore & A. M. Isen (Eds), *Affect and social behavior* (pp. 89–125). New York: Cambridge University Press.

Baumeister, R. F. (1986). *Identity: Cultural change and the struggle for self.* New York: Oxford University Press.

Baumeister, R. F., & Bushman, B. J. (2013). *Social psychology and human nature* (3rd ed.). Belmont, CA: Wadsworth.

Baumeister, R. F., Campbell, J. D., Krueger, J. I., & Vohs, K. D. (2003). Does high self-esteem cause better performance, interpersonal success, happiness, or healthier lifestyles? *Psychological Science in the Public Interest, 4,* 1–44.

Baumeister, R. F., & Leary, M. R. (1995). The need to belong: Desire for interpersonal attachments as a fundamental human motivation. *Psychological Bulletin, 117,* 497–529.

Beck, A. T. (1967). *Depression: Causes and treatment.* Philadelphia: University of Pennsylvania Press.

Beer, N., & Moneta, G. B. (2010). Construct and concurrent validity of the Positive Metacognitions and Positive Meta-Emotions Questionnaire. *Personality and Individual Differences, 49,* 977–982.

Beer, N., & Moneta, G. B. (2012). Coping and perceived stress as a function of positive metacognitions and positive meta-emotions. *Individual Differences Research, 10*, 105–116.

Beghetto, R. A., & Kaufman, J. C. (2007). Toward a broader conception of creativity: A case for 'mini-c' creativity. *Psychology of Aesthetics, Creativity, and the Arts, 2*, 73–79.

Beghetto, R. A., & Plucker, J. A. (2006). The relationship among schooling, learning, and creativity: 'All roads lead to creativity' or 'You can't get there from here?' In J. C. Kaufman & J. Baer (Eds), *Creativity and reason in cognitive development* (pp. 316–332). Cambridge, UK: Cambridge University Press.

Bem, S. L. (1974). The measurement of psychological androgyny. *Journal of Consulting and Clinical Psychology, 42*, 152–162.

Benson, H. (1975). *The relaxation response*. New York: Morrow.

Bergdahl, J., & Bergdahl, M. (2002). Perceived stress in adults: Prevalence and association of depression, anxiety and medication in a Swedish population. *Stress and Health, 18*, 235–241.

Berscheid, E. (1983). Emotion. In H. H. Kelly, E. Berscheid, A. Christensen, J. H. Harvey, T. L. Huston, G. Levinger, E. McClintock, L. A. Peplau, & D. R. Peterson (Eds), *Close relationships* (pp. 110–168). San Francisco, CA: Freeman.

Berscheid, E., & Walster, E. (1969). *Interpersonal attraction*. Reading, MA: Addison-Wesley.

Bharadwaj, S., & Menon, A. (2000). Making innovation happen in organizations: Individual creativity mechanisms, organizational creativity mechanisms or both? *Journal of Product Innovation Management, 17*, 424–434.

Biggs, J. B. (1992). Learning and schooling in ethnic Chinese: An Asian solution to a Western problem. Unpublished manuscript, University of Hong Kong, Hong Kong.

Bishop, S. R., Lau, M., Shapiro, S., Carlson, L., Anderson, N. D., Carmody, J., Segal, Z. V., Abbey, S., Speca, M., Velting, D., & Devins, G. (2004). Mindfulness: A proposed operational definition. *Clinical Psychology: Science and Practice, 11*, 230–241.

Blankstein, K. R., Flett, G. L., & Koledin, S. (1991). The Brief College Student Hassles Scale: Development, validation, and relation with pessimism. *Journal of College Student Development, 32*, 258–264.

Bledow, R., Rosing, K., & Frese, M. (2013). A dynamic perspective on affect and creativity. *Academy of Management Journal, 56*, 432–450.

Block, J. (1971). *Life through time*. Berkley, CA: Bancroft Books.

Block, J. (1993). Studying personality the long way. In D. C. Funder, R. D. Parke, C. Tomlinson-Keasey, & K. Widaman (Eds), *Studying lives through time* (pp. 9–41). Washington: American Psychological Association.

Block, J. H., & Block, J. (1980). The role of ego control and ego resiliency in the organization of behavior. In W. A. Collins (Ed.), *Development of cognitive, affect, and social relations: The Minnesota symposium in child psychology* (pp. 39–101). Hillsdale, NJ: Erlbaum.

Bloom, B. S. (1964). *Stability and change in human characteristics*. New York: Wiley.

Blumenthal, J. A. (1985). Relaxation therapy, biofeedback, and behavioral medicine. *Psychotherapy, 22*, 516–530.

Boland, A., & Cappeliez, P. (1997). Optimism and neuroticism as predictors of coping and adaptation in older women. *Personality and Individual Differences, 22*, 909–919.

Bouman, T. K., & Meijer, K. J. (1999). A preliminary study of worry and metacognitions in hypochondriasis. *Clinical Psychology and Psychotherapy, 6*, 96–101.

Boyatzis, R. E. (1973). Affiliation motivation. In D. McClelland (Ed.), *Human motivation: A book of readings* (pp. 252–278). Morristown, NJ: General Learning Press.

Brackett, M. A., & Mayer, J. D. (2003). Convergent, discriminant, and incremental validity of competing measures of emotional intelligence. *Personality and Social Psychology Bulletin, 29*, 1147–1158.

Branden, N. (1984). In defense of self. *Association for Humanistic Psychology*, August–September, 12–13.

Brandtstadter, J., & Renner, G. (1990). Tenacious goal pursuit and flexible goal adjustment: Explication and age-related analysis of assimilation and accommodation strategies of coping. *Psychology and Aging, 5*, 58–67.

Brannon, L. (2005). *Gender: Psychological perspectives* (4th ed.). Boston, MA: Allyn & Bacon.

Brdar, I., & Kashdan, T. B. (2010). Character strengths and well-being in Croatia: An empirical investigation of structure and correlates. *Journal of Research in Personality, 44*, 151–154.

Bridges, K. R. (2001). Using attributional style to predict academic performance: How does it compare to traditional methods? *Personality and Individual Differences, 31*, 723–730.

Brief, A. P., Butcher, A. H., Georage, J. M., & Link, K. E. (1993). Integrating bottom-up and top-down theories of subjective well-being: The case of health. *Journal of Personality and Social Psychology, 64*, 646–653.

Brockmann, H., Delhay, J., Yuan, H., & Welzel, C. (2008). The China puzzle: Declining happiness in a rising economy. *Journal of Happiness Studies, 10*, 387–405.

Brown, K. W., & Ryan, R. M. (2003). The benefits of being present: Mindfulness and its role in psychological well-being. *Journal of Personality and Social Psychology, 84*, 822–848.

Buchanan, G. M., & Seligman, M. E. P. (Eds) (1995). *Explanatory style*. Hillsdale, NJ: Erlbaum.

Bunderson, J. S., & Sutcliffe, K. M. (2003). Management team learning orientation and business unit performance. *Journal of Applied Psychology, 88*, 552–560.

Buss, D. M. (1987). Selection, evocation, and manipulation. *Journal of Personality and Social Psychology, 53*, 1214–1221.

Buss, D. M. (1991). Evolutionary personality psychology. *Annual Review of Psychology, 42*, 459–491.

Buss, D. M. (2000). The evolution of happiness. *American Psychologist, 54*, 15–23.

Butler, A. C., Chapman, J. E., Forman, E. M., & Beck, A. T. (2006). The empirical status of cognitive-behavioral therapy: A review of meta-analyses. *Clinical Psychology Review, 26*, 17–31.

Butt, D. S., & Beiser, M. (1987). Successful aging: A theme for international psychology. *Psychology and Aging, 2*, 87–94.

Campbell, A., Converse, P. E., & Rodgers, W. L. (1976). *The quality of American life*. New York: Russell Sage Foundation.

Campbell, D. T. (1960). Blind variation and selective retention in creative thought as in other knowledge processes. *Psychological Review, 67*, 380–400.

Cantor, N., & Kihlstrom, J. F. (1987). *Personality and social intelligence*. Englewood Cliffs, NJ: Prentice-Hall.

Cantor, N. (1990). From thought to behaviour: 'having' and 'doing' in the study of personality and cognition. *American Psychologist, 45*, 735–750.

Carli, M., Delle Fave, A., & Massimini, F. (1988). The quality of experience in the flow channels: Comparison of Italian and U.S. students. In M. Csikszentmihalyi & I. S. Csikszentmihalyi (Eds), *Optimal experience: Psychological studies of flow in consciousness* (pp. 266–306). New York: Cambridge University Press.

Cartwright-Hatton, S., & Wells, A. (1997). Beliefs about worry and intrusions: The metacognitions questionnaire and its correlates. *Journal of Anxiety Disorders, 11*, 279–296.

Carver, C. S. (1997). You want to measure coping but your protocol's too long: Consider the brief COPE. *International Journal of Behavioral Medicine, 4*, 92–100.

Carver, C. S. (2001). Affect and the functional bases of behavior: On the dimensional structure of affective experience. *Personality and Social Psychology Review, 5*, 345–356.

Carver, C. S., & Scheier, M. F. (1981). *Attention and self-regulation: A control-theory approach to human behavior*. New York: Springer.

Carver, C. S., & Scheier, M. F. (1990). Origins and functions of positive and negative affect: A control-process view. *Psychological Review, 97*, 19–35.

Carver, C. S., & Scheier, M. F. (2000). Scaling back goals and recalibration of the affect system are processes in normal adaptive self-regulation: Understanding 'response shift' phenomena. *Social Science & Medicine, 50*, 1715–1722.

Carver, C. S., & Scheier, M. F. (2003). Three human strengths. In L. G. Aspinwall & U. M. Staudinger (Eds), *A psychology of human strengths: Fundamental questions and future directions for a positive psychology* (pp. 87–102). Washington: American Psychological Association.

Carver, C. S., Scheier, M. F., & Segerstrom, S. C. (2010). Optimism. *Clinical Psychology Review, 30*, 879–889.

Carver, C. S., Scheier, M. F., & Weintraub, J. K. (1989). Assessing coping strategies: A theoretically based approach. *Journal of Personality and Social Psychology, 56*, 267–283.

Cassady, J. C., & Johnson, R. E. (2002). Cognitive test anxiety and academic performance. *Contemporary Educational Psychology, 27*, 270–295.

Cattell, R. B. (1943). The description of personality: Basic traits resolved into clusters. *Journal of Abnormal and Social Psychology, 38*, 476–506.

Cattell, R. B., Eber, H. W., & Tatsuoka, M. M. (1970). *Handbook for the 16PF*. Champaign, IL: Institute for Personality and Ability Testing.

Cawley, M. J. III, Martin, J. E., & Johnson, J. A. (2000). A virtues approach to personality. *Personality and Individual Differences, 28*, 997–1013.

Cermakova, L., Moneta, G. B., & Spada, M. M. (2010). Dispositional flow as a mediator of the relationships between attentional control and approaches to studying during academic examination preparation. *Educational Psychology, 30*, 495–511.

Chang, E. C. (1998). Does dispositional optimism moderate the relation between perceived stress and psychological well-being? A preliminary investigation. *Personality and Individual Differences, 25*, 233–240.

Chang, E. C., Asakawa, K., & Sanna, L. J. (2001). Cultural variations in optimistic and pessimistic bias: Do Easterners really expect the worst and Westerners really expect the best when predicting future life events? *Journal of Personality and Social Psychology, 81*, 476–491.

Chang, E. C., Maydeu, O. A., & D'Zurilla, T. J. (1997). Optimism and pessimism as partially independent constructs: Relationship to positive and negative affectivity and psychological well-being. *Personality and Individual Differences, 23*, 433–440.

Chang, E. C., & Sanna, L. J. (2001). Optimism, pessimism, and positive and negative affectivity in middle-aged adults: A test of a cognitive-affective model of psychological adjustment. *Psychology & Aging, 16*, 524–531.

Chang, H. C., & Holt, R. G. (1994). *A Chinese perspective on face as inter-relational concern*. New York: State University of New York Press.

Chao, R. K. (1995). Chinese and European American cultural models of the self reflected in mothers' childrearing beliefs. *Ethos, 23*, 328–354.

Chen, H. (2006). Flow on the net: Detecting Web users' positive affect and their flow states. *Computers in Human Behavior, 22*, 221–233.

Cheng, C., & Cheung, M. W. L. (2005a). Cognitive processes underlying coping flexibility: Differentiation and integration. *Journal of Personality, 73*, 859–886.

Cheng, C., & Cheung, M. W. L. (2005b). Processes underlying gender-role flexibility: Do androgynous individuals know more or know how to cope? *Journal of Personality, 73*, 645–673.

Cheng, S. T., & Hamid, P. N. (1995). An error in the use of translated scales: The Rosenberg Self-Esteem Scale for Chinese. *Perceptual and Motor Skills, 81*, 431–434.

Cheung, K. F. M. (1996). Cultural adjustment and differential acculturation among Chinese new immigrant families in the US. In S. Lau (Ed.), *Growing up the Chinese way* (pp. 287–320). Hong Kong: Chinese University Press.

Cho, W., & Cross, S. E. (1995). Taiwanese love styles and their association with self-esteem and relationship quality. *Genetic, Social, and General Psychology Monographs, 121*, 283–309.

Choy, W. C. W., & Moneta, G. B. (2002). The interplay of autonomy and relatedness in Hong Kong Chinese single mothers. *Psychology of Women Quarterly, 26*, 186–199.

Christian, M. S., Garza, A. S., & Slaughter, J. E. (2011). Work engagement: A quantitative review and test of its relations with task and contextual performance. *Personnel Psychology, 64*, 89–136.

Clark, A., Frijters, P., & Shield, M. (2008). Relative income, happiness, and utility: An explanation for the Easterlin paradox and other puzzles. *Journal of Economic Literature, 46*, 95–144.

Clark, D. A., Beck, A. T., & Alford, B. A. (1999). *Scientific foundations of cognitive theory and therapy of depression.* New York: John Wiley.

Cohen, R. (2011). The happynomics of life. *The New York Times.* Available at: http://www.nytimes.com/2011/03/13/opinion/13cohen.html

Cohn, M. A., Fredrickson, B. L., Brown, S. L., Mikels, J. A., & Conway, A. M. (2009). Happiness unpacked: Positive emotions increase life satisfaction by building resilience. *Emotion, 9*, 361–368.

Collins, A. M., & Loftus, E. F. (1975). A spreading activation theory of semantic processing. *Psychological Review, 82*, 407–428.

Conte, H. R., & Plutchik, R. (1981). A circumplex model for interpersonal personality traits. *Journal of Personality and Social Psychology, 40*, 701–711.

Conway, J. M., & Huffcutt, A. I. (1997). Psychometric properties of multisource performance ratings: A meta-analysis of subordinate, supervisor, peer, and self-ratings. *Human Performance, 10*, 331–360.

Coombs, C. H., & Avrunin, G. (1977). A theorem on single-peaked preference functions in one dimension. *Journal of Mathematical Psychology, 16*, 261–266.

Coopersmith, S. (1967). *The antecedents of self-esteem.* San Francisco, CA: W. H. Freeman.

Costa, P. T., Jr, & McCrae, R. R. (1992). *Revised NEO Personality Inventory (NEO-PI-R) and NEO Five-Factor Inventory (NEO-FFI) manual.* Odessa, FL: Psychological Assessment Resources.

Costa, P. T., Jr, Terraciano, A., & McCrae, R. R. (2001). Gender differences in personality traits across cultures robust and surprising findings. *Journal of Personality and Social Psychology, 81*, 322–331.

Csikszentmihalyi, M. (1975/2000). *Beyond boredom and anxiety: Experiencing flow in work and play* (2nd ed.). San Francisco, CA: Jossey Bass.

Csikszentmihalyi, M. (1982). Toward a psychology of optimal experience. In L. Wheeler (Ed.), *Review of personality and social psychology* (pp. 13–36). Beverly Hills, CA: Sage Publications.

Csikszentmihalyi, M. (1988). Society, culture, and person: A systems view of creativity. In R. J. Sternberg (Ed.), *The nature of creativity: Contemporary psychological perspectives* (pp. 325–339). New York: Cambridge University Press.

Csikszentmihalyi, M. (1990). *Flow: The psychology of optimal experience.* New York: Harper & Row.

Csikszentmihalyi, M. (1996). *Creativity: Flow and the psychology of discovery and invention*. New York: Harper & Collins.

Csikszentmihalyi, M. (1997). *Finding flow: The psychology of engagement with everyday life*. New York: Basic Books.

Csikszentmihalyi, M., & Csikszentmihalyi, I. (1988). *Optimal experience: Psychological studies of flow in consciousness*. Cambridge, UK: Cambridge University Press.

Csikszentmihalyi, M., & Larson, R. (1987). Validity and reliability of the experience-sampling method. *The Journal of Nervous and Mental Disease, 175*, 526–536.

Csikszentmihalyi, M., Larson, R., & Prescott, S. (1977). The ecology of adolescent activity and experience. *Journal of Youth and Adolescence, 6*, 281–294.

Csikszentmihalyi, M., & LeFevre, J. (1989). Optimal experience in work and leisure. *Journal of Personality and Social Psychology, 56*, 815–822.

Csikszentmihalyi, M., & Massimini, F. (1985). On the psychological selection of bio-cultural information. *New Ideas in Psychology, 3*, 115–138.

Csikszentmihalyi, M., & Rathunde, K. (1993). The measurement of flow in everyday life: Toward a theory of emergent motivation. In J. Jacobs (Ed.), *Nebraska symposium on motivation, 1992: Developmental perspectives on motivation, current theory and research in motivation, 1992* (Vol. 40, pp. 57–97). Lincoln, NE: University of Nebraska Press.

Csikszentmihalyi, M., Rathunde, K., & Whalen, S. (1993). *Talented teenagers: A longitudinal study of their development*. New York: Cambridge University Press.

Csikszentmihalyi, M., & Schneider, B. (2000). *Becoming adult: How teenagers prepare for the world of work*. New York: Basic Books.

Dahlsgaard, K., Peterson, C., & Seligman, M. E. P. (2005). Shared virtue: The convergence of valued human strengths across culture and history. *Review of General Psychology, 9*, 203–213.

David, J. P., Green, P. J., Martin, R., & Suls, J. (1997). Differential roles of neuroticism, extraversion, and event desirability for mood in daily life: An integrative model of top-down and bottom-up influences. *Journal of Personality and Social Psychology, 73*, 149–159.

Davies, K. A., Lane, A. M., Devonport, T. J., & Scott, J. A. (2010). Validity and reliability of a Brief Emotional Intelligence Scale (BEIS-10). *Journal of Individual Differences, 31*, 198–208.

Davies, M., Stankov, L., & Roberts, R. D. (1998). Emotional intelligence: In search of an elusive construct. *Journal of Personality and Social Psychology, 75*, 989–1015.

deCharms, R. (1968). *Personal causation: The internal affective determinants of behavior*. New York: Academic Press.

Deci, E. L. (1971). Effects of externally mediated rewards on intrinsic motivation. *Journal of Personality and Social Psychology, 18*, 105–115.

Deci, E. L., & Ryan, R. M. (1985a). *Intrinsic motivation and self-determination in human behavior*. New York: Plenum Press.

Deci, E. L., & Ryan, R. M. (1985b). The General Causality Orientations Scale: Self-determination in personality. *Journal of Research in Personality, 19*, 109–134.

Deci, E. L., Ryan, R. M., Gagne, M., Leone, D. R., Usunov, J., Kornazheva, B. P. (2001). Need satisfaction, motivation, and well-being in the work organizations of a former Eastern Block country: A cross-cultural study of self-determination. *Personality and Social Psychology Bulletin, 27*, 930–942.

De Cuyper N., Notelaers G., & De Witte H. (2009). Job insecurity and employability in fixed-term contractors, agency workers, and permanent workers: Associations with job satisfaction and affective organizational commitment. *Journal of Occupational Health Psychology, 14*, 193–205.

Delle Fave, A., & Bassi, M. (2000). The quality of experience in adolescents' daily life: Developmental perspectives. *Genetic, Social, and General Psychology Monographs, 126*, 347–367.

Delle Fave, A., & Massimini, F. (2003). Optimal experience in work and leisure among teachers and physicians: Individual and bio-cultural implications. *Leisure Studies, 22*, 323–342.

Delle Fave, A., & Massimini, F. (2004). The cross-cultural investigation of optimal experience. *Ricerche di Psicologia, 1*, 79–102.

Delle Fave, A., & Massimini, F. (2005). The investigation of optimal experience and apathy: Developmental and psychosocial implications. *European Psychologist, 10*, 264–274.

Demorest, A. P. (1995). The personal script as the unit of analysis for the study of personality. *Journal of Personality, 63*, 569–592.

Deponte, A. (2004). Linking motivation to personality: Causality orientations, motives and self-descriptions. *European Journal of Personality, 18*, 31–44.

De Raad, B., & Van Oudenhoven, J. P. (2011). A psycholexical study of virtues in the Dutch language, and relations between virtues and personality. *European Journal of Personality, 25*, 43–52.

Derryberry, D. (2002). Attention and voluntary self-control. *Self and Identity, 1*, 105–111.

Derryberry, D., & Reed, M. A. (2002). Anxiety-related attentional biases and their regulation by attentional control. *Journal of Abnormal Psychology, 111*, 225–236.

Derryberry, D., & Reed, M. A. (2009). Information processing approaches to individual differences in emotional reactivity. In R. J. Davidson, K. R. Scherer, & H. H. Goldsmith (Eds), *Handbook of affective sciences* (2nd ed.) (pp. 681–697). New York: Oxford University Press.

Diener, E. (2000). Subjective well-being: The science of happiness and a proposal for a national index. *American Psychologist, 55*, 34–43.

Diener, E., & Diener, M. (1995). Cross-cultural correlates of life satisfaction and self-esteem. *Journal of Personality and Social Psychology, 68*, 653–663.

Diener, E., Diener, M., & Diener, C. (1995). Factors predicting the subjective well-being of nations. *Journal of Personality and Social Psychology, 69*, 851–864.

Diener, E., & Emmons, R. A. (1984). The independence of positive and negative affect. *Journal of Personality and Social Psychology, 47*, 1105–1117.

Diener, E., Emmons, R. A., Larsen, R. J., & Griffin, S. (1985). The satisfaction with life scale. *Journal of Personality Assessment, 49*, 71–75.

Diener, E., & Lucas, R. (1999). Personality and subjective well-being. In D. Kahneman, E. Diener, & N. Schwarz (Eds), *Well-being: The foundations of hedonic psychology* (pp. 213–229). New York: Russell Sage Foundation.

Diener, E., Lucas, R. E., Oishi, S., Suh, E. M. (2002). Looking up and down: Weighting good and bad information in life satisfaction judgments. *Personality and Social Psychology Bulletin, 28*, 437–445.

Diener, E., Sapyta, J. J., & Sub, E. (1998). Subjective well-being is essential to well-being. *Psychological Inquiry, 9*, 33–37.

Diener, E., Smith, H., & Fujita, F. (1995). The personality structure of affect. *Journal of Personality and Social Psychology, 69*, 130–141.

Diener, E., & Suh, E. M. (1998). Subjective well-being and age: An international analysis. *Annual Review of Gerontology and Geriatrics, 17*, 4–24.

Diener, E., Suh, E. M., Lucas, R. E., & Smith, H. E. (1999). Subjective well-being: Three decades of progress. *Psychological Bulletin, 125*, 276–302.

Diener, E., Suh, E., & Oishi, S. (1997). Recent findings on subjective well-being. *Indian Journal of Clinical Psychology, 24*, 25–41.

Diener, E., Wolsic, B., & Fujita, F. (1995). Physical attractiveness and subjective well-being. *Journal of Personality and Social Psychology, 69*, 120–129.

Dimotakis, N., Scott, B. A., & Koopman, J. (2011). An experience sampling investigation of workplace interactions, affective states and employee well-being. *Journal of Organizational Behavior, 32*, 572–588.

Di Tella, R., Haisken-De New, J., & MacCulloch, R. (2010). Happiness adaptation to income and to status in an individual panel. *Journal of Economic Behavior & Organization, 76*, 834–852.

Drury, J., Cocking, C., Reicher, S., Burton, A., Schofield, D., Hardwick, A., Graham, D., & Langston, P. (2009). Cooperation versus competition in a mass emergency evacuation: A new laboratory simulation and a new theoretical model. *Behavior Research Methods, 41*, 957–970.

Dwek, C. (1986). Motivational processes affecting learning. *American Psychologist, 41*, 1040–1048.

Easterlin, R. A. (1974). Does economic growth improve the human lot? In P. A. David & M. W. Reder (Eds), *Nations and households in economic growth: Essays in honour of Moses Abramovitz*. New York: Academic Press.

Easterly, W. (2011). The happiness wars. *The Lancet, 377*, 1483–1484. Available at: http://www.thelancet.com/journals/lancet/article/PIIS0140-6736%2811%2960587-4/fulltext.

Eisenberger, R., Huntington, R., Hutchison, S., & Sowa, D. (1986). Perceived organizational support. *Journal of Applied Psychology, 71*, 500–507.

Ekman, P. (1992). An argument for basic emotions. *Cognition and Emotion, 6*, 169–200.

Elangovan, A. R. (2001). Causal ordering of stress, satisfaction and commitment, and intention to quit: A structural equations analysis. *Leadership & Organization Development Journal, 22*, 159–165.

Elliot, A. J. (1997). Integrating the 'classic' and 'contemporary' approaches to achievement motivation: A hierarchical model of achievement. In M. Maehr & P. Pintrich (Eds), *Advances in motivation and achievement* (pp. 243–279). Greenwich, CT: JAI Press.

Elliot, A. J., & McGregor, H. A. (2001). A 2 × 2 Achievement Goal Framework. *Journal of Personality and Social Psychology, 3*, 501–519.

Ellis, A. (1987). The impossibility of achieving consistently good mental health. *American Psychologist, 42*, 364–375.

Ellis, G. D., Voelkl, J. E., & Morris, C. (1994). Measurements and analysis issues with explanation of variance in daily experience using the flow model. *Journal of Leisure Research, 26*, 337–356.

Emmons, R. A. (1986). Personal strivings: An approach to personality and subjective well-being. *Journal of Personality and Social Psychology, 51*, 1058–1068.

Emmons, R. A. (1989). The personal striving approach to personality. In L. A. Pervin (Ed.), *Goals concepts in personality and social psychology* (pp. 87–126). Hillsdale, NJ: Erlbaum.

Emmons, R. A. (1992). Abstract versus concrete goals: Personal striving level, physical illness, and psychological well-being. *Journal of Personality and Social Psychology, 62*, 292–300.

Emmons, R. A., & Diener, E. (1985). Personality correlates of subjective well-being. *Personality and Social Psychology Bulletin, 11*, 89–97.

Emmons, R. A., & King, L. A. (1988). Conflict among personal strivings: Immediate and long-term implications for psychological and physical well-being. *Journal of Personality and Social Psychology, 54*, 1040–1048.

Emmons, R. A., & McAdams, D. P. (1991). Personal strivings and motive dispositions: Exploring the links. *Personality and Social Psychology Bulletin, 17*, 648–654.

Engeser, S. (Ed.) (2012). *Advances in flow research*. New York: Springer.

Engeser, S., & Rheinberg, F. (2008). Flow, moderators of challenge-skill-balance and performance. *Motivation and Emotion, 32*, 158–172.

Engeser, S., & Schiepe-Tiska, A. (2012). Historical lines and an overview of current research. In S. Engeser (Ed.), *Advances in flow research* (pp. 1–22). New York: Springer.

Epstein, S. (1998). *Constructive thinking: The key to emotional intelligence*. Westport, CT: Praeger.

Erikson, E. H. (1959). *Identity and the life cycle*. New York: International Universities Press.

Erikson, E. H. (1963). *Childhood and society* (2nd ed.). New York: Norton.

Erikson, E. H. (1968). *Identity: Youth and Crisis*. New York: Norton.

Erikson, E. H. (1982). *The life cycle completed: A review*. New York: Norton.

Extremera, N., Ruiz-Aranda, D., Pineda-Galán, C., & Salguero, J. M. (2011). Emotional intelligence and its relation with hedonic and eudaimonic well-being: A prospective study. *Personality and Individual Differences, 51*, 11–16.

Eysenck, H. J., & Eysenck, S. B. G. (1975). *Manual of the Eysenck Personality Questionnaire (adult and junior)*. London: Hodder & Stoughton.

Eysenck, S. B. G., Eysenck, H. J., & Barrett, P. (1985). A revised version of the psychoticism scale. *Personality and Individual Differences, 6*, 21–29.

Feist, G. J. (1998). A meta-analysis of personality in scientific and artistic creativity. *Personality and Social Psychology Review, 2*, 290–309.

Ferrándiz, C., Marín, F., Gallud, L., Ferrando, M., López Pina, J. A., & Prieto, Mª D. (2006). Validez de la escala de inteligencia emocional de Schutte en una muestra de estudiantes universitarios [Validity of Schutte's scale of emotional intelligence in a sample of university students]. *Ansiedad y Estrés, 12*, 167–179.

Findlay, C. S., & Lumsden, C. J. (1988). The creative mind: Towards an evolutionary theory of discovery and innovation. *Journal of Social and Biological Structures, 11*, 3–55.

Finkbeiner, A. (2011). Crystal method. *The University of Chicago Magazine, 104*, 32–37.

Fiori, M., & Antonakis, J. (2011). The ability model of emotional intelligence: Searching for valid measures. *Personality and Individual Differences, 50*, 329–334.

Firth, L., Mellor, D. J., Moore, K. A., & Loquet, C. (2004). How can managers reduce employee intention to quit? *Journal of Managerial Psychology, 19*, 170–187.

Flavell, J. H. (1979). Metacognition and metacognitive monitoring: A new area of cognitive-developmental inquiry. *American Psychologist, 34*, 906–911.

Fleishman, E. A. (1953). The description of supervisory behavior. *Journal of Applied Psychology, 37*, 1–6.

Floderhus-Myrhed, B., Pedersen, N., & Rasmuson, I. (1980). Assessment of heritability for personality, based on a short form of the Eysenck Personality Inventory: A study of 12,898 twin pairs. *Behavior Genetics, 10*, 153–162.

Folkman, S. (1997). Positive psychological states and coping with severe stress. *Social Science Medicine, 45*, 1207–1221.

Folkman, S., & Lazarus, R. S. (1980). An analysis of coping in a middle-aged community sample. *Journal of Health and Social Behavior, 21*, 219–239.

Folkman, S., & Lazarus, R. S. (1985). If it changes it must be a process: Study of emotion and coping during three stages of examination. *Journal of Personality and Social Psychology, 48*, 150–170.

Føllesdal, H., & Hagtvet, K. A. (2009). Emotional intelligence: The MSCEIT from the perspective of generalizability theory. *Intelligence, 37*, 94–105.

Fontaine, K. R., & Seal, A. (1997). Optimism, social support and premenstrual dysphoria. *Journal of Clinical Psychology, 53* (3), 243–247.

Francis, L. J., & Wilcox, C. (1998). The relationship between Eysenck's personality dimensions and Bem's masculinity and femininity scales revisited. *Personality and Individual Differences, 25*, 683–687.

Fredrickson, B. L. (1998). What good are positive emotions? *Review of General Psychology, 2*, 300–319.

Fredrickson, B. L. (2000). Cultivating positive emotions to optimize health and well-being. *Prevention & Treatment, 3*, March, no pagination.

Fredrickson, B. L. (2001). The role of positive emotions in positive psychology: The broaden-and-build theory of positive emotions. *American Psychologist, 56*, 218–226.

Fredrickson, B. L., Cohn, M. A., Coffey, K. A., Pek, J., & Finkel, S. M. (2008). Open hearts build lives: Positive emotions, induced through loving-kindness meditation, build consequential personal resources. *Journal of Personality and Social Psychology, 95*, 1045–1062.

Fredrickson, B. L., & Joiner, T. (2002). Positive emotions trigger upward spirals toward emotional well-being. *Psychological Science, 13*, 172–175.

Fredrickson, B. L., & Levenson, R. W. (1998). Positive emotions speed recovery from the cardiovascular sequelae of negative emotions. *Cognition and Emotion, 12*, 191–220.

Fredrickson, B. L., & Losada, M. F. (2005). Positive affect and the complex dynamics of human flourishing. *American Psychologist, 60*, 678–686.

Fredrickson, B. L., Mancuso, R. A., Branigan, C., & Tugade, M. M. (2000). The undoing effect of positive emotions. *Motivation and Emotion, 24*, 237–258.

Fresco, D. M., William, N. L., & Nugent, N. R. (2006). Flexibility and negative affect: Examining the associations of explanatory flexibility and coping flexibility to each other and to depression and anxiety. *Cognitive Therapy and Research, 30*, 201–210.

Freud, S. (1910). *Three contributions to the theory of sex.* New York and Washington: N.M.D. Pub. Co.

Freud, S. (1925). *Collected papers, Vol. 3, Case histories.* London: Hogarth Press and the Institute of Psycho-Analysis.

Freudenberger, H. J. (1974). Staff burn-out. *Journal of Social Issues, 30*, 159–165.

Frey, B., & Stutzer, A. (2002). What can economists learn from happiness research? *Journal of Economic Literature, 40*, 402–435.

Frijda, N. H. (2009). Emotion experience and its varieties. *Emotion Review, 1*, 264–271.

Fulmer, A. C., Gelfand, M. J., Kruglanski, A. W., Kim-Prieto, C., Diener, E., Pierro, A., & Higgins, E. T. (2010). On 'feeling right' in cultural contexts: How person-culture match affects self-esteem and subjective well-being. *Psychological Science, 21*, 1563–1569.

Funder, D. C. (2001). *The personality puzzle.* New York: Norton.

Funder, D. C., & Block, J. (1989). The role of ego-control, ego-resiliency, and IQ in delay of gratification in adolescence. *Journal of Personality and Social Psychology, 57*, 1041–1050.

Gable, S. L. (2006). Approach and avoidance social motives and goals. *Journal of Personality, 74*, 175–222.

Gaines Jr, S. O. (1998). Communication of emotions in friendships. In P. A. Andersen & L. K. Guerrero (Eds), *Handbook of communication and emotion: Research, theory, applications, and contexts* (pp. 507–531). San Diego, CA: Academic Press.

Gallagher, M. W., & Lopez, S. J. (2009). Positive expectancies and mental health: Identifying the unique contributions of hope and optimism. *Journal of Positive Psychology, 4*, 548–556.

Garland, E. L., Fredrickson, B., Kring, A. M., Johnson, D. P., Meyer, P. S., & Penn, D. L. (2010). Upward spirals of positive emotions counter downward spirals of negativity: Insights from the broaden-and-build theory and affective neuroscience on the treatment of emotion dysfunctions and deficits in psychopathology. *Clinical Psychology Review, 30*, 849–864.

Gasper, K., & Clore, G. (2002). Attending to the big picture: Mood and global versus local processing of visual information. *Psychological Science, 13*, 34–40.

Geschwind, N., Peeters, F., Drukker, M., van Os, J., & Wichers, M. (2011). Mindfulness training increases momentary positive emotions and reward experience in adults vulnerable to depression: A randomized controlled trial. *Journal of Consulting and Clinical Psychology, 79*, 618–628.

Getzels, J. W. (1964). Creative thinking, problem solving, and instruction. In E. R. Hilgard (Ed.), *Theories of learning and instruction: 63rd yearbook of the National Society for the Study of Education* (pp. 240–276). Chicago, IL: University of Chicago Press.

Getzels, J. W., & Csikszentmihalyi, M. (1976). *The creative vision: A longitudinal study of problem finding in art.* New York: Wiley.

Getzels, J. W., & Jackson, P. J. (1962). *Creativity and intelligence: Explorations with gifted students.* New York: Wiley.

Gilman, R., Dooley, J., & Florell (2006). Relative levels of hope and their relationship with academic and psychological indicators among adolescents. *Journal of Social and Clinical Psychology, 25,* 166–178.

Glucksberg, S. (1962). The influence of strength of drive on functional fixedness and perceptual recognition. *Journal of Experimental Psychology, 63,* 36–41.

Goldberg, L. R. (1990). An alternative 'description of personality': The Big-Five factor structure. *Journal of Personality and Social Psychology, 59,* 1216–1229.

Goldberg, L. R. (1993). The structure of phenotypic personality traits. *American Psychologist, 48,* 26–34.

Goleman, D. (1995). *Emotional intelligence.* New York: Bantam Books.

Gottman, J. M. (1994). *What predicts divorce? The relationship between marital processes and marital outcomes.* Hillsdale, NJ: Erlbaum.

Gottman, J. M., Katz, L. F., & Hooven, C. (1997). *Meta emotion: How families communicate emotionally.* Mahwah, NJ: Erlbaum.

Grant, A. M., & Schwartz, B. (2011). Too much of a good thing: The challenge and opportunity of the inverted U. *Psychological Science, 6,* 61–76.

Greenberg, L. (2002). *Emotion-focused therapy: Coaching clients through their feelings.* Washington: American Psychological Association.

Gross, J. J., & John, O. P. (2003). Individual differences in two emotion regulation processes: Implications for affect, relationships, and well-being. *Journal of Personality and Social Psychology, 85,* 348–362.

Gudykunst, W. B., Matsumoto, Y., Ting-Toomey, S., Nishida, T., Kim, K., & Heyman, S. (1996). The influence of cultural individualism-collectivism, self construals, and individual values on communication styles across cultures. *Human Communication Research, 22,* 510–543.

Guilford, J. P. (1967). *The nature of human intelligence.* New York: McGraw-Hill.

Guisinger, S., & Blatt, S. J. (1994). Individuality and relatedness. *American Psychologist, 49,* 104–111.

Haaga, D. A. F., & Stewart, B. L. (1992). Self-efficacy for recovery from a lapse after smoking cessation. *Journal of Consulting and Clinical Psychology, 60,* 24–28.

Hackman, J. R. (1987). Design of work teams. In J. W. Lorsch (Ed.), *Handbook of organizational behavior* (pp. 315–342). Englewood Cliffs, NJ: Prentice-Hall.

Hackman, J. R. (2002). *Leading teams: Setting the stage for great performances.* Boston, MA: Harvard Business School Press.

Hackman, J. R., & Oldham, G. R. (1974). The Job Diagnostic Survey: An instrument for the diagnosis of jobs and the evaluation of job redesign projects. *JSAS Catalog of Selected Documents in Psychology, 4* (148) (Ms. No. 810).

Hackman, J. R., & Oldham, G. R. (1980). *Work redesign.* Reading, MA: Addison-Wesley Publishing Company.

Hall, J. A., & Taylor, M. C. (1985). Psychological androgyny and the masculinity X femininity interaction. *Journal of Personality and Social Psychology, 49,* 429–435.

Harari, Y. N. (2008). Combat flow: Military, political, and ethical dimensions of subjective well-being in war. *Review of General Psychology, 12,* 253–264.

Harrington, D. M., Block, J. H., & Block, J. (1987). Testing aspects of Carl Rogers's theory of creative environments: Child-rearing antecedents of creative potential in young adolescents. *Journal of Personality and Social Psychology, 52,* 851–856.

Harris, M. M., & Schaubroeck, J. (1988). A meta-analysis of self-supervisor, self-peer, and peer-supervisor ratings. *Personnel Psychology, 41,* 43–62.

Harter, S. (1983). Developmental perspectives on the self-esteem. In P. H. Mussen (Ed.), *Handbook of child psychology: Socialization, personality, and social development* (Vol. 4, pp. 275–386). New York: Wiley.

Harter, S. (1993). Causes and consequences of low self-esteem in children and adolescents. In R. Baumeister (Ed.), *Self-esteem: The puzzle of low self-regard* (pp. 87–116). New York: Plenum Press.

Hatfield, E. (1988). Passionate and companionate love. In R. J. Sternberg & M. L. Barnes (Eds), *The psychology of love* (pp. 191–217). New Haven, CT: Yale University Press.

Hatfield, E., & Rapson, R. L. (1993). *Love, sex, and intimacy: The psychology, biology, and history*. New York: Harper Collins.

Hatfield, E., & Rapson, R. L. (1996). *Love and sex: Cross-cultural perspectives*. Boston: Allyn and Bacon.

Haworth, J., & Evans, S. (1995). Challenge, skill and positive subjective states in the daily life of a sample of YTS students. *Journal of Occupational and Organizational Psychology, 68*, 109–121.

Hayamizu, T. (1997). Between intrinsic and extrinsic motivation: Examination of reasons for academic study based on the theory of internalization. *Japanese Psychological Research, 39*, 98–108.

Hayes, S. C., Strohsahl, K., Wilson, K. G., Bissett, R. T., Pistorello, J., Toarmino, D., Polusny, M. A., Dykstra, T. A., Batten, S. V., Bergan, J., Stewart, S. H., Zvolensky, M. J., Eifert, G. H., Bond, F. W., Forsyth J. P., Karekla, M., & McCurry, S. M. (2004). Measuring experiential avoidance. A preliminary test of a working model. *Psychological Record, 54*, 553–578.

Headey, B., & Wearing, A. (1992). *Understanding happiness: A theory of subjective well-being*. Melbourne: Longman Cheshire.

Hemingway, E. (2009). *A moveable feast: The restored edition* (edited by S. Hemingway). New York: Scribner.

Hendrick, S. S. (1988). A generic measure of relationship satisfaction. *Journal of Marriage and the Family, 50*, 93–98.

Hendrick, C., & Hendrick, S. S. (1986). A theory and method of love. *Journal of Personality and Social Psychology, 50*, 392–402.

Hendrick, S. S., & Hendrick, C. (1987). Multidimensionality of sexual attitudes. *Journal of Sex Research, 23*, 502–526.

Hendrick, S. S., & Hendrick, C. (2005). Love. In C. R. Snyder & S. J. Lopez (Eds), *Handbook of positive psychology* (pp. 472–484). New York: Oxford University Press.

Hills, P., & Argyle, M. (2002). The Oxford Happiness Questionnaire: A compact scale for the measurement of psychological well-being. *Personality and Individual Differences, 33*, 1073–1082.

Hirt, E. R., Levine, G. M., McDonald, H. E., Melton, R. J., & Martin, L. L. (1997). The role of mood in quantitative and qualitative aspects of performance: Single or multiple mechanisms? *Journal of Experimental Social Psychology, 33*, 602–629.

Ho, D. Y. F. (1986). Chinese patterns of socialization: A critical review. In M. H. Bond (Ed.), *Psychology of the Chinese people* (pp. 1–37). Hong Kong: Oxford University Press.

Hodgins, H., Koestner, R., & Duncan, N. (1996). On the compatibility of autonomy and relatedness. *Personality and Social Psychology Bulletin, 22*, 227–245.

Hoffer, J., Bush, H., & Kiessling, F. (2008). Individual pathways to life satisfaction: The significance of traits and motives. *Journal of Happiness Studies, 9*, 503–520.

Hofstede, G. (2001). *Culture's consequences, comparing values, behaviors, institutions, and organizations across nations*. Thousand Oaks, CA: Sage Publications.

Hofstede, G., & McCrae, R. R. (2004). Personality and culture revisited: Linking traits and dimensions of culture. *Cross-Cultural Research, 38*, 52–88.

Hollon, S. D., Stewart, M. O., & Strunk, D. (2006). Cognitive behavior therapy has enduring effects in the treatment of depression and anxiety. *Annual Review of Psychology, 57*, 285–315.

Hong, Y. Y., Chiu, C. Y., & Kung, T. M. (1997). Bringing culture out in front: Effects of cultural meaning system activation on social cognition. In K. Leung, Y. Kashima, U. Kim, & S. Yamaguchi (Eds), *Progress in Asian social psychology* (Vol. 1, pp. 135–146). Singapore: Wiley.

Horley, J., & Lavery, J. J. (1995). Subjective well-being and age. *Social Indicators Research, 34*, 275–282.

Hudson, W. W. (1998). Index of Sexual Satisfaction. In C. M. Davis, W. L. Yarber, R. Bauserman, G. Schreer, & S. L. Davis (Eds), *Handbook of sexuality-related measures* (pp. 512–513). London: Sage Publications.

Hudson, W. W., Harrison, D. F., & Crosscup, P. (1981). A short-form scale to measure sexual discord in dyadic relationships. *Journal of Sex Research, 17*, 157–174.

Hume, D. (1739/1896). *A treatise of human nature* (reprinted from the original edition in three volumes and edited, with an analytical index, by L. A. Selby-Bigge). Oxford: Clarendon Press.

Huth, T. (2008). *Organizing cross-functional new product development projects: The phase-specific effects of organizational antecedents*. Wiesbaden, Germany: Gabler.

Ilies, R., & Judge, T. A. (2002). Understanding the dynamic relationships among personality, mood, and job satisfaction: A field experience sampling study. *Organizational Behavior and Human Decision Processes, 89*, 1119–1139.

Inglehart, R. F. (1990). *Culture shift in advanced industrial societies*. Princeton, NJ: Princeton University Press.

Ip, G. W. M., & Bond, M. H. (1995). Culture, values, and the spontaneous self-concept. *Asian Journal of Psychology, 1*, 29–35.

Isen, A. M., Daubman, K. A., & Nowicki, G. P. (1987). Positive affect facilitates creative problem solving. *Journal of Personality and Social Psychology, 52*, 1122–1131.

Iyengar, S. S., & Lepper, M. R. (1999). Rethinking the value of choice: A cultural perspective on intrinsic motivation. *Journal of Personality and Social Psychology, 76*, 349–366.

Izard, C. E. (1977). *Human emotions*. New York: Plenum Press.

Izard, C. E. (2011). The many meanings/aspects of emotion: Definitions, functions, activation, and regulation. *Emotion Review, 2*, 363–370.

Jackson, S. A., & Csikszentmihalyi, M. (1999). *Flow in sports: The keys to optimal experiences and performances*. Champaign, IL: Human Kinetics.

Jackson, S. A., & Eklund, R. C. (2002). Assessing flow in physical activity: The Flow State Scale-2 and Dispositional Flow Scale-2. *Journal of Sport and Exercise Psychology, 24*, 133–150.

Jackson, S. A., & Eklund, R. C. (2004). *The flow scale manual*. Morgantown, WV: Fitness Information Technology, Inc.

Jackson, S. A., & Roberts, G. C. (1992). Positive performance states of athletes: Toward a conceptual understanding of peak performance. *The Sport Psychologist, 6*, 156–171.

Jäger, C., & Bartsch, A. (2006). Meta-Emotions. *Grazer Philosophische Studien, 73*, 179–204.

James, W. (1892/1963). *Psychology*. Greenwich, CT: Fawcett.

Jang, H., Reeve, J., & Deci, E. L. (2010). Engaging students in learning activities: It is not autonomy support or structure but autonomy support and Structure. *Journal of Educational Psychology, 102*, 588–600.

Jerusalem, M., & Schwarzer, R. (1992). Self-efficacy as a resource factor in stress appraisal processes. In R. Schwarzer (Ed.), *Self-efficacy: Thought control of action* (pp. 195–213). Washington: Hemisphere.

Judge, T. A., & Hurst, C. (2007). The benefits and possible costs of positive core self-evaluations: A review and agenda for future research. In D. Nelson & C. L. Cooper (Eds), *Positive organizational behavior* (pp. 159–174). London: Sage Publications.

Judge, T. A., Thoresen, C. J., Bono, J. E., & Patton, G. K. (2001). The job satisfaction-job performance relationship: A qualitative and quantitative review. *Psychological Bulletin, 127*, 376–407.

Kahneman, D., & Krueger, A. B. (2006). Developments in the measurement of subjective well-being. *Journal of Economic Perspectives, 20*, 3–24.

Kahn, W. A. (1990). Psychological conditions of personal engagement and disengagement at work. *Academy of Management Journal, 33*, 692–724.

Kahoe, R. D., & McFarland, R. E. (1975). Interactions of task challenge and intrinsic and extrinsic motivations in college achievement. *Journal of Educational Psychology, 67*, 432–438.

Kamarck, T. W., Peterman, A. H., & Raynor, D. A. (1998). The effects of the social environment on stress-related cardiovascular activation: Current findings, prospects, and implications. *Annals of Behavioral Medicine, 20*, 247–256.

Kant, I. (1781/1787/1997). *Critique of pure reason* (trans. by P. Guyer & A. Wood). Cambridge and New York: Cambridge University Press.

Kashdan, T. B. (2004). The assessment of subjective well-being (issues raised by the Oxford Happiness Questionnaire). *Personality and Individual Differences, 36*, 1225–1232.

Kaviani, H., Javaheri, F., & Hatami, N. (2011). Mindfulness-Based Cognitive Therapy (MBCT) reduces depression and anxiety induced by real stressful setting in non-clinical population. *International Journal of Psychology and Psychological Therapy, 11*, 285–296.

Keele S. M., & Bell R. C. (2008). The factorial validity of emotional intelligence: An unresolved issue. *Personality and Individual Differences, 44*, 487–500.

Keenan, A., & Newton, T. J. (1985). Stressful events, stressors and psychological strains in young professional engineers. *Journal of Occupational Behaviour, 6*, 151–156.

Keller, J., & Bless, H. (2008). Flow and regulatory compatibility: An experimental approach to the flow model of intrinsic motivation. *Personality and Social Psychology Bulletin, 34*, 196–209.

Keller, J., Bless, H., Blomann, F., & Kleinbohl, D. (2011). Physiological aspects of flow experiences: Skills-demand-compatibility effects on heart rate variability and salivary cortisol. *Journal of Experimental Social Psychology, 47*, 849–852.

Kenrick, D. T., Sadalla, E. K., Groth, G., & Trost, M. R. (1990). Evolution, traits and the stages of human courtship: Qualifying the parental investment model. *Journal of Personality, 58*, 97–116.

Keyes, C. L. M. (1998). Social well-being. *Social Psychology Quarterly, 61*, 121–140.

Keyes, C. L. M. (2002). The mental health continuum: From languishing to flourishing in life. *Journal of Health and Social Behavior, 43*, 207–222.

Keyes, C. L. M. (2005). Mental illness and/or mental health? Investigating axioms of the complete state model of health. *Journal of Consulting and Clinical Psychology, 73*, 539–548.

Keyes, C. L. M. (2006). Mental health in adolescence: Is America's youth flourishing? *American Journal of Orthopsychiatry, 76*, 395–402.

Keyes, C. L. M., Dhingra, S. S., & Simoes, E. J. (2010). Change in level of positive mental health as a predictor of future risk of mental illness. *American Journal of Public Health, 100*, 2366–2371.

Keyes, C. L. M., Shmotkin, D., & Ryff, C. D. (2002). Optimizing well-being: The empirical encounter of two traditions. *Journal of Personality and Social Psychology, 82*, 1007–1022.

Keyes, C. L. M., Wissing, M., Potgieter, J., Temane, M., Kruger, A., & van Rooy, S. (2008). Evaluation of the mental health continuum: Short Form (MHC-SF) in Swetsana-speaking South Africans. *Clinical Psychology and Psychotherapy, 15*, 181–192.

Kim, J., & Hatfield, E. (2004). Love types and subjective well-being: A cross-cultural study. *Social Behavior and Personality, 32*, 173–182.

King, L. A., McKee Walker, L., & Broyles, S. J. (1996). Creativity and the five-factor model. *Journal of Research in Personality, 30*, 189–203.

Kirton, M. (1976). Adaptors and innovators: A description and measure. *Journal of Applied Psychology, 61*, 622–629.

Klinger, E. (1977). *Meaning and void: Inner experience and the incentives in people's lives.* Minneapolis, MI: University of Minnesota Press.

Kuhn, M., & McPartland, T. S. (1954). An empirical investigation of self-attitudes. *American Sociological Review, 19*, 68–77.

Kuhn, T. (1969). *The structure of scientific revolutions.* Chicago: University of Chicago Press.

Kundera, M. (1984). *The unbearable lightness of being* (trans. by Michael Henry Heim). London: Harper & Row.

Kundera, M. (1988). *The art of the novel* (trans. by Linda Asher). London: Faber and Faber.

Kundera, M. (1998). *Identity* (trans. by Linda Asher). London: Faber and Faber.

Kupfer, D. J., Frank, E., Perel, J. M., Cornes, C., Mallinger, A. G., Thase, M. E., McEachran, A. B., & Grochocinski, V. J. (1992). 5-year outcome for maintenance therapies in recurrent depression. *Archives of General Psychiatry, 49*, 769–773.

Kuyken, W., Byford, S., Taylor, R. S., Watkins, E., Holden, E., White, K., Barrett, B., Byng, R., Evans, A., Mullan, E., & Teasdale, J. D. (2008). Mindfulness-based cognitive therapy to prevent relapse in recurrent depression. *Journal of Consulting and Clinical Psychology, 76*, 966–978.

Kwan, V. S. Y., Bond, M. H., & Singelis, T. M. (1997). Pancultural explanations for life satisfaction: Adding relationship harmony to self-esteem. *Journal of Personality and Social Psychology, 73*, 1038–1051.

LaFromboise, T., Coleman, H. L., & Gerton, J. (1993). Psychological impact of biculturalism: Evidence and theory. *Psychological Bulletin, 114*, 395–412.

Lai, J. C. L. (1997). Relative predictive power of the optimism versus the pessimism index of a Chinese version of the Life Orientation Test. *The Psychological Record, 47*, 399–410.

Lai, J. C. L., Cheung, H., Lee, W. M., & Yu, H. (1998). The utility of the revised Life Orientation Test to measure optimism among Hong Kong Chinese. *International Journal of Psychology, 33* (1), 45–56.

Lam, C. B., & McBride-Chang, C. A. (2007). Resilience in young adulthood: The moderating influences of gender-related personality traits and coping flexibility. *Sex Roles, 56*, 159–172.

Langer, E. J., & Imber, L. G. (1979). When practice makes imperfect: Debilitating effects of overlearning. *Journal of Personality and Social Psychology, 37*, 2014–2024.

Larsen, R. J., & Cutler, S. E. (1996). The complexity of individual emotional lives: A within-subject analysis of affect structure. *Journal of Social and Clinical Psychology, 15*, 206–230.

Larsen, R. J., & Diener, E. (1987). Affect intensity as an individual difference characteristic: A review. *Journal of Research in Personality, 21*, 1–39.

Larsen, R. J., & Diener, E. (1992). Promises and problems with the circumplex model of emotion. *Review of Personality and Social Psychology, 13*, 25–59.

Larson, R., Hansen, D. M., & Moneta, G. B. (2006). Differing profiles of developmental experiences across types of organized youth activities. *Developmental Psychology, 42*, 849–863.

Lazarus, R. S. (1991). *Emotion and adaptation.* London: Oxford University Press.

Lazarus, R. S. (1993). From psychological stress to the emotions: A history of changing outlooks. *Annual Review of Psychology, 44*, 1–21.

Lazarus, R. S., & Folkman, S. (1984). *Stress, appraisal and coping*. New York: Springer.

Lee, R. T., & Ashforth, B. E. (1996). A meta-analytic examination of the correlates of the three dimensions of job burnout. *Journal of Applied Psychology, 81*, 123–133.

Leiter, M. P. (1993). Burnout as a development process: Consideration of models. In W. B. Schaufeli, C. Maslach, & T. Marek (Eds), *Professional burnout: Recent developments in theory and research* (pp. 237–250). Washington: Taylor & Francis.

Leu, J., Wang, J., & Koo, K. (2011). Are positive emotions just as 'positive' across cultures? *Emotion, 11*, 994–999.

Lewinsohn, P. M., & Gotlib, I. H. (1995). Behavioral theory and treatment of depression. In E. E. Beckham & W. R. Leber (Eds), *Handbook of depression* (2nd ed.) (pp. 352–375). New York: Guilford.

Leys, S. (1997). *The analects of Confucius: Translation and notes*. New Yok: Norton.

Linley, P. A., Joseph, S., Harrington, S., & Wood, A. M. (2006). Positive psychology: Past, present, and (possible) future. *The Journal of Positive Psychology, 1*, 3–16.

Little, B. R. (1983). Personal projects: A rationale and method for their investigation. *Environment and Behavior, 15*, 273–309.

Little, B. R. (1987). Personal projects analysis: A new methodology for counselling psychology. *NATCOM, 13*, 591–614.

Little, B. R. (1989). Personal projects analysis: Trivial pursuits, magnificent obsessions, and the search for coherence. In D. M. Buss & N. Cantor (Eds), *Personality psychology: Recent trends and emerging directions* (pp. 15–31). New York: Springer.

Loehlin, J. C. (1992). *Genes and environment in personality development*. Newbury Park, CA: Sage Publications.

Loevinger, J. (1976). *Ego development: Conceptions and theories*. San Francisco, CA: Jossey-Bass.

Loevinger, J. (1985). Revision of the Sentence Completion Test for ego development. *Journal of Personality and Social Psychology, 48*, 420–427.

Loevinger, J. (1993). Measurement in personality: True or false. *Psychological Inquiry, 4*, 1–16.

Loher, B. T., Noe, R. A., Moeller, N. L., & Fitzgerald, M. P. 1985. A meta-analysis of the relation of job characteristics to job satisfaction. *Journal of Applied Psychology, 70*, 280–289.

Lucas, R. E., Diener, E., Grob, A., Suh, E. M., & Shao, L. (2000). Cross-cultural evidence for the fundamental features of extraversion. *Journal of Personality and Social Psychology, 79*, 452–468.

Luttmer, E. (2005). Neighbors as negatives: Relative earnings and well-being. *Quarterly Journal of Economics, 120*, 963–1002.

Lykken, D. T., & Tellegen, A. (1996). Happiness is a stochastic phenomenon. *Psychological Science, 7*, 186–189.

Lyubomirsky, S. (2001). Why are some people happier than others? The role of cognitive and motivational processes in well-being. *American Psychologist, 56*, 239–249.

Lyubomirsky, S., Boehm, J., Kasri, F., & Zehm, K. (2011a). The cognitive and hedonic costs of dwelling on achievement-related negative experiences: Implications for enduring happiness and unhappiness. *Emotion, 11*, 1152–1167.

Lyubomirsky, S., Dickerhoof, R., Boehm, J. K., & Sheldon, K. M. (2011b). Becoming happier takes both a will and a proper way: An experimental longitudinal intervention to boost well-being. *Emotion, 11*, 391–402.

Lyubomirsky, S., & Lepper, H. (1999). A measure of subjective happiness: Preliminary reliability and construct validation. *Social Indicators Research, 46*, 137–155.

Lyubomirsky, S., & Ross, L. (1997). Hedonic consequences of social comparison: A contrast of happy and unhappy people. *Journal of Personality and Social Psychology, 73*, 1141–1157.

Lyubomirsky, S., & Ross, L. (1999). Changes in attractiveness of elected, rejected, and precluded alternatives: A comparison of happy and unhappy individuals. *Journal of Personality and Social Psychology, 76*, 988–1007.

Lyubomirsky, S., Tkach, C., & Dimatteo, M. R. (2006). What are the differences between happiness and self-esteem? *Social Indicators Research, 78*, 363–404.

Lyubomirsky, S., Tucker, K. L., & Kasri, F. (2001). Responses to hedonically conflicting social comparisons: Comparing happy and unhappy people. *European Journal of Social Psychology, 31*, 511–535.

Macdonald, C., Bore, M., Munro, D. (2008). Values in Action Scale and the Big 5: An empirical indication of structure. *Journal of Research in Personality, 42*, 787–799.

MacDonald, R., Byrne, C., & Carlton, L. (2006). Creativity and flow in musical composition: An empirical investigation. *Psychology of Music, 34*, 292–306.

Maehr, M. L. (1989). Thoughts about motivation. In C. Ames & R. Ames (Eds), *Research on motivation in education* (Vol. 3, pp. 299–315). New York: Academic Press.

Magnus, K., Diener, E., Fujita, F., & Pavot, W. (1993). Extraversion and neuroticism as predictors of objective life events: A longitudinal analysis. *Journal of Personality and Social Psychology, 65*, 1046–1053.

Maier, S. F., & Seligman, M. E. P. (1976). Learned helplessness: Theory and evidence. *Journal of Experimental Psychology: General, 105*, 3–46.

Marcia, J. E., (1966), Development and validation of ego identity status. *Journal of Personality and Social Psychology, 3*, 551–558.

Marcia, J. E. (1980). Identity in adolescence. In J. Adelson (Ed.), *Handbook of adolescent psychology* (pp. 159–187). New York: Wiley.

Markus, H. R., & Kitayama, S. (1991). Culture and the self: Implications for cognition, emotion, and motivation. *Psychological Review, 98*, 224–253.

Markus, H. R., & Kitayama, S. (1994). A collective fear of the collective: Implications for selves and theories of selves. *Personality and Social Psychology Bulletin, 20*, 568–579.

Markus, H. R., Kitayama, S., & Heiman R. J. (1996). Culture and basic psychological principles. In E. T. Higgins & A. W. Kruglanski (Eds), *Social psychology: Handbook of basic principles* (pp. 857–913). New York: Guilford.

Marques, S. C., Pais-Ribeiro, J. L., & Lopez, S. J. (2009). Cross-sectional and longitudinal predictors of early adolescents' academic achievement. Paper presented at the 11th European Congress of Psychology, Oslo, Norway.

Marshall, G. N., & Lang, E. L. (1990). Optimism, self-mastery, and symptoms of depression in women professionals. *Journal of Personality and Social Psychology, 59* (1), 132–139.

Martin, L. L., Ward, D. W., Achee, J. W., & Wyer, R. S. (1993). Mood as input: People have to interpret the motivational implications of their moods. *Journal of Personality and Social Psychology, 64*, 317–326.

Maslach, C., Jackson, S. E., & Leiter, M. P. (1996). *The Maslach Burnout Inventory: Test manual* (3rd ed.). Palo Alto, CA: Consulting Psychologists Press.

Maslow, A. H. (1968). *Toward a psychology of being*. New York: Van Nostrand.

Massimini, F., & Carli, M. (1988). The systematic assessment of flow in daily experience. In M. Csikszentmihalyi & I. S. Csikszentmihalyi (Eds), *Optimal experience: Psychological studies of flow in consciousness* (pp. 266–287). New York: Cambridge University Press.

Massimini, F., Csikszentmihalyi, M., & Carli, M. (1987). The monitoring of optimal experience: A tool for psychiatric rehabilitation. *The Journal of Nervous and Mental Diseases, 175*, 545–549.

Massimini, F., Inghilleri, P., & Delle Fave, A. (Eds) (1996). *La selezione psicologica umana* [Human psychological selection]. Milan: Cooperativa Libraria IULM.

Mather, M., & Carstensen, L. L. (2003). Aging and attentional biases for emotional faces. *Psychological Science, 14*, 409–415.

Mathews, A., Yiend, J., & Lawrence, A. D. (2004). Individual differences in the modulation of fear-related brain activation by attentional control. *Journal of Cognitive Neuroscience, 16*, 1683–1694.

Matlin, M., & Stang, D. (1978). *The Pollyanna principle.* Cambridge, MA: Schenkman.

Matsumoto, D. (1991). Cultural influences on facial expressions of emotion. *The Southern Communication Journal, 56*, 128–137.

Mayer, J. D., Caruso, D., & Salovey, P. (1999). Emotional intelligence meets traditional standards for an intelligence. *Intelligence, 27*, 267–298.

Mayer, J. D., & Salovey, P. (1997). What is emotional intelligence? In P. Salovey & D. Sluyter (Eds), *Emotional development and emotional intelligence: Implications for educators* (pp. 3–31). New York: Basic Books.

Mayer, J. D., Salovey, P., & Caruso, D. (2002a). *Mayer-Salovey-Caruso Emotional Intelligence Test (MSCEIT), Version 2.0.* Toronto, Canada: Multi-Health Systems.

Mayer, J. D., Salovey, P., & Caruso, D. (2002b). *MSCEIT technical manual.* Toronto: Multi-Health Systems.

McAdams, D. P. (1984). Human motives and personal relationships. In V. J. Derlega (Ed.), *Communication, intimacy, and close relationships* (pp. 41–70). Orlando, FL: Academic Press.

McAdams, D. P. (1996). Personality, modernity, and the storied self: A contemporary framework for studying persons. *Psychological Inquiry, 7*, 295–321.

McAdams, D. P. (2008). Personal narratives and the life story. In O. John, R. Robins, & L. A. Pervin, *Handbook of personality: Theory and research* (pp. 241–261). New York: Guilford Press.

McAdams, D. P., Healy, S., & Krause, S. (1984). Social motives and patterns of friendship. *Journal of Personality and Social Psychology, 47*, 828–838.

McAdams, D. P., Josselson, R., & Lieblich, A. (2006). *Identity and story: Creating self in narrative.* Washington: American Psychological Association.

McAuley, E., Duncan, T., & Tammen, V. V. (1987). Psychometric properties of the Intrinsic Motivation Inventory in a competitive sport setting: A confirmatory factor analysis. *Research Quarterly for Exercise and Sport, 60*, 48–58.

McClelland, D. C. (1985). *Human motivation.* Glenview, IL: Scott, Foresman.

McClelland, D. C. (1961). *The achieving society.* Princeton, NJ: Van Nostrand.

McClelland, D. C., Atkinson, J. W., Clark, R. A., & Lowell, E. L. (1953). *The achievement motive.* New York: Appleton-Century-Crofts.

McCrae, R. R. (1987). Creativity, divergent thinking, and openness to experience. *Journal of Personality and Social Psychology, 52*, 1258–1265.

McCrae, R. R., & Allik, J. (2002). *The five-factor model of personality across cultures.* New York: Kluwer Academic/Plenum.

McCrae, R. R., & Costa, P. T., Jr (1989). Reinterpreting the Myers-Briggs Type Indicator from the perspective of the five-factor model of personality. *Journal of Personality, 57*, 17–40.

McCullers, J. C., & Martin, J. A. G. (1971). A reexamination of the role of incentive in children's discrimination learning. *Child Development, 42*, 827–837.

Meilman, P. W. (1979). Cross-sectional age change in ego identity status during adolescence. *Developmental Psychology, 15*, 230–231.

Milam, J. E., Richardson, J. L., Marks, G., Kemper, C. A., & McCutchan, A. J. (2004). The roles of dispositional optimism and pessimism in HIV disease progression. *Psychology and Health, 19*, 167–181.

Mitmansgruber, H., Beck, T. N., Höfer, S., & Schüßler, G. (2009). When you don't like what you feel: Experiential avoidance, mindfulness and meta-emotion in emotion regulation. *Personality and Individual Differences, 46*, 448–453.

Moneta, G. B. (2004). The flow model of state intrinsic motivation in Chinese: Cultural and personal moderators. *Journal of Happiness Studies, 2*, 181–217.

Moneta, G. B. (2010). Chinese short form of the Personal Attributes Questionnaire: Construct and concurrent validity. *Sex Roles, 62*, 334–346.

Moneta, G. B. (2012a). On the measurement and conceptualization of flow. In S. Engeser (Ed.), *Advances in flow research* (pp. 23–50). New York: Springer.

Moneta, G. B. (2012b). Opportunity for creativity in the job as a moderator of the relation between trait intrinsic motivation and flow in work. *Motivation and Emotion, 36*, 491–503.

Moneta, G. B., Amabile, T. M., Schatzel, E., & Kramer, S. J. (2010). Multi-rater assessment of individual creative contributions to team projects in organizations. *European Journal of Work and Organizational Psychology, 2*, 150–176.

Moneta, G. B., & Csikszentmihalyi, M. (1996). The effect of perceived challenges and skills on the quality of subjective experience. *Journal of Personality, 64*, 275–310.

Moneta, G. B., & Csikszentmihalyi, M. (1999). Models of concentration in natural environments: A comparative approach based on streams of experiential data. *Social Behavior and Personality, 27*, 603–637.

Moneta, G. B., & Siu, C. M. Y. (2002). Trait intrinsic and extrinsic motivations, academic performance, and creativity in Hong Kong college students. *Journal of College Student Development, 43*, 664–683.

Moneta, G. B., Spada, M. M., & Rost, F. (2007). Approaches to studying when preparing for final exams as a function of coping strategies. *Personality and Individual Differences, 43*, 191–202.

Moore, R. L. (1998). Love and limerence with Chinese characteristics: Student romance in PRC. In V. C. de Munck (Ed.), *Romantic love and sexual behavior: Perspectives from the social sciences* (pp. 251–283). London: Praeger.

Moran, S., & John-Steiner, V. (2003). Creativity in the making: Vygotsky's contemporary contribution to the dialectic of development and creativity. In R. K. Sawyer, V. John-Steiner, S. Moran, R. J. Sternberg, D. H. Feldman, J. Nakamura, & M. Csikszentmihalyi (Eds), *Creativity and development* (pp. 61–90). New York: Oxford University Press.

Morrison, M., Tay, L., & Diener, E. (2011). Subjective well-being and national satisfaction: Findings from a worldwide survey. *Psychological Science, 22*, 166–171.

Moss, J. (2011). Virtue makes the goal right: Virtue and phronesis in Aristotle's ethics. *Phronesis: A Journal for Ancient Philosophy, 56*, 204–261.

Mowrer, O. H. (1960). *Learning theory and behavior.* New York: Wiley.

Murgatroyd, S. (1985). Introduction to reversal theory. In M. J. Apter, D. Fontana, & S. Murgatroyd (Eds), *Reversal theory: Applications and developments* (pp. 1–19). Cardiff, Wales: University College Cardiff Press, and New Jersey, NJ: Erlbaum.

Muris, P., Mayer, B., van Lint, C., & Hofman, S. (2008). Attentional control and psychopathological symptoms in children. *Personality and Individual Differences, 44*, 1495–1505.

Muris, P., Meesters, C., & Rompelberg, L. (2007). Attention control in middle childhood: Relations to psychopathological symptoms and threat perception distortions. *Behaviour Research and Therapy, 45*, 997–1010.

Muris, P., Merckelbach, H., & Bögels, S. (1995). Coping, defense, and fear in college students. *Journal of Personality and Individual Differences, 18*, 301–304.

Murray, H. A. (1938). *Explorations in personality.* New York: Oxford University Press.

Myers, D. G. (1999). Close relationships and quality of life. In D. Kahneman, E. Diener, & N. Schwarz (Eds), *Well-being: The foundations of hedonic psychology.* New York: Russell Sage Foundation.

Myers, D. G. (2000). The funds, friends, and faith of happy people. *American Psychologist, 55,* 56–67.

Myers, D. G., & Diener, E. (1995). Who is happy? *Psychological Science, 6,* 10–19.

Myers, I. B. (1962). *Manual: The Myers-Briggs Type Indicator.* Palo Alto, CA: Consulting Psychologists Press.

Myers, I. B., & McCaulley, M. H. (1985). *Manual: A guide to the development and use of the Myers-Briggs Type Indicator.* Palo Alto, CA: Consulting Psychologists Press.

Nakamura, J., & Csikszentmihalyi, M. (2005). The concept of flow. In C. R. Snyder & S. Lopez (Eds), *Handbook of positive psychology* (pp. 89–105). New York: Oxford University Press.

Nelson, T. O., & Narens, L. (1990). Metamemory: A theoretical framework and some new findings. In G. H. Bower (Ed.), *The psychology of learning and motivation* (Vol. 26, pp. 125–173). New York: Academic Press.

Neumark, D., & Postlewaite, A. (1998). Relative income concerns and the rise in married women's employment. *Journal of Public Economics, 70,* 157–183.

Nicholls, J. G. (1984). Achievement motivation: Conceptions of ability, subjective experience, task choice, and performance. *Psychological Review, 91,* 328–346.

Nikitin, J., & Freund, A. M. (2010a). When wanting and fearing go together: The effect of co-occurring social approach and avoidance motivation on behavior, affect, and cognition. *European Journal of Social Psychology, 40,* 783–804.

Nikitin, J., & Freund, A. M. (2010b). Age and motivation predict gaze behavior for facial expressions. *Psychology and Aging, 26,* 695–700.

O'Connell, K. A., & Calhoun, J. E. (2001). The telic/paratelic state instrument (T/PSI): Validating a reversal theory measure. *Personality and Individual Differences, 30,* 193–204.

Oishi, S., Diener, E., Lucas, R. E., & Suh, E. M. (1999). Cross-cultural variations in predictors of life satisfaction: Perspectives from needs and values. *Personality and Social Psychology Bulletin, 25,* 980–990.

Oishi, S., & Kurtz, J. L. (2011). The positive psychology of positive emotions: An avuncular view. In K. M. Sheldon, T. B. Kashdan, & M. E. Steger (Eds), *Designing positive psychology: Taking stock and moving forward* (pp. 101–114). New York: Oxford University Press.

Papageorgiou, C., & Wells, A. (2003). An empirical test of a clinical metacognitive model of rumination and depression. *Cognitive Therapy and Research, 27,* 261–273.

Park, N., Peterson, C., & Seligman, M. E. P. (2004). Strengths of character and well-being. *Journal of Social and Clinical Psychology, 23,* 603–619.

Pashler, H., Johnston, J. C., & Ruthroff, E. (2001). Attention and performance. *Annual Review of Psychology, 52,* 629–651.

Pennebaker, J. W. (1997). Writing about emotional experiences as a therapeutic process. *Psychological Science, 9,* 162–166.

Peterson, C. (2000). The future of optimism. *American Psychologist, 55,* 44–55.

Peterson, C. (2009). The future of positive psychology: Science and practice. *Psychology Today.* Available at: http://www.psychologytoday.com/blog/the-good-life/200912/the-future-positive-psychology-science-and-practice.

Peterson, C., & Barrett, L. (1987). Explanatory style and academic performance among university freshmen. *Journal of Personality and Social Psychology, 53,* 603–607.

Peterson, C., & Park, C. (1998). Learned helplessness and explanatory style. In D. F. Barone, V. B. Van Hasselt, & M. Hersen (Eds), *Advanced personality* (pp. 287–310). New York: Plenum Press.

Peterson, C., Park, N., & Seligman, M. E. P. (2006). Greater strengths of character and recovery from illness. *The Journal of Positive Psychology, 1,* 17–26.

Peterson, C., Ruch, W., Beermann, U., Park, N., & Seligman, M. E. P. (2007). Strengths of character, orientations to happiness, and life satisfaction. *The Journal of Positive Psychology, 2,* 149–156.

Peterson, C., & Seligman, M. E. P. (2001). *VIA Inventory of Strengths (VIA-IS)*. Available at: http://www.authentichappiness.sas.upenn.edu/questionnaires.aspx

Peterson, C., & Seligman, M. E. P. (2004). *Character strengths and virtues: A handbook and classification*. Washington: American Psychological Association.

Peterson, C., Semmel, A., von Baeyer, C., Abramson, L. Y., Metalsky, G. I., & Seligman, M. E. P. (1982). The Attributional Style Questionnaire. *Cognitive Therapy and Research, 6*, 287–299.

Petrides, K. V., & Furnham, A. (2000). On the dimensional structure of emotional intelligence. *Personality and Individual Differences, 29*, 313–320.

Pfister, R. (2002). *Flow im alltag: Untersuchungen zum quadrantenmodell des flow-erlebens und zum konzept der autotelischen persönlichkeit mit der Experience Sampling Method (ESM)* [Flow in everyday life: Studies on the quadrant model of flow experiencing and on the concept of the autotelic personality with the experience sampling method (ESM)]. Bern: Peter Lang.

Piaget, J. (1976). *The psychology of intelligence*. Totowa, NJ: Littlefield, Adams and Co.

Plomin, R., Chipuer, H. M., & Loehlin, J. C. (1990). Behavior genetics and personality. In L. A. Pervin (Ed.), *Handbook of personality: Theory and research* (pp. 225–243). New York: Guilford.

Plutchik, R. (1980). A general, psychoevolutionary theory of emotion. In R. Plutchik & H. Kellerman (Eds), *Emotion: Theory, research and experience* (Vol. 1, pp. 3–34). New York: Academic Press.

Plutchik, R. (1997). The circumplex as a general model of the structure of emotions and personality. In R. Plutchik & H. R. Conte (Eds), *Circumplex models of personality and emotions* (pp. 17–45). Washington: American Psychological Association.

Posner, M. I., & Rothbart, M. K. (1998). Attention, self-regulation and consciousness. *Philosophical Transactions of the Royal Society of London B, 353*, 1915–1927.

Puca, R. M., Rinkenauer, G., & Breidenstein, C. (2006). Individual differences in approach and avoidance movements: How the avoidance motive influences response force. *Journal of Personality, 74*, 979–1014.

Quevedo, R. J. M., & Abella, M. C. (2011). Well-being and personality: Facet-level analyses. *Personality and Individual Differences, 50*, 206–211.

Ramírez-Esparza, N., Gosling, S. D., Benet-Martínez, V., Potter, J. P., & Pennebaker, J. W. (2006). Do bilinguals have two personalities? A special case of cultural frame switching. *Journal of Research in Personality, 40*, 99–120.

Rapkin, B. D., & Fischer, K. (1992). Framing the construct of life satisfaction in terms of older adults' personal goals. *Psychology and Aging, 7*, 138–149.

Rashid, T., & Anjum, A. (2005). *340 ways to use VIA character strengths*. Available at: http://www.viastrengths.org/Applications/Exercises/tabid/132/Default.aspx

Rathunde, K. (1988). Optimal experience and the family context. In M. Csikszentmihalyi & I. Csikszentmihalyi (Eds), *Optimal experience: Psychological studies of flow in consciousness* (pp. 342–363). New York: Cambridge University Press.

Reilley, S. P., Geers, A. L., Lindsay, D. L., Deronde, L., & Dember, W. N. (2005). Convergence and predictive validity in measures of optimism and pessimism: Sequential studies. *Current Psychology, 24*, 43–59.

Rheinberg, F. (2008). Intrinsic motivation and flow-experience. In H. Heckhausen & J. Heckhausen (Eds), *Motivation and action* (pp. 323–348). Cambridge, UK: Cambridge University Press.

Rheinberg, F., Vollmeyer, R., & Engeser, S. (2003). Die Erfassung des Flow-Erlebens [The assessment of flow experience]. In J. Stiensmeier-Pelster & F. Rheinberg (Eds), *Diagnostik von Selbstkonzept, Lernmotivation und Selbstregulation* [Diagnosis of motivation and self-concept] (pp. 261–279). Göttingen: Hogrefe.

Roberts, R. D., Zeidner, M., & Matthews, G. (2001). Does emotional intelligence meet traditional standards for an intelligence? Some new data and conclusions. *Emotion, 1*, 196–231.

Rogaten, J., Moneta, G. B., & Spada, M. M. (in press). Academic performance as a function of approaches to studying and affect in studying. *Journal of Happiness Studies*.

Rogers, C. R. (1954). Towards a theory of creativity. *ETC: A Review of General Semantics, 11*, 249–260.

Rogers C. R. (1963). The actualizing tendency in relation to 'motives' and to consciousness. In M. R. Jones (Ed.), *Nebraska Symposium on Motivation* (pp. 1–24). Lincoln, NE: University of Nebraska Press.

Rosenberg, M. (1979). *Conceiving the self.* New York: Basic Books.

Rothbart, M. K., & Derryberry, D. (1981). Development in individual differences in temperament. In M. E. Lamb & A. L. Brown (Eds), *Advances in developmental psychology* (Vol. 1, pp. 37–86). Hilsdale, NJ: Erlbaum.

Rothbart, M. K., Ellis, L. K., & Posner, M. I. (2004). Temperament and self-regulation. In R. F. Baumeister & K. D. Vohs (Eds), *Handbook of self-regulation: Research, theory, and applications* (pp. 357–370). New York: Guilford.

Rotter, J. B. (1966). Generalized expectancies for internal versus external control of reinforcements. *Psychological Monographs, 80* (Whole No. 609).

Runco, M. A. (2005). Motivation, competence, and creativity. In A. Elliott & C. Dweck (Eds), *Handbook of achievement motivation and competence* (pp. 609–623). New York: Guilford Press.

Rusbult, C. E., Martz, J. M., & Agnew, C. R. (1998). The Investment Model Scale: Measuring commitment level, satisfaction level, quality of alternatives, and investment size. *Personal Relationships, 5*, 357–391.

Russell, J. A. (1997). How shall an emotion be called? In R. Plutchik, & H. R. Conte (Eds), *Circumplex models of personality and emotions* (pp. 205–220). Washington: American Psychological Association.

Russell, J. A., & Carroll, J. M. (1999). On the bipolarity of positive and negative affect. *Psychological Bulletin, 125*, 3–30.

Russell, J. A., Lewicka, M., & Niit, T. (1989). A cross-cultural study of a circumplex model of affect. *Journal of Personality and Social Psychology, 57*, 848–856.

Ryan, R. M., Chirkov, V. I., Little, T. D., Sheldon, K. M., Timoshina, E., & Deci, E. L. (1999). The American dream in Russia: Extrinsic aspirations in two cultures. *Personality and Social Psychology Bulletin, 25*, 1509–1524.

Ryan, R. M., & Deci, E. L. (2000). Self-Determination Theory and the facilitation of intrinsic motivation, social development, and well-being. *American Psychologist, 55*, 68–78.

Ryan, R. M., & Deci, E. L. (2001). On happiness and human potentials: A review of research on hedonic and eudaimonic well-being. *Annual Review of Psychology, 52*, 141–166.

Ryan, R., & Grolnick, W. S. (1986). Origins and pawns in the classroom: Self-report and projective assessments of individual differences in children's perceptions. *Journal of Personality and Social Psychology, 5*, 550–558.

Ryff, C. D. (1989). Happiness is everything, or is it? Explorations on the meaning of psychological well-being. *Journal of Personality and Social Psychology, 57*, 1069–1081.

Ryff, C. D., & Keyes, C. L. M. (1995). The structure of psychological well-being revisited. *Journal of Personality and Social Psychology, 69*, 719–727.

Ryff, C. D., & Singer, B. H. (1998). The contours of positive human health. *Psychological Inquiry, 9*, 1–28.

Saklofske, D. H., Austin, E. J., & Minski, P. S. (2003). Factor structure and validity of a trait emotional intelligence measure. *Personality and Individual Differences, 34*, 707–721.

Salami, S. O. (2010). Emotional intelligence, self-efficacy, psychological well-being and students' attitudes: Implications for quality education. *European Journal of Educational Studies, 2*, 247–257.

Salili, F. (1994). Age, sex and cultural differences in the meaning and dimensions of achievement. *Personality and Social Psychology Bulletin, 2*, 635–648.

Salovey, P., Bedell, B. T., Detweiler, J. B., & Mayer, J. D. (2000). Current directions in emotional intelligence research. In M. Lewis & J. M. Haviland-Jones (Eds), *Handbook of emotions* (2nd ed.) (pp. 504–520). New York: Guilford.

Salovey, P., & Mayer, J. D. (1990). Emotional intelligence. *Imagination, Cognition, and Personality, 9*, 185–211.

Salovey, P., Mayer, J. D., & Caruso, D. (2005). The positive psychology of emotional intelligence. In C. R. Snyder & S. J. Lopez (Eds), *Handbook of positive psychology* (pp. 159–171). New York: Oxford University Press.

Sato, I. (1988). Bosozoku: Flow in Japanese motorcycle gangs. In M. Csikszentmihalyi & I. S. Csikszentmihalyi (Eds), *Optimal experience: Psychological studies of flow in consciousness* (pp. 92–117). New York: Cambridge University Press.

Schaufeli, S. W., Bakker, A. B., & Salanova, M. (2006). The measurement of work engagement with a short questionnaire: A cross-national study. *Educational and Psychological Measurement, 66*, 701–716.

Schaufeli, W. B., Salanova, M., González-Romá, V., & Bakker, A. (2002). The Measurement of burnout and engagement: A confirmatory factor analytic approach. *Journal of Happiness Studies, 3*, 71–92.

Schaufeli, W. B., Taris, T., & Bakker, A. B. (2006). Dr. Jeckyll or Mr. Hyde: On the differences between work engagement and workaholism. In R. Burke (Ed.), *Workaholism in organizations* (pp. 194–217). Cheltenham, UK: Edward Elgar.

Scheier, M. F., & Carver, C. S. (1985). Optimism, coping, and health: Assessment and implication of generalized outcome expectancies. *Health Psychology, 4*, 219–247.

Scheier, M. F., & Carver, C. S. (1992). Effects of optimism on psychological and physical well-being: Theoretical overview and empirical update. *Cognitive Therapy and Research, 16*, 201–228.

Scheier, M. F., Carver, C. S., & Bridges, M. W. (1994). Distinguishing optimism from neuroticism (and trait anxiety, self-mastery, and self-esteem): A reevaluation of the Life Orientation Test. *Journal of Personality and Social Psychology, 67*, 1063–1078.

Scheier, M. F., Carver, C. S., & Bridges, M. W. (2001). Optimism, pessimism, and psychological well-being. In E. C. Chang (Ed.), *Optimism and pessimism: Implications for theory, research, and practice* (pp. 189–216). Washington: American Psychological Association.

Scheier, M. F., Matthews, K. A., Owens, J. F., Magovern, G. J., Lefebvre, R. C., Abbott, R. A., & Carver, C. S. (1989). Dispositional optimism and recovery from coronary artery bypass surgery: The beneficial effects on physical and psychological well-being. *Journal of Personality and Social Psychology, 57*, 1024–1040.

Scheier, M. F., Weintraub, J. K., & Carver, C. S. (1986). Coping with stress: Divergent strategies of optimists and pessimists. *Journal of Personality and Social Psychology, 51*, 1257–1264.

Schimmack, U., Oishi, S., & Diener, E. (2002). Cultural influences on the relation between pleasant emotions and unpleasant emotions: Asian dialectic philosophies or individualism-collectivism? *Cognition and Emotion, 16*, 705–719.

Schmutte, P. S., & Ryff, C. D. (1997). Personality and well-being: Reexamining methods and meanings. *Journal of Personality and Social Psychology, 73*, 549–559.

Schroevers, M. J., & Brandsma, R. (2010). Is learning mindfulness associated with improved affect after mindfulness-based cognitive therapy? *British Journal of Psychology, 101*, 95–107.

Schüler, J. (2010). Achievement incentives determine the effects of achievement-motive incongruence on flow experience. *Motivation and Emotion, 34*, 2–14.

Schüler, J., & Brunner, S. (2009). The rewarding effect of flow experience on performance in a marathon race. *Psychology of Sport & Exercise, 10*, 168–174.

Schüler, J., & Pfenninger, M. (2011). Flow impairs risk perception in kayakers. In B. D. Geranto (Ed.), *Sport Psychology* (pp. 237–246). New York: Nova.

Schulte, M. J., Ree, M. J., & Carretta, T. R. (2004). Emotional intelligence: Not much more than g and personality. *Personality and Individual Differences, 37*, 1059–1068.

Schutte, N. S., Malouff, J. M., Hall, L. E., Haggerty, D. J., Cooper, J. T., Golden, C. J., & Dornheim, L. (1998). Development and validation of a measure of emotional intelligence. *Personality and Individual Differences, 25*, 167–177.

Schwartz, B., & Sharpe, K. E. (2006). Practical wisdom: Aristotle meets positive psychology. *Journal of Happiness Studies, 7*, 377–395.

Schweizer, K., Beck-Seyffer A., & Schneider, R. (1999). Cognitive bias of optimism and its influence on psychological well-being. *Psychological Reports, 84*, 627–636.

Sears, R. R. (1977). Sources of life satisfaction of the Terman gifted men. *American Psychologist, 32*, 119–128.

Seligman, M. E. P. (1998). *Learned optimism* (2nd ed.). New York: Pocket Books (Simon and Schuster).

Seligman, M. E. P. (2002). *Authentic happiness: Using the new positive psychology to realize your potential for lasting fulfillment*. New York: Free Press.

Seligman, M. E. P., & Csikszentmihalyi, M. (2000). Positive psychology: An introduction. *American Psychologist, 55*, 5–14.

Seligman, M. E. P., Maier, S. F., & Geer, J. (1968). The alleviation of learned helplessness in dogs. *Journal of Abnormal Psychology, 73*, 256–262.

Seligman, M. E. P., Reivich, K., Jaycox, L., & Gillham, J. (1995). *The optimistic child*. New York: Houghton Mifflin.

Seligman, M. E. P., Steen, T. A., Park, N., & Peterson, C. (2005). Positive psychology progress: Empirical validation of interventions. *American Psychologist, 60*, 410–421.

Seligman, M. E. P., Castellon, C., Cacciola, J., Schulman, P., Luborsky, L., Ollove, M., & Downing, R. (1988). Explanatory style change during cognitive therapy for unipolar depression. *Journal of Abnormal Psychology, 97*, 13–18.

Selye, H. (1983). *Selye's guide to stress research, Vol. 3*. New York: Van Nostrand Reinhold.

Sharpe, J. P., Martin, N. R., & Roth, K. A. (2011). Optimism and the Big Five factors of personality: Beyond neuroticism and extraversion. *Personality and Individual Differences, 51*, 946–951.

Shaver, P., Schwartz, J., Kirson, D., & O'Connor, C. (1987). Emotional knowledge: Further explorations of a prototype approach. *Journal of Personality and Social Psychology, 52*, 1061–1086.

Sheldon, K. M., Elliot, A. J., Kim, Y., & Kasser T. (2001). What is satisfying about satisfying events? Testing 10 candidate psychological needs. *Journal of Personality and Social Psychology, 80*, 325–339.

Sheldon, K. M., Kashdan, T. B., & Steger, M. E. (2011). *Designing positive psychology: Taking stock and moving forward*. New York: Oxford University Press.

Shepperd, J. A., Maroto, J. J., Pbert, L. A. (1996). Dispositional optimism as a predictor of health changes among cardiac patients. *Journal of Research in Personality, 30*, 517–534.

Shifren, K., & Bauserman, E. (1996). The relationship between instrumental and expressive traits, health behaviors and perceived physical health. *Sex Roles, 34*, 841–864.

Shorey, H. S., Little, T. D., Rand, K. L., Snyder, C. R., Monsson, Y., & Gallagher, M. (2007). Validation of the Revised Snyder Hope Scale: The will, the ways, and now the goals for positive future outcomes. Unpublished manuscript, University of Kansas, Lawrence.

Simonton, D. K. (2000). Creativity: Cognitive, personal, developmental, and social aspects. *American Psychologist, 55,* 151–158.

Simonton, D. K. (2011). Positive psychology in historical and philosophical perspective: Predicting its future from the past. In K. M. Sheldon, T. B. Kashdan, & M. E. Steger (Eds), *Designing positive psychology: Taking stock and moving forward* (pp. 447–454). New York: Oxford University Press.

Singh, K., & Choubisa, R. (2010). Empirical validation of Values in Action-Inventory of Strengths (VIA-IS) in Indian context. *Psychological Studies, 55,* 151–158.

Smith, C. P. (1992). *Motivation and personality: Handbook of thematic content analysis.* New York: Cambridge University Press.

Snyder, C. R. (2000). The past and the future of hope. *Journal of Social and Clinical Psychology, 19,* 11–28.

Snyder, C. R. (2002). Hope theory: Rainbows in the mind. *Psychological Inquiry, 13,* 249–275.

Snyder, C. R., Harris, C., Anderson, J. R., Holleran, S. A., Irving, L. M., Sigmon, S. T., Oshinoubu, L., Gibb, J., Langelle, C., & Harney, P. (1991). The will and the ways: Development and validation of an individual-differences measure of hope. *Journal of Personality and Social Psychology, 60,* 570–585.

Snyder, C. R., Lopez, S. J., Shorey, H. S., Rand, K. L., & Feldman, D. B. (2003). Hope theory, measurements, and applications to school psychology. *School Psychology Quarterly, 18,* 122–139.

Snyder, C. R., Rand, K. L., & Sigmon, D. R. (2005). Hope theory: A member of the positive psychology family. In C. R. Snyder & S. J. Lopez (Eds), *Handbook of positive psychology* (pp. 257–266). New York: Oxford University Press.

Somers, M. J., & Casal, J. C. (1994). Organizational commitment and whistle-blowing: A test of the reformer and the organization man hypotheses. *Group & Organization Management, 19,* 270–284.

Spada, M. M., Georgiou, G. A., & Wells, A. (2010). The relationship among meta-cognitions, attentional control, and state anxiety. *Cognitive Behaviour Therapy, 39,* 64–71.

Spada, M. M., Mohiyeddini, C., & Wells, A. (2008). Measuring metacognitions associated with emotional distress: Factor structure and predictive validity of the Metacognitions Questionnaire 30. *Personality and Individual Differences, 45,* 238–242.

Spada, M. M., & Moneta, G. B. (2012). A metacognitive-motivational model of surface approach to studying. *Educational Psychology, 32,* 45–62.

Spada, M. M., & Moneta, G. B. (in press). Metacognitive and motivational predictors of surface approach to studying and academic examination performance. *Educational Psychology.*

Spence, J. T., & Helmreich, R. L. (1978). *Masculinity and femininity: Their psychological dimensions, correlates, and antecedents.* Austin, TX: University of Texas Press.

Spence, J. T., Helmreich, R. L., & Stapp, J. (1974). The Personal Attributes Questionnaire: A measure of sex role stereotypes and masculinity-femininity. *JSAS: Catalog of Selected Documents in Psychology, 4,* 43–44.

Spence, J. T., Helmreich, R. L., & Stapp, J. (1975). Ratings of self and peers on sex role attributes and their relation to self-esteem and conceptions of masculinity and femininity. *Journal of Personality and Social Psychology, 32,* 29–39.

Spinks, J. A., Mei-Oi Lam, L., & Van Lingen, G. (1996). Cultural determinants of creativity: An implicit theory approach. In S. Dingli (Ed.), *Creative thinking: New perspectives.* La Valletta, Malta: Malta University Press.

Stangor, C. (2011). Research methods for the behavioral sciences (4th ed.). Mountain View, CA: Cengage.

Steger, M. F., Frazier, P., Oishi, S., & Kaler, M. (2006). The Meaning in Life Questionnaire: Assessing the presence of and search for meaning in life. *Journal of Counseling Psychology, 53,* 80–93.

Sternberg, R. J. (1986). *Construct validation of a triangular theory of love.* Unpublished manuscript. Yale University: New Haven.

Sternberg, R. J. (1988). *The triangle of love: Intimacy, passion, commitment.* New York: Basic Books.

Sternberg, R. J. (1998). *Cupid's arrow: The course of love through time.* Cambridge, UK: Cambridge University Press.

Sternberg, R. J. (2006). *Cognitive psychology* (4th ed.). Belmont, CA: Wadsworth.

Sternberg R. J., & Lubart, T. I. (1996). Investing in creativity. *American Psychologist, 51,* 677–688.

Stetter, F., & Kupper, S. (2002). Autogenic training: A meta-analysis of clinical outcome studies. *Applied Psychophysiology and Biofeedback, 27,* 45–98.

Stoll, O., & Lau, A. (2005). Flow-erleben beim marathonlauf: Zsammenhänge mit anforderungspassung und leistung [Experiencing flow during a marathon: Association with the fit between demand and ability]. *Zeitschrift für Sportpsychologie, 12,* 75–82.

Stutzer, A. (2004). The role of income aspirations in individual happiness. *Journal of Economic Behavior and Organization, 54,* 89–109.

Sugihara, Y., & Katsurada, E. (2002). Gender role development in Japanese culture: Diminishing gender role differences in a contemporary society. *Sex Roles, 47,* 443–452.

Tay, L., & Diener, E. (2011). Needs and subjective well-being around the world. *Journal of Personality and Social Psychology, 101,* 354–365.

Tellegen, A., Lykken, D. T., Bouchard, T. J., Jr, Wilcox, K., Segal, N., & Rich, S. (1988). Personality similarity in twins reared apart and together. *Journal of Personality and Social Psychology, 54,* 1031–1039.

Thatcher, A., Wretschko, G., & Fridjhon, P. (2008). Online flow experiences, problematic Internet use and Internet procrastination. *Computers in Human Behavior, 24,* 2236–2254.

The Gallup Organization (1999–2013). *Worldwide research methodology.* Available at: http://www.gallup.com/se/128147/Worldwide-Research-Methodology.aspx

The Internet Classics Archive by Daniel C. Stevenson, Web Atomics (1994–2009a). *The doctrine of the mean by Confucius.* Available at: http://classics.mit.edu/Confucius/doctmean.html

The Internet Classics Archive by Daniel C. Stevenson, Web Atomics (1994–2009b). *Nicomachean ethics by Aristotle* (trans. by W. D. Ross). Available at: http://classics.mit.edu/Aristotle/nicomachaen.html

Thompson, E. R. (2007). Development and validation of an internationally reliable short-form of the Positive and Negative Affect Schedule (PANAS). *Journal of Cross-Cultural Psychology, 38,* 227–242.

Tiger, L. (1979). *Optimism: The biology of hope.* New York: Simon & Schuster.

Torrance, E. P. (1965). *Rewarding creative behavior.* Englewood Cliffs, NJ: Prentice-Hall.

Torrance, E. P. (1972). Predictive validity of the Torrance Tests of Creative Thinking. *Journal of Creative Behavior, 6,* 236–252.

Trapnell, P. D., & Wiggins, J. S. (1990). Extension of the Interpersonal Adjectives Scales to include the Big Five dimensions of personality. *Journal of Personality and Social Psychology, 59,* 781–790.

Tugade, M. M., & Fredrickson, B. L. (2004). Resilient individuals use positive emotions to bounce back from negative emotional experiences. *Journal of Personality and Social Psychology, 86,* 320–333.

Valle, M. F., Huebner, E. S., & Suldo, S. M. (2006). An analysis of hope as a psychological strength. *Journal of School Psychology, 44*, 393–406.

Vosburg, S. K. (1998). The effects of positive and negative mood on divergent-thinking performance. *Creativity Research Journal, 11*, 165–172.

Ward, C. A., & Sethi, R. R. (1986). Cross-cultural validation of the Bem Sex Role Inventory. *Journal of Cross-Cultural Psychology, 17*, 300–314.

Ward, C., & Chang, W. (1997). 'Cultural fit': A new perspective on personality and sojourner adjustment. *International Journal of Intercultural Relations, 21*, 525–533.

Watson, D., Clark, L. A., & Carey, G. (1988). Positive and negative affectivity and their relations to anxiety and depressive disorders. *Journal of Abnormal Psychology, 97*, 346–353.

Watson, D., Clark, L. A., & Tellegen, A. (1988). Development and validation of brief measures of positive and negative affect: The PANAS scales. *Journal of Personality and Social Psychology, 54*, 1063–1070.

Watson, D., & Tellegen, A. (1985). Toward a consensual structure of mood. *Psychological Bulletin, 98*, 219–235.

Weisberg, J. (1994). Measuring workers' burnout and intention to leave. *International Journal of Manpower, 15*, 4–14.

Wells, A. (2000). *Emotional disorders and metacognition: Innovative cognitive therapy.* Chichester, UK: Wiley.

Wells, A. (2009). *Metacognitive therapy for anxiety and depression.* New York: Guilford.

Wells, A., & Carter, K. (2001). Further tests of a cognitive model of generalized anxiety disorder: Metacognitions and worry in GAD, panic disorder, social phobia, depression, and non patients. *Behavior Therapy, 32*, 85–102.

Wells, A., & Cartwright-Hatton, S. (2004). A short form of the Meta-Cognitions Questionnaire: Properties of the MCQ-30. *Behaviour Research and Therapy, 42*, 385–396.

Wells, A., & Matthews, G. (1994). *Attention and emotion: A clinical perspective.* Hove, UK: Erlbaum.

Westerhof, G. J., & Keyes, C. L. M. (2008). Geestelijke gezondheid is meer dan de afwezigheid van geestelijke ziekte [Mental health is more than the absence of mental illness]. *Maandblad Geestelijke Volksgezondheid, 63*, 808–820.

Westerhof, G. J., & Keyes, C. L. M. (2010). Mental illness and mental health: The two continua model across the lifespan. *Journal of Adult Development, 17*, 110–119.

Wheeler, L., Reis, H. T., & Bond, M. H. (1989). Collectivism-individualism in everyday social life: The middle kingdom and the melting pot. *Journal of Personality and Social Psychology, 57*, 79–86.

White, R. W. (1959). Motivation reconsidered: The concept of competence. *Psychological Review, 66*, 297–333.

White, R. W. (1960). Competence and the psychosexual stages of development. In M. R. Jones (Ed.), *Nebraska symposium on motivation* (Vol. 8, pp. 97–141). Lincoln, NE: University of Nebraska Press.

White, R. W. (1963). Sense of interpersonal competence: Two case studies and some reflections on origins. In R. W. White (Ed.), *The study of lives* (pp. 72–93). New York: Prentice-Hall.

Whitley, M. P. (1998). Sexual Satisfaction Inventory. In C. M. Davis, W. L. Yarber, R. Bauserman, G. Schreer, & S. L. Davis (Eds), *Handbook of sexuality-related measures* (pp. 519–521). Thousand Oaks, CA: Sage Publications.

Wiggins, J. S., & Broughton, R. (1985). The interpersonal circle: A structural model for the integration of personality research. In R. Hogan & W. H. Jones (Eds), *Perspectives in personality* (Vol. 1, pp. 1–47). Greenwich, CT: JAU Press.

Wiggins, J. S., & Broughton, R. (1991). A geometric taxonomy of personality scales. *European Journal of Personality, 5*, 343–365.

Windsor, T. D., Anstey, K. J., & Rodgers, B. (2008). Volunteering and psychological well-being among young-old adults: How much is too much? *The Gerontologist, 48*, 59–70.

Winter, D. G. (1973). *The power motive*. New York: Free Press.

Winter, D. G. (1993). Power, affiliation, and war: Three tests of a motivational model. *Journal of Personality and Social Psychology, 65*, 532–545.

Winter, D. G. (2002). Motivation and political leadership. In L. Valenty & O. Feldman (Eds), *Political leadership for the new century: Personality and behavior among American leaders* (pp. 25–47). Westport, CT: Praeger.

Wong, C. S., Tinsley, C., Law, K. S., & Mobley, W. H. (2003). Development and validation of a multidimensional measure of Guanxi. *Journal of Psychology in Chinese Societies, 4*, 43–69.

Woodman, R. W., Sawyer, J. E., & Griffin, R. W. (1993). Toward a theory of organizational creativity. *Academy of Management Review, 18*, 293–321.

World Health Organization (2005). *Promoting mental health: Concepts, emerging evidence, practice*. Geneva: WHO.

World Health Organization (2010). *International Classification of Diseases (ICD)*. Geneva: World Health Organization. Available at: http://www.who.int/classifications/icd/en/

World Health Organization (2012). *Depression: A global public health concern*. Geneva: World Health Organization. Available at: http://www.who.int/mental_health/management/depression/en/

World Values Study Association (1981–2013). *The world's most comprehensive investigation of political and sociocultural change*. Available at: http://www.worldvaluessurvey.org/

Wright, R. (2000). *Nonzero: The logic of human destiny*. New York: Pantheon.

Wright, T. A. (2005). The role of 'happiness' in organizational research: Past, present and future directions. In P. L. Perrewe & D. C. Ganster (Eds), *Research in occupational stress and well-being* (pp. 221–264). Amsterdam: JAI Press.

Wyer, R. S., Clore, G. L., & Isbell, L. M. (1999). Affect and information processing. In M. P. Zanna (Ed.), *Advances in experimental social psychology* (Vol. 31, pp. 1–77). San Diego, CA: Academic Press.

Wylie, R. (1979). *The self-concept, Vol. 2: Theory and research on selected topics*. Lincoln, NE: University of Nebraska Press.

Yang, K. S. (1993). Chinese social orientation: An integrative analysis. In W. L. Y. C. Cheng, E. M. C. Cheung, & C. N. Chen (Eds), *Psychotherapy for the Chinese* (pp. 19–56). Hong Kong: Department of Psychiatry, Chinese University of Hong Kong.

Yates, A. J. (1970). *Behavior therapy*. New York: Wiley.

Yerkes, R. M., & Dodson, J. D. (1908). The relation of strength of stimulus to rapidity of habit-formation. *Journal of Comparative Neurology and Psychology, 18*, 459–482.

Yik, M., Bond, M. H., & Paulhus, D. L. (1998). Do Chinese self-enhance or self-efface? It's a matter of domain. *Personality and Social Psychology Bulletin, 24*, 399–406.

Yukl, G. (2002). *Definitions of managerial behaviors from leadership in organizations* (5th ed.). Upper Saddle River, NJ: Prentice Hall.

Zelenski, J. M., Murphy, S. A., & Jenkins, D. A. (2008). The happy-productive worker thesis revisited. *Journal of Happiness Studies, 9*, 521–537.

Zuckerman, M., & Gagne, M. (2003). The COPE revised: Proposing a 5-factor model of coping strategies. *Journal of Research in Personality, 37*, 169–204.

Index